The Doctrine of Vibration

The Doctrine of Vibration

An Analysis of the Doctrines and Practices of Kashmir Shaivism

Mark S. G. Dyczkowski

State University of New York Press

Published by
State University of New York Press, Albany

Printed in the United States of America

For information, address State University of New York
Press, State University Plaza, Albany, N.Y., 12246

Library of Congress Cataloging-in-Publication Data

Dyczkowski, Mark S. G.
The doctrine of vibration.

(SUNY series in Kashmir Śaivism)
Includes index.
1. Kashmir Śaivism—Doctrines. I. Title. II. Series.
BL1281.1545.D93 1986 294.5'513'09546 86-14552
ISBN 0-88706-431-0
ISBN 0-88706-432-9 (pbk.)

10 9 8 7 6 5 4 3 2 1

This book is dedicated to my
PARENTS

For you every vision has become like the words of a sealed book.
You give it to someone able to read and say, "Read that."
He replies, "I cannot, because the book is sealed."
Or else you give the book to someone who cannot read and say,
"Read that."
He replies, "I cannot read."

Isaiah 29/11-12.

CONTENTS

ACKNOWLEDGEMENTS

This book was originally researched and written in Oxford. I will always be grateful to Richard Gombrich, at present Boden professor of Sanskrit at Oxford University, who gave me the opportunity to do this work. I also wish to thank Mr. G. S. Sanderson, at present lecturer in Sanskrit at the same university, whose zeal and scholarship inspired me. My gratitude also extends to a close disciple of the Late Mahāmahopādhyāya Gopinatha Kaviraj, Professor Heman Chakravarti with whom I read my first Kashmiri Śaiva works in India before going to Oxford and the late Pandit Ambikadatta Upadhyaya who taught me Sanskrit.

Above all I cannot be thankful enough to my parents whose support has been constant and unremitting, both through my stay in Oxford, and for more than fifteen years in India. Finally, I wish to acknowledge the help of Giovanna, who has been both a wife for me and a mother for our children.

Introduction

The Land of Kashmir

The ancient Himalayan kingdom of Kashmir is now part of the province of Jammu and Kashmir situated in the extreme northwest of India. The heart of modern Kashmir is, as it was in the past, the wide and fertile valley of the river Vitasta. Set at an altitude of five thousand feet, the valley's beautiful lakes and temperate climate nowadays attract tourists in large numbers during the summer months when temperatures rise high into the forties Centigrade on the North Indian plains. Although most of the population is at present Muslim, before the advent of Islam in the thirteenth century, Kashmir enjoyed an unparalleled reputation as a centre of learning amongst both Buddhists and Hindus. Kashmiris excelled not only in religious studies but also in the secular fields of Sanskrit literature, literary criticism and grammar as well as the sciences, including medicine, astronomy and mathematics. They had a uniquely realistic sense of history clearly evidenced in Kalhaṇa's twelfth century chronicle of the kings of Kashmir, the *Rājataraṅgiṇī*, which is virtually the only history of its kind in India.

Remarkable as Kashmir has been as a seat of Hindu spirituality and learning, it was no less so as a centre of Buddhism. Possibly introduced into Kashmir as early as the third century B.C., Buddhism had already developed there to such a degree by the first century of our era that the Kushan king, Kaniṣka, chose Kashmir as the venue of a major Buddhist Council. It was a huge gathering, attended by more than five hundred Buddhist monks and scholars. The previously uncodified portions of the Buddha's discourses and the theoretical portion of the canon (the *Abhidharma*) were codified and the rest extensively revised. The entire early canon, the *Tripiṭaka*, was then inscribed on copper plates and deposited in a *stūpa*. In the centuries that followed most forms of Indian Buddhism flourished in Kashmir. Of the early schools the *Sarvāstivāda* was particularly well developed. Similarly, the schools of the Great Vehicle, both those of the Middle Way and the idealist Yogācāra, were taught and practiced extensively. Kashmir also produced many fine Buddhist logicians in the line of Diṅnāga and Dharmakīrti, amongst whom Vinītadeva and Dharmottarācārya, who lived in the eighth century, are the most famous.

The borders of Kashmir at that time extended further west beyond the roads to Asia which ran through the Swat and Chitral valleys in Gilgit. For this reason Kashmir was the first to make a substantial contribution to the spread of Buddhism in Central Asia, which began about the fourth century A.D. and travelled along these routes. Many Buddhists, attracted by Kashmir's reputation, came from distant lands to learn Sanskrit and train as translators and teachers. One of the earliest and most brilliant was Kumārajīva (334-413 A.D.). Born into an aristocratic family of the Central Asian kingdom of Khotan, he came to Kashmir in his youth and learnt there the scriptures of the Great Vehicle from Bandhudatta. He then went to China, where he lived and worked for the rest of his life, translating Buddhist scriptures. The Kashmiri Buddhabhadra, his contemporary, did the same. Yoga teachers like Dharmabhikṣu attracted a large number of Chinese and Kashmiri students at the end of the fifth century when there was a growing foreign interest in Buddhist Yoga. It was also during this period that the Kashmiri Buddhasena translated a major work of the idealist Buddhist Yogācāra school—the *Yogācārabhūmi*—into Chinese for the first time. In 631 A.D., Hsüan Tsang, one of China's most famous Buddhist pilgrims, came to study in Kashmir leaving us an account of his two-year stay which eloquently testifies to Buddhism's popularity and influence.

Such was Kashmir's reputation that it was from here that Tibet originally chose to receive its religion. The first king of Tibet, Srong-bcan-sgampo, sent Thon-mi Saṃbhota to Kashmir during the reign of Durlabhavardhana (616 A.D.). He learnt Sanskrit from Devātītasiṃha and returned to Tibet with a modified thirty-letter version of the Kashmiri script.[1] Kashmir continued to play a role in the transmission of Buddhism from India into Tibet although other routes (particularly through Nepal) later became more important. By the eleventh century, when the Kashmiri Śaiva schools were reaching the peak of their development, Kashmir was also, as Tucci says, "one of the places where Buddhism prospered most, even if not as state religion, certainly as the home of the greatest scholars and exegetes of the time."[2]

The rich spiritual and intellectual climate of Kashmir helped to foster an important and far reaching development that affected every aspect of Indian religious life, namely, Tantra. About the middle of the first millennium of our era, Tantra began to assume a clearly defined, although immensely varied, identity through the emergence of vast corpuses of sacred literature that defined themselves specifically as Tantric. There can be no doubt, despite the fragmentary and as yet poorly researched evidence, that Kashmir was an important centre of a wide range of Tantric cults, both Hindu and Buddhist. Many famous Buddhist Tantric teachers lived in or near Kashmir at that time. Naropā and even Padmasambhava (who is said to have introduced Tantric Buddhism into Tibet) sometimes figure in Tibetan sources as Kashmiris.[3] Uḍḍiyāna (Tibetan: U-rgyan), important as Padmasambhava's birthplace and as a major centre of Tantric Buddhism and Hinduism, may well have been located in the nearby Swat valley.

Both of Tantra's major Hindu streams, one centred on the worship of Viṣṇu and the other on Śiva, evolved a bewildering number of Tantric cults, some large others small. Kashmir contributed substantially to these developments not only on the Śaiva side but also on the Vaiṣṇava. Indeed, the earliest known references drawn from Vaiṣṇava Tantric sources are found in the writings of Kashmiris.[4] Nowadays the form of Vaiṣṇavism that looks to these scriptures as authoritative, namely, the Pāñcarātra, survives only in South India; however, the earliest Southern teachers of this school looked to Kashmir as one of their oldest seats of learning and spiritual culture.[5] But although the worship of Viṣṇu, whether performed according to the norms prescribed by the Tantras or otherwise, was certainly an important feature of Kashmiri religious life and was patronised extensively by the Hindu kings of the valley, even so, Śaivism remained, on the whole, the dominant form of Hinduism.

The Śaivism of Kashmir and Kashmiri Śaivism

We know very little of the origins of Śaivism in Kashmir, although tradition testifies to its antiquity in this part of India. The written records confirm that it has always occupied an important place in the religious life of Kashmir. Thus Kalhaṇa records (possibly from earlier chronicles) the existence of an already ancient temple dedicated to Śiva in emperor Aśoka's time. Although this is hardly possible, as temples were not constructed in India as early as the third century B.C., this reference illustrates the then[6] common Kashmiri belief in Śaivism's ancient presence in Kashmir.[7] Certainly the many newly constructed temples, as well as the old ones renovated throughout the period covered in Kalhaṇa's history, testify to Śaivism's continuing popularity. In the early ninth century A.D., when the first Kashmiri Śaiva works were written, there were numerous Śaiva groups in the valley of Kashmir. Amongst them were those that came to form a part of what we nowadays call Kashmiri Śaivism of which the Spanda school, whose teachings we are concerned with here, was the first development.

All these Śaiva groups, diverse though they were, accepted the Śaiva Tantras (also known as Āgamas) as their scriptural authority. Some groups would look to one section of the Āgamas, others to another. They thus ordered themselves quite naturally into lineages of Tantric masters who initiated disciples into the rituals and other practices of their chosen Tantras. We know of the existence of these Tantric subcultures not only from epigraphic and other sources including other Hindu scriptures, particularly the Purāṇas, but also from the Āgamas themselves. Although the Āgamas are all considered to be divine revelation and hence, in a sense, eternal, they do nonetheless reflect the growth of these Śaiva groups for they not only studied them but also contributed to them. Thus, one way in which we can understand how these groups are related is to see how the Śaiva Tantras have ordered themselves in relation to one another. The brief account that follows of the Śaiva canon[8] will hopefully serve to indicate in broad terms how the Śaiva groups that have contributed to the formation of Kashmiri Śaivism are related to Tantric Śaivism as a whole. According to an important system of classification we find in the Āgamas themselves, they can be divided into the following sections.

Śaivasiddhānta. The Āgamas generally agree that there are twenty-eight principal Siddhāntāgamas and about two hundred Śaiva scriptures (called *Upāgamas*) affiliated to them.[9] All the main Āgamas, and many of the secondary ones, are still extant in South India, although only a relatively small number have as yet been edited from the manuscript sources. The cults of these Āgamas are largely concerned with the worship of Sadāśiva which is generally conducted in public temples and is centred on the Liṅga, Sadāśiva's phallic symbol. Descriptions of the temples, Liṅga and iconic forms of the gods and goddesses of the Siddhānta constitute an important part of these Āgamas. They also deal extensively with the rituals related to them. These include the regular daily rites as well as occasional ones such as consecration ceremonies and festivals. Other important rituals are those that concern the initiation of the neophyte into this form of Śaivism or the priesthood.

The Āgamas are primarily concerned with ritual and devote relatively little space to philosophical matters or even yoga. Even so, the philosophical standpoint of these Tantras can, broadly speaking, be said to be a dualism of a more or less tempered form although not one consistently maintained throughout them. The homonymous philosophical school inspired by these Āgamas, however, ultimately developed a well defined dualism, according to which there are three basic realities, namely, Śiva (*pati*), the fettered soul (*paśu*) and the factors that bind it (*pāśa*). The Kashmiri Śaiva tradition records that the founder of dualist Śaivism was called Āmardaka. This name recurs in inscriptions and other sources as that of an important founder figure believed to have lived in the eighth century. This Āmardaka had predecessors and so cannot really be said to have founded this branch of Śaivism; even so, he is important as the founder of a major Siddhānta monastic centre (*maṭha*). This centre, named Āmardaka after its founder, was located in Ujjain. Purandara, Āmardaka's successor, also founded a Siddhānta order, namely, the Māttamayūra. This order was named after the capital of the Cālukya empire in the Punjáb where its headquarters were located. A third important order was the Mādhumateya founded by Pavanaśiva to which belonged the royal preceptors of the Kalacuri kings of Central India.

Siddhānta ascetics, full of missionary zeal, used the influence of their royal patrons to propagate their teachings in the neighbouring kingdoms, especially in South India. From the oldest capital of the Cālukyas, Mattamayūra, they established monasteries in Mahārāṣṭra, the Koṅkan, Karnāṭaka, Āndhra and Kerala. The Siddhānta flourished in the areas where it spread, until it was devastated by the Muslim invasions, which started in the eleventh century, or supplanted by other forms of Hinduism. It survived, however, in South India where it changed its medium of expression from Sanskrit to Tamil in which form it is better known and persists to this day.[10] Although Śaivasiddhānta survives at present only in South India, we know that a number of the earliest commentators of the Āgamas and important authors of independent works expounding the philosophy of the Siddhānta were Kashmiris.[11] Monist Kashmiri Śaiva[12] authors quote them with great reverence as their predecessors, although they do not always agree with them. There can be no doubt that the Siddhānta greatly influenced Kashmiri Śaivism which largely adopted it, reshaping it on non-dualist lines.

Bhūta and Gāruḍa Tantras. These two groups of Āgamas have been almost entirely lost. They are considered together as they appear to have much in common. We know that both dealt with magical cures (particularly of snakebite), exorcism of malevolent ghosts and spirits, the protection of children from such entities as well as the acquisition of magical powers and other such matters. References to these two groups is common in the Siddhāntāgamas, and Kashmiri Śaivites also knew of them although already at this time (viz., the ninth century A.D. onwards) they were clearly on the decline, at least in Kashmir.[13]

The Vāmatantras. According to the classification we are following in this account, each group of Āgamas constitutes a 'current' (*srotas*) of scriptures spoken by one or other of Sadāśiva's five faces. The Siddhānta belongs to the Upper current, spoken by the Upper face, while the Bhūta and Gāruḍatantras belong to the Western and Eastern currents. The Vāmatantras were spoken by the Northern face. This face, located to the left of centre (which is in the eastern direction), is that of the left-hand current, not to be confused with the Tantric distinction between 'left' and 'right-hand' paths.

The only Tantra belonging to this group that has been recovered so far is the *Vīṇāśikhatantra* recently edited from just two Nepalese manuscripts by Dr. T. Goudriaan.[14] Although this group of Tantras is regularly mentioned in the primary sources when they refer to the Śaiva canon and its divisions, the cults associated with it seem to have had little success in India and practically died out after the first millennium of our era. The dominant form of Śiva in these Tantras appears to have been Tumburubhairava.[15] He is described as having four faces, each one of which spoke one of the major Tantras of this group, namely, the Tantra of the Severed Head (*Śiraścheda*), the Tantra of the Crest of the Vīṇā (*Vīṇāśikha*), the Tantra of Delusion (*Saṃmohana*) and the Tantra of the Higher Law (*Nayottara*).[16]

These Tantras, and with them the cult of Tumburu, spread from India to Southeast Asia sometime before the end of the eighth century. We know from a Cambodian inscription discovered at Sdok Kok Thom dated 1052 A.D. that these Tantras were known there at the time. This inscription commemorates the history of a lineage of royal priests founded by Śivakaivalya who was the priest of Jayavarman II who returned to Cambodia from exile in Java in 802 A.D.. At that time a Brahmin called Hiraṇyadāma taught the four Tantras to Śivakaivalya and several rites described in them were performed for the benefit of the king. We also find references to Tumburu in Sanskrit hymns and fragments from Bali, some of which go back to an early period of Hindu influence in Indonesia.[17] The absence of further reference to these Tantras and their cults in Southeast Asia seems to indicate that, as happened in India, they did not survive much beyond the eleventh century. Similarly, although the Vāmatantras were known in Kashmir, monistic Kashmiri Śaivites clearly preferred the Siddhāntāgamas and the Bhairavatantras to which we now turn.

The Bhairavatantras. As their name suggests, the Bhairavatantras were especially (but not exclusively) concerned with the worship of Bhairava. Bhairava is an important form of Śiva known and worshipped throughout India. He is popular both in the literate Sanskrit tradition as well as in many non-literate vernacular traditions. Bhairava, whose name literally means 'the Terrible One', is the 'wrathful', 'frightening' form of Śiva Who is 'peaceful' and 'auspicious'. Abhinavagupta, an important Kashmiri Śaiva teacher (see below), explains the popular Tantric etymology of the word *Bhairava* as follows:

> 1) Bhairava is He Who bears all things and is supported by the universe, filling it and sustaining it on the one hand, while uttering it or conceiving it on the other.[18]
>
> 2) Bhairava is He Who protects those frightened by the rounds of rebirth.[19]
>
> 3) Bhairava is the One born in the heart of those who, terrified by transmigratory existence, call on Him for help.[20]
>
> 4) Bhairava is He Who arouses by His grace a fear of transmigration.
>
> 5) Bhairava is He Whose light shines in the minds of those yogis who are intent on assimilating time (*kālagrāsa*) into the eternal presence of consciousness and thus exhaust the energy of time said to be the driving force behind the machine of the galaxies.[21]
>
> 6) Bhairava is the Lord of the powers of the senses whose shouting (*rāvaṇa*) frightens the souls in bondage.[22]
>
> 7) Bhairava is the Lord Who calls a halt to transmigration and thus is very terrible.[23]

There are countless forms of Bhairava, each with their own name. A typical and widely-known form is that of Mahākālabhairava. He is worshipped in major centres in India including Ujjain, Benares and Kathmandu. He is the protector of these three cities. One could add, incidentally, that Mahākāla is also an important Buddhist god and as such is the guardian of Lhasa, the capital of Tibet. He is described as dark blue or black[24] and fierce in appearance. He carries the skull of the creator-god, Brahmā, as penance for having cut off his head to save the world from its great heat generated within it by Brahmā's pride.[25] Bhairava's furious drunkenness and body aflame with the fire of cosmic destruction has served for centuries as an archetype of the liberated state for numerous Śaiva cults. All these cults shared the view that liberation is essentially freedom from the opposites of good and evil; thus the adept who seeks it must break through them to a higher state of expanded, inebriated and blissful consciousness that, unaffected by them, encompasses both.

In the Kashmiri Śaiva tradition, Bhairava is understood as the divine form of the absolute realised as the exertive force (*udyama*) that drives the senses and mind at the microcosmic level along with the universe at the macrocosmic level.[26] Much of Kashmiri Śaiva practice—particularly that of the Doctrine of Vibration with which this volume is concerned—deals with how to lay hold of this inner power and identify with it. One way is to arouse the spiritual and cosmic energy latent in the soul through an expansion of consciousness brought about by the performance of rituals and the practice of yoga. Unlike the rituals of the Siddhānta, which generally take place in public, many of these rituals were originally performed in cremation grounds or lonely places for the benefit of a few select initiates. Again, unlike the Siddhānta rituals, many of them involve the offering of meat and wine to the deity and, at times, ritual intercourse.

The Bhairavatantras were not the only Tantras to advocate such practices. Moreover, they were numerous and of varied content and not all of them considered these practices important. Thus a Bhairavatantra well known to Kashmiri Śaivites, the *Svacchandabhairavatantra*, allows such practices, but even so generally advocates 'tamer' procedures similar to the rituals of the Siddhāntāgamas. The Bhairavatantras are conventionally said to number sixty-four but must have been many more. They were major sources for Kashmiri Śaivites.

Other Śaiva Groups. Important precursors of the Āgamic Śaiva groups were the Pāśupatas. References to them are found in the earliest portions of the *Mahābhārata* and in Patañjali's commentary on Pāṇini's grammar written in the second century B.C. Unfortunately, we do not possess any original scriptures of these early Śaiva sects. The *Pāśupatasūtra*, the only work we have, is relatively late although earlier than the tenth century A.D..[27] It enjoins, amongst other things, that Pāśupatas should behave in a manner contrary to accepted norms. They should laugh and cry like madmen, make lewd gestures at young women and abuse those that approach them. The aim was thereby to overcome the ego and gain magical power through transgression. Those who behaved in this way were the votaries of the Great Vow (*mahāvrata*). Other extremist Śaiva sects that adhered to the Great Vow were the skull-bearing ascetics of the Kāpālika order and other Śaiva groups collectively said to belong to the Higher Path (*atimārga*).[28]

Other important Śaiva groups are those of the Kaulas. In a sense, successors of the early extremist Śaiva sects belonging to the Higher Path, these groups are closely affiliated to other Śaivāgamic groups, particularly those of the Bhairavatantras. They are very important in the history of Kashmiri Śaivism as it later developed extensively by integrating into itself a number of Kaula systems, largely divested of their outer ritual forms. Monist in outlook, the original Tantras of these groups were, as were the Bhairava and Vāmatantras, strongly Śākta in tone. Although they remained essentially and consistently Śaiva, they stressed the worship of female divinities. Thus they represent the precursors of the later Śākta Tantric tradition. Indeed the word 'Kula' itself denotes the power of consciousness—Śakti, the Goddess Who is the emission (*visarga*) of the absolute (called Akula), through which the universe is created.[29]

Amongst the many Kaula schools, the most important for Kashmiri Śaivites were these of the Krama and Trika. The Krama School is important because it deals with what were considered to be the most secret doctrines and practices of Kashmiri Śaivism, namely, those involved in the worship of Kālī. Basing itself on concepts already developing in the original Tantras and the oral traditions associated with them, the Kashmiri Śaiva Krama elevated the worship of Kālī to a level beyond outer ritual. Ritual came to be understood as an inner process of realisation through which the initiate discovered his essential identity with Kālī Who is the flow (*krama*) of the power of consciousness through the polarities of subject, object and means of knowledge in consonance with their arising and falling away in each act of perception. The experience of this process coupled with the arousing of man's spiritual potential (*kuṇḍalinī*) and the expansion of consciousness that brings it about is the most esoteric practice of Kashmiri Śaivism. The Kaula character of this school is evidenced by the fact that it advocates the ritual consumption of meat and wine as well as ritual intercourse, as a possible means of developing this consciousness.

Abhinavagupta and the Flowering of Trika Śaivism

In order to complete our general survey of the forms of Āgamic Śaivism incorporated into Kashmiri Śaivism, before we turn to those schools that originated in the hands of monist Kashmiri Śaivite philosophers, we turn now to that of the Trika and to Abhinavagupta who developed and made of it the culmination of Kashmiri Śaivism. Abhinavagupta lived in Kashmir from about the middle of the tenth century into the eleventh. He was, without a doubt, the most brilliant of the Kashmiri Śaiva teachers and one of the greatest spiritual and intellectual giants India has produced. He wrote more than sixty works, some very extensive, and all remarkable for the beauty of their Sanskrit and profundity of thought. His literary activity falls into three periods. In chronological order these are:[30]

1) Tāntrika. This, the first period of Abhinavagupta's literary life, extends probably up to his early forties, and concerns us particularly here. In this period Abhinava sought in his writings to establish the superiority of Trika above all other schools of Āgamic Śaivism. His most important work during this period is the *Light of the Tantras* (*Tantrāloka*). It is an extensive and difficult text in which he quotes from numerous Āgamic sources belonging to all (or most) types known in Kashmir. If not the most important, certainly one of the most important works of Tantric Hinduism, it reads as an exposition of Śaivāgamic ritual and practice couched in the monistic philosophy of Kashmiri Śaivism (i.e., the Pratyabhijñā). Abhinava's aim was to bring together the major Śaivāgamic schools into that of Trika Śaivism and in so doing he has provided us with a unique account of Āgamic Śaivism, albeit from his point of view.

2) Poetics and Dramaturgy. In the second period of his life Abhinava wrote important works in these fields. Indeed, it is for this contribution that he is best known. His commentary on the *Nāṭyaśāstra*, the foremost treatise in Sanskrit dramaturgy, is the only one preserved, a fact that testifies to its excellence and influence. Similarly, his commentary on Ānandavardhana's *Mirror of Suggestion* (*Dhvanyāloka*) is justly famous. In this work Ānandavardhana and Abhinavagupta expound the theory that the soul of poetry is its power of suggestion through which sentiment is conveyed to the reader.

3) Philosophical. In the last period of his life Abhinava wrote extensive and profound commentaries on Utpaladeva's *Stanzas on the Recognition of God* (*Īśvarapratyabhijñākārikā*). In these commentaries he elucidates the Doctrine of Recognition (*pratyabhijñā*) which is the monistic philosophy proper of Kashmiri Śaivism to which we shall refer later.

We know that Abhinavagupta was a Brahmin belonging to the *Atrigotra* and that his ancestors were distinguished scholars in the court of Kanauj. They were brought to Kashmir by King Lalitāditya about the middle of the eighth century. Abhinava's grandfather was Varāhagupta and his father Narasiṃhagupta, also known as Cukhala. Despite the Vaiṣṇava connotations of his father's name, he was an ardent devotee of Śiva. Abhinava refers to him reverently in several places as the teacher who taught him, amongst other things, the fundamentals of Sanskrit grammar, logic and literature.[31] His mother, for whom he had great affection, died when he was a child.[32] Abhinava took full advantage of the many Śaiva Masters and teachers of other branches of learning who lived in Kashmir. Even in this, his formative period, he shunned the company of the impious and so, as he tells us, "lived a solitary life devoted to the quest for truth."[33] When Abhinava wrote the *Light of the Tantras* (*Tantrāloka*) in his early middle age, he seems to have had just a small group of close disciples, almost all of whom were members of his family. He tells us that his brother Manoratha was one of the first to learn from him[34] and that he was later joined by Karṇa, the husband of his sister Ambā. Karṇa's premature death, which left his wife alone with their only son, led her to devote herself entirely to the worship of Lord Śiva and the service of her brother. Karṇa's father was a minister who had left the court to become "a minister of the Lord."[35] His sister, Vatsalikā, was the aunt of Mandra, Karṇa's cousin and close friend. All these in-laws of Abhinava's sister were devoted to him and served him faithfully. Thus Mandra invited him to stay in his town outside Pravarapura (modern Srinagar) where, in the house of Vatsalikā, he wrote his *Light of the Tantras* for the benefit of his disciples who, Abhinava tells us at the end of his work, wanted to gain "a perfect knowledge of the Tantras."[36] Almost all the other disciples he refers to here were the sons of his paternal uncle. Amongst them was one called "Kṣema" who may possibly have been none other than Kṣemarāja, his most distinguished disciple. It must have been in this period of his life that Madhurāja, an aged itinerant ascetic, came from South India to Kashmir and wrote his eulogy of Abhinavagupta entitled, *Reflections on the Master* (*Gurunāthaparāmarśa*). There he describes Abhinavagupta as still young and seated in the midst of a great congregation of religious leaders, preceptors and female ascetics (*yoginī*) who recognised him to be the foremost preceptor of all the Śaiva groups then prevalent in Kashmir, including the Siddhānta, Vāma, Bhairava, Kaula and Trika.[37]

Abhinavagupta's works can be said to represent the climax of a hermeneutics of synthesis and exegesis of the Śaivāgama initiated by the revelation of the *Aphorisms of Śiva* (*Śivasūtra*) to Vasugupta in the beginning of the ninth century (see below). In his *Light of the Tantras* which, according to Abhinava, is a manual of the rituals and attendant doctrines of the *Anuttaratrikakula*[38] (also known simply as Trika), he introduced a unified exegetical scheme inspired by Śambhunātha, his teacher in Trika Śaivism. This scheme brings together what he saw as the essential elements of all Śaiva ritual and doctrine. Thus he sought to fill out and complete the theology and praxis of the Trika school.[39] As we know that Śambhunātha came to Kashmir from Jālandharapīṭha (Punjab? Himachal?), and that his teacher, Sumati, came from "some sacred place in the southern land,"[40] it seems therefore that Trika, in the form Abhinavagupta learned it, was not originally Kashmiri. Trika, so called because triads feature prominently in its presentation of the nature of reality and praxis, is said (in the Kashmiri tradition) to look to three scriptures as its primary authorities, namely, the *Mālinīvijayottaratantra*, the *Siddhayogeśvarīmata* and the (*A*)*nāmakatantra*. The *Mālinīvijaya* is quoted by authors prior to Abhinavagupta as was another Trikatantra, the *Trikasāra*.[41] The Triad of Supreme (*Parā*), Middling (*Parāparā*) and Inferior (*Aparā*) goddesses, who are the focus of worship in this school, were also known and venerated[42] in Kashmir before Abhinavagupta's time. Even so, it was he who made Trika the focal point of non-dualist Kashmiri Śaivism.

In order to trace the history of Trika Śaivism we must eventually come to grips directly with Āgamic Śaivism in its original scriptural sources. It is also there that we must seek to uncover the origins of two other Tantric systems scholars have discerned as syncretized in the works of these Kashmiri Śaivites, namely, the Kula and Krama.[43] We must seek out the origins of these systems in the Āgamas because it is in them, and through them, that these systems developed until they emerged, as it were, from out of the dark, mysterious anonymity of scripture and revealed their essential purport in the works of known authors who were the recipients of a traditional interpretation of these scriptures.

This aspect of Kashmir Śaivism is the hardest to deal with because the origins of these systems, with their attendant lineages, are easily lost in their antecedents and in the broader context of the greater cultic milieu of Āgamic Śaivism as a whole. In order to understand Abhinava's Trika (and hence to know an important aspect of Kashmiri Śaivism) we cannot just limit ourselves to the Kula and Krama. Nor is it possible to understand the limit of even these two systems. For although the Krama and Trika can be treated as Tantric systems in the Kashmiri Śaiva context (and we understand Kashmiri Śaivism here in the restricted sense noted above), if we inquire into their antecedents we find that they do not have the same clearly defined identity in their scriptural sources. Thus Kula is not a Tantric school or system in the same sense as are the Trika and Krama insofar as 'Kula' is a broader generic term for a number of major traditions, each with its own secondary branches. Again, in both the Āgamic context and Abhinava's *Light of the Tantras*, "Kula" is not only a blanket term for Kaula Śaivism (as a distinct category of the Śaivāgama)[44] but also indicates a liturgical type or archetypal pattern which Abhinava terms *Kulaprakriyā*, the 'Kula Method'. This method is contrasted with, as complementary to, the basic Tantric Method—*Tantraprakriyā*. The rituals of the Krama school, which involve the consumption and offering of meat and wine to the deity, as well as ritual intercourse,[45] fall into the former pattern. Those of the Trika (as we would expect since it integrates every form into itself) contain both. That Trika and Krama (at least as presented in the Kashmiri Śaiva context) share common Kaula roots is clear from the fact that the masters who are traditionally said to have brought the Kula scriptures to earth are equally venerated in both traditions.[46] This does not mean that the Trika school is to be simply identified with Kula for Abhinava clearly distinguishes between the two in a number of places, usually indicating the superiority of the former over the latter. We understand this to mean not that Trika excludes Kaula Śaivism but that Trika, as presented by Abhinava, completes it, so to say, as its finest flower. Indeed, from Abhinava's point of view, which he supports by reference to scripture and sustains on the authority of his teacher Śambhunātha, Trika comes as the culmination of the entire Śaivāgamic tradition and encompasses it.[47] Heading a hierarchy of Āgamic 'systems', arranged in such a way that the higher members include the lower, Trika (and hence Kashmiri Śaivism) contains them all. Abhinava thinks of Tantric systems in their original Āgamic contexts. He makes observations on the level and relationship between initiates belonging to the different currents (*srotas*) of Śaiva scripture.[48] This is coupled, following a method of exegesis already worked out in the Āgamas themselves, with the hierarchy of forces and metaphysical principles which constitute reality.[49] It makes sense, therefore, that Abhinava should insist that in order to study and understand Kashmiri Śaivism, it is essential not only to have studied grammar, logic and the orthodox philosophical systems, but also to have a sound knowledge of the Śaivāgamas.[50]

Sumati, who was Abhinava's grandteacher in the Trika, was reputed to have a thorough understanding of the five currents of Śaiva scripture as well as the Pāśupata and kindred schools that constitute the Higher Path (*atimārga*).[5]. Trika, Krama and Kula are therefore just a part of what Abhinava and Kashmiri authors have attempted to bring together into one system. Although they are certainly very important, they are far from being the only components. In fact, we should even reckon the dualist Śaivasiddhānta amongst them, not to mention the Āgamas of the Bhairava current of Śaiva scripture. The former is important because it constitutes the backbone of the ritual of Abhinava's Trika, which he presents as blended predominantly with that of the *Mālinīvijaya*, the *Svacchandabhairavatantra* and other Tantras such as the *Triśirobhairava* and *Devyāyāmala*. The latter is important because at least the *Siddhayogeśvarīmata*, one of the most authoritative of the triad of scriptures to which Abhinava's Trika looks for scriptural support, belongs to the Bhairava group of Śaivāgamas.

Tantra, Kashmiri Śaivism and Kashmiri Society in the Eleventh Century

Despite Kalhaṇa's frequent references to temple building and endowments and the pains he takes to note prominent figures in Kashmir's history, and although he himself was Śaivite,[52] he ignores Śaiva teachers of the non-dualist faction. The one exception is a well-known reference to Kallaṭabhaṭṭa,[53] a key figure in the Spanda tradition to whom we shall have occasion to refer later. Clearly what we nowadays call Kashmiri Śaivism was not a religion of the masses. Abhinavagupta himself declares that it is very hard to find even one person who is qualified to follow the Śaivism of his *Light of the Tantras*. Nonetheless, he wishes that "at least someone impelled by Śiva should make an effort to achieve perfection in this system".[54] Here Abhinava is referring specifically to the form of Trika Śaivism he elaborates in this work. He implies that those who dedicated themselves to this system were a minority amongst the followers of that type of Āgamic Śaivism to which the Trika was affiliated, namely, that of the Kaulas and of the Bhairavāgamas. Although the members of these Āgamic traditions were themselves probably a minority of the Hindu population, they must have been a notable feature of Kashmiri society, certainly larger in number than their absence in Kalhaṇa's work would lead one to suppose. This is probably due to the fact that Kalhaṇa, being the son of a minister, was particularly concerned with the history of the Kashmiri courts and their vicissitudes, rather than with the religious history of Kashmir. Although Abhinavagupta, for example, must have been an intellectual of repute, Kalhaṇa never refers to him. This is probably because Abhinava lived a life away from the Kashmiri political scene, never attaching himself to the court despite his reputation among his contemporaries.

Another reason for Kalhaṇa's silence was that the type of Śaiva culture represented in the elevated and refined works of these authors was a source of scandal and the object of active repression. Kalhaṇa himself entertained but scant regard for the individuals who posed as its privileged hierophants. What he has to say about King Kalaśa and his associates exemplifies his attitude well. King Kalaśa (1063-89 A.D.) lived a particularly dissolute life choosing to surround himself with rogues, procurers, and teachers of Tantric cults that encouraged depravity and licentiousness. One such was the 'Cat Merchant' whose influence over the king and the learned of his court suggests that belief in these 'extremist' Bhairava-centred Śaiva cults prevailed at times even in these circles. Thus Kalhaṇa writes:

> These honourable and learned men (*bhaṭṭapāda*) who knew how to behave fearlessly at great [Tantric] rites and who, grimly conscious of their power and thus immune to terror, were heedless even to Bhairava, would fall to the ground in fear and bend their knees before the 'Cat Merchant', who put them at ease again by placing his hand on their heads ... Deceitful of his ignorance and vaunting his [learning] as a physician and Guru, he gradually established a position [for himself] as the Guru of dyers and other craftsmen.[55]

Abhinava, for his part, wrote eulogies of the land of Kashmir as a place where Tantric adepts, male and female, met to drink the wine for which his beloved land was famous and "inspired timid lovers with confidence"[56] to play in this garden strewn with saffron flowers growing as an offering to the Three Goddesses of Trika Śaivism. Kṣemendra, a well-known Kashmiri poet and younger contemporary of Abhinava,[57] on the contrary, was struck by the hypocrisy, greed and lasciviousness of the masters of the Tantric cults belonging to the culture from which Abhinavagupta drew inspiration. He felt it his moral duty to write biting satires on this and other aspects of what he considered to be the corruption that afflicted Kashmiri society in his day.[58] In this spirit he describes in his *Garland of Satire* (*Narmamālā*) a Kaula ritual centred on a maṇḍala in which are drawn male and female sexual organs coupled in union. The rite is officiated by Trighaṇṭika, a Bhairavācārya (also called Kulācārya) who, already in a drunken state, is brought to the house where the rite is to take place, supported by two disciples. His other disciples are a motley crowd of low caste reprobates including shoemakers, butchers, fishermen, fake ascetics, old prostitutes, pimps, liquor distillers and drunken Brahmin bards. Kṣemendra describes him as:

> The Śaiva master (*śaivācārya*), Trighaṇṭika, [disfigured] like the root of an elephant's ear, his eyes wrathful, throat swollen with goitre and nose severed, he performs the Great Vow [*mahāvrata* of antinomian behaviour] and his face is [withered and distorted in appearance like] the female sexual organ. Naked, he attends to the vow of observing the auspicious times [to perform ritual intercourse—*velāvratin*], both silent and a composer of hymns, his knees [are round and swollen like] bells. Exalting, surrounded by dogs and mad women, his body smeared with faeces he knows the Mantras, practices alchemy, magic, and ritual intercourse. Full of wisdom, he knows the nature of lust.[59]

Supposedly learned Brahmins who belonged to the higher levels of society were also among Kṣemendra's favourite targets. Kaula doctrines were, it seems, particularly deleterious for them. He writes:

> [Here], come to his preceptor's house, is the learned Brahmin (*bhaṭṭa*) initiated [into Kaula practice]. In his hands a fish and a jar [of liquor], his mind made up to drink, freed by Kaula doctrine of the sense of shame [he should feel] by virtue of his caste.
>
> Filling himself with [the wine which is] Bhairava, making the sound "gala gala" of a jar as it fills, he seems carried away in its flow and is bent over by its flood [like a jar tipping over in a torrent of water that makes that same sound as it fills].
>
> Passing thus the night [he leaves] drunk, vomiting his wine; his face licked by a dog, the Brahmin in the morning is purified by his prostration in the midst of other learned men.[60]

Cakrabhānu was an important Kashmiri master of the Kālīkrama. According to Kalhaṇa, he was the son of a minister who, for his objectionable practices, was branded on the forehead with the mark of a dog's foot.[61] A manuscript of one of his works, possibly written in prison, is preserved in Nepal. There he writes about how he longs to be released from prison so that he can go out at night to the cremation ground, his forehead covered with the edge of his turban, to offer human sacrifice to the goddess Kālī.[62] Somadeva, a Jain monk living in South India in the tenth century, refers in the *Yaśastilaka* to the Kaulas whom he identifies with the followers of the Trika. He is very critical of the Trika Kaulas whose antinomian behaviour he took to be no more than a sign of their depravity. If salvation were the fruit of reckless living, he says, then it would sooner come to thugs and butchers than to Kaulas. Even though this is almost the only independent reference we have to Trika Śaivism, it is nonetheless solid evidence for the existence of Trika as a distinct school and to its presence far outside the confines of Kashmir.[63] Somadeva also tells us in this way that the followers of the Āgamic Trika were (or at least seemed to him to be) far different from the refined, spiritual Kashmiris, like Abhinavagupta, in whose hands Trika came to finally blossom.

The Philosophy of Recognition and the Doctrine of Vibration

Up to now we have dealt with the components of Kashmiri Śaivism that are derived directly from the Tantric traditions of the Śaivāgamas, namely, the Kula, Krama and Trika. The two schools of Kashmiri Śaivism left to consider, namely, those concerned with the philosophy of Recognition (*Pratyabhijñā*) and the Doctrine of Vibration (*Spanda*), unlike the others, do not extend back directly into Āgamic traditions. Both have, for this reason, a peculiar importance of their own and merit separate consideration as independent schools although they share much in common and have deeply influenced each other. We turn first to the philosophy of Recognition and conclude with the Doctrine of Vibration, the subject of this book.

The Pratyabhijñā represents the fullest expression of Śaiva monism, systematically worked out into a rational theology of Śiva and philosophy of absolute consciousness with which He is identified. The Pratyabhijñā takes its name from the Stanzas on the Recognition of God (*Īśvarapratyabhijñākārikā*) written by Utpaladeva towards the beginning of the tenth century. Utpaladeva understood the ultimate experience of enlightenment to consist essentially of a profound and irreversible recognition that one's own authentic identity is Śiva Himself. According to him:

> The man blinded by ignorance (*Māyā*) and bound by his actions (*karma*) is fettered to the round of birth and death, but when knowledge inspires the recognition of his divine sovereignty and power (*aiśvarya*) he, full of consciousness alone, is a liberated soul.[64]

According to Utpaladeva, the soul is bound because he has forgotten his authentic identity and can only achieve liberation, the ultimate goal of life, by recognising his true universal nature. Realising that everything is a part of himself, extending his being in wonderfully diverse forms, the fettered soul achieves this recognition and with it the conviction that he is not a slave of creation (*paśu*) but its master (*pati*). In this way he who thought himself weak discovers his spiritual might. Failing to recognise his identity with Śiva, the one reality Who is the life and Being of every existing thing, the soul perceives only their individual identity and thus severs them from one another and from himself. For this reason he is seemingly sullied by his actions and afflicted by the myriad conditions that stand as obstacles to the realisation of his goals.[65] Yearning for liberation, he is like a young woman betrothed by arrangement to a handsome man. Hearing of his many fine qualities she comes to love him even though she has never seen him. One day they chance to meet but she remains indifferent to him until she notices that he possesses the qualities of the man she is to marry and so, to her great delight, she recognises him.[66] Similarly, just as man and wife become one in spirit, so the fettered soul becomes one with Śiva by recognising his identity with him, and is liberated.

Utpaladeva's teacher was Somānanda whose *Vision of Śiva* (*Śivadṛṣṭi*) is the first work of the Recognition school. Somānanda lived towards the end of the ninth century and was, he says, the nineteenth in line from Tryambaka. Tryambaka, according to Somānanda,[67] was the mind-born son of Durvāsas,[68] who taught him the principles of Śaiva monism he had learnt on Mount Kailasa from Śrīkaṇṭha, a form of Śiva.[69] Tryambaka figures again in another account, this time one which refers to the origin of Trika.[70] According to this story, Durvāsas was instructed by Śrīkaṇṭha (here represented as an incarnation of Śiva) that "he may spread the wisdom of Trika (*ṣaḍardhakrama*) which is the essence of the secret of all Śaiva scripture."[71] Durvāsas then generated from his mind three perfected yogis, namely, Tryambaka, Āmardaka and Śrīnātha, who taught Śaiva monism, dualism and unity-in-difference, respectively.[72] Of these, the lineage (*sampradāya*) founded by Tryambaka that transmitted monistic Śaivism was none other than that of the Trika.[73]

On the basis of this connection J. C. Chatterjee thought the Pratyabhijñā to be the "philosophy proper of the Trika" and identified the two as did K. C. Pandey.[74] At the same time Pandey simply took the Tryambaka of these accounts to be Somānanda's legendary ancestor[75] and distinguished between monistic Śaivism as a whole founded by Tryambaka and the Pratyabhijñā started by Somānanda.[76] Presumably Pandey believed that Trika was the original form of monistic Śaivism of which the Pratyabhijñā was a later development, initiated by Somānanda. It seems more likely, however, that Trika was traditionally identified in this way with monistic Śaivism as a whole to enhance its importance. In the same way, Somānanda attributed the beginnings of his own system to a popular mythical figure associated with the origins of Āgamic Śaivism in order to lend it the authority of a tradition grounded in the scriptures. To do this he sought the support of an already existing mythical account of the origin of the monistic strains in the Āgamas. Utpaladeva, therefore, is justified in referring to the Pratyabhijñā taught by Somānanda as a 'New Path'.[77] It is, moreover, an entirely Kashmiri product. Jayaratha, Abhinavagupta's commentator, accordingly says that this, the doctrine of the 'oneness of the Lord' (*Īśvarādvayavāda*), initiated by Somānanda, flourished in Kashmir and it is from there that it spread to other parts of India where it was received as a product of that land, as precious and unique to it as saffron itself.[78]

The importance of the Pratyabhijñā in the development of Kashmiri Śaivism lies in its rigorously philosophical exposition of those fundamental principles of monistic Śaivism that Kashmiri Śaivites considered to be essentially common to all the schools of Kashmiri Śaivism. Through the Pratyabhijñā the monism of the Tantric schools and their idealism was supported by sound argument and an analysis of the fundamental problems that any thoroughgoing Indian philosophy must tackle. These problems include the nature of causality, the problem of change and continuity, the nature of the absolute and its relationship to its manifestations and the relationship between God and man.

Somānanda and Utpaladeva enjoy the distinction of having introduced a number of fundamental concepts previously unknown or poorly understood. Certainly the most important of these new ideas was the concept of the Superego. According to these philosophers ultimate reality is Śiva Who is the identity of all beings as pure 'I' consciousness. This entirely original idea had important repercussions in the later monistic philosophies through which the Tantras were interpreted. Worth noting also is the fact that the precedents of what is less original in this philosophy are found not so much in the Āgamas (although it is certainly, as it professes, in harmony with their monistic strains), but in the works of earlier philosophers and so should be considered to belong to the history of Indian philosophy rather than religion.

An important source of the Pratyabhijñā is, for example, the philosophy of the Śaivasiddhānta (not to be confused with the Siddhāntāgamas). Although Śaivasiddhānta is dualist in orientation and insists on a distinction between God and the individual soul, nonetheless it prefigures many of the essential elements of the philosophy of Recognition. Particularly important in this respect is the Siddhānta's phenomenological analysis of Being which stresses the reality of experience. The world is quite real[79] and consciousness is the essential nature of both God and the soul despite their equally essential differences. Consciousness is the direct perception of entities just as they are in themselves, insofar as it is experience-as-such (*anubhava*) free of thought-constructs.[80]

Somānanda was concerned with refuting rival Hindu schools; he does not tackle the traditional enemy of the Hindu philosopher, namely, the Buddhist. Utpaladeva, on the contrary, builds up the Pratyabhijñā as a critique of the Buddhist doctrine of 'no-self' (*anātma-vāda*)[81] and in this way he is clearly following in the tracks of his dualist Śaiva precursors. In a manner reminiscent of Utpaladeva's latter argumentation, the Siddhānta pointed to the phenomenon of recognition as proof that objects are not momentary and that they are essential for language to be possible.[82] Moreover, a conscious Self, the Siddhānta argued, must persist unchanged in order to connect a previous perception with a subsequent perception as a necessary condition for recognition.[83] In Somānanda's work, the term 'recognition' appears just once and does not bear the specific technical sense it has for Utpaladeva. Somānanda does seek to establish that a unity must exist between the perception of a previously perceived object and its recollection in order that its recognition as the same be possible, but he does this merely to prove that an essential unity underlies the two perceptions.[84] He does not think of recognition as the intuitive capacity of consciousness to grasp its own nature. This extension of the recognitive faculty common to every act of determinate perception occurs for the first time with Utpaladeva.

The development of the meaning and implication of the concept of recognition is emblematic of the logical development of this phase of the history of Indian philosophical thought from dualist to monistic Śaivism. It serves to stress the fact that the Pratyabhijñā developed in the milieu of philosophical and theological speculation. The Spanda school and its Doctrine of Vibration, with which this book is concerned, is best understood, however, as a development of the practical application of the yogic doctrines of the esoteric Āgamic traditions of Kashmir.

The Doctrine of Vibration

Just as the Pratyabhijñā school is named after Utpaladeva's *Stanzas on the Recognition of God*, so the Spanda school takes its name from one of its root texts, namely, the *Spandakārikā*, the *Stanzas on Vibration*. The philosophy of the Pratyabhijñā focuses on the liberating recognition of the soul's authentic identity as Śiva while the

Doctrine of Vibration stresses instead the importance of experiencing Spanda, the vibration or pulse of consciousness. The mainstay of the Doctrine of Vibration is the contemplative experience the awakened yogi has of his true nature as the universal perceiving and acting consciousness. Every activity in the universe, as well as every perception, notion, sensation or emotion in the microcosm, ebbs and flows as part of the universal rhythm of the one reality, which is Śiva, the one God Who is the pure conscious agent and perceiver. According to the Doctrine of Vibration, man can realise his true nature to be Śiva by experiencing Spanda, the dynamic, recurrent and creative activity of the absolute.

The Spanda school, like the Pratyabhijñā, originated and developed in Kashmir through the works of known authors, not in anonymous Tantras. Indeed, the origins of this school mark the beginnings of Kashmiri Śaivism in our modern sense of the term. In the first half of the ninth century, a Śaiva ascetic called Vasugupta received, Kṣemarāja tells us, a revelation from Śiva in a dream in which he was told that an important message for all mankind lay hidden on Mount Mahādeva in Kashmir. Going to the spot indicated to him, he found a boulder on which were inscribed the *Aphorisms of Śiva* (*Śivasūtra*).[85] Consisting of some eighty brief statements, the *Śivasūtra* summarizes the essentials of monistic Śaiva Yoga. Although its authorship is traditionally attributed, as is scripture, to Śiva Himself, it is nonetheless the first Kashmiri Śaiva work. Concise as it is profound, the *Śivasūtra* required explanation and so commentaries came to be written, four of which survive. The most extensive is the *Vimarśinī* by Kṣemarāja, Abhinavagupta's closest disciple. It has already been translated into a number of languages. Varadarāja, Kṣemarāja's junior contemporary, wrote another commentary largely based on Kṣemarāja's work. Although lacking originality it does contain a few novel ideas. It is not just a summary of it, as is the anonymous *Śivasūtravṛtti.* A fourth commentary, by Bhāskara, however, differs from it in many respects. Predating Kṣemarāja's work, it appears to represent an independent commentatorial tradition. It is, as yet, untranslated.[86]

Vasugupta's most prominent disciple was Kallaṭabhaṭṭa who lived during the reign of King Avantivarman (855-883 A.D.).[87] *The Stanzas on Vibration* (*Spandakārikā*) are, according to some Kashmiri Śaiva authors,[88] the work of Kallaṭabhaṭṭa who wrote them with the intention of summarizing the teachings of the *Śivasūtra.* Although we cannot be sure whether it was he who wrote the *Stanzas* or, as Kṣemarāja maintains, Vasugupta himself, there can be no doubt that he wrote a short commentary (*vṛtti*) on it which was the first of a series of commentaries by various authors, including two by Kṣemarāja who took a special interest in this branch of Kashmiri Śaivism. Indeed, it seems that Kṣemarāja's very first work was a commentary on the first verse of the *Stanzas* which he called the *Essence of Vibration* (*Spandasaṃdoha*). After writing his commentary on the *Aphorisms*, he wrote an extensive commentary on all the *Stanzas* called the *Determination of Vibration* (*Spandanirṇaya*). This work has been translated.[89]

In a companion volume we shall publish a translation and study of Kallaṭa's commentary along with Kṣemarāja's *Essence of Vibration* and the remaining two surviving commentaries that have not yet been translated, namely, the *Lamp of Spanda* (*Spandapradīpikā*) by Bhagavatotpala and the *Extensive Commentary* (*vivṛti*) by Rājānaka Rāma.[90] Although both predate Kṣemarāja, they are later than Utpaladeva whom they quote and so belong to the latter half of the tenth century. The reader is referred to our volume of translations for a detailed account of these authors and the historical development of the Doctrine of Vibration as reflected in their works.

Notes on Methodology and Synopsis of Contents

This book can be read from two points of view: as an introduction to the doctrines and practices of the Spanda school of Kashmiri Śaivism as well as to Kashmiri Śaivism as a whole. The reader is thus free to read this volume alone or else to make use of it as an introductory study to the companion volume of translations. The scope of the present work covers the exposition of the Doctrine of Vibration in its most complete expression as presented by Kṣemarāja in his commentaries on the *Stanzas on Vibration*, a work which, although considered to be the root text of the Spanda school, Kṣemarāja effectively treats as a concise and direct exposition of the essentials of Kashmiri Śaivism as a whole. It seems that for this reason he boasts of the superiority of his commentary over that of others who failed to present such a complete synthesis of the essential doctrines of all the schools of Kashmiri Śaivism.[91] Insofar as the fifty-one *Stanzas on Vibration* present the essential teachings of the *Aphorisms of Śiva*,[92] which Kṣemarāja characterizes as "a compendium of secret Śaiva doctrine,"[93] they are a succinct exposition of monistic Śaiva yoga—the 'secret' of the Śaivāgama.[94]

Following in Kṣemarāja's tracks, this exposition presents Spanda as a doctrinal formulation of the dynamic character of the absolute and its manifestations at every level of existence and experience. Appearing in many forms, it is a fundamental feature of the Śaiva absolute, both in the primary Āgamic sources and in their exegesis at the hands of Kashmiri authors. In the present work we have therefore chosen to cut across the internal distinctions between schools and traditions within Kashmiri Śaivism to present Spanda as a concept which represents an important point of contact between them, on the one hand, ond on the other to see how each of these schools contribute to the development of the Doctrine of Vibration within the context of the Spanda tradition. In our companion work, particularly in our analysis of the *Stanzas of Vibration* and their commentaries, we note differences in emphasis and terminology and points of divergence between this and other schools of Kashmiri Śaivism. We also indicate how the commentators who have drawn from other traditions have modified the original Spanda doctrine and how it has, in its turn, influenced these other schools. In other words, the presentation of the Doctrine of Vibration in the present work is systematic and generic, whereas in the later it is historical and particular.

These two approaches are possible and valid because Kashmiri Śaivism can be studied as a unit and does indeed constitute, according to its authors, a single corpus of literature. Even so, when we study these works we find ourselves drawn in two directions, one being to consider them as part of a whole, and the other to discern in them different schools or systems.[95] Thus on the one hand we can study each system in the process of its development within the context of Kashmiri Śaivism (and in some cases, through their Āgamic antecedents); on the other hand, we can study Kashmiri Śaivism as a collective development of these various schools. Each system develops to varying degrees, and in different ways, by the accretion of elements from others and can be explained in terms of the other systems. Thus the study of any one of these systems is impossible without reference to the others. This is particularly true of the Spanda tradition because, as already noted, it eventually came to represent a focal point of synthesis of all these schools. From this point of view Spanda presents in general and essential terms the whole of Kashmiri Śaivism.

Thus although this book is about Spanda, the Pratyabhijñā serves as an important source, particularly for the first two chapters because, despite differences in both doctrine and terminology, it has served, within the extended ambit of the Spanda tradition presented by Rājānaka Rāma and Kṣemarāja, as a definitive statement and defence, in philosophical terms, of Spanda doctrine. The point of contact is the idealism of both systems. Consciousness rather than Being is the most perfect representation of the absolute. It is not just a consciousness which observes but one that actively perceives itself as its object through, and as, each act of perception. The fundamental concept of consciousness as a universally active and absolute principle is common to both Spanda and Pratyabhijñā. Indeed, it is common to every formulation of the nature of ultimate reality we find expressed in the varying terminology of the doctrinal systems which constitute the semantic manifold of Kashmiri Śaivism as a whole.

Spanda is the spontaneous and recurrent pulsation of the absolute objectively manifest as the rhythm of the arising and subsidence of every detail of the cosmic picture that appears within its infinite expanse. At the same time, Spanda is the inner universal vibration of consciousness as its pure perceptivity (*upalabdhṛtā*) which constitutes equally its cognizing subjectivity (*jñātṛtva*) and agency (*kartṛtva*). Common to all these systems is this liberating insight into the nature of the outer recurrence of reality through its manifest forms as an expression of its inner freedom and inherent power. It is for this reason that it is possible to move from the world of discourse of one system to that of another to form a single universe of expression.

In Chapter One the Śaiva concept of the absolute is contrasted with that developed through an exegesis of the Upaniṣads by Śaṅkara in his Advaita Vedānta. Although this form of non-dualist Vedānta was unknown to these authors, it represents, typologically, forms of absolutism they knew well, namely, those that understood non-duality solely as the transcendental unity of the absolute. This transcendental absolute is the infinite, supreme reality (*paramārtha*) contrasted with the finite as the ground of its apparent existence. The finite, although not totally unreal, is a lesser reality of undefinable status (*anirvacanīya*), much as an illusion exists in relation to its real ground.

This approach is contrasted with that of monistic Śaivism, which establishes that reality can be one and undivided only if it is understood to be a creative, infinite absolute that manifests itself actively through the finitude and transitoriness of phenomena perpetually changing in consonance with the absolute's activity. Thus we encounter Spanda in its most fundamental form when we deal with the Śaiva solution to the problem of relating the finite to the absolute—a problem common to all absolutisms. It is Spanda, the inscrutable pulse of consciousness, that moves and yet moves not, that changes and yet remains eternally itself, that ensures that both manifestation and the absolute, its unmanifest source, form part of a single process which passes freely from one to the other in such a way that both poles are at the same level and equally real.

Somānanda lists a number of Vedāntas in terms of their most characteristic doctrines. Amongst them are the *bhrāntivādins*, who maintain that the world is an illusion and hence unreal.[96] Thus, although he did not know about Śaṅkara's Advaita, Somānanda was well aware that the world of manifestation can be understood to be less than real, and he is careful to refute this view in various places throughout his work. Later Pratyabhijñā authors, particularly Abhinavagupta, follow suit. The Pratyabhijñā doctrine of manifestation (*ābhāsavāda*) differs radically from that formulated by the forms of Vedānta typified by Śaṅkara's Advaita. From the Advaita point of view, manifestation is an appearing to be (*ābhāsa*) in the place of actual existence. The unity of being appears to be a multiplicity in the sense of its *seeming* to appear as such. Those ignorant of the underlying unity behind this apparent diversity assume that the latter is all that exists whereas it has no real independent existence. The Pratyabhijñā also understands manifestation to be an appearance (*ābhāsa*)—not, however, in the sense of a semblance, but as the manifest form of the absolute. The everyday world of diversity is not a world of semblances contrasted with an absolute that preserves its authenticity and absolute nature by never being actually and phenomenally manifest.

Although these Kashmiri schools are idealist, they affirm the reality of the world and the common commerce of daily life (*vyavahāra*). Even so, the reality status of appearances is variously conceived in the works of Pratyabhijñā authors, and in Kashmiri Śaivism as a whole. To quote extreme examples, we can observe a contrast between the uncompromising realism of Somānanda—for whom even illusions are real insofar as they are manifest appearances—and Abhinava's adaptation of the *Paramārthasāra*, in which we find a clear-cut distinction between levels of manifestation in the absolute, such that the higher levels are fuller expressions of its essential nature, and therefore are more 'real' than the lower levels. Similarly, we can observe a range of views in the commentaries on the *Stanzas on Vibration*. Bhagavatotpala, for example, influenced by monistic Kashmiri Vaiṣṇavism,[97] maintains that the universe is, in a sense, both a real as well as an apparent transformation of the absolute (*pariṇāma* and *vivarta*).[98] Rājānaka Rāma, on the other hand, tends to interpret the *Stanzas* as positing a distinction between a real, ultimate reality (*paramārtha*) and the unreal (*asat*) experience of pleasure, pain and dullness.[99] Kṣemarāja, for his part, maintains that in reality "nothing arises or falls away" but, even so, asserts that manifestation is real in the sense that it is the shining appearing of the power of consciousness.[100] The divergence and contrast between the presentation of Spanda doctrine and its original form in the *Stanzas* is a measure of the divergence of views within the wider ambit of the works by Kashmiri Śaiva authors and those they accepted as authoritative.

Our point of departure here is the presentation of the world-affirming realism of Śaiva absolutism as a whole. Despite the fact that it was variously tempered in the course of its exposition and development, this realism remained essentially unchanged.

Chapter Two deals with the Pratyabhijñā representation of the Śaiva absolute as Light (*prakāśa*) and reflective awareness (*vimarśa*), terms which denote the pure Light of the absolute and its infinite appearing. The absolute is Śiva Who is universal consciousness and man's authentic nature (*ātman*) Who, reflecting on Himself, actively generates and discerns His own manifestations.[101] Thus a striking feature of Pratyabhijñā literature in its original sources is the regular use made of analogies with the properties of light to express and explain the nature of manifestation. It is common in these works for the author to express the notion that an object is manifest, appears, is visible, or just simply exists, by saying that "it shines." Thus, typically, the Pratyabhijñā establishes that all things participate in the one reality by arguing that nothing 'shines' (i.e., appears, manifests or exists in its apparent form) if it is not illuminated by the light of consciousness. If phenomena were to be anything but 'light', they could not 'shine', that is, exist. One cannot help recalling here a famous passage from the *Śvetāśvataropaniṣad:*

> The sun shines not there, neither moon nor stars. There these flashes of lightning do not shine nor does fire. It is that by whose shining all things shine. It is the light of That which illumines all this.[102]

Light and its attendant phenomena fascinated Kashmiri minds. Thus the dualist Kashmiri Siddhāntins also make use of light analogies freely, as do monistic Kashmiri Vaiṣṇavas and Kashmiri poets such as Ratnākara (the author of the *Haravijaya*) who uses words for 'light' or 'brilliance' to express the appearance of the details which fill out and decorate his poetic descriptions. Even so, it is with Utpaladeva and Abhinavagupta that this terminology really comes into its own. Somānanda makes but sparse use of it, while in the *Aphorisms of Śiva* and the *Stanzas on Vibration* which predate Somānanda, the terms 'light' (*prakāśa*) and 'reflective awareness' (*vimarśa*) are entirely absent.

Consequently, Spanda doctrine (and so, one could add, Kashmiri Śaivism at its inception) originally lacked an important characterisation of absolute consciousness which clearly distinguishes it from other Indian absolutisms, namely, its existential status as a Superego (*ahaṃbhāva*). Utpaladeva was later to insist that if the light of consciousness were devoid of reflective awareness, it would be as inert and lifeless as the light of a crystal.[103] He meant to say that the light of consciousness not only illumines and makes manifest all things, but that it is a living light which, reflecting on itself, is an infinite, self-conscious subjectivity. This subjectivity, as the pure 'I' sense, is the very "life of all living beings."[104] Somānanda also refers to Śiva as the pure egoity of 'myself' (*asmad*)[105] and in so doing clearly distinguishes his view from that of his senior predecessors who were the custodians of the doctrines of the *Aphorisms of Śiva* and the *Stanzas on Vibration.*

A careful, unprejudiced reading of the *Stanzas* without reference to its later commentaries (all of which postdate Utpaladeva) reveals that despite the fact that commentators found the Superego hidden in these verses, it was not really there. The original concept of the Self in these early works was, in fact, generally closer to that of the Āgamas, which understood liberation as a freedom from egoity that entailed no loss of personal identity. Accordingly, in the *Stanzas*, this self-identity is neither understood as an impersonal *'ātman'* nor as a Superego, but rather as one's own being (*svabhāva*) which, belonging to none other, is intimately one's own (*svasvabhāva*) as one's own fundamental state of being (*svasthiti*). This personal identity is the living soul (*jīva*) who is none other than Śiva Himself.[106] The soul's inherent and authentic attribute (*akṛtrimadharma*) is cognizing subjectivity (*jnātṛtva*) coupled with agency (*kartṛtva*).[107] Yet although it is thus both the agent and knower, the soul is nowhere identified with an ego-consciousness (*ahambhāva*) even though it is said to be a state of pure perceiving subjectivity (*upalabdhṛtā*). In this way the soul is not confused with the individual subject (*grāhaka*) set in opposition to its object.[108] In the *Stanzas* and in Kallaṭa's commentary, the ego is consistently relegated to the level of a notion or conception of oneself (*ahaṃpratyaya*) which inevitably figures as a part of an idea or mental representation of the type: "I am happy, sad or dull." It is never found as a pure ego outside such patterns of representation.

Of the commentators, only Bhagavatotpala observes this feature of Spanda doctrine without overlaying and obscuring it with ulterior interpretations. This is because he is not concerned to integrate Pratyabhijñā into Spanda doctrine, as are the other commentators who stress, in typically Pratyabhijñā terms, that the goal of the Spanda teachings is the recognition (*pratyabhijñā*) of Spanda as the activity of consciousness. In this way, they say, it is possible to lay hold of one's own authentic identity as the universal agent and perceiver, understood as the universal vibration (*sāmānyaspanda*) of the pure ego. Although Bhagavatotpala does talk of recognition, and even quotes Utpaladeva's

Stanzas on Recognition, his intention is to refer to nothing more than a faculty of individualised consciousness which enables one to recognise past experience and link it with the present. He does this in order to establish the permanence of a personal identity constantly and universally present in all experience. He never represents recognition as an intuitive insight into reality. Bhagavatotpala is in this instance (as he is in general) more consistent with original Spanda doctrine than are other commentators. This is not just because he seeks to be faithful to the text, but also because the monistic Vaiṣṇavism he integrates into Spanda doctrine agrees with it more exactly, in this respect, than does the Pratyabhijñā.

Even so, Spanda is generally represented as the activity of the pure 'I' and more particularly as a manner of characterising the reflective awareness (*vimarśa*) of its universal Light. This identification has been so thorough that the doctrine of Self as 'one's own nature' (*svabhāva* or *svasvabhāva*) no longer features evidently in the works of Kashmiri Śaivas. Although it is in fact a technical term charged with a very specific meaning in its own right, 'own nature' (*svabhāva*) seems in these works to be merely a manner of referring to oneself as an immediate qualification of the ultimate principle and, as such, to pure 'I' consciousness.[109]

In this way the doctrinal identity of the Spanda teachings has been worn away, so much so, that as eminent a scholar as K. C. Pandey has been led to say that the *Stanzas on Vibration* is only a minor treatise dealing with certain aspects of the *Pratyabhijñā* system, particularly with what is termed 'reflective awareness' (*vimarśa*) in Utpaladeva's *Stanzas on Recognition.*[110] Pandey has been misled by the equations made in the Spanda commentaries as well as in the Pratyabhijñā of cognate concepts and terms in the two systems. Thus, for example, *'sphurattā'*, meaning literally 'radiant pulse' or 'glittering', is an inherent quality of the light of consciousness in the Pratyabhijñā world of discourse. It also means 'pulsation' or 'vibration', and so quite naturally is equated with Spanda by Abhinavagupta,[111] who sees it as corresponding to the activity of the reflective awareness of consciousness which reflects upon its manifestations within its own pure noetic continuum. Thus Light (*prakāśa*) represents consciousness as its own illuminating knowledge, and awareness (*vimarśa*) its activity.

In Chapter Two we discuss this dimension of Spanda in Pratyabhijñā terms. In Chapter Three we examine what is meant by 'Spanda' in its own terms as a movement which proceeds from the interior domain of undifferentiated consciousness, out to the exterior domain of its manifestation which is created as it moves outward and is destroyed when it returns to the inner state of undifferentiated unity.

Just as the step from a personal self-identity, which is at the same time the universal perceiving and acting subjectivity identified with Śiva Himself, to a universal 'I' consciousness is a short one, so too that from Spanda (as the creative-cum-destructive activity of Reality) to its representation as power is easily made. In the original Spanda doctrine 'Spanda' is a neutral term simply denoting this recurrent activity, whether it be that of the Supreme Principle in itself (equivalent to Śiva, the male polarity) or that of its power (the female polarity)—a power that extends and withdraws as the will or intent to manifestation. The commentators are, however, generally more struck by the power of this activity, than by the activity itself, and so Kṣemarāja goes so far as to talk of the power of Spanda as *'Spandaśakti'*, a term unknown to other commentators. Once again it is Kṣemarāja and Rājānaka Rāma who depart most distinctly from the original form of Spanda doctrine. Kṣemarāja, who everywhere in his works finds equivalents in Krama doctrine for the essential principles of other systems, here sees *Spandaśakti* as the Krama Goddess of Consciousness (*saṃviddevī*). Rājānaka Rāma, who is not concerned to integrate Krama into the Doctrine of Vibration, finds equivalents in the Śāktism of Pradyumnabhaṭṭa. Thus, universal Spanda, which he equates with the 'principle of power' (*śāktatattva*),[112] is none other than the Supreme Goddess (*parameśvarī*), who manifests Herself as all the principles (*tattva*) constituting the one reality—including Śiva Himself. Therefore, according to Rājānaka Rāma, Spanda is the Goddess Who is the highest principle.

It is not surprising, therefore, that a number of modern scholars consider Spanda doctrine to be Śākta-oriented.[113] Indeed, Spanda regularly figures as Śakti in Kashmiri Śaiva works in general and so is presented in this way in Chapter Four where Śaṅkara and His Spanda nature are viewed as the equivalents of Śiva and Śakti. The relationship between these polarities within the unity of the absolute is examined from various points of view, as presented in the works of Kashmiri Śaiva authors, and in the Āgamas which serve as their sources. The dynamic recurrence which characterises their relationship is, in this exposition, the focus of attention. The pulse of their union and separation is the archetype of the fusion and divergence of opposites, through the interplay of the elements constituting the cosmic order that takes place in harmony with their recurrent emergence and subsidence into the absolute. Although not discussed in these terms in Spanda literature, it finds a place here as a feature of monistic Śaiva (as well as Śākta) metaphysics and its verbalization in these symbolic terms. The relationship between Śaṅkara and Spanda is in this way explained as that which exists between the absolute, as the power-holder, and its power. This relationship is itself Spanda.

Chapter Five discusses a subject which is clearly an element of original Spanda doctrine, namely, the Wheel of Energies (*śakticakra*) of which Śaṅkara is both the source and master. This is a very important topic for Kṣemarāja who comments extensively on the nature of the Wheel of Energies. He is motivated primarily by the intention to demonstrate (as was his teacher Abhinavagupta) that the most secret, and hence highest Śaiva doctrine, is that of the cycle of powers as presented in the Krama tradition, particularly that of the Twelve Kālīs (which Abhinava describes in his *Light of the Tantras*)[114] and that of Vāmeśvarī. The Wheel of Energies is in this way presented as the cycle of universal consciousness which expresses itself at the individual level as, and through, the powers of the senses.

It follows that the next topic is the body of consciousness to which belongs the power of perception operating through the circle of the senses. Thus this is the subject of Chapter Six. The yogi and his experience have gradually come to the fore in the course of our exposition and it is this that concerns us primarily in the remaining portion of this work, just as it does Spanda doctrine. Thus we discuss two forms of contemplative absorption, which Kṣemarāja says are the subject of the entire Spanda teachings, namely, that 'with the eyes closed' and that 'with the eyes open' (*nimīlana* and *unmīlanasamādhi*). Spanda doctrine equates the opening and closing of Śiva's eyes (*unmeṣa* and *nimeṣa*) with His pulsation. It seems obvious to equate it also with the introverted and extroverted phases of the enlightened yogi's contemplation who, one with Śiva, similarly creates and destroys the world of his objectified perceptions by opening and closing his eyes in these two phases of contemplation. Even so, only Kṣemarāja actually makes this connection. In fact, these terms themselves are peculiar to his vocabulary. The concept is attested in the works of earlier authors, just as it is in the primary sources, but these terms, as such, are not previously found elsewhere, not even in Abhinavagupta's works. Thus, although Kṣemarāja most likely derived these formats of representation of yogic states from Krama sources, his application of these categories both fills them out and further contributes to Spanda doctrine. We therefore discuss them in this chapter because they are connected with the operation of the senses and with the yogi's experience of them in consonance with their authentic nature as the powers of consciousness operating in the field of its own manifestation.

In Chapter Seven we discuss the nature of bondage and the means to liberation. Although our concern is primarily with Spanda practice, we present it here in terms of the system of classification of the means to liberation (*upāya*) described by Abhinavagupta. Abhinavagupta quotes the *Mālinīvijayottaratantra* as his authority when defining the fundamental characteristics of these categories;[115] even so, there is no evidence to suggest that this system of classification is applied extensively, if at all, in the Āgamas or elsewhere. On the other hand, it appears that he learnt it from Śambhunātha who taught him Trika doctrine. Thus instructed by the oral tradition, he went on to add it to the patrimony of literate Kashmiri Śaivism. It is for this reason that we find no trace of it in any of the works that predate him. Even so, Kṣemarāja considered that the three sections into which the *Aphorisms of Śiva* are divided dealt separately with these three orders of practice and that the Spanda doctrine of the *Stanzas* could similarly be analysed in terms of these categories. We conclude this work, therefore, with an exposition of these categories in relation to Spanda practice and refer the reader to our translation and analysis of the *Stanzas on Vibration* for its specific features and further details.

I

The Integral Monism of Kashmiri Śaivism

In India, metaphysics serves as a theoretical framework supporting a body of spiritual discipline; it is never merely abstract speculation. More than a reasoned opinion, it indicates the seeker's attitude to his own experience, an attitude that forms the path he treads to salvation. When the seeker acts upon the conclusions he has reached, philosophy blends imperceptibly into religion. To the degree in which he participates in this new attitude, death yields to immortality and the darkness of doubt and ignorance is banished by the light of spiritual illumination. Underpinning the quest is the ultimate goal: gnosis, which is not a knowledge of things but insight into their essential nature. Metaphysical insight is the pinnacle of knowledge. Long ago those who attained this absolute knowledge exclaimed: "no longer can anyone bring before us anything that we have not already found understood or known."[1] It is essentially a state or experience of recognition.

The ways to this realisation are various. We can tread the Path of Wisdom (*jñānamārga*) and seek to intuit the Real, illumined by its own brilliance, in the directness of (an essentially mystical) insight developed through meditative practice and disciplined reasoning (*viveka*). Another way is that of Devotion (*bhaktimārga*) to the embodiment of truth experienced with religious awe and wonder as Deity. A third way is to follow the Path of Yoga and seek freedom directly through mastery (*aiśvarya*) of the Self and with it the All which it contains and governs. From the yogi's point of view this is the most direct approach, for all paths tend towards this achievement. As Karl Potter remarks:

> The ultimate value recognised by classical Hinduism in its most sophisticated sources is not morality but freedom, not rational self-control in the interests of the community's welfare but complete control over one's environment—something which includes self-control but also involves control of others and even control of the physical sources of power in the universe.[2]

Freedom (*svātantrya*) in the sense of both autonomy (*kaivalya*) and mastery (*aiśvarya*) is the goal. It can be attained only if we manage to rid ourselves of outer constraints and limitations. To do this we must be able to homologise with a single, all-embracing reality from which nothing is excluded—neither the world nor ourselves. The dualism of most devotional approaches, however tempered, understands reality in terms which preclude the possibility of ultimate release. If we are to attain salvation, reality can only be one and absolute. In the Hindu tradition the nature of this absolute has been understood in a wide variety of ways. Here we shall consider only two. One is embodied in the metaphysics of Kashmiri Śaivism and the other in that of Advaita Vedānta.

Advaita Vedānta emerged, to a large extent, as a critique of Sāṃkhya dualism. Classical Sāṃkhya posits two realities, both eternal but of contrary nature. One is *Puruṣa*, 'the Person', the other *Prakṛti* or 'Nature'. The Person is the Self who, as pure sentient consciousness, is the witness of the activity of all that lies in the sphere of objectivity. The latter includes not only the outer physical world but also the body and mind the Person inhabits, vitalising and illumining it with his conscious presence. Although varied and constantly changing, all that lies in the sphere of objectivity shares a common nature. All thoughts, perceptions or physical phenomena are equally part of the play of Nature—*Prakṛti*—which manifests in this way to fulfil the need of the Person for phenomenal experience. In this experience the Person represents the principle of sentience and Nature that of change and activity. Just as insentient Nature cannot view itself, and so is as if blind, similarly the Person does not act or change, and so is as if lame.[3] The two together make experience possible. The content of this experience is real but unsatisfactory. The Person is bound by Nature; it experiences the changes in Nature as if they were its own and so suffers their painful consequences. The Person is freed when he discriminates between himself and Nature. The latter then retires into its original unmanifest state severing its association with the Person.

Īśvarakṛṣṇa explains:

> Just as a dancing girl retires from her dance after performing for the audience, in the same way Nature (*Prakṛti*) retires after exhibiting herself to the Person.[4]

In this way the Person achieves a state of transcendental detachment (*kaivalya*). But because the Person is an independent reality, already separate from Nature, he can in fact neither be bound nor released.

> Therefore, no one is actually bound, no one released and no one transmigrates. [It is] Nature, the abode of diversity that transmigrates, is bound and released.[5]

Ultimately, bondage is unreal and no relationship is possible between an eternal subject and an equally eternal object. The problem is that they cannot be related to one another unless this relationship is also eternal. In order to preserve the transcendental integrity of the Person, the reality of Nature must be denied. Not only does the Advaita Vedānta do this, but it also denies that there is a plurality of Persons. The Self, each individual's most authentic identity, is beyond the specifications of the qualities of Nature, and so nothing can distinguish one 'self' from another. The Self is one only and hence none other than the Brahman, the absolute, free of all specification. From this point of view the one reality can only be grasped through negation.[6] However, although this safeguards it from predication it also implies that the empirical (*vyavahāra*) is itself a negation of absolute reality. As Kṣemarāja puts it: "the Brahman is what the world is not."[7] And so the world is less than real. The Brahman is always empirically unmanifest (*avyakta*).[8] It is beyond the reach of the senses but, like the Person, is the witness (*sākṣin*) of all things. It can never be an object of knowledge for "who can know the knower?"[9] Ultimately it is that which cannot be grasped or perceived. The world which is 'grasped' and 'perceived' cannot be the Brahman and is consequently less than real.

Absolute Being is not an existing quality to be found in things; it is not an object of thought or the result of production. It is that from which both speech and mind turn back, unable to comprehend its fullness.[10] To make this point Śaṅkara quotes a passage from a lost Upaniṣad in his commentary on the *Brahmasūtra*. Baṣkali, an Upaniṣadic sage, is being questioned by his disciple about the nature of the absolute. He sits motionless and silent. "Teach me, sir," prayed the disciple.

The teacher continued to be silent. When addressed a second and third time he said: "I am teaching, but you do not follow. The Self is silence."[11]

The undetermined and unthinkable character of the Brahman is a consequence of the absolutes's eternal and immutable nature.[12] To concede the existence of a real universe is, from the Vedāntin's point of view,[13] to posit the existence of a reality apart from the Brahman. Nor can we simply identify a real universe with the absolute unless we are prepared to compromise its unchanging, absolute status. The criterion of authenticity is immutability. Reality never changes; only that which is less than real can appear to do so. Reality is constant in the midst of change. What this means essentially is that there is change although nothing changes. This impossible situation is reflected in the ultimate impossibility of change itself. That which does not exist prior to its changing and at the end, after it has changed, must be equally non-existent between these two moments. Although the world of change appears to be real, it cannot be so.[14] Change, according to the Vedāntin, presupposes a loss of identity. Reality cannot suffer transformation; if it were to do so, it would become something else and the real would be deprived of its reality. The immortal can never become mortal, nor can the mortal become immortal. The ultimate nature of anything cannot change.[15] Change of any sort is merely apparent (*vivarta*); the world of change and becoming is a false superimposition (*adhyāropa, adhyāsa*) on the absolute.[16]

In cosmic terms, the mistake (*bhrānti*) consists of the supposition that the real Brahman is the unreal universe and the unreal universe is the real Brahman. In microcosmic terms, it is the mistake of falsely conceiving the body, mind or even one's personality to be the Self. In the same way as the image of a snake is falsely superimposed on a rope, similarly the universe is falsely projected onto the real substratum, the Brahman. Ignorance is not merely a personal lack of knowledge, but a cosmic principle. As such it is called "Māyā," the undefinable factor (*anirvacanīyā*) that brings this mistake in identity about. The reality status of this cosmic illusion is also undefinable: on the one hand it is not Brahman, the sole reality; on the other hand it is not absolutely non-existent like a hare's horn or the son of a barren woman.

Brahman is the source of world appearances only in the sense of being their unconditioned ground or essential nature. The universe is false not because it has no nature of its own but because it does have one. Just as the illusion of a snake disappears when one sees that it is nothing but a rope, similarly cancellation (*bādha*) of the empirically real occurs when the absolute reality of the Brahman is realised. Thus, according to Vedānta, appearance implies the real, while the real need not imply appearance. To appear is essentially to appear in place of the real, but to be real is not necessarily to appear. All things exist because the absolute exists. It is their Being. Thus the very existence of phenomena implies their non-existence as independent realities. When they are known to be as they are, in the fullest sense of their existence, their phenomenal nature disappears leaving the ground of Being naked and accessible. This approach was validated by a critique of experience. The Vedānta established that space, time and the other primary categories of our daily experience can have no absolute existence. It was therefore necessary to make a distinction between a relative truth—that accepted by the precritical common man—and an absolute truth discovered at a higher level of consciousness.

The Śaiva absolutist[17] rejects any theory that maintains that the universe is less than real. From his point of view a doctrine of two truths, one absolute and the other relative, endangers the very foundation of monism. The Kashmiri Śaiva approach is integral:[18] everything is given a place in the economy of the whole. It is equally wrong to say that reality is either one or diverse. Those who do so fail to grasp the true nature of things which is neither as well as both.[19]

> "We, do not" says Abhinavagupta, "base our contention that [reality] is one because of the contradictions inherent in saying that it is dual. It is your approach (*pakṣa*) that accepts this [method]. [While], if [duality and oneness] were in fact [to contradict each other], they would clearly be two [distinct realities]."[20]

The Vedāntin, who maintains that non-duality is the true nature of the absolute by rejecting duality as only provisionally real, is ultimately landed in a dualism between the real and illusory by the foolishness of his own excessive sophistry (*vācāṭadurvidyā*). Oneness is better understood as the coextensive unity (*ekarasa*) of both duality and unity.[21] They are equally expressions of the absolute.[22] As Gopinath Kaviraj says:

> According to Śaṅkara, Brahman is truth and Māyā is inexplicable (*anirvacanīyā*). Hence the [Advaitin's] endeavour to demonstrate the superiority of Advaita philosophy is turned against his own system. It tarnishes the picture of its philosophical perfection and profundity. It cannot accept Māyā to be a reality, therefore his non-dualism is exclusive. The whole system is based on renunciation and elimination and thus is not all-embracing . . . . By accepting Māyā to be Brahman (*brahmamayī*), eternal (*nityā*) and real (*satyarūpa*), Brahman and Māyā [in the Tantra] become one and coextensive.[23]

The Vedāntin seeks to preserve the integrity of the absolute by safeguarding it from all possible predication. The Śaiva[24] defends the absolute status of the absolute by ensuring that it is in every way self-subsistent (*svatantra*) and all-embracing (*pūrṇa*). The integral nature of the absolute allows for the existence of the world of objectively perceivable phenomena along with the pure subjectivity of consciousness. The two represent opposite polarities of a single reality. Of these two, objectivity is insignificant (*tuccha*) with respect to the ultimacy (*paramārthatva*) of the subject.[25] It is the sphere of negation, in which objectivity presents itself as a void (*śūnya*) in relation to the fullness of the subject.[26] Thus it appears in some Kashmiri Śaiva works that objectivity is said to be false with respect to the ultimate reality of absolute consciousness.[27] What is meant, however, is that nothing can exist apart from the absolute; not merely in the sense that only the absolute exists, but also that nothing exists separated from it. All things are as if nothing in themselves apart from the absolute in this sense alone—it does not mean that they do not exist.[28] The world, in other words, represents a level of manifestation within the absolute which in the process of its emanation must, at a certain stage, radically contrast one aspect of its nature with another to appear as the duality and multiplicity of manifestation.[29] The One is not any one thing because it is all things;[30] excluding nothing from its omniformity, it cannot be defined in any other way than as the Supremely Real (*paramārtha*).

The Real is, from this point of view, the All (*nikhila*). It is the pure absolute because nothing stands outside it which can in any way qualify its absoluteness; on this point at least, Śaiva and Vedāntin are in agreement. It is the Śaiva's approach to establishing the absoluteness of the absolute which differs from the Vedānta. The Śaiva method is one of an ever widening inclusion of phenomena mistakenly thought to be outside the absolute. The Vedāntin, on the other hand, seeks to understand the nature of the absolute by excluding (*niṣedha*) every element of experience which does not conform to the criterion of absoluteness, until all that remains is the unqualified Brahman. The Śaiva's approach is one of affirmation and the Vedāntin's one of negation. They arrive at the absolute from opposite directions. The Vedāntin's way is a path of renunciation founded on dispassion (*vairāgya*) born of discrimination (*viveka*) between the absolutely real and the provisionally relative. It is only when all attachment and, ultimately, perception and thought of the illusory world of phenomena—Māyā—have been abandoned, that the true nature of the absolute is realised to be as it really is, that is, free of all phenomenality. The realisation of the true nature of the relative accompanies the realisation of the absolute.

It is to realise that the world never existed, just as it does not at present, nor ever will.[31] It is just a magic show.

One could say that in this approach the field of consciousness is increasingly restricted to exclude the 'unreal' and focus on the real. It is the Way of Transcendence, and we progress along it by denying all ultimate significance to the transitory. The doctrine is one of world denial. Thus Gauḍapāda, Śaṅkara's teacher, says:

> Constantly reflecting that everything is full of misery, (*sarvaṃ duḥkham*) one should withdraw the mind from the pleasures nurtured by desire. Recalling constantly that the birthless Brahman is all things, one no longer perceives creation.[32]

The Advaitic path leads to a freedom 'from'. Desire is denied because it individualises attention, dispersing it among the objects of desire which are defined as impure matter and ultimately unreal as opposed to the absolute, which is spirit and reality itself. Freedom is ignorance of 'matter-unreality'; conversely, ignorance of the spirit is equivalent to knowledge of matter. These correspond to:

> A) A knowledge of qualities and conditions through acts of determining knowledge (*vikalpa*).
>
> B) A direct experience (*sākṣātkāra*) of the unqualified (*nirguṇa*) free of determinate perception (*nirvikalpa*).

Case A implies a contrast between subject and object, which is unreal or illusory; case B implies the disappearance of the subject-object distinction by denying the reality of the object, and thus expresses the real state of affairs. A and B are not really opposites because A is unreal; consequently the contrast between A and B comes under category A and so is illusory. In other words, our spiritual ignorance (*avidyā*) consists of the false conception that there is a real relationship between the finite and the infinite. Herein we find the philosophical justification for an attitude of detachment. The relationless absolute is realised by the elimination of the finite.

The New Way (*navamārga*)[33] taught in Kashmiri Śaiva doctrine is transcendence through active participation. Not freedom 'from', but freedom 'to'. Desire is not denied, but accepted at a higher level as the pure will or freedom (*svātantrya*) of the absolute. Desire is to be eliminated only if it is desire 'for' (*ākāṅkṣā*), rather than desire 'to' (*icchā*). Matter cannot sully the absolute, nor is it unreal. Freedom is achieved by knowing 'matter-unreality' completely; ignorance of the spirit is ignorance of the true nature of matter. From this point of view ignorance is failure to experience directly the intimate connection (*saṃbandha*) between the infinite and the finite, thus justifying an active participation in the infinite-finite continuum. Following this New Way the transition from the finite to the infinite does not require that we postulate any ontological distinction between them. The finite is a symbol of the infinite. The infinite stamps its seal (*mudrā*) onto its own nature replete with all possible forms of the finite.[34] This is the transcendental attitude of the absolute, namely its impending manifestation as the finite. Reality is the state of eternal emergence (*satatodita*) of the finite from the infinite and vice versa. Expansion of the relative distinction (*bheda*) between the elements constituting the All is equivalent to contraction of the undivided (*abheda*) awareness of its totality and vice versa. Neither excludes the other, but together they participate in the all-embracing fullness (*pūrṇatā*) of the pulsation (*spanda*) of the absolute in its different phases of being. True knowledge (*sadvidyā*) from this point of view, is to know that the apparent opposites normally contrasted with one another, such as subject and object, unity and diversity, absolute and relative, are aspects of the one reality.

The Vedāntin's way is one of withdrawal from the finite in order to achieve a return (*nivṛtti*) to the infinite. This process, however, from the Śaiva point of view is only the first stage. The next stage is the outward journey (*pravṛtti*) from the infinite to the finite. When perfection is achieved in both movements, that is, from the finite to the infinite and back, man participates in the universal vibration of the absolute and shares in its essential freedom. Thenceforth, he no longer travels 'to' and 'from' but eternally 'through' the absolute, realised to be at once both infinite and finite.[35] The highest level of dispassion (*paravairāgya*) is not attained by turning away from appearance but by realising that the absolute manifests as all things.[36] The absolute freely makes diversity (*bheda*) manifest through its infinite power. The wise know that this power pours into the completeness of the All (*viśvamaṇḍala*) and in so doing, flows only into itself.[37] Standing at the summit of Being (*parakāṣṭhā*) the absolute is brimming over with phenomena. The streams of cosmic manifestation flow everywhere from it as does water from a tank full to overflowing.[38] Replenished inwardly by its own power, it emerges spontaneously as the universe, and makes manifest each part of the cosmic totality as one with its own nature.[39]

The involution of phenomena and their reassimilation into the absolute is not enough. True knowledge and perfect dispassion can only be achieved when we realise that the universe is the expansion (*vikāsa*) of the absolute void of content (*śūnyarūpa*).[40] The absolute will (*icchā*) is the driving force behind this cosmic expansion. It is the pure intent of Being to act and exist which although, in a sense, is similar to mundane desire is unsullied by any object of its intent (*iṣyamāna*)[41] and so differs fundamentally from it. The absolute yearns for nothing other than itself. Desire is not to be abandoned but elevated to the level of this pure will (*icchāmātra*). This is achieved not by restraint or suppression of desire, but by merging it with the divine creative will of the absolute. This is the spontaneity of the Way of Wholeness. Quotes Jayaratha:

> Those who went before said that [desire] is checked by the practice of dispassion; we teach that this is achieved by desisting from all effort.[42]

The absolute oscillates between a 'passion' (*rāga*) to create and 'dispassion' (*virāga*) from the created. This is the eternal pulsation—Spanda—of the absolute. Through it the absolute transforms itself into all things and then returns back into the emptiness (*śūnya*) of its undifferentiated nature. Both poles of this movement are equally real; both are equally absolute. Allowing for the reality of manifestation, the Śaiva absolute is called the Great Oneness (*mahādvaya*).[43] An experienced music lover, hearing a fast sequence of notes played on the *vīṇā* can distinguish whether the microtones are high or low.[44] Similarly the well-practiced yogi can discern the unity of reality while phenomena are manifest to him. If duality and unity were in fact absolute contraries, the moment they appeared together, they would cancel each other out. This, however, is not the case. We continue to experience the diversity of daily life (*vyavahāra*).[45] The Vedāntin who distinguishes between duality and unity, saying that the former is false while the latter is true, is under the spell of Māyā—the ignorance he seeks so hard to overcome. All forms of relative distinction, even that between the dual and the non-dual, are due to Māyā; none of them are applicable to the uncreated, self-existent reality, free of all limitation.[46] Abhinava writes:

> Where duality, unity and both unity and duality are equally manifest is said to be [true] unity. To those who object that in that case diversity (*bheda*) must also exist, [we say:] so be it: we do not want to speak overmuch. We neither shun nor accept [anything] that [manifests to us] here [in this world] as you do. If you wish to be supported by the view that favours all then resort to the doctrine of Supreme Unity, the great refuge you should adopt.[47]

The one reality is manifest both as unity and diversity. There can be no real unity unless diverse elements are united in the wholeness of totality. On the other hand, without unity, diversity would be unintelligible. A total dispersion of elements does not constitute diversity but a number of single, unrelated units.[48] Just as everything that falls into a salt mine becomes salty, so all this diversity, grounded in unity, shares in the single flavour of oneness.[49] There is an undeniable difference between individual phenomena, but the distinction we perceive between two entities which leads us to think that one differs from the other is merely external.[50] Relative distinction is not an inherent quality of things that can divide their innate nature, not because this division (*bheda*) is in any way unreal, but because it operates within the domain of the real, which appears as phenomenally manifest. Division (*bheda*) is merely the relative distinction between two manifest entities; it is based on the difference between their manifest form.

> "Relative distinction between two realities (*tattva*)," writes Abhinava, "is not impossible. This is the doctrine of Supreme Unity in which relative distinction is neither shunned nor accepted. While there is [an external] difference between phenomena, there is none [inwardly], established as they are in their own essential nature."[51]

Reality is the One (*eka*) which becomes manifest as the many (*bahu*). Universal Being moves between two poles, viz., diversification of the one and unification of the many. Thought (*vikalpa*) interferes with our direct intuitive understanding of this fact and splits up the two aspects of this movement into separate categories. Reality is a structured whole consisting of a graded hierarchy (*tāratamya*) of metaphysical principles corresponding to the planes of existence (*daśā*). On the lowest planes up to the level of Māyā, we experience division (*bheda*) between objects and ourselves; at the highest level we reach the plane of unity (*abheda*) which pervades and contains within itself all the others. Maheśvarānanda writes:

> We maintain that the basis of duality (*bheda*) in the [empirical] universe is a phase (*vibhāga*) [of reality]. The separation between things is certainly not adventitious (*upādhi*) for then they [i.e., the object and its separatedness] being two, unity would stand contradicted.[52]

He goes on to say:

> The various categories of existence (*padārtha*), though distinct from one another in their [outer form] must be, in terms of their essential specific nature, a single collective reality.[53]

This understanding of reality allows for a range of insights into its nature which complement and sustain each other without conflict. Almost every school of Indian thought aspires to lead us to a plane of being and an experience which it believes to be the most complete and satisfying. This is the liberation it offers. All these views are correct insofar as they correspond to an actual experience. But this is because the absolute, through its inherent power, assumes the form of all the levels of realisation (*bhūmikā*) which correspond to the ultimate view (*sthiti*) each system upholds.[54] Dualism is not an incorrect view of reality although it corresponds to only one of the levels within the absolute.

Citing the well-known Jaina example, Abhinava explains that the exponents of different systems are like blind men who, presented with an elephant, touch one part or another and argue amongst themselves about what it could be. This is not because they disagree completely but because their agreement is only partial.[55] Ultimately, differing views of reality are the result of the capacity (*śakti*) of the absolute to appear in different forms.[56] Rather than reject all views as incorrect because they are not completely true, the Kashmiri Śaiva prefers to accept them all because they are partially true. System builders are all equally concerned with reality, but are like children of feeble intellect (*sukumāramati*) who have not yet reached the supreme summit (*parakāṣṭhā*) of the absolute, the experience of Supreme Oneness. They cannot, as yet, look down to the lower planes and see their role within the whole. Accordingly Maheśvarānanda says:

> Not accepting each others' point of view they talk of Your universal nature in terms of that which is to be refuted and that which refutes it in order to reject [their] opponents' position.[57]

Why does this phasing or hierarchy of planes not divide the absolute? The answer to this question will emerge through a closer examination of the nature of the Śaiva absolute. Śaivism equates the absolute wholly with consciousness. Reality is pure consciousness alone (*saṃvid*). Consciousness and Being are synonymous.[58] To experience the essential identity between them is to enjoy the bliss (*ānanda*) of realisation.[59] The Advaita Vedāntin maintains that in a primary sense reality cannot be characterised in any particular way, but affirms that secondarily we can conceive it to be 'Being-Consciousness-Bliss (*saccidānanda*). Being, understood as an absolute substance (which is not substantial in a material sense), is the model for the Advaita conception of consciousness. Monistic Śaivism, on the other hand, considers consciousness to be the basic model through which we understand Being. Consciousness from the Vedāntin's point of view is the microcosmic parallel of macrocosmic Being. Being is the real substratum of the universe and consciousness that of the individual personality (*jīva*). Hence consciousness, like Being, is perfectly inactive, a pure noetic plenum: knowledge as such, without an object of knowledge or even self-awareness. He maintains that consciousness is autonomous; it is an eternal reality that does not depend on the mind or body for its existence. On this point, the Śaivite and Vedāntin agree. Abhinava pours scorn on materialist views; making no pretence at politeness, he says,

> Some fools consider that nothing apart from the body exists because movement arises from the body, whose property is consciousness, which in its turn is one with the vital breath. This conception, peculiar to individuals (of low status) such as children, women and idiots is, by the materialists, elevated to the status of a system.[60]

The concept of consciousness is the firm foundation upon which Kashmiri Śaiva metaphysics is constructed. One could almost describe it as a psychology of absolute consciousness. Consciousness is more than the awareness an individual has of himself and his environment; it is an eternal all-pervasive principle. It is the highest reality (*paramārtha*) and all things are a manifestation of this consciousness (*cidvyakti*).[61] All entities, without distinction, are of the nature of consciousness[62] and hence reality can be positively affirmed to be a 'compact mass of consciousness and bliss' (*cidānandaghana*). There are no holes or gaps anywhere in reality where consciousness is absent. It is eternally and blissfully at rest within its own nature (*svātmaviśrānta*), free of all association with anything outside itself.[63] Free of all craving for anything (*nirākāṅkṣa*) and independent (*nirapekṣa*), it looks to none other but itself (*ananyamukhaprekṣin*).

The essential nature (*svabhāva*) of this pure universal consciousness is the true nature of the Self. As the supreme subject who illumines and knows all things, it is called the 'Great Light' (*mahāprakāśa*) which is uncreated and can never be taught (*aśrauta*). Figuratively described as the sun of consciousness, its light absorbs duality in its brilliance, bathing the whole universe with the splendour of its divine radiance. Making all things one with its nature, it transforms them into the sacred circle (*maṇḍala*) of its own rays.[64] Not only is consciousness absolute, it is also divine. It is Śiva, the Lord (*cinnātha*) of the universe.[65] As the authentic identity (*ātman*) of all living beings, consciousness is the supreme object of worship, the true nature of Deity.[66] Consciousness is God and God is consciousness by virtue of its very nature; omnipotence, omniscience and all the other divine attributes are in fact attributes of consciousness. Bhagavatotpala, commenting on the *Stanzas on Vibration*, quotes:

> In none of Your states [O Lord] is consciousness absent. Therefore, You are worshipped as the yogi's dense mass of consciousness alone.[67]

Consciousness is not a passive witness (*sākṣin*), but is full of the conscious activity (*citikriyā*) through which it generates the universe[68] and reabsorbs it into itself at the end of each cycle of creation. The freedom (*svātantrya*) of consciousness to do this is its sovereign power (*aiśvarya*) by virtue of which it is the one God Who governs the entire universe. Absolute freedom to know and do all things is the primary characteristic of Deity:

> The governing power of the Supreme Lord Whose nature is His own unique eternal nature as pure agency (*kartṛtā*) whose essence is the divine pulsing radiance (*sphurattā*) of the light of consciousness.[69]

Both dynamic and creative, this divine power is Spanda—the vibration of consciousness. Its universal activity is the basis of Śiva's divine sovereign status. Indeed, Spanda is Śiva's most essential nature for without it He would not be God. As Kṣemarāja says:

> Thus God (*bhagavat*) is always the Spanda principle with its dependent categories—He is not motionless (*aspanda*) as those who say, 'the supreme reality is perfectly inactive (*aspanda*)'. If that were so, His nature would be a self-confined stasis (*śāntasvarūpa*) and so He would not be God at all.[70]

The supreme reality which is 'perfectly inactive' is like the Vedāntin's Brahman. Although the Vedāntin says that 'God alone is the source of all things',[71] Brahman cannot be a creator God (*īśvara*) for His supposed creation is unreal. A creator implies that His creation is a separate reality and this would contravene the fundamental principles on which Advaita Vedānta bases its concept of non-duality. Accordingly, Śaṅkara says:

> God's rulership, omniscience and omnipotence are contingent to limiting adjuncts conjured up by nescience: in reality such terms as ruler and ruled, omniscience etc., cannot be used with regard to the Self shining in its own nature.[72]

Kashmiri Śaivism, on the contrary, believes in a personal absolute God Who is the one reality (*īśvarādvayavāda*). The planes within the absolute correspond to a hierarchy of deities which rule over them, empowered to do so by the Supreme Deity: consciousness. Absolute Deity is the highest level of consciousness which stands at the supreme summit of Being (*parakāṣṭhā*). It is attained by a process of ascent through higher levels or, in other words, through increasingly expanded states of consciousness, until we reach the highest and most complete state of expansion possible (*pūrṇavikāsa*). The Supreme Lord rests at the end of the expansion or evolution of objectivity from the lowest level to the supramental state (*unmanā*) of pure consciousness.[73]

This supreme state is named variously in the differing traditions syncretised into Kashmiri Śaivism. Thus Bhairava (the 'wrathful' form of Śiva) figures as the supreme God in Abhinavagupta's works when he deals with the doctrine and ritual of the Kaula schools (including Trika and Krama) and those in various ways linked to them. This male principle is associated with corresponding female ones such as Kālī, Kālasaṅkarṣiṇī (the 'Attractress of Time'), Mātṛsadbhāva (the 'Essence of Subjectivity') and Parā (the 'Supreme'). In the Spanda school the supreme male deity is Śiva Who is also called Śaṅkara, while Spanda is by some identified with the Goddess. When no sectarian distinctions are intended, the supreme is simply called Parameśvara (the Supreme Lord), Paramaśiva or just Śiva.[74]

Śaiva Idealism

Interiority (*antaratva*) is the keynote of both Kashmiri Śaiva metaphysics and practice: it is a 'doctrine which maintains that everything is internal' (*antarārthavāda*).[75] Everything, according to this view, resides within one absolute consciousness. It is the great abode of the universe.[76] Full (*pūrṇa*) of all things, it sustains them all and embraces them within its infinite, all-pervasive nature. Utpaladeva writes:

> O Lord, some, greatly troubled, move perplexed (*bhramanti*) within themselves while others, well established [in themselves], wander in that which is their own Self alone.[77]

All events are consciously experienced happenings. According to Somānanda, only that which hypothetically exists outside consciousness can be said to be non-existent (*avastu*) and hence false. Daily life carried on without knowledge that everything is manifest within consciousness is illusory or unreal in that sense alone.[78] Things are more real or more tangibly experienced according to their own essential nature (*svabhāva*) to the degree in which we recognise that they are appearances (*ābhāsa*) within absolute consciousness. As Jayaratha says:

> Just as images manifest in a mirror, for example, are essentially mere appearances, so too are [phenomena] manifest within consciousness. Thus, beause they are external, [phenomena] have no being (*sattva*) of their own. The Lord says this [not with the intention of saying anything about the nature of things] but in order to raise the level of consciousness of those people who are attached to outer things; thus everything in this sense is essentially a mere appearance. [Knowing this], in order to quell the delusion of duality, one should not be attached to anything external.[79]

The ultimate experience is the realisation that everything is contained within consciousness. We can discover this in two ways. Either we merge the external world into the inner subject, or we look upon the outer as a gross form of the inner. In these two ways we come to recognise that all things reside within our own consciousness just as consciousness resides within them.

This all-embracing inwardness is only possible if there is an essential identity between the universe and consciousness. The events which constitute the universe are always internal events happening within consciousness because their essential nature is consciousness itself.[80] We can only account for the fact that things appear if there is an essential identity between consciousness and the object perceived.[81] If a physical object were really totally material, that is, part of a reality independent of, and external to, consciousness, it could never be experienced.[82] Abhinava says:

> The existence or non-existence of phenomena within the domain of the empirical (*iha*) cannot be established unless they rest within consciousness. In fact, phenomena which rest within consciousness are apparent (*prakāśamāna*). And the fact of their appearing is itself their oneness (*abheda*) with consciousness because consciousness is nothing but the fact of appearing (*prakāśa*). If one were to say that they were separate from the light of [that consciousness] and that they appeared [it would be tantamount to saying that] 'blue' is separate from its own nature. However, [insofar as it appears and is known as such] one says: 'this is blue'. Thus, in this sense, [phenomena] rest in consciousness; they are not separate from consciousness.[83]

The universe and consciousness are two aspects of the whole, just as quality and substance constitute two aspects of a single entity. The universe is an attribute (*dharma*) of consciousness which bears (*dharmin*) it as its substance.

> It is said that 'substance' is that resting in which this entire group of categories manifests and is made effective. Now, if you don't get angry [we insist that] this entire class of worlds, entities, elements and categories (*tattva*) rests in consciousness and [resting in it] is as it is.[84]

Thus consciousness contains everything in the sense that it is the ground or basis (*ādhāra*) of all things, their very being (*sattā*) and substance from which they are made. But, unlike the Brahman of the Advaita Vedānta, it is not the real basis (*adhiṣṭhāna*) of an unreal projection or illusion. Consciousness and its contents are essentially identical and equally real. They are two forms of the same reality. Consciousness is both the substratum and what it supports: The perceiving awareness and its object.[85] In this respect, the Kashmiri Śaiva is frankly and without reserve an idealist. Although he does not deny the reality of the object, his position is at odds with most commonly accepted forms of realism. The realist maintains that the content perceived is independent of the act of perception. The content is only accidentally an object of perception and undergoes no change in the process of being perceived. His contention, however, is essentially unverifiable; to verify it, we would have to know an object without perceiving it. This, from the Kashmiri Śaiva point of view, is not possible. Objects of which we have no knowledge may indeed exist, but they are knowable as objects only if they are related to subjects who perceive them. In this sense, if there were no subjects, there could be no objects.[86] The subject, however, as opposed to the object is, in terms of the phenomenology of perception, apparent to himself. He is self-luminous (*svaprakāśa*). Thus, consciousness (the essence of subjectivity) is one's own awareness by virtue of which all things exist.[87]

The realist maintains that consciousness clearly differs from its object insofar as their properties are contrary to each other. The Śaivite idealist, however, says that the object is a form of awareness (*vijñānākāra*).[88] The objective status of the object is cognition itself.[89] Perception manifests its object and renders it immediately apparent (*sphuṭa*) to those who perceive it.[90] It does not appear at any other time.[91] If 'blue' were to exist apart from the cognition of 'blue', two things would appear: 'blue' and its cognition, which is not the case.[92] It is the perception of the object which constitutes its manifest nature. An entity becomes an object of knowledge not by virtue of the entity itself but by our knowledge of it. If objects had the property of making other objects appear, it would be possible for one object to make another appear in its own likeness. 'Blue' is perceived to be 'blue' because it is manifest as such to the perceiver.[93] As Abhinava points out:

> The [nature of an] object of knowledge could not be established through a means of knowledge totally unrelated to it—a crow does not become white because a swan [sitting next to it] is white.[94]

Perception, on the other hand, is immediately apparent to consciousness. It is self-luminous in the sense that it is directly known without need of being known by any ulterior acts of perception and makes its object known at the same time.[95] Adopting the Buddhist Yogācāra doctrine that things necessarily perceived together are the same (*sahopalambhaniyamavāda*), the Śaivite affirms that because the perceived is never found apart from perception, they are in fact identical.[96] Reality (*satya*) is the point where the intelligible and the sensible meet in the common unity of being; it cannot be said to exist in itself outside, and apart from, knowledge or vision. Bhagavatotpala in his commentary on the *Stanzas on Vibration* quotes:

> Once the object is reduced to its authentic nature, one knows [the true nature of] consciousness. What then [remains of] objectivity? What [indeed could be] higher than consciousness?[97]

Consciousness is essentially active. Full of the vibration of its own energy engaged in the act of perception, it manifests itself externally as its own object. When the act of perception is over, consciousness reabsorbs the object and turns in on itself to resume its undifferentiated inner nature.[98]

> Knowledge (*jñāna*) manifests internally and externally as each individual entity . . . . Once knowledge has assumed that form it falls back [into itself].[99]

The Yogācāra Buddhist similarly maintains that consciousness creates its own forms. But, according to him, because the perceived and perception are identical, there is no perceived object at all. The so-called outer world is merely a flux of cognitions, it is not real. He is firmly committed to a doctrine of illusion. The reality of consciousness from his point of view is established by proving the unreality of the universe.

"All this consists of the act of consciousness alone", says Vasubandhu, "because unreal entities appear, just as a man with defective vision sees unreal hair or a moon, etc.".[100]

He points to dreams as examples of purely subjective constructs which appear to be objective realities. The apparent reality dreams possess is not derived from any concrete, objective world, but merely from the idea of objectivity. While the Yogācāra does not say that an idea has, for example, spatial attributes, it does have a form manifesting them. While he agrees with the Śaiva idealist that appearances have no independent existence apart from their appearing to consciousness, he maintains that for this reason they are unreal. The creativity of consciousness consists in its diversification in many modes having apparent externality; it is not a creation of objects.

While the Kashmiri Śaivite agrees that the world is pure consciousness alone, he maintains that it is such because it is a real creation of consciousness. The effect is essentially identical with the cause and shares in its reality. Matter and the entire universe are absolutely real, as 'congealed' (*styāna*) or 'contracted' (*saṃkucita*) forms of consciousness. "This God of consciousness", writes Kṣemarāja, "generates the universe and its form is a condensation of His own essence (*rasa*)."[101] By boiling sugarcane juice it condenses to form treacle, brown sugar and candy which retains its sweetness. Similarly, consciousness abides unchanged even though it assumes the concrete material form of the five gross elements.[102] The same reality thus abides equally in gross and subtle forms.[103] Consequently no object is totally insentient. Even stones bear a trace (*vāsanā*) of consciousness, although it is not clearly apparent because it is not associated with the vital breath (*prāṇa*) and other components of a psycho-physical organism.[104] Somānanda goes so far as to affirm that physical objects, far from being insentient, can only exist insofar as they are aware of themselves as existing.[105] The jar performs its function because it knows itself to be its agent.[106] Indeed, all things are pervaded by consciousness and at one with it and hence share in its omniscience.[107] Thus, Śiva, Who perceives Himself in the form of physical objects, is the one ultimate reality.[108]

> "The jar knows because it is of my nature", writes Somānanda, "and I know it because I am of the jar's nature. I know because I am of Sadāśiva's nature and He knows because He is of my nature; Yajñadatta [knows] because he is of Śiva's nature and Śiva [knows] because He is of Yajñadatta's nature".[109]

Everything in this sense is directly perceived by absolute consciousness, and this direct perception (*pratyakṣa*) unifies the knowable into a single, undivided whole. This is the central concept behind a doctrine originally expounded by Narasiṃha called 'the non-dualism of direct perception' (*pratyakṣādvaita*).[110] This states that consciousness is essentially perceptive and that its perception of all things operates throughout the universe.[111] Insofar as phenomena are clearly evident (*sphuṭa*) to us, everything is directly perceived by absolute consciousness, with which our individual consciousness is identical. This direct perception unfolds everywhere; the one true reality, it is alone and without companion or rival (*niḥsapatna*). Even though it remains one, it can, by its very nature, perceive distinctions (*bheda*) between one entity and another, without this engendering any division within it.[112]

We distinguish between two entities in empirical terms on the basis of their mutual exclusion (*anyonyābhāva*). The relative distinction (*bheda*) between them is essentially the perceived difference between their respective characteristics. Despite this difference they are united within the purview of a single cognition insofar as they are equally both manifest appearances. This cognition is the undivided essence (*rasa*) or 'own nature' (*svabhāva*) of both. Encompassed by the 'fire of consciousness', there is no essential difference between them. Just as when an emerald and ruby reflect each other's light, the ruby is reddish-green and the emerald greenish-red, similarly everything is connected with everything else as part of the single variegated (*vicitra*) cognition of absolute consciousness.[113] Maheśvarānanda writes:

> The Supreme Lord's unique state of emotivity (*asādhāraṇabhāva*) is the outpouring of pure Being (*mahāsattā*). It is manifest as the brilliance (*sphurattā*) of the universe which, if we ponder deeply, [is realized to be] the single flavour (*ekarasa*) of the essence of Beauty which is the vibration of the bliss of one's own nature.[114]

In this way all things are in reality one although divided from the one another sharing as they do the 'single flavour' (*ekarasa*) of the pure vibration of consciousness.

Kashmiri Śaiva Realism

Kashmiri Śaivism as a whole has been variously called a form of 'realistic idealism',[115] 'monistic idealism',[116] 'idealistic monism'[117] and 'concrete monism'.[118] It is easy to understand why Kashmiri Śaivism is said to be 'idealistic' and 'monistic', but in what sense is it also 'realistic'? The answer to this question is of no small importance in trying to understand the central idea behind its metaphysics and the fundamental importance of the concept of Spanda, in this seemingly impossible marriage between monistic idealism and pluralistic realism.

The Kashmiri Śaiva approach understands the world to be a symbol of the absolute, that is, as the manner in which it presents itself to us. Again we can contrast this view with that of the Advaita Vedānta. The Advaita Vedānta understands the world to be an expression of the absolute insofar as it exists by virtue of the absolute's Being. Being is understood to be the real unity which underlies empirically manifest separateness and as such is never empirically manifest. It is only transcendentally actual as 'being-in-itself'. The Kashmiri Śaiva position represents, in a sense, a reversal of this point of view. The nature of the absolute, and also that of Being, is conceived as an eternal becoming (*satatodita*), a dynamic flux or Spanda,[119] 'the agency of the act of being'.[120] It is identified with the concrete actuality of the fact of appearing, not passive unmanifest Being. Appearance (*ābhāsa*) alone is real.[121] Appearing (*prakāśamānatva*) is equivalent to the fact of being (*astitva*).[122] Kṣemarāja writes in his commentary on the *Stanzas on Vibration:*

> Indeed, all things are manifest because they are nothing but manifestation. The point being that nothing is manifest apart from manifestation.[123]

The absolutely unmanifest, from this point of view, can have as little existence as the space in a lattice window of a sky-palace. Nay, even less, because even that space can appear as an imagined image manifest within consciousness.[124] Everything is real according to the manner in which it appears.[125] Even an illusion is in this sense real, insofar as it appears and is known in the manner in which it appears. The empirical and the real are identical categories of thought. As Abhinava says:

> Thus this is the supreme doctrine (*upaniṣad*), namely that, whenever and in whatever form [an entity] appears, that then is its particular nature.[126]

Perhaps at this stage a brief comparison with Heidegger's ideas might prove to be enlightening and not altogether out of place. According to Heidegger's phenomenology of Being, reality is intelligible in a two-fold manner as 'phenomenon' and 'logos'. Heidegger defines what he means by 'phenomenon' as: "that-which-shows-itself. The manifest . . . phenomena are then the collection of that which lies open in broad daylight or can be brought to the light of day—what the Greeks at times implicitly identified as 'ta onta' (the things-which-are)".[127] In his later writings Heidegger drops the term 'phenomenon' in preference for the verbal form 'phainesthai' in order to emphasize even more the actuality or presentational property of Being. Explaining this new form of the term he writes: "Being disclosed itself to the ancient Greeks as 'physis'. The etymological roots 'phy-' and 'pha-' designate the same thing: 'phyein', the rising-up or upsurge which resides within itself as 'phainesthai', lighting-up, self-showing, coming-out, appearing-forth."[128]

Heidegger contrasted his notion of phenomenon with semblance (*Schein*) and with appearing (*Erscheinung*). In the case of semblance a thing can show itself as that which it is not, as when fool's gold shows itself to be gold. The ancients always allied semblance with non-being. Heidegger points out, however, that semblances are grounded in showings, and so does Abhinava. Both Heidegger and Abhinava consequently maintain that all semblances have a real basis and are to be treated as instances of phenomena along with the so-called real showing or manifestation of non-deceptive objects. So Heidegger states that: 'however much seeming, just that much being'.[129] Thus self-showing or appearing defines Being as phenomenon, but this definition of Being is as yet incomplete. Being is not only self-showing but 'logos' which Heidegger explains means 'discourse' (*Rede*) in the sense of 'apophansis': 'letting-be-seen'. Phenomenology, which according to Heidegger is the only correct study of Being, means 'letting-be-seen-that-which-shows-itself'. This is true of Śaiva *Paramādvaita* as well.

The reality of the world demands recognition; we are forced to accept the direct presentation of the fact of our daily experience. As Abhinava says: "if practical life, which is useful to all persons at all times, places and conditions were not real, then there would be nothing left which could be said to be real."[130] A thousand proofs could not make 'blue' other than the colour blue.[131] The reality of whatever appears in consciousness cannot be denied. Objects appear; they do not cease to do so by a mere emphatic denial.[132] The manifestation of an entity in its own specific form is a fact at one level of consciousness; it is real. The appearing of the same entity in the same form but recognised to be a direct representation of the absolute is also a fact, but at another level of consciousness.[133] It is no more or less real than the first. 'As is the state of consciousness, so is the experience,' says Abhinava.[134] Although the nature of the absolute is discovered at a higher level of consciousness, nonetheless it presents itself to us directly in the specific form in which we perceive things; otherwise there would be no way in which we could penetrate from the level of appearing to that of its source and basis. Abhinava writes:

> Real is the entity (*vastu*) that appears in the moment of direct perception (*sākṣātkāra*), that is to say, within our experience of it. Once its own specific form has been clearly determined one should, with effort, induce it to penetrate into its pure conscious nature.[135]

All things are known to be just as they present themselves. The concrete actuality of being known (*pramiti*), irrespective of content, is itself the vibrant (*spanda*) actuality of the absolute. Liberating knowledge is gained not by going beyond appearances but by attending closely to them. "The secret," Maheśvarānanda says, "is that liberation while alive (*jīvanmukti*) is the profound contemplation of Māyā's nature."[136] No ontological distinction can be drawn between the absolute and its manifestations because both are an appearing (*ābhāsa*), the latter of diversity and the former of 'the true light of consciousness which is beyond Māyā and is the category Śiva'.[137]

> Those who have attained the category of Pure Knowledge above Māyā and have thus gone beyond the category of Māyā, see the entire universe as the light of consciousness . . . Just as the markings [on a feather] are nothing apart from the feather, the feather [is nothing apart from] them, similarly, when the light of consciousness is manifest, the whole group of phenomena is manifest as the light of consciousness itself.[138]

Within the sphere of Māyā, every entity's 'own nature' (*svabhāva*) corresponds to its specific manifest form. Accordingly it is defined as that which distinguishes it from all else and from which it never deviates.[139] Above the sphere of Māyā, that is, above the level of objectivity, is the domain of the subject. At this level, everything is realised to be part of the fullness of the experiencer[140] and hence no longer bound by the conditions which impinge on the object. Here the part is discovered to be the whole, that is, consciousness *in toto*. In this sphere beyond relative distinctions, the yogi realises that (all) the categories of existence are present in every single category.[141] The yogi experiences every individual particular as the sum total of everything else. He recognises that all things have one nature and that every particular is all things.[142] This is the 'essence' (*sāra*) or co-extensive unity (*sāmarasya*) of all things.

> We have established that reality is manifest according to how [and the degree in which] the freedom of consciousness reveals it and that [this freedom] is the womb of all forms. Just as 'sweetness' is present in its entirety in every atom of the sugarcane, so each and every atom [of the universe] bears within itself the emanation of all things.[143]

This is the level of consciousness in which the absolute reflects on itself realising to its eternal delight and astonishment (*camatkāra*) its own integral nature.[144] The reality of the world of diversity is not denied, but experienced in a new mode of awareness free of time and space in the eternal omnipresence of the Here and Now.

> [Phenomenal forms of awareness] such as 'this [exists]', born of the colouring [imparted to the absolute] by the limitations engendered by the diversifying power of time (*kālakalanā*) also emanate within the Supreme Principle. There [at that level], Fullness (*pūrṇatā*) is the one nature [of all things] and so everything is omnipresent; otherwise, associated with division (*khaṇḍana*), the Fullness [of the absolute] would not be full.[145]

The content of absolute consciousness consists of diverse appearings (*ābhāsa*) which, because they are manifest through it in this way, do not compromise the wholeness of consciousness. Everything we perceive is a momentary collocation of a number of such manifestations which combine together like 'a row of altar lamps' (*dīpāvalī*) to form the single radiant picture of the universe. The individual objects which constitute the universe are specific collocations of such 'atomic' appearings. Together they form a single unified particular which appears according to its own defining features (*svalakṣaṇa*). A jar, for example, consists of a number of appearances such as 'round', 'fat', 'earthen', 'red', etc., which together discharge a single function (*arthakriyā*), in this case, that of carrying the appearance 'water'. They unite with each other much as the scattered rays of a lamp come together when focused, or as the various currents of the sea together give rise to waves.[146] Atomic appearings can combine in any number of ways, provided that they are not contrary to one another as established by the dictates of natural law (*niyati*). An appearance of 'form', for example, cannot combine with that of 'air'.[147]

Insofar as they share a common basis (*sāmānyādhikaraṇya*), a given cluster of appearances appears as a single whole. This common basis is the most prominent member of the group; the appearance 'jar' is such in the example quoted above. Any one appearance in a cluster may assume a more important or subordinate role. The result is a specific awareness of an object of the form: 'here this is such.'[148] While individual appearances do not lose their separate identity (*svarūpabheda*) when they rest on a common basis, even so the particular object which appears according to its own characteristics (*svalakṣaṇa*) is an individual reality in its own right. It is a different kind of appearance characterised by its association with the appearance of the specific location and time in which it is made manifest.[149] The form of our experience is thus 'I now see this here'.[150] But when we perceive each particular constituent appearance separately, each assumes a separate fixed function. Abhinava cites the following colourful example to illustrate how the various combinations of appearances account for the variety of experience:

> Thus even though the appearance of the beloved may manifest externally, it is as if far away in the absence of another appearance, namely, that of 'embracing'. So when the [appearing of the beloved] is associated with another appearance [namely that of 'far away'] the power (*arthakriyā*) it formerly had of giving pleasure appears as its contrary.[151]

The form our experience assumes depends, not only on the nature of the object perceived, but also on personal factors entirely peculiar to ourselves. This theory explains this in two ways. In one sense, the object remains the same, but one or other of its constituent appearances comes to the fore according to the inclinations of the perceiver. From another point of view, we can say that the perceived object is different for each perceiver according to the difference in the prominent appearance manifest to him. Abhinava, citing as an example a golden jar, illustrates how the same object appears differently to different perceivers according to the use they wish to make of it and to their state of mind:

> When a person who is depressed and feels that there is nothing [of value for him in the world] sees the jar, he merely perceives the appearance 'exists' [in the form of the awareness that] 'it is'. He is not conscious of any other [of its constituent appearances] at all. An individual who desires to fetch water [perceives] the appearance 'jar'. The man who simply wants something that can be taken somewhere and then brought back, [perceives] the appearance 'thing'. The man who desires money [perceives] the appearance 'gold'. The man who desires a pleasing object [perceives] the appearance 'brightness' while he who wants something solid sees the appearance 'hardness'.[152]

These 'atomic events' or appearances emerge from the pure subject's consciousness and combine together to form a total event at each moment.

Daily life (*vyavahāra*) goes on by virtue of this ever renewed flux of appearances.[153] They are connected together and work towards a single unified experience because they appear within the field of consciousness of the universal subject.

> The aggregate of appearances arises in the [supreme] subject as do [sprouts in] a rice field. Even though each sprout germinates from its own seed, they are perceived as a collective whole.[154]

Appearances rest in this way within the universal subject. 'Externality' is itself another appearance;[155] it arises from a distinction between appearances and the individual subject.[156] So, although all manifestation always occurs within the subject, it appears to be external due to the power of Māyā[157] which separates the individual subject from his object. This split must occur for daily life to be possible. Only externally manifest appearances can perform their functions; when they are merged within the subject and at one with him, they cannot do so.[158] Daily life proceeds on the basis of the operation and withdrawal of the conditions necessary for fruitful action to be possible. Appearance in this sense represents the actualisation of a potential hidden in consciousness made possible by virtue of its dynamic, Spanda nature which is both the flow from inner to outer and back as well as the power that impels it. The emergence from, and submergence into, pure consciousness of each individual appearance is a particular pulsation (*viśeṣaspanda*) of differentiated awareness. Together these individual pulsations constitute the universal pulse (*sāmānyaspanda*) of cosmic creation and destruction. Thus, every single thing in this way forms a part of the radiant vibration (*sphurattā, sphuraṇa*) of the light of absolute consciousness.

II

Light and Awareness: The Two Aspects of Consciousness

Absolute consciousness understood as the unchanging ontological ground of all appearing is termed *'Prakāśa'*. As the creative awareness of its own Being, the absolute is called *'Vimarśa'*. *Prakāśa* and *Vimarśa*—the Divine Light of consciousness and the reflective awareness this Light has of its own nature—together constitute the all-embracing fullness (*pūrṇatā*) of consciousness. The Recognition (*pratyabhijñā*) school of Kashmiri Śaivism develops this concept of the absolute which finds its fullest expression in Utpaladeva's *Stanzas on the Recognition of God.* Even though neither of these two key terms appear in the *Stanzas on Vibration* or the *Aphorisms of Śiva*, they recur frequently in their commentaries. Thus, although the original formulation of the Doctrine of Vibration differs from the theology of Recognition in this respect, it was extended in the course of its development to accommodate this concept of the absolute as well. This was possible, and quite justified, insofar as the absolute understood in Pratyabhijñā terms does not, as we shall see, differ essentially from that of the Spanda school. We can, as Kashmiri Śaivites themselves have done, explain one in terms of the other.

Prakāśa: The Light of Consciousness

Prakāśa is the pure 'luminosity' (*bhāna*) or 'self-showing' that constitutes the essence and ultimate identity (*ātman*) of phenomena.[1] That things appear at all is due to the light of consciousness, and their appearing (*avabhāsana*) is itself this Light which bestows on all things their evident, manifest nature.[2] Established in the light of consciousness everything appears there according to its own specific nature (*svabhāva*). Anything that supposedly does not rest in this Light is as unreal as a sky-flower.[3] Thus, according to Rājānaka Rāma, unlike the light of the sun, or any other light, this Light not only makes all things apparent, it is also their ultimate source.[4] Full of its divine vibration the Light makes all things manifest and withdraws them into itself. This supra-temporal activity characterises it most specifically; devoid of it, it would be no better than an inert physical phenomenon.[5] At the same time, this light is the conjunction (*śleṣa*) or oneness (*aikātmya*) of its countless manifest forms,[6] and the collective whole (*sampiṇḍana*) of all the categories of existence.[7] The universe is nothing but the shining of the Light within itself. It is the radiant vibration (*sphurattā*) of this Light, the state (*avasthāna*) in which consciousness becomes manifest.[8]

Although the Light shines as all things at all times and hence also makes their diversity manifest,[9] penetrating each object individually as well as collectively, it is not totally 'merged' (*magna*) or identified with the object so as to suffer any division within itself.[10] Our experience of any object is of the form: 'I see this': it is not itself an object, but the manifest form the object assumes as a luminous principle of experience.[11] The Light is ever revealed and can never be obscured; objectivity can never cast a shadow on the light of consciousness.[12] The *Stanzas on Vibration* declare:

> That in which all this creation is established and from whence it arises is nowhere obstructed because it is unconditioned by [its very] nature.[13]

This Light is the highest reality (*paramārtha*). It is the 'Ancient Light' (*purāṇaprakāśa*) that makes all things new and fresh every moment.[14] It is 'always new and secret, ancient and known to all'.[15] It is the form of the Present (*vartamānarūpa*), the Eternal Now. Time and space are relations between the contents of consciousness; they cannot impinge on the integrity of the absolute itself.[16] Neither space nor time can divide it, for they are one with the Light that illumines them and makes them known as elements of experience. But this Light is the shining of the absolute, it is not an impersonal principle. It is the living Light of God, indeed it is God Himself,[17] the Master Who instructs the entire universe.[18] Śiva is this 'auspicious lamp', Who illumines all things.[19] He is the Light of consciousness that reveals the presence of both the real and the unreal, of 'light' and 'darkness'.[20] Abhinavagupta writes:

> Thus Bhairava, the Light, is self-evident (*svataḥsiddha*); without beginning, He is the first and last of all things, the Eternal Present. And so what else can be said of Him? The unfolding of the categories of existence (*tattva*) and creation, which are the expansion of His own Self, He illumines, luminous with His own Light, in identity with Himself, and because He illumines Himself, so too He reflects on His own nature, without His wonder (*camatkāra*) being in any way diminished.[21]

The Kashmiri Śaiva concept of consciousness is clearly more akin in the West to the Christian mystic's understanding of the nature of Deity than to that of consciousness as conceived by most western psychologists and philosophers of mind. Dionysius the Aeropagite talks of God, in the passage cited below, in much the same terms as the Kashmiri Śaivite would about the light of absolute consciousness.

> [God] being One communicates His unity into every part of the world and also unto the Whole, both unto that which is one and that which is many. He is One and unchangeable in a superessential manner being neither a multiplicity of things, nor yet the sum total of such units . . . . He is a unity in a manner far different from this . . . He is indivisible plurality, insatiable, yet brimful, producing, perfecting and maintaining all unity and plurality.[22]

The central mystical experience of enlightenment is aptly symbolised by light in most of the numerous forms of mysticism; Deity and all that surrounds the higher reaches of existence are universally symbolised by light. The vision of Light is one of the most characteristic features of higher mystical experiences. When the Kashmiri Śaiva talks of Deity or Reality as Light, he is trying to express his direct experience of the Real; this is more important to the mystic than any concept of reality. The yogi's concern is realisation, not philosophical speculation or theological discussion.

If the mystic is to traverse the boundary between the transitory and the eternal, he must die to the profane condition. He must depart from a world devoid of light to be reborn into the higher, sacred state of enlightenment, into a world he recognises to be full of light. The result is an increase in consciousness; that is, the previous condition is augmented by formerly unconscious contents. The new condition carries with it more insight, which is symbolised by more light. It is a vision of the world radiant with the light and life of the divine reality within all things, and yet beyond them. The most profoundly satisfying experience possible is the recognition that the light of one's own consciousness is all things.

> "[This] Bliss", writes Abhinava, "is not like the intoxication of wine or that of riches, nor similar to union with the beloved. The manifestation of the light of consciousness is not like the ray of light from a lamp, sun or moon. When one frees oneself from accumulated multiplicity, the state of bliss is like that of putting down a burden; the manifestation of the Light is like the acquiring of a lost treasure, the domain of universal non-duality."[23]

This is the central experience upon which the Kashmiri Śaiva bases his understanding of the nature of reality. In the transition from experience (mysticism) to a concept of reality (metaphysics), we can only carry with us ideas symbolic of the original experience. Philosophy, from this point of view, can only serve a descriptive function. It is a 'systematic symbolism' which serves primarily to generate insight into the nature of reality by a process of elevating the philosopher's power of recognition (*pratyabhijñā*), allowing him to couple the concept with the experience which lies behind it.

> Philosophy is an elaboration of different kinds of spiritual experiences. The abstractions of high-grade metaphysics are based on spiritual experience and derive their whole value from the experiences they symbolise. No metaphysical concept is entirely intelligible without reference to the spirit.[24]

Light (*prakāśa*), Sound (*nāda*), Vibration (*spanda*), Taste (*rasa*) and a host of others all serve this symbolic function in this universe of discourse. Amongst these, Light (*prakāśa*) and Vibration (*spanda*) feature prominently. Light symbolism helps us to grasp the inner relationship between things understood as integral parts of the absolute in static juxtaposition and mutual interpenetration. Vibration (*spanda*) symbolism serves to represent the dynamic, self-regenerative character of the absolute. It symbolises the active participation of the infinite in the finite as the process of its transformation into the finite and the reconversion of the finite into the infinite. Space is the model for the former and time for the latter. Light aptly symbolises an absolute conceived as a pure noetic plenum. The absolute is called 'Light' because it is the universal knowledge of the supreme subject which makes the entire knowable manifest.[25] It represents consciousness as the unchanging witness of all the events in the universe, the power of the absolute to know the universe (*jñānaśakti*) merged within it:

> We bow to Siva Who eternally illumines by the lamp of the power of his knowledge the many objects lying in the Great Cave of Māyā.[26]

In the cognitive sphere, the dynamic character of the light of consciousness is represented by the flux of cognitions. This is the pulsation—Spanda—of its noetic activity (*jñānātmikakriyā*) of which it is itself the conscious agent (*kartṛ*) as well as perceiver. Knowledge cannot exist independently of the knower.[27] The object is grounded in knowledge and knowledge in the subject which thus connects them together like a powerful glue.[28] Ultimately, these three are identical:

> Nothing perceived is independent of perception and perception differs not from the perceiver, therefore the universe is nothing but the perceiver [himself].[29]

The one universal consciousness, therefore, has three aspects: it is the illuminator (*prakāśaka*), the illumined universe (*prakāśya*) and the light of knowledge (*prakāśa*) which illumines it. The universe, Light and Self are one.[30] Subject, object and means of knowledge necessarily attend each act of perception and make cognitive awareness (*pramā*) possible. Manifested by the creative power (*sṛṣṭiśakti*) of the Great Light,[31] they are always present together whenever anything is perceived objectively, and so embrace, as it were, the entire universe in their nature:[32]

> The group of subjects, the various means of knowledge, the multiple kinds of knowledge and the objects of knowledge—all this is consciousness alone. The Supreme Goddess is the absolute freedom of our own consciousness which assumes these various forms.[33]

When they are made manifest, the universe appears within the field of universal consciousness. When they cease to operate, and the tension between subject and object is resolved again into their primordial unity, the universe is again withdrawn into undifferentiated consciousness. Thus the devout yogi addresses the divine Light with the words:

> Your playful desire is the cause of the diversity between the perceiver, perceiving, perception and perceptible; when Your playful desire is over, that diversity disappears somewhere. Seldom does man realise this.[34]

As aspects of the dynamic consciousness (*caitanya*) which is Śiva's freedom to act as the agent of cognition,[35] they are phases of His vibration (*spanda*). This movement of conscious energy, incandescent with the light of consciousness, generates cognitions that appear as manifestations (*ābhāsa*) of consciousness within it. Thus, taken together as a single whole, they are the inner light of the innate nature of all things (*svarūpa-jyotis*).[36] United, they are the supreme subject (*parapramātṛ*) identified with the state of pure awareness (*pramitibhāva*) that constitutes their essence. This higher subject is Paramaśiva Who assumes these three aspects through a process of self-limitation (*saṃkoca*), all the while continuing to exist as the undifferentiated unity of pure consciousness.[37]

As aspects of the light of consciousness, these three are appropriately symbolised as three great luminaries, namely, the Fire, Sun and Moon.[38] The means of knowledge, like the Sun, illumines the object. The object shines, like the Moon, by its reflected light. Again, like the moon, according to the common Indian way of thinking, it exudes nectar in the sense that the object delights the senses.[39] Fire aptly symbolises the subject because fire is said to have three abodes, as ordinary fire on earth, as lightning in the sky and the god of fire in heaven. The subject too is three-fold as the object, the means of knowledge and the subject itself. Moreover the subject, like fire, flames upwards, consuming all things within the pervasive field of its consciousness, ultimately digesting them within itself when perception is over and he rests tranquil.

Even though the light of consciousness experiences all three, it does not require another to be perceived, but illumines itself in the course of making the universe manifest. Consciousness is the ultimate principle of revelation. The Light that reveals everything does not require a second for its own revelation.[40] If consciousness were not self-conscious but required another consciousness to reveal its nature, that too would require another and the third a fourth and so on *ad infinitum*.[41]

This Light, as we have seen, unfolds or expands (*prasarati*) everywhere, shining this way and that as each particular aspect of our experience. Śiva does this by creating and freely imposing on Himself countless limiting conditions (*upādhi*) through which He becomes manifest in limited forms, just as a light shining through a lattice window appears diverse. At the same time He abides unchanged as the supreme experiencer. Rājānaka Rāma in his commentary on the *Stanzas on Vibration* writes:

> If we could anywhere, at any time, or in any way conceive of You apart from [universal] manifestation, then we could say that Your diversity (*vicitratā*) is due to the diverse limiting conditions (*upādhi*) [that reflect Your light] like outer crystal.[42]

The formless, pervasive nature of consciousness makes it possible for objects to be related to each other. The Light (*prakāśa*) does not exhaust itself as the luminosity of the outer object, for although every object is separate from every other, it is not totally unrelated to other objects. We do in fact experience a variety of objects in a single act of perception.[43] This is only possible if the light of consciousness is fundamentally one and the same for each object. Even so, the Kashmiri Śaiva denies that consciousness is a formless (*nirākāra*), undivided reality, set apart from the object it perceives. We know from our own experience that consciousness does not view all things equally; some objects are more clearly apparent than others.[44] Moreover, if the Light (*prakāśa*) were to be one and entirely homogeneous, there would be no difference between the knowledge of 'blue' and that of 'yellow'.[45] Objects would become confused with one another and the world of perceptions would collapse into a chaos (*saṃkara*).[46] How could the same Light by virtue of which we know 'blue' to be 'blue', illumine 'yellow' so that we know it to be 'yellow', if consciousness were in no way affected by the object perceived?[47] The way we experience things is therefore only explicable if we agree that the Light which illumines them is somehow both formless and omniform at the same time.

We can explain how consciousness can have these two aspects only if we admit that it is free to be both single and diverse.[48] It cannot be just one or the other for then we would have to posit the existence of a second reality to make up for the deficiency of one or other of these two aspects. Indeed, we cannot say that the Light is either single or diverse for that would imply a division (*bheda*) within it.[49] One way for solving this problem, without recourse to some form of dualism, is to say that unity alone is real and that diversity is merely apparent. All that exists is consciousness which seems to assume diverse forms. This is the Advaitin's view.

We can, however, approach this problem in a different way through a deeper understanding of the properties of consciousness. The light of consciousness is absolute and hence free of the limitations inherent in all that is relative. This freedom from limitations characterises the Light most specifically.[50] It is by virtue of this freedom that it is not bound to a single fixed form, as are common objects.[51] Vibrant with life, the Light assumes countless forms. Pure consciousness is equivalent to absolute freedom. A lifeless unconscious object, on the contrary, is hemmed in on every side by spatial and temporal limitations. Unlike the light of consciousness, it is not free to be other than the form in which it appears to be.

According to the dualist Sāṃkhya consciousness is always formless. It is matter that assumes diverse forms although it remains substantially the same, as does the clay from which pots of different sizes and shape are fashioned. This cannot be correct, says the Kashmiri Śaiva, because matter, however subtle we may conceive it to be, is objective and, as such, cannot be both one and diverse. Our experience testifies to the fact that 'the states of unity and division are distinct in all objective phenomena'.[52] But as Abhinava writes:

> Both characteristics, unity and diversity, are found in that which does not fall to the level of an object but which, because it is consciousness, is the supremely real Light. It has only one characteristic, namely, consciousness which is the perfect medium of reflection (*svaccha*). This is what experience tells us.[53]

The experience we all have to which Abhinava is alluding in this passage is that we perceive various objects in the scan of one perception without it being divided. The same holds true of the universal perception absolute consciousness has of the universe. Accordingly, the Light of Śiva's consciousness is symbolically conceived to be an infinite, perfectly polished (*svaccha*) mirror within which the entire universe is reflected. In this way the Kashmiri Śaiva explains how the one conscious reality can at once be immanent and transcendent without this either compromising its unity or denying the reality of the manifest universe. Abhinava quotes a Tantra as saying:

> Deity is both formless and omniform, pervading all things both moving and immobile, as does water or a mirror [the image reflected in it].[54]

Consciousness, like a mirror, can reflect objects within itself. It has the power to manifest entities that are separate from it as if they were one with it, without this in any way affecting its nature.[55] Conversely, it also makes manifest these reflected images as if they were distinct from it although they are not.[56] Again, the variety of manifest forms (*ābhāsa*) appear separate from one another, without this compromising the oneness of consciousness, just as happens with the reflections in a mirror.[57] However, in one respect at least, the mirror analogy does not hold good. Reflections in a mirror correspond to outer objects; this is not the case with consciousness. The All (*viśva*) is entirely a reflection (*pratibimbamātra*).[58] From the point of view of consciousness, the original object is as much a reflection as the image reflected in the mirror. Although the universe is like a reflection, there is no object outside the mirror of consciousness that, reflected within it, appears as the universe. Abhinava points out:

> The image reflected [in a mirror] is deposited [there] by the original external object. Now, if this too is a reflected image, what remains of the original object?[59]

The object apprehended by the senses cannot be the original object because the perception of the object is never immediate; it occurs through a series of causes.[60] The perception of the object is real enough, but it is always perceived as a reflection within the mind and senses. An outer world may indeed exist, but the form in which it appears is always as a reflection, never as the original object. An opponent may object that no reflection can exist without an original reflected object. Abhinava replies that this is true of reflections in a mirror but not of those within consciousness. Anyway, even in the case of a mirror, the object is never one with the reflected image.[61] Nor are they one in the way that a particular can be said to be one with its universal.[62] Moreover, when we perceive a reflection in a mirror, we do not perceive the original object at the same time. The cognition of one follows the other; they are not simultaneous. Similarly, we hear an echo when the original sound has ceased,[63] and we can perceive a shadow without seeing the hand that makes it.[64] The bashful maiden can secretly view the charming form of her lover standing behind her, reflected in a mirror without having to look at him directly.[65] Thus Abhinava prefers to cut short all argument and boldly state:

> If then, even though [the universe] clearly bears the characteristics [of a reflected image], you still insist on calling it the original object (*bimba*), go ahead. The wise attend to the facts, not to commonly accepted convention.[66]

The only way to account for the appearing of this cosmic reflection is to accept that consciousness itself creates it spontaneously. Consciousness is free (*svatantra*) to be 'the agent of the act of manifestation'.[67] Consciousness in this sense is the cause of both the original object and its reflection.[68] Otherwise, if this were not the case, we would be forced to seek another reality apart from consciousness which deposits these reflections within it;[69] as this is impossible, nothing would appear at all. Abhinava concludes:

> The truth is therefore this: the Supreme Lord manifests freely (*anargala*) all the varied play of emissions and absorptions in the sky of His own nature.[70]

The creation of reflections within the mirror of consciousness is spontaneous, like play. In the Spanda tradition, Kṣemarāja personifies the power of consciousness that plays the game of manifestation as the Goddess Spanda. Consciousness is the fecund womb from which all things are born and in which they ultimately unite to rest blissfully.[71] The Goddess is therefore not just the power of consciousness that generates the cosmic reflection, but is also the mirror in which it appears. Thus it is the Goddess Spanda Who is:

> . . . . . the Lord's power of freedom that, although undivided, displays on the screen of Her own nature all the cycles of creation and destruction. [She reflects them within Herself] in such a way that although they are at one with Her, they appear to be separate from Her, like a city reflected in a mirror . . . . Therefore, the Supreme Being is always one with the Spanda principle and never otherwise.[72]

The vibration of consciousness is manifest as the forms which emerge within it. In the mental, subjective sphere, these include thoughts, memories and cognitions; in the objective sphere objects, universals and words—none of which could exist if consciousness did not have the power to generate them. Thus our exposition of the Kashmiri Śaiva concept of the absolute as Light and its manifestations as reflections has led us to consider its universal power apparent through its recurring pulsations of activity. This same power both generates forms within itself and is conscious of them. Therefore, this, the absolute's power of self-awareness, to which we now turn, is also Spanda—its vibration.

Self-Awareness and Consciousness

As we have seen, the absolute is the light of consciousness (*prakāśa*) because it makes all things manifest by shining in its universal form. The phenomena that appear in the field of consciousness are experienced directly in this way at the initial instant of perception when they are still at one with the perceiving subject. The light of consciousness is itself this direct experience[73] had before thought-constructs interpose themselves between subject and object, thus degrading the latter to the level of objectivity, which obscures the light of the subject's immediate perception. But although the light of consciousness accounts for the appearing of phenomena in this way, it does not by itself fully account for our experience of them. No experience is possible without self-awareness. Experience must be personal to be experience at all. As Jung suggests:

> Experience is not possible without reflection, because experience is a process of assimilation without which there could be no understanding.[74]

From the Kashmiri Śaivite point of view, this reflection is an awareness of the images that appear within the mirror of the Light. For the psycho-cosmic processes occurring at the level of universal consciousness (*saṃvid*) to be accessible to experience, consciousness must reflect (literally 'bend back') on itself to know itself and what appears within it:

> The Supreme Lord bears within Himself the reflection of the universe and the [reflection] is His nature as all things. Nor is He unconscious of His nature as such because that which is conscious necessarily reflects on itself.[75]

This act of reflective awareness is termed *'vimarśa'*. The word is derived from the root *'mṛś'* which means to touch, feel, understand, perceive, reflect or examine. Thus *'vimarśa'* is the power of consciousness by virtue of which it can understand or perceive itself, feel, reflect on and examine the events that occur within it—in short, behave like a limitless, living being. This ability to reflect on itself is inherent in the very nature of the light of consciousness; indeed it is its most specific characteristic[76] and the very life of its sentient nature. Deprived of reflective awareness, the light of consciousness would amount to no more than the more appearing of phenomena unknown to anyone[77] like the light that shines reflected in a common mirror or crystal.[78]

Through this awareness, the Light knows itself to be the sole reality and so rests in itself, but not as does a self-confined, lifeless object.[79] It enjoys perfect freedom and is satisfied (*caritārtha*) in the knowledge that it is all that exists, be it subject, object or means of knowledge.[80] Self-awareness is God's omniscience, the fullness (*pūrṇatā*) of all-embracing consciousness, its bliss (*ānanda*) or aesthetic rapture (*camatkāra*) that contains within itself the infinite variety of things.[81] As such, it is the pulse of pure contemplation, the inner activity of the absolute's power of action (*kriyāśakti*);[82] in it all the powers of the absolute[83] merge to form its uncreated 'I' consciousness (*ahaṃ*), whose radiant vibration (*sphuraṇa*) is manifest as the form, emanation and reabsorption of the universe.[84] By contemplating its own nature, consciousness assumes the form of all the planes of existence from the subtlest to the most gross.[85] The power of reflection is thus the inherent creative freedom of the light of consciousness to either turn in on itself introspectively and be free of its outer forms, or move out of itself to view its outer manifestations.[86] In harmony with the oscillation of awareness between these polarities, the universe of manifestation is incessantly renewed and is the essence of the vitality of its pulsation.[87] The vibration of awareness serves, in short, to account for the manifestation of phenomena without either material cause or essential change in consciousness, and distinguishes the Light as a primary, uncaused principle from its creations.

Awareness is the oneness of the unlimited vision of the All. Lack of awareness results in incomplete vision and divides the All into parts, each separately seen as a specific 'this' (*idam*) contrasted and distinguished from all that it is not. Turning away from the unity of self-awareness, we become obsessed with the part and ignore the Whole. But when awareness rests in itself and contemplates its own nature, it sees itself as the pure subject that unfolds as the unity of all things.[88] This awareness (*vimarśa*) can therefore be said to have two aspects:

Internal. This is the act of awareness when the light of consciousness rests in itself alone. It is the pure awareness of 'I' (*ahaṃvimarśa*), devoid of all thought-constructs (*nirvikalpa*), said to be 'total freedom and unsullied wonder'.[89]

External. This aspect corresponds to the act of reflection directed away from the subject to the object he perceives as separate from himself. Reality then becomes accessible to discursive representation (*vikalpa*) and amenable to empirical definition.

Awareness serves to relate objectivity with subjectivity in such a way that the object ultimately comes to rest in the self-awareness of the subject. In reality, reflective awareness is always awareness of 'I' (*ahaṃvimarśa*); it never objectivises even when, in the form of the awareness of 'this' (*idaṃvimarśa*), it reflects upon the object. The experience we have of things existing outside consciousness is due to a lack of self-awareness. The awareness of the object is never 'out there'; it is registered and known within the subject. All forms of awareness come to rest in the subject:

"Just as every drop of water comes to rest in the ocean, so all acts and cognitions [come to rest] in the Great Lord, the ocean of consciousness. Even a little water on the ground drunk by the sun's rays goes, as rain, to the great ocean. Similarly all knowledge and action in the universe merge in the ocean of Śiva either spontaneously and evidently (*sphuṭam*), by itself or [indirectly] through a series of other [processes]."[90]

Individual and universal consciousness are one. The same processes operate in both; the only difference between them is that in the case of individual consciousness these processes are restricted or limited (*saṃkucita*) representations of the maximally expanded (*vikāsita*) operation of universal consciousness. The activity of the mind is that of consciousness itself, or to be more precise, of its reflective awareness, the power of Spanda.[91] Thus, on the individual level, reflective awareness:

> Is the capacity of the Self to know itself in all its purity in the state of perfect freedom from all kinds of affections; to analyse all its states of varying affections, due either to the internal or the external causes; to retain these affections in the form of residual traces (*saṃskāra*); to take out, at will, at any time, anything out of the existing stock of the *saṃskāras* and bring back an old affected state of itself as in the case of remembrance; to create an altogether new state of self-affection by making a judicious selection from the existing stock and displaying the material so selected on the background of the *prakāśa* aspect as at the time of free imagination.[92]

Cognition would be impossible if consciousness were incapable of it. This capacity is the reflective awareness it has of itself as pure 'I' consciousness. When it is conditioned by the object of knowledge, which is in its turn conditioned by the forces and laws that govern the physical universe (all of which are aspects of the power of Māyā), it operates as cognition, memory and all the other functions of the mind.[93] Cognition, in other words, is the reflective awareness of 'I' limited by the affections imposed upon it by the variety of external manifestations generated by this 'I' consciousness itself. Freed from all association with outer objects, the individual shares in God's bliss, which is the experience He enjoys at rest in His own nature.[94] This blissful self-awareness (*vimarśa*) is the abiding condition of the subject even while he perceives the world and reacts to it. It is the inner activity of the Spanda principle, which is the inspired wonder (*camatkāra*) of consciousness from which the powers of will, knowledge and action flow out as phases in its vibrating rhythm (*spanda*).[95]

Normally, the individual subject fails to recognise the creative nature of this flow of awareness (*jñānadhārā*) to and from the object in the act of cognition. He is unaware that he fashions from his own consciousness the various forms which populate his objective field of awareness. On the universal level of subjectivity, however, this movement from inner to outer and back is experienced within consciousness as the coming into being and destruction of the entire universe. Consequently, reflective awareness (*vimarśa*) is characterized as action (*kriyā*) which is the flux of Becoming, while the Light (*prakāśa*) is knowledge (*jñāna*) or passive Being.[96] In other words, awareness is the creative act of making reality known, while the Light is the actuality of its being known. The latter without the former would be an inactive principle, a state of pure potential that could never actualize into an act of awareness. From this point of view the two aspects of awareness are:

> *Karma Vimarśa.* When the act of awareness is directed externally and coincides with the unfolding (*vikāsa*) of the expansion of the universe (*prapañca*) out of the absolute.
>
> *Kriyā Vimarśa.* When this activity is still unlimited and infinite, completely internalized within the absolute as its agency (*kartṛtva*), undisturbed by any goal of action (*kārya*) as the pure vibration or stir (*saṃrambha*) of consciousness.[97]

The Śaiva rejects the Vedāntin's view that knowledge is incommensurable with action. Knowledge and action together constitute the basis of daily life and the life of all living beings.[98] One is never without the other; they function hand in hand. At the universal level, the power of action evolves forms out of the pleroma of consciousness, while the power of knowledge makes them manifest. On the individual level, they represent the objective and subjective poles of all sentient activity. As the inner awareness that 'I am' (*ahaṃ*), knowledge is the stable referent of all actions. It persists undivided throughout all action, however diverse. If it did not, then running, for example, would be impossible,[99] nor would we be able to understand a sentence spoken in haste.[100]

While our own self-awareness (*svasaṃvedana*) informs us of its existence, action, thus illumined by knowledge, is the awareness that 'I act'. Together they are the pure awareness of 'I' (*ahaṃ*) as the knowing and acting subjectivity which is the inner Spanda nature of consciousness.

Awareness and the Integral Nature of the Absolute

Although diverse elements may appear within consciousness, they must be distinguished from one another. Individual appearances share a common nature as appearances and so cannot divide themselves off from one another; otherwise the severed elements, disassociated from their essential nature, would not appear at all.[101] Established in its own undifferentiated (*aviśiṣṭa*) nature, the universe would not be a universe unless the light of consciousness itself differentiates the diverse forms it creates by its spontaneous shining. It does this by the various ways in which it reflects upon its own nature. Although the Light is always undivided on the lower level of Māyā as well as on the higher level of pure consciousness, the reflective awareness it has of its own nature is not.[102] Thus while Light expresses the unity of consciousness, awareness, when distinguished from it, expresses the diversity of perceptions. At the microcosmic level we can say:

> The one light of consciousness consists of such types of reflective awareness as: 'this is a jar' and 'this is a cloth'; 'these two are divided from each other and from other subjects as well as from me'.[103]

At the macrocosmic level:

> The Light is the supreme reality (*paramārtha*) that encompasses [the categories] from Earth to Paramaśiva, [while] the unfolding (*unmeṣa*) of the reflective awareness of the Heart [of 'I' consciousness] within it, distinguishes between them.[104]

This does not mean that *vimarśa* is diverse. Although it is due to the awareness of the unity or relative distinction between the phenomena illumined by the light of consciousness that they are experienced as one or diverse, this is only possible because awareness is the same in both cases.[105] This then is another aspect of the dynamic nature of awareness: it is the "freedom [of consciousness] to unite, separate and hold things together."[106] This distinguishes consciousness from inert objects "devoid of the freedom to conjoin and disjoin."[107] It is the vibration of consciousness which generates the universe by a process of uniting and dividing the elements contained within it in an undifferentiated state.[108] Thus *vimarśa* is said to operate in four ways: (1) it negates its true nature and (2) identifies with something else, (3) merges both into one and (4) denies both once they have been merged together.[109] These four functions correspond to three levels of reflective awareness, namely, the awareness of the separation, of the holding together and of the union of the manifestations of consciousness. First, by 'negating its true nature and identifying with something else', consciousness, through its power of awareness, freely identifies with the psychophysical organism and denies its true nature as consciousness. The result is the emergence of seemingly individual locii of consciousness distinct from the object and from each other. Secondly, through the same power of awareness, subject and object are held together and different objects related to one another in a single field of consciousness during the act of cognition. Thirdly, the individual subject and object, together with all diversity, merge in the reflective awareness the light of consciousness has of its nature as the universal subject.

These three levels of awareness correspond to the three-fold appearing of consciousness:

> *Division* (*Bheda*) corresponding to the awareness of separation between objects.
>
> *Awareness of unity-in-difference* (*bhedabheda*) represented by the means of knowledge which serves as a link between the unity (*abheda*) of the subject and the diversity (*bheda*) of the object.
>
> *Awareness of the undivided unity* (*abheda*) of all things as the pure subject.

These three levels are held together in the fullness (*pūrṇatā*) of consciousness as the wave of vibration (*spanda*) of awareness moves from the lower contracted level of diversity in the process of ascent (*ārohakrama*) to the expanded state of unity, and down from unity to diversity in the process of descent (*avarohakrama*). We can understand this movement from two points of view. Firstly, 'vertically' as a movement from the absolute down to its manifestation and back in consonance with the emanation (*sṛṣṭi*) and withdrawal (*saṃhāra*) of diversity. Secondly, 'horizontally' as the movement of awareness towards and away from the object during the act of perception. Perception serves in this way as a paradigm for cosmogenesis and as a means of realising the oneness and creativity of the absolute.

An aspect of the pulsing power of awareness operates at each level as a separate energy generating, sustaining and annulling the dimension of experience to which it corresponds. Thus there are three energies, namely, those of will, knowledge and action corresponding to the supreme (*parā*), middling (*parāparā*) and inferior (*aparā*) levels. These three are emanations or aspects of the pure 'I-ness' of the undifferentiated power of the reflective awareness of consciousness.[110] This is the pure vibration of its Bliss which contains and pours forth all the powers operating on every plane of existence. It is the simultaneous awareness of the unity of all three planes in the oneness of undistracted contemplation. Self-realisation is the recognition that this integral 'I-ness' (*pūrṇāhantā*) manifests on these three levels and is the yogi's true Śiva-nature which encompasses all possible formats of experience, from the unity of transcendental consciousness to the diversity of its immanent manifestations. Spanda is thus the powerful wave of energy released through the act of self-awareness which carries consciousness from the lower contracted level to the supreme state of expansion, freeing the unawakened from the torments of limitation and awakening them to the fullness of universal consciousness.

III

Spanda: The Universal Activity of Absolute Consciousness

We have seen how the dynamic (*spanda*) character of absolute consciousness is its freedom to assume any form at will through the active diversification of awareness (*vimarśa*) in time and space, when it is directed at, and assumes the form of, the object of awareness. The motion of absolute consciousness is a creative movement, a transition from the uncreated state of Being to the created state of Becoming. In this sense Being is in a state of perpetual Becoming (*satatodita*); it constantly phenomenalises into finite expression. The shining of inner Being is the manifestation of outer Becoming[1] and, as such, is the constantly self-renewing source of its own appearing as Becoming. Thus, the universal character (*sāmānya*) of Being is expressed in the radiant form (*sphurattā*) of each phenomenon. Rightly understood, Being and Becoming are the inner and outer faces of universal consciousness which becomes spontaneously manifest, through its inherent power, as this polarity.[2] The inner face (*antarmukha*) of consciousness is the pure subject which, devoid of all objective content, abides beyond the realms of time and space. The *Stanzas on Vibration* declare: "That inner being is the abode of omniscience and every other divine attribute. It can never cease to exist because nothing else can be perceived [outside it]."[3]

The outer face of consciousness represents the diversity and continuous change of the manifest universe—the object.[4] While the outer appears to be a distinct reality set apart from the inner, the inner contains the totality of the outer which appears within it without dividing its nature: "Internality", writes Utpaladeva, "is a state of oneness with the subject, while externality is the state of separation from it."[5]
Again:

> Having made itself manifest consciousness abides as both the inner [subject] and outer [object]. It shines there [within itself] in such a way that it appears to be illumining [some] other [reality].[6]

The emergence of a particular object within the field of awareness is accompanied by a mental representation through which the subject identifies the object and distinguishes it from others.[7] Thus, the manner in which the objective universe is experienced is governed by the same principles as those upon which thought is based. Phenomena follow one another linked in a causal chain, much as one thought leads to the next in a chain of associations (*prapañca*). This is not only true of individual objects but applies equally to individual perceivers. The manifestation of the universe and the emergence of Becoming, consisting of both individual subjects and objects, from the inner state of pure Being is equivalent to the emergence of thought in universal consciousness. Although introverted and inherently free of all dichotomysing mental activity, consciousness, through its inner vibration (*spanda*), conceives the world-thought (*viśvavikalpa*). As it thinks, it turns away from its pure 'I-ness' (*ahantā*) to plunge into its opposite—'thisness' (*idantā*), which is the essence of all empirically definable distinctions (*bhedavyavahāra*). Thus the movement from inner to outer engenders a split within consciousness between subject and object that gives rise to the perception of relative distinctions. This corresponds to the loss of a direct, thought-free intuition of the essential unity between inner and outer.[8] In the supreme state—that is the 'inner' reality of consciousness—there is no difference between 'inner' and 'outer'. Everything is experienced as part of one, undivided compact mass of consciousness (*saṃvidghana*). The pure Being (*sattā*) of universal consciousness assumes the form of Becoming and is involved in time and space only when a contrast appears within it between the perceiver and the perceived:

> It is Lord Śiva alone Who, by virtue of His freedom, playfully gives rise to the subject and the object, the enjoyer and the enjoyed, which are the basis of every activity in this world of duality.[9]

When the power of awareness gives rise to a sense of separation between subject and object with all the consequent limitations it imposes upon itself, it is called 'Māyā'. As Māyā, it veils consciousness and obscures the individual subject's awareness of its essential unity.[10] While non-dualist Vedānta maintains that Māyā is an undefinable principle that gives rise to the cosmic illusion of multiplicity falsely superimposed on the undivided unity of the absolute, according to Kashmiri Śaivism, Māyā is the power of the absolute to appear in diverse forms. The separation between subject and object is the product of a creative act and not of an illusion:

> The variety of subjects and objects with their characteristic differences is made manifest by the creative power of the Lord, Who knows them.[11]

The creative freedom (*svātantrya*) of the absolute and its deluding power of Māyā are identical. When the power of consciousness is recognised to be the spontaneous expression of the absolute made manifest in the variety of forms it assumes without compromising its essential unity, it is experienced as the pure vibration (*spanda*) of its freedom. If, however, the cosmic outpouring (*viśvollāsa*) of consciousness is felt to consist of diverse and conflicting elements, the same power is called Māyā. The field of operation of the freedom of the absolute is the kingdom of universal consciousness, while that of its power of Māyā is the world of transmigratory existence. The difference between them is based on the degree of insight we have into the nature of reality. Due to this power the object appears to be projected outside the subject even though it is always manifest within it and is the inner reality of the object. The creation of diversity is accordingly defined as 'the projection (*kṣepa*) of one's own nature into the Self from the Self'.[12] Abhinava explains:

> Creation is to make that which shines within, externally manifest while it still preserves its original internal nature. Therefore [the object] must be made manifest by that in relation to which it is said to be internal and which makes the internal externally manifest.[13]

Conversely, the moment-to-moment destruction of the objective content of consciousness occurs by a reversal of the movement from inner to outer. The object, in other words, is never destroyed, but merely withdrawn into the inner reality of the subject.[14] The Spanda teachings agree with the Buddhist doctrine of momentariness only insofar as it applies to outer objectivity.[15] Although perception and every phenomenal occurrence can be analysed into a series of moments (*kṣaṇa*), daily life cannot entirely be understood in terms of such moment-units. Change is an activity within the absolute which can only be properly understood in terms of conscious action and not as a mechanical process. Each act is part of a single continuous motion which proceeds from the agent—the pure Being of introverted consciousness—to its final completion in the result, which is the object or deed (*kārya*). The outer reality of Becoming is the effect which emerges from the cause, the inner reality of Being, just as action emerges from the agent. It is a wave of activity which rises out of the infinite potential of the agent. Every event is a part of the greater rhythm of the total, cosmic event. Every object is part of the universal object and every subject shares in the agency of the universal subject. Kṣemarāja writes:

> Hence the Lord creates and destroys only the objective aspect of the perceiver, i.e., the body, etc., but not the subjective aspect which is the light of 'I' consciousness because although embodied, the subject is, in reality, one with the Lord. Thus of the two—subject and object—the latter is perishable while the former is the freedom of consciousness and immortal. For even when the world is emanated and absorbed [the subject] does not waver from his true nature. If he were to do so, the emanation and absorption of the world would not be manifest [for there would be none to perceive it].[16]

The inner is the domain of Being, where the subject's power of knowledge (*jñānaśakti*) operates within itself, while the outer is the domain of the subject's power of action (*kriyāśakti*). Knowledge turns into action and action leads to knowledge. Thus every individual phenomenon has two aspects: its outer form and its inner nature. Its outer form is apparent to us as the manner in which it behaves, its properties and pragmatic efficacy (*arthakriyā*). This aspect differentiates each individual object from other objects and renders it accessible to conceptual representation (*savikalpa*). Its inner nature the Kashmiri Śaiva equates with its pure Being as an appearance (*ābhāsa*) within universal consciousness at one with pure 'I-ness' and hence inaccessible to conceptual representation (*nirvikalpa*). Thus the movement from Being to Becoming is essentially an act of perception. Perception is the connecting link between the outer manifest form of the object and its inner nature. The movement of awareness from inner to outer is equivalent to a movement from an awareness of the unity of the inner nature of all things to the diversity of their outer forms. The activity of consciousness gives rise to diversity in this sense alone.

Although it would not be wrong to say that the absolute is in a constant state of transformation or is full of vibration—Spanda—from another point of view we could say that no change or movement occurs in the absolute at all. Movement (*saṃrambha*) and rest (*viśrānti*) in the absolute presuppose one another. The freedom (*svātantrya*) of consciousness to do what seems, according to reason, to be impossible explains how the absolute can at once be motionless and yet full of activity. Abhinava explains:

> By 'vibration' (*spandana*) [we mean] subtle movement. It is subtle [in the sense that] although it moves not, it manifests as motion. The light of consciousness is not at all separate [from manifestation] yet it appears to be so. Thus, that which is immobile, associated with the variety of manifestation, manifests [as movement].[17]

Motion normally implies a movement between two separate points, which entails the existence of at least two distinct entities between which motion can occur. But as all things are equally consciousness there are no two such distinct realities between which motion, as we understand it, can take place. Abhinava explains that Spanda—the pulsation of consciousness—is defined as a 'subtle movement' (*kiñciccalana*) because "if that movement [were] to entail motion towards another entity, it would not be 'subtle' [but merely gross motion]; if not, [on the other hand], it is not motion at all."[18]

The cosmic process consists of a cyclic series of creations and destructions which follow one another like buckets fixed on a water-wheel.[19] Although change is manifest through this process, and change is the basis of time, the pulsation of the absolute is a movement outside the confines of time. Śiva is eternally engaged in all the phases of the creative act simultaneously and yet performs them one after another. So Utpaladeva sings of Śiva's glory thus:

> Salutations to the Lord Who eternally delights in emission (*sṛṣṭi*) and is always comfortably seated in persistence (*sthiti*), and is eternally satisfied with the Three Worlds for His food.[20]

Although the creative activity of consciousness is not divided by time or set in space, it is the basis of all sequentially definable spatial and temporal manifestations (*deśakrama* and *kālakramābhāsa*). Action, therefore, is of two kinds. The first is the kind of activity that can be broken down into a series (*krama*) or sequence of actions set in time and space. The second type is the non-successive (*akramika*) action that takes place within the absolute. It is the source of time and space and hence beyond the spatial and temporal distinctions which characterize all sequences.

"Worldly action", writes Utpaladeva, "can be said to be successive due to the power of time; but the eternal activity of the Highest Lord, like the Highest Lord Himself, cannot."[21]

Reality contemplated from the highest (*para*) level of consciousness is experienced as a single, unchanging (*akrama*) whole. At the lower (*apara*) level we experience this same reality as a sequence (*krama*) of events—as changing positions in space and a continuous transition from one moment in time to the next. At the intermediate (*parāpara*) level, reality is experienced at the instant of cosmic manifestation into which it blossoms with the suddenness and energy of a lightning flash.[22] This cosmic expansion (*viśvasphāra*) occurs in a single, non-sequential flash which transcends both the successive change and the non-successive, simultaneous manifestation of all its phases at once.[23] Kṣemarāja quotes the *Sārasvatsaṃgraha* as saying: "This Self has shone forth but once; it is full [of all things] and can nowhere be unmanifest."[24]

Abhinava explains:

> Moreover, consciousness does not issue forth in succession, as do the seed, sprout, stalk, petals, flowers and fruit, etc.. The sprout issues from the seed, and the stalk from the sprout, not the seed. In this case, however, absolute consciousness (*saṃvittattva*) is manifest here in every circumstance (*sarvataḥ*) [of daily life because] it is everywhere full and perfect. [Consciousness] is said to be the cause of all things because it is everywhere emergent (*udita*) [as each manifest entity].[25]

A sequence is only intelligible as a series of differing elements. From the point of view of absolute consciousness, events do not occur successively. Succession (*krama*) depends upon difference, and difference on the existence of a certain manifestation (*ābhāsa*) and the (simultaneous) non-existence of another.[26] On the other hand, cosmic events cannot be said to occur simultaneously either, because simultaneity of being is only possible between two different entities.[27] In reality, succession and its absence are not objective properties of an entity but only formats of perception.[28] Succession is a function of time which is not to be understood as a self-existent reality but merely as the perception of 'prior' and 'subsequent' based on the recollection of past events in relation to the present or possible future events in the field of awareness. Thus

Utpaladeva writes:

> Time is in reality nothing but the succession observable in the movement of the sun, etc., and the birth of different flowers [in their due season], or [the transition from] summer [to] winter.[29]

The transition or movement of awareness from one perception to the next is the basis of our sense of time passing. It is only possible because we sense separation between individual phenomena, both from each other and from the individual subject. This happens when consciousness freely obscures itself by turning away from its own self-awareness to become extroverted and contracted. In the essentially introverted nature of consciousness there is no time. Time operates within the sphere of objectivity; it cannot divide the inner subjectivity of consciousness.[30] To think that time can divide consciousness is like seeking nourishment from lumps of sugar cut from the sky by a whirling sword.[31] As consciousness is the source and basis of all appearances, it makes time manifest as well and hence cannot be affected by it.

Kṣemarāja insists that all talk of processes occurring within universal consciousness in terms of a sequence of events does not really refer to the actual state of affairs (*vastu*), but serves merely to impart instruction about the nature of consciousness in the only manner in which language permits.[32] The incessant creative activity of the absolute does not involve it in any temporal diversification. The emergence and submergence of each total-event from the body of consciousness does not divide it in any way. Even so, we experience change. Abhinava says:

> As there is no succession within [consciousness], there is no simultaneity; and as there is no simultaneity, there is no succession either. The extremely pure conscious reality transcends all talk of succession and its absence.[33]

In reality nothing arises and nothing falls away. It is the vibrating power of consciousness which, though free of change, becomes manifest in this or that form and thus appears to be arising and falling away:[34]

> [All things] exist in Śiva just as blue rays reside in the opal; in reality they nowhere come into being nor cease to exist.[35]

Reality presents itself to reason as a paradox: though it is one, yet it is diverse; though changing, it changes not at all. All the concepts we may have of it necessarily fall short of the truth. To know reality we must experience it directly. "Why speak much?" ask the *Stanzas on Vibration*, "[the yogi] will experience it for himself!"[36] When the yogi is plunged in the contemplative absorption of the 'Fourth State' (*turīya*) beyond waking, dreaming and deep sleep, he shares in Śiva's experience, enjoying its vibrant creative power personified as the Goddess, Śiva's consort:

> This Goddess of Consciousness, the Fourth State (*turīyā*) consists of the union of emission, preservation and destruction. She emits and withdraws [into Herself] each particular phase of emission, etc.. Containing all things within Herself She is eternally 'full' and, [void of all particulars], 'thin'. She is both as well as neither of the two, abiding [eternally] as the vibrating radiance [of consciousness] in a manner free of all succession (*akrama*).[37]

Cosmic creation and destruction is not a mechanical process. The emergence of the universe from consciousness and its submergence back into it are not simply a matter of withdrawing or replacing an object from a locus in space. The world does not come out of the absolute as do walnuts out of a bag.[38] The change from the pre-cosmic to the cosmic state is a transformation from one form of consciousness to another. The transition from one form of consciousness to another marks the creation of a new experience and the destruction of the old. Thus the power of awareness potentially contains within itself every possible experience—every cycle of creation and destruction. It is the inner blissful vibration (*antaḥspanda*) which impels the movement (*vibhrama*) of the universe made manifest as the outer cosmic rhythm (*bahiḥspanda*) of creation and destruction.[39] Kṣemarāja writes:

> The vibrating power of awareness (*spandaśakti*) is the bliss which is the wonder of the one compact mass of 'I' consciousness embracing the endless cycles of creation and destruction. Its true nature is the manifestation of the expansion and contraction of the perceiver and the perceived which represent the entire pure and impure creation.[40]

Universal creation is like the individual creation of the world of waking life when a person wakes from sleep. Conversely, just as when a person sleeps all the activities and ideas of waking life cease and merge back into his self-consciousness, so during cosmic destruction, in the sleep (*nimeṣa*) of consciousness, everything is withdrawn and brought to rest within it. Abhinava prayerfully addresses Śiva with the words:

> When Your nature expands, You, I and the entire universe come into being; when it is withdrawn, neither You nor I nor the universe [exist].[41] The universe awakes when You awake and is destroyed when You sleep. Thus the entire universe of being and non-being is one with You.[42]

The *Stanzas on Vibration* explain that the universe comes into being when Śiva, as it were, opens His eyes to see it, and is again destroyed when He closes His eyes to observe His own nature and no longer views the universe.[43] Śiva's power to know the universe is one with His power to create it:

> Then, when the Lord desires to discern something within the abode of the Void, the universe spontaneously unfolds and is established within consciousness and the Lord's unfolding power of knowledge perceives it.[44]

In this way, consciousness expands to assume the form of the universe by withdrawing back into itself. In other words, by veiling His undivided nature, Śiva appears as the diverse play of multiplicity. Conversely, when Śiva reveals His own nature and withdraws the veil which contracts consciousness, the universe is destroyed:[45]

> The Supreme Lord is the light of the absolute (*anuttara*). Concealing His own nature, by the glory of His free will alone, He rests on the plane of objectively definable knowledge (*pramāṇa*), etc., and makes phenomena manifest [as if] separate [from His own nature].[46]

The universe is the wonderful variety (*vicitratā*) of Śiva's nature created by Him when he reflects on Himself and thinks 'I am diverse'.[47] Śiva contemplates none other than Himself, whether He knows Himself as the multiplicity of things or as their undivided source. At one with Śiva, the enlightened yogi recognises that the expansion (*unmeṣa*) of the universe of diversity coincides with the expansion of his own undivided consciousness which appears as "the dawning of absolute reality to the exclusion of the external world."[48] Thus the two phases in the pulse of consciousness coincide. Oscillating like the pans of an evenly weighted balance,[49] they are perfectly equivalent. Kṣemarāja writes:

> The state of cosmic contraction (*nimeṣa*) is identical with the state of expansion (*unmeṣa*) even though the [universe reverts to a pure

consciousness] which assimilates everything within itself to form an undivided unity.[50]

Again:

The contracted state (*nimeṣa*), corresponding to the withdrawal of previously emitted diversity, is itself the expanding (*unmeṣa*) awareness of the unity of consciousness. [Conversely] the expanded state (*unmeṣa*), indicative of forthcoming diversity, is itself the contraction (*nimeṣa*) of the awareness of the unity of consciousness.[51]

Thus, the expansion and contraction of consciousness are brought about by Śiva's pulsating power, which is simultaneously identical with both. They are the internal and external aspects of the same energy. Similarly, cosmogenesis and lysis do not essentially differ:

Cosmic lysis (*pralaya*) corresponds to the state of [Śiva's] power in which external [objectivity] is predominantly withdrawn (*nimeṣa*). It is the unfolding (*unmeṣa*) of the innate nature which corresponds to the emergence of a state of unity (*abheda*) and the withdrawal of diverse multiplicity (*bheda*). Therefore we maintain that lysis (*pralaya*) is the same as the genesis (*udaya* of consciousness) and that genesis is also the same as lysis.[52]

There are many passages in the *Upaniṣads* which explicitly state that the universe emerges from Brahman and that it is ultimately reabsorbed back into It.[53] Even so, Śaṅkara's Vedānta cannot accept that creation is a real process. Following the lead of his predecessor, Gauḍapāda, Śaṅkara maintains that no universe is ever actually created. The real is unborn and uncreated;[54] hence creation can only occur within the domain of illusion (*māyā*). From the Advaita Vedāntin's point of view, to state that the universe arises from, and subsides into, the absolute Brahman is another way of saying that the universe is transitory and hence illusory. Illusions also appear and disappear; only their real ground continues to exist unchanged:

"As the spaces within pots or jars," writes Śaṅkara, "are non-different from cosmic space, or as water in a mirage is non-different from a [sandy] desert—*since they sometimes appear and sometimes vanish away*, and as such their nature cannot be defined, even so is it to be understood that this phenomenal world of experiences, things experienced and so on, has no existence apart from Brahman."[55]

Kashmiri Śaivism maintains that all things are spontaneously emanated by consciousness in such a way that the original source of the emitted product remains unchanged and one with its emanation. The plenitude of universal manifestation emerges out of the fullness of the absolute; both are perfect expressions of the all-encompassing totality of reality which, thus emitting itself, suffers no loss.[56] The manifestation of the universe is, in this sense, a real event, not just an apparent change (*vivarta*) in the essentially undivided nature of the absolute. Even so, as the absolute undergoes no change when becoming manifest as the universe, diversity is, in a sense, merely an apparent deviation from unity. Again, in one sense, cosmogenesis involves a real transformation (*pariṇāma*) of consciousness into the form of a universe, much as a ball of clay changes when fashioned into a jar. Yet, in another sense, consciousness undergoes no transformation at all. Bhagavatotpala quotes the *Light of Consciousness* (*Saṃvitprakāśa*) in his commentary on the *Stanzas on Vibration* to illustrate this seeming paradox:

> In no circumstance is the All-Pervasive Lord subject in this way to change, either apparent or real. Even if He were subject to both His nature would remain undivided.[57]

The Kashmiri Śaivite agrees with the Vedāntin that everything appears just as it is without any real change occurring in the essential nature of the absolute. Even so, he maintains that the production of diversity is not merely an apparent change in the unity of the absolute if this implies the production of unreal entities, for they could never be made manifest.[58] Thus, the Kashmiri Śaivite accepts the view that an effect is a real transformation (*pariṇāma*) of its cause, although he does so with certain reservations. Even when the light of consciousness is apparent to us as the universe of our experience, there is no question of its becoming anything else. The effect is the cause appearing as the effect without changing in any way. Abhinava writes:

> [A real transformation of cause into effect] entails the obscuring of the preceding form [of the changing substance] and the coming into being of another. In the case of the light of consciousness this is impossible because it has no other form. [Moreover], if [the light of consciousness] were to be obscured [the entire universe] would be as if blind. Again, [if the new form] were other than the light of consciousness it could not appear. In either case the universe [could not be perceived and hence] would be as if asleep, [which runs contrary to our] experience.[59]

A change can involve two types of transformation (*pariṇāma*). The first type is total. The material cause becomes its effect (*kāryapariṇāma*) in such a way that it is completely and irreversibly absorbed into it. The example given is that of a log burnt to ashes. This type of change the Kashmiri Śaiva rejects, and so denies that the substance of a material cause undergoes any real change to produce its effect. However, he does accept the possibility of a real change occurring in its qualities (*dharma-pariṇāma*). This second type of change does not entail the total destruction of the cause and allows for the possibility of a reversion of the effect back into it. All that has happened is that the qualities of the material cause—its form, texture, physical properties, etc., have temporarily changed.[60]

This concept of causality fits with the manner in which the Kashmiri Śaivite describes the process of manifestation. Consciousness spontaneously evolves through a series of stages ranging from the most subjective or 'inner' states of Śiva-consciousness to the most 'outer' or objective forms of awareness. The process of descent into matter is a progressive self-limitation (*rodhana*) of consciousness. As we have seen, the different orders or levels in the hierarchy (*tāratamya*) of being do not, in reality, become manifest consecutively. Even so, the only way we can understand the process of manifestation is to conceive the different categories of existence (*tattva*) as progressively emerging from consciousness in a single causal chain. Each member of this chain is the effect of all the preceding members and a constituent cause of the lower, grosser orders which follow it.[61] Kṣemarāja explains:

> When [the Lord] feels a playful desire to veil His own nature and appears in the order of descent, the preceding [members in the sequence] . . . fall into the background and the succeeding forms come to the fore, in such a way that the preceding members serve as the substratum for the succeeding [phases].[62]

In this way the cause contains within itself the effect in a potential form while the effect contains the cause as its actualization. Abhinava explains:

> Thus, even though the final element [in the series] is such as it is, it nonetheless contains within itself all the other countless aspects that, step by step, precede it and are encompassed by it in such a way that they are inseparable from its own nature. [Consciousness] thus illumines and contemplates itself as full and perfect (*pūrṇa*). The members which precede [any given phase] likewise have their being in the same reflective awareness and light of consciousness which, full and perfect, has already

> unfolded through the succeeding members. Thus, [none of the phases] are divorced from the fullness [of consciousness] and they embrace all the other members which precede them and forcibly induce them to form a part of their own nature. Each of these phases illumining itself thus, and reflecting on its own nature, is full and perfect.[63]

The two phases of the pulsation of consciousness from inner to outer and outer to inner are equivalent, respectively, to the processes of self-limitation or coagulation (*rodhana*) of consciousness and the dissolution (*drāvaṇa*) of the gross into the subtler forms of consciousness. They represent the sequence of descent into matter and ascent into consciousness.[64] As consciousness descends, its manifestations become increasingly subject to the power of natural law (*niyati*) and so progressively more conditioned. Conversely, as it ascends it frees itself, step by step, of constraints until it reaches its fullest manifestation as the absolute beyond all relativity.[65] Therefore, from one point of view, we can think of the process of descent as a movement into the fettered condition and the process of ascent as the movement towards liberation. This is how it appears to those who have not realised the true nature of the pulse of consciousness—Spanda—in its two phases. For the enlightened, however, these movements represent the spontaneous activity of consciousness. Creation is the manifestation of difference within the unity of consciousness through which it immanentalises into its cosmic form. Destruction is the reverse of this. Diversity merges into unity and consciousness assumes its transcendental formless aspect. These two aspects represent, respectively, the 'lower' (*apara*) and 'supreme' (*para*) forms of Śiva.

Three Moments in the Vibration of Consciousness

The transformation from one aspect to the other can be analysed in terms of a number of successive phases. This, as we have seen, is no more than a convenient way of conceiving the activity of consciousness. Even so, it serves not only to explain in conceptual terms what happens, but it also serves as a means to realise the liberating experience of Spanda. One way this movement can be understood is to analyse it into three stages corresponding to three aspects of the universal power of Śiva's consciousness, namely, will, knowledge and action. All things come into being through an act of will, with action as its immediate instrumental cause and knowledge of its application as the intermediary between the will to create and the act itself.[66] Insofar as the emergence of an object within the field of awareness through the act of perception, and its subsequent subsidence when it has been perceived, are part of the radiant pulse (*sphuraṇa*) of awareness,[67] this three-fold vibration constitutes the essential nature of all things as elements of experience.[68] The intent on making the object manifest, the actual act of manifestation and the manifest state, which are the result of these three powers in their due order, represent the beginning, middle and end of all things, held together as aspects of the universal flow of the absolute (*anuttara*).[69] Śiva's 'lower' (*apara*) form is the unfolding (*unmeṣa*) of the flow (*prasara*) of this universal will[70] in which His powers of will, knowledge and action manifest in relation to their respective fields of operation.[71] In Śiva's supreme (*para*) form His powers merge into one energy that comes to rest within Śiva where it naturally resides.[72] As Bhāskarācārya explains:

> [Śakti's] own abode is understood to be the place of Being (*sat*) called Śiva. It is [Śiva's] vitality (*vīrya*), [His] energy of the nature of knowledge and action. [Energy's] stable state is absorption (*līnatā*), that is, penetration into the agential aspect [of consciousness]. That same [state] is the light of intuition (*pratibhā*) which is the solitary churner of the light of consciousness [that thus aroused issues forth as the universe].[73]

In His supreme, transcendental state, Śiva's knowledge is the awareness He has of Himself as full of all things (*pūrṇo 'ham*). It is one with His activity as the inner vibration of His all-embracing 'I-ness', the creative movement of the will. Thus, together, these three powers represent aspects of Śiva's bliss,[74] which is His Spanda nature as the enjoying subjectivity (*bhoktṛtva*). They are the Lordship (*īśvaratā*), agency of knowledge (*jñātṛtva*) and agency of action (*kartṛtva*) of universal consciousness.[75] The vibration of consciousness is the power of one's own true nature (*svabala*) which brings about the incessant coming together and separation of these energies in the supreme state of universal consciousness and on the lower level of individual consciousness.[76] So let us now examine these three powers in greater detail.

The Conative Power of Consciousness

The self-revealing (*svataḥsiddha*) character of Being corresponds to the incessant flow of consciousness through its will to Be. The outpouring of the will to exist expresses itself both as the active cause of individual beings and the passive assent (*abhyupagama*) to Being expressed through the individuality (*svabhāva*) of all that partakes of Being. The will is thus both the agent and the act of Being:

> Thus the will of the Lord Who wills to appear as the jars or cloths, etc., constituting the world as the manifestations (*ābhāsa*) of consciousness, is the cause, the agent and the action.[77]

The will is coextensive with its own conscious intent. As such it is a form of awareness (*vimarśa*) associated with a specific goal which it reflects on as its objective. The generic nature (*sāmānyarūpa*) of awareness is thus restricted and directed to a single object.[78] The potter's intention to make a pot relates to the action he is about to perform. If his intent were not limited to its own specific object, the potter could just as well set about weaving a cloth or do anything else.[79] When we walk down the road, we are conscious of our ultimate destination and move towards it; even though we may pause to admire the scenery, the will remains fixed (*niyata*) on its goal.[80] Similarly, cooking involves a number of separate actions; even so, the awareness that 'I cook' remains one and unbroken. The conscious intent remains constant throughout. Although it may manifest at different times through different actions, the same will necessarily precedes every action and perception. The existence of another will, prior to, and instigating the will to act or perceive entails that this second will require another to initiate it and that another, leading to an infinite regress. Nor can we deny the existence of the will. Without an original desire to act, activity would be aimless: nothing would determine that one action should occur rather than another. Similarly, no intrinsic necessity ordains that the perception of a particular object should follow that of another. The reason why all other possible perceptions are excluded from the field of awareness is that the will freely chooses to direct attention towards the intended object of perception.

Preceding both perception and action, the will is most clearly manifest (*sphuṭa*) when it begins to assert itself in the subject before either perception or action take place. The first moment or intent (*aunmukhya*) of the will towards its objective conditions the inherent contentment of consciousness at rest in itself, by the act upon which it is intent.[81] Even so, it coincides with the final moment in the movement of the will when the previous desire to act is satisfied and consciousness abides in a state of pure intent free of all specific goals and full of the power of bliss.[82] Abhinava explains:

> [The universal will] in the form of desire (*kāmanā*) blossoms forth through the individual subject. Thus actualized, it is apparent as a desire for sense objects. It does not proceed through the succeeding phases [mechanically] step by step like the feet of the blind. Rather, after it has been aroused and has initially decided upon its goal, thus stimulated, it bounds forward with delight to forcibly lay hold of its goal like a far-sighted man when walking. The will is clearly evident in the initial state when it has [just] arisen and is similarly full and perfect (*pūrṇa*) in its final state of rest.[83]

Thus, we can distinguish between two moments in the movement of the will. The first is the initial state of tension or intent (*aunmukhya*) and the second when it goes on to develop into a conscious desire for a specific object (*iṣyamāna*), discursively representable (*savikalpa*) at the individual level of awareness. At this stage the object of desire appears to be projected outside the subject who desires it, although at the universal level their essential unity remains unchanged. In reality, it is the subject who is always the object of his own desire.[84] But insofar as the subject is now caught up in the object he desires, the first moment is, from the point of view of practice, more important. So for the rest of this section we shall devote our attention to it.

Prior to their manifestation, all things reside within consciousness in a potential form just as in a peacock's egg, we find all the peacock's limbs with its feathers large and small, colours and patterns.[85] In the state of involution (*nimeṣa*) all things mingle with one another in the all-embracing egoity (*pūrṇāhantā*) of Śiva's nature.[86] When consciousness evolves (*unmeṣa*) out of itself to become the diversified universe of experience, this pre-existent potential is actualized. In this way differentiated awareness pours out of the body of undifferentiated consciousness, heralded by a subtle stress or vibration (*ghūrṇana*) of aesthetic delight set up in its causal matrix.[87] This is Spanda in its purest form, free of all differentiation. Bhagavatotpala defines it accordingly: "[This] pulsation (*spanda*) is consciousness free of mental constructs. It is the state in which the Supreme Soul actively tends towards [manifestation]. It simultaneously operates everywhere [although the Supreme Soul is in Himself] motionless (*nistaraṅga*)".[88]

At this stage all the powers of the absolute are activated and merged in the unity of the bliss (*ānanda*) Śiva experiences contemplating His own nature. Subject, object and means of knowledge form a single undivided whole, like the clay ball (*piṇḍa*) a potter is about to fashion into a jar.[89] It is the matrix of all cosmic vibrations, both of the physical order and the extra-physical or metaphysical. In this state consciousness is like a seed swelling to bursting point (*ucchūna*), abounding with infinite possibilities.[90] Somānanda explains:

> When a waveless stretch of water becomes violently agitated, one may notice, if one observes carefully, an initial tension [which forms within it] just when this begins to happen. When the open fingers of the hand are clenched into a fist, one may notice at the outset of this action, a [slight] movement. Similarly, when the desire to create begins to unfold in consciousness, at rest tranquil in itself, a tension [arises within it].[91]

This initial instant (*tuṭi*) is as fleeting and full of energy as a lightning flash.[92] Preceding the spatial-temporal continuum of the lower (*apara*) or immanent level of consciousness, it is not a moment fully set in time. The subtle influence the power of time exerts on the, as yet, unclearly differentiated objectivity (*idantā*) made manifest at this level[93] serves as a link between the eternal and the temporal, the unmanifest consciousness and the manifest universe. He who pays close attention to the initial welling up of desire when it is especially intense is afforded an opportunity to realise the fullness of consciousness by merging into the force of his intention. As Utpaladeva puts it:

> Here [during the initial movement of the will], worldly men who desire to ascend to the plane of ultimate reality can experience in this way the entire aggregate of energies.[94]

In states of heightened psychic intensity all the powers operating through the mind and senses are suddenly withdrawn into the pulsing core of one's own nature, just as a tortoise contracts its limbs in fright,[95] and the continuity of mental life is suddenly broken. The ordinary man, hopelessly distracted, is carried away by this flood of energy (*śaktivisarga*). The yogi, however, master of himself, can by the sheer intensity of this energy penetrate through the flux of his feelings to the 'firmly fixed vibration' (*pratiṣṭhaspanda*) of his own nature. He must learn to do this the instant fear arises in him or when he begins to feel depressed or disgusted, no less than when he is confused and wondering what to do. Equally he must try to penetrate into the source of the vitality (*vīrya*) which intensifies the activity of the senses during the ecstasy of love or of joy at beholding a beautiful object or seeing a close relative after a long time.[96] Overcome with the awe (*vismaya*) of self-realisation (*ātmalābha*), the yogi intuits the intense feelings welling up inside him as aspects of the aesthetic rapture of consciousness (*ciccamatkāra*)[97] in which all emotions blend together like rivers in the ocean of his blissful consciousness. The *Stanzas on Vibration* teach:

> Spanda is stable in that state one enters when extremely angry, extremely excited, running or wondering what to do.[98]

The alert yogi (*prabuddha*) reflects upon his own nature and in so doing instantly penetrates into the initial tension of the will during these heightened states of emotivity. The instant they arise he is elevated beyond his conditioned state of consciousness and so is never entangled in them. The unawakened, however, overcome by Māyā, falls a victim to these states believing mistakenly that his many perceptions and actions are independent of the universal pulsation of his own authentic nature. Thus in order to achieve the direct intuitive insight (*upalabdhi*) that they are grounded in the universal movement of consciousness (*sāmānyaspanda*), one must desist from the tendency, engendered by one's lack of self-awareness, to make distinctions between the functions (*vṛtti*) of consciousness to will, exert itself, know and act, etc.[99]. In this way, the yogi discovers that they are all aspects of the one undivided pulse of consciousness.

This awareness can be achieved by attending to the first movement of the will, discovered when we are fully present to ourselves in the actuality of our situation. Every instant is a new beginning which abides in the eternity of the self-perpetuating present where all 'beginnings' cease.[100] The closer we come to experiencing the moment in which the impulse to action arises, the more directly we come in contact with the concrete actuality of the present and the authenticity of our Being. Thus the Spanda teachings instruct the yogi to maintain an alert awareness of the continuity of his consciousness throughout his every action. When running in fear, for example, he should attend closely to the desire he feels to lift his foot; then to the exertion he applies to lift it and the attention he directs to the place where he is going to place it, as well as the actual act of doing so. He must similarly attend to each phase in the production of words and sentences (*śabdaniṣpatti*) uttered in the excitement of a vivacious conversation, or the movement of the fingers while playing a musical instrument.[101]

The same holds true of the impulse to perceive. The yogi must fix his attention on the thought-free (*nirvikalpa*) intent of the unfolding (*unmeṣa*) of awareness which marks the initial impulse to perception (*didṛkṣā*). For an instant the individual subject (*kṣetrajña*) experiences the same identity between the entities he desires to perceive and his own consciousness, as does the supreme subject between Himself and every entity in the universe.[102] He shares in the Great Pervasion (*mahāvyāpti*) of universal consciousness present in all the categories of existence (*tattva*). Abhinava explains:

> Immersing himself in the supreme reality, clearly aware that consciousness is all things, [the yogi's consciousness] vibrates. This vibration (*ghūrṇi*) is the Great Pervasion (*mahāvyāpti*).[103]

Always on the alert to discern the activity of his own vibrating consciousness, the yogi's attitude (*mudrā*) is kept secret (*rahasya*) in the privacy of his own experience. Established in his own nature, the yogi's awareness is intent (*unmukha*) on discerning the All (*sarvabhāva*) as his true nature through the on-going expansion (*vikāsavṛtti*) of his own consciousness the instant his senses are set in motion:

> The yogi should abide firmly fixed in his own nature by the power of the exertion of [his] expanding consciousness (*vikāsavṛtti*). [Thus he is] established on the plane of Bliss relishing the objects of sense that spontaneously appear before him. Perfected yogis (*siddha*), devoted to bliss, are ever steadfast in this, the Supreme Gesture (*mudrā*), the perfect and unobstructed expansion of the Awakened.[104]

Intent in this way on the initial movement of the will, the power of the yogi's awareness free of thought-constructs (*nirvikalpa*) transcends the limitations imposed upon it by the diversity of perceptions and he is awakened to the higher reality of his all-embracing (*pūrṇa*) nature. Penetrating into the universal vibration (*sāmānyaspanda*) of consciousness, he shares in its unfolding vision (*unmeṣa*)[105] and comes to recognise every state, whether in the mental or in the physical sphere, to be Śiva.[106] Every phase in the unfolding and withdrawal of the activity of the will is now illumined by the yogi's reflective awareness. Perceiving the totality of his experience through the undivided vision of universal consciousness, he experiences the subject, object and means of knowledge as a single whole reposing in the supreme subject with which he is now identified. Having burnt away the sense of diversity (*vibhāgabodha*) in the fire of awareness and transmuted it into the unity of his true nature, the yogi is established in the supreme flow (*paradhārā*) of the powers of consciousness.[107] He maintains a state of self-awareness throughout every moment of his experience, be it while waking, dreaming or in deep sleep.[108] Space, time, change and form are recognised to be modalities of the one consciousness and no longer condition it. The awakened yogi is now constantly mindful of the pulsing power of his true nature not only in the beginning but in every phase of his activity and perception. He realises that all things exist by virtue of their identity with the supreme subject which he recognises himself to be and so no longer wanders in *saṃsāra*.[109]

The Cognitive Power of Consciousness

The apparent gap between the unmanifest, perceiving consciousness and the manifest, perceived object is bridged by understanding their distinctive status as two modes of perception. The cognitive power of consciousness operates both as the immediate, intuitive awareness consciousness has of its own nature and as the mediated perception of objectively manifest particulars. The will to create represents the first movement (*ādyaspanda*) out of the absolute, unmanifest condition into the relative, phenomenally manifest state. The first movement (*ādya-spanda*) of awareness that occurs within the sphere of manifestation is the perception of the undifferentiated totality projected into it by the universal will. The activity of the power of knowledge coincides with the expansion (*unmeṣa*) of objectivity in the field of awareness. In the primordial emptiness of consciousness the faint traces of cosmic manifestation appear as 'the inner desire to know the universe [consciousness] wills to create'.[110] This unfolding awareness successively evolves through the various states of consciousness ranging from deep sleep to the waking state,[111] where the totality of occurrences making up the world of experience is set apart from the individual locus of awareness. The perceptions occasioned by the operation of the cognitive power of consciousness are now fully formed and the universe of experience is manifest in all its plenitude:

> This is the expansion of the power of knowledge which unfolds [spontaneously] through its own energy (*tejas*); phenomena become fully manifest through the persistence of cognition (*jñānasthiti*).[112]

The vibrating power (*spandaśakti*) of knowledge is thus the pure cognitive awareness (*upalabdhṛtā*) of consciousness,[113] which both links perceptions together and accounts for their individual emergence within the field of awareness. These two functions correspond to the quiescent and emergent aspects of consciousness, which together account for the possibility of phenomenal experience. The quiescent aspect represents absolute, undivided consciousness and the emergent, its finite manifestations. Perceptions could not take place were consciousness to be constantly at rest within itself. Completely immersed in its own indeterminate nature, nothing could be made manifest at all. On the other hand, if consciousness were to be entirely emergent as the manifest universe, it could never be consciously experienced. The apparent ontological distinction between the absolute and the relative, the infinite and the finite, is thus reducible to an epistemic distinction between two different modes of knowledge. The cognitive power of consciousness is its capacity to shift back and forth between these two modes and, as it does so, select some of the countless potential forms merged within it to make them externally manifest.[114] The light of consciousness, full to overflowing with innumerable phenomena, thus separates some of them from itself, while at the same time limiting its own nature to apear as the individual (*māyīya*) subject set apart from the object. Perception takes place when this limited subject is affected by the 'shade' (*chāyā*) cast upon it by the object. As the pulse of awareness moves from the expanded, undivided state to the contracted, limited condition and back again at each instant, novel perceptions are generated and the world of experience is thus constantly renewed. Thus this energy, like those of will and action, is essentially Śiva's creative power (*svātantrya*) which is the vibration (*spanda*) of consciousness through which He generates all things.[115]

The Power of Action

Śiva's conative energy becomes fully evident in all its plenitude when the activity of consciousness is manifest (*prasṛta*) on the phenomenal plane.[116] The creative will is the freedom of the absolute and so is equated both with its power to act (*kriyāśakti*) and its power to fashion the diverse forms of the universe (*nirmāṇaśakti*). It is the action of the creative subjectivity (*nirmātṛtā*) of consciousness.[117] As 'the agency of the act of Being' the power of action is the essence (*sāra*) of universal Being (*sattāmātra*)[118] of all things[119] both as their pragmatic efficacy and manifest nature.[120]

This autonomous act of Being is free in every way. It is an act of awareness, the agent of which is the Light of the Heart of consciousness. Being can only be directly experienced within the domain of the subject. We cannot grasp the pure Act of universal Being in the sphere of objectivity. The object is a product of the act of Being of which the subject is the agent. Only the agent is completely autonomous and self-existent. As such he is one and absolute and so can be none other than Śiva Himself, Whose agency is free in all respects.[121] The potter is an agent and is free to make his pot because he shares in Śiva's nature as the agent.[122] It is Śiva Himself Who fashions the jar through the potter and weaves a cloth through the weaver, just as at the universal level He is the guide and impeller (*pravartaka*) of the flux of cosmic forces and of the powers of consciousness:

> Listen! Our Lord, Whose nature is consciousness, is unlimited, the absolute master of the arising and dissolving away of every power.[123]

Śiva, the universal agent, eternally active is never bound by His activity. The universe is the unfolding effect of Śiva's agency (*kartṛprathā*) while He, as the agent, always remains true to His essential, autonomous nature.[124] The law of action and reaction (*karma*) binds only the ignorant.[125] At the lower level, outer activity contrasts with inner awareness. The unfolding of the power of action coincides with the withdrawal of self-awareness. At the higher level, the universal outpouring of consciousness is experienced as the inner Being of all things which spontaneously rise out of it without obscuring it in any way:

> Thus action is said to be one and born of no other inner nature [but itself, which, as such] emerges out of the innate nature [of all things]. It is [the goddess] Śivā, the inner nature, which spontaneously emerges out of itself.[126]

The Doctrine of Vibration urges us to be conscious of Spanda, the recurrent activity of consciousness. In all its outer phases, be they will, knowledge or action, we can catch a glimpse of our authentic identity and realise our inherent freedom. The inner activity of consciousness, free of all restrictions, is bliss itself. The experience of Spanda is wonder, an abiding bliss far higher than the transitory pleasures of life. We can experience Spanda through the activity of the senses, mind and body, because its foundation is universal consciousness, our authentic Śiva nature. Thus the Spanda yogi finds freedom where those who, failing to attend to the vibration of consciousness, are bound.

IV

Śiva and Śakti

As do the Tantras that are their original source and inspiration, all Kashmiri Śaiva traditions speak of God as an inconnumerable and perfect Identity between two contrasted principles, distinguishable in all composite things, but coincident without composition in the One Who is everything. Encompassed by the vision of Śiva's all-embracing consciousness, all contrasts and contradictions are resolved in the harmony of opposites.[1] This unity is the Wholeness of the All in which the opposites are transfigured into a divine polarity, each member of which fully represents the absolute through its inherent identity with its opposite counterpart.

In the Hindu tradition this primal opposition and its reconciliation in the unity of opposites is understood as the intimate, inner relationship between God and His omnipotent power. God is the formless and transcendent unity Who as, and through, His power manifests diversity. God and His creation are not two contrasting realities. Intimately bound together as heat is with fire[2] or coolness with ice,[3] Śakti—God's power, and Śiva—its possessor, are never separate.[4] Even so, if we are to understand their relationship we must provisionally distinguish between them in the realms of manifestation. First, we have the finite vision in which they are seen apart and then the infinite vision in which we realise their unity. Without the experience of duality that of unity would have no meaning. Unity is not mere negation of distinction, but the absence of difference in diversity. The realisation of unity (*tādātmya*) consists of the insight that apparently different things are identical.

As expressions of this polarity, the Doctrine of Vibration focuses on the continuity and change which characterize every experience. Accordingly, Kṣemarāja represents the primordial couple as Śaṅkara and His Spanda energy. Spanda is the immanent, actively emergent aspect, while Śaṅkara, although 'one with the Spanda principle and never otherwise',[5] is the pure, unchanging experiencer Who represents the element of continuity—the passive, quiescent aspect of consciousness. In the Trikakula school the latter is called Bhairava and the former His emission (*visarga*):

> "Bhairava and His power of emission," explains Abhinava, "constitute the couple (*yāmala*). One member (*Bhairava*) rests in His own eternal, unchanging nature, and is therefore called 'repose' (*viśrama*). The other is His primordial vibration (*prathamaspanda*) and is therefore called 'emergence' (*udaya*)."[6]

The opposites separate and merge in rhythm with the pulsing union of Śiva and Śakti. This play of opposites is itself the absolute, the supreme form of Spanda.[7] When Śiva and Śakti unite, the universe, formerly experienced as a reality set apart from consciousness, ceases to exist. When they separate, it is once more created. The eternal rhythm of cosmic creation and destruction is consonant with the pulse of their union and separation. Spanda is the blissful relationship between these two aspects through which the universe unfolds.[8] The emission of cosmic manifestation (*visarga*) pours out between these two poles. It is the result of their conjunction, just as through the bliss of orgasm (*visarga*) the male and female seeds mingle, and man—the microcosm—is born. The yogi who witnesses this union experiences the birth of a higher level of consciousness within himself. He recognises the all-powerful pulsation of his consciousness as it moves between Śaṅkara's transcendental bliss[9] and the radiant emission of His immanent power within Himself. One fixed and the other moving, these two poles are like firesticks that, rubbing together, generate within Śaṅkara His pure Spanda energy.[10] In the bliss of self-realisation, the yogi experiences this as the simultaneous unfolding of cosmic consciousness and the pure undifferentiated consciousness of the absolute. He experiences them together as the universal vibration of the supreme subject beyond all contradictions and distinctions. Abhinava instructs:

> Just as a female ass or mare [in orgasm], enters into the [delight of her own] Abode, the Temple of Bliss repeatedly expanding and contracting and is overjoyed in her own heart, so [the yogi] must establish himself in the Bhairava couple, expanding and contracting, full of all

things, dissolved and created by them again and again.[11]

Jayaratha explains that the contraction of Śakti marks the withdrawal of the universe and the expansion of transcendental Śiva-consciousness. Conversely, the contraction of Śiva-consciousness marks the expansion of Śakti as the cosmos.[12] The yogi attains the supreme state of consciousness by experiencing the pulsing rhythm of this divine couple (*yāmalabhāva*) through which he realises that the absolute is at once both Śiva and Śakti and yet neither of the two:

> The couple (*yāmala*) is consciousness itself, the unifying emission and the stable abode. It is the absolute, the noble cosmic bliss consisting of both [Śiva and Śakti]. It is the supreme secret of Kula [the ultimate reality]; neither quiescent nor emergent, it is the flowing fount of both quiescence and emergence.[13]

Both Śaṅkara and His Spanda energy have two aspects. Śaṅkara is Spandaśakti, the active aspect, as well as being Śaṅkara, the passive aspect. Equally, Spanda is Śaṅkara, the passive aspect, as well as being Spanda, the active aspect:

> "These two aspects, passive (*śānta*) and active (*udita*)," explains Abhinava, "arise at the same time in the power and its possessor. The active passes from one domain to the other, the passive is confined within the Self [the essential nature of both]. But even so, in reality, each of them form a couple (*yāmala*). Hence the emergent is the quiescent."[14]

Despite the one aspect being the other, Spandaśakti is still the active aspect and the cause of creation:

> Even though the awareness proper to these two aspects, passive and active, pertains to them equally, nonetheless it is power, not its possessor, that nurtures His emission (*visarga*).[15]

Maheśvarānanda explains the manner in which we can perceive Śiva and Śakti as a gestalt. It is like a picture of a bull and an elephant drawn together in such a way that we see either one or the other depending on the way in which we view it.[16] There is a movement (*spanda*) of awareness from one to the other as Śiva becomes Śakti and Śakti becomes Śiva. They are reflected within one another like two mirrors facing each other. Exchanging roles repeatedly, they penetrate each other in the intimacy of their union.[17] In this way consciousness contemplates itself as both Śiva and Śakti simultaneously. In other words, the moment in which it is aware of itself as transcending all things, it is also aware of its immanence. These two moments of transcendence and immanence imply one another while remaining distinct.[18]

The *Play of Passion and its Power* (*Kāmakalāvilāsa*), a text of the Śākta Śrīvidyā tradition explains the dynamics of this process in some detail. Śiva and Śakti are represented in this work as the universal subject and His cosmic object. Their infinite nature is symbolized by two trans-dimensional points of absolute consciousness (*bindu*). Śiva is represented by a white point (*śuklabindu*) and Śakti by a red point (*śoṇitabindu*): both expand and contract. 'White Śiva' penetrates 'Red Śakti'. This results in the creation of the universe and Śiva's transformation into Śakti and Śakti's transformation into Śiva. Śiva becomes 'Red Śiva' and acts as the supreme reality and transcendental ground of 'White Śakti'—the manifest universe. Then 'Red Śiva' penetrates into 'White Śakti' and 'White Śiva' withdraws from 'Red Śakti'. This phase of their pulsation marks the moment of transcendence and the withdrawal of the universe. 'White Śakti' is retransformed into 'White Śiva' and 'Red Śiva' into 'Red Śakti'. Śakti then merges in Śiva as the introverted awareness He has of Himself as pure transcendental 'I' consciousness. They thus exchange roles. When one comes to the fore and becomes manifestly apparent, the other recedes into the background as the unmanifest, inner nature of the other. The two moments of transcendence and immanence, Śiva and Śakti, thus imply one another.[19]

The two points make up the two aspects of *Visarga*—the last member of the vowel series, written in Sanskrit as ':' and pronounced 'ḥ'. This is the form (*svarūpa*) of Kāmeśvarī—the Mistress of Passion Who is the power of reflective awareness (*vimarśaśakti*) through which the absolute unfolds and withdraws its cosmic form. She is called 'Kalā'—the 'Divine Power' of consciousness manifest as the incessant transformation or Spanda of Śiva and Śakti. When Śiva and Śakti, the two aspects of the pure vibration of consciousness, are understood as one reality, their symbol is a single dot (pronounced 'ṃ') called a 'mixed point' (*miśra-bindu*). It represents both the integral unity of the absolute and the fertile potential of consciousness which, like a seed, is swollen (*ucchūna*) ready to germinate into cosmic manifestation.[20] This 'mixed point' is the seed of consciousness known as the 'Sun of Knowledge'. It is Kāmeśvara—the Lord of Passion.[21] He is the Self worshipped by yogis as the highest reality and the form or body (*piṇḍa*) of the absolute symbolized as the sexual embrace of Śiva and Śakti,[22] the Divine Husband and Wife. He is called 'Passion' (*kāma*) because His state is sought and desired (*kāmyate*) by great yogis.[23]

Śiva is symbolized in the mystic alphabet by the first letter—'A'—which stands for the absolute. Śakti is represented by 'H', the last letter of the Sanskrit alphabet, which symbolises the ongoing emanation (*prasara*) of the universe. Each letter of the alphabet stands for an aspect or phase in the cycle of cosmic manifestation and withdrawal. 'A' and 'H', Śiva and Śakti, the two ends of the cycle, are united by their 'Passion' (*kāma*), in the totality of 'Ahaṃ' ('I' consciousness). This pure 'I' is the universal vibration of consciousness[24] which embraces the universe in its nature.[25] It is *Kāmakalā* sometimes called the 'Supreme Power',[26] and at other times the Supreme Śiva.[27] The identity and distinction between them is thus reiterated in different ways at higher and lower levels of consciousness in more or less comprehensive terms.

Despite their essential identity, the Śaivite stresses Śiva's superiority over Śakti and the Śākta that of His power. Thus, although all schools of Kashmiri Śaivism are essentially Śaivite, some tend to emphasise the importance of one or the other. The Spanda school, however, maintains that power and the power-holder are equally important. Śaṅkara is the source of power[28] and so is, in this respect, superior to the Goddess Who is its embodiment. On the other hand, this power is the means by which we can discover our authentic identity to be Śiva—the power-holder. The flow of the supreme power is Śaṅkara's path.[29] Herein lies Spanda's importance; while Śaṅkara is the goal (*upeya*), Spanda is the means (*upāya*).[30] We must recognise the activity of Spandaśakti in every moment of our lives. By knowing the divine energy which creates and animates the world, we know ourselves to be its possessor. Only through Spanda's power can we realise our identity with Śiva. But it alone is not enough; power without a power-holder to regulate its activity is blind and potentially destructive.

Śaṅkara

The Spanda yogi experiences the absolute in intimately personal terms as an infinite and perfect divine Being. Although not an object of thought, and hence, Nameless (*nirnāma*),[31] this divine reality is present in all named things.[32] It is the Nameless Whose name is All-Names. It is man who gives It a name to aid in his quest for enlightenment and endear it to his own heart.[33] As a male deity Vasugupta and Kallaṭa call Him Śaṅkara, Śiva, Vīreśa and Bhairava. His commentators add to this list common synonyms of Śiva such as Maheśvara, Parameśvara, Īśa, Śambhu, etc.. Of all these names for Śiva, 'Śaṅkara' is the one preferred by the teachers of the Spanda tradition. Intent solely on gracing man in every way, Śaṅkara is so-called because He bestows the best of things (*śam*).[34] Like the Wishfulfilling Gem, He gives man all he desires.[35] As Abhinava says:

> Once one has achieved the Supreme Lord's state (*pārameśvaratā*) all the good things that came from it are automatically attained just as all the jewels [in the world] are acquired by acquiring Rohaṇa, the Mountain of Gems. Other achievements are vain if one has missed the supreme reality, the Self. But once one has attained this reality (*paramārtha*), there is nothing left one could desire.[36]

Through Śaṅkara's grace man overcomes all the limitations that contract his consciousness and he comes to recognise that it fills the entire universe. Encompassing all things in itself it is blissfully at rest. Kṣemarāja says:

> We praise Śaṅkara Who is one's own nature. He bestows the grace to recognise the total expansion of one's own consciousness which is the non-duality of Supreme Bliss wherein all troubles cease.[37]

Śaṅkara bestows both the peace of liberation from suffering (*apavarga*), and the delight (*bhoga*) of recognising all things to be nothing but Śaṅkara Himself.[38] Man achieves liberation (*mokṣa*) and becomes tranquil through Śaṅkara's gracious withdrawal (*nimeṣa*) of the binding activity of Māyā. Through the concomitant expansion (*unmeṣa*) of his consciousness, he enjoys divine bliss (*bhoga*) in countless forms,[39] even while delighting in the world. Kṣemarāja quotes Utpaladeva as saying: "This is Śaṅkara's Path wherein pain becomes pleasure, poison turns to nectar and *saṃsāra* becomes liberation."[40]

As the innate nature (*svabhāva*) common to all (*sāmānya*) phenomena[41] none equal Śaṅkara nor are like Him (*niḥsāmānya*).[42] He is the supreme good realised at the 'summit of all summits'.[43] None is greater than He along the scale of Being and so can only be discovered at the very peak of man's spiritual endeavour:

> O Lord, those who have achieved the supreme path (*gati*) of renunciation, the supreme wealth of knowledge and the supreme summit of desirelessness, bear You, the Lord, [always before them].[44]

The gods who rule over the worlds pale before Śiva's glory; they are like mere bubbles in the vast ocean of His consciousness.[45] The many powerful gods, including Viṣṇu and Brahmā, reside within the sphere of Māyā and owe their divine status to a mere spark of Śiva's power.[46] Arranged in order of precedence, the gods are like flowers in bloom on the creeper of Śiva's power.[47] They all aspire to attain Śiva's abode and race along the garland-like ladder of yogic practice (*karma*) in their attempt to reach it.[48] Again, while they have fixed forms, Śaṅkara appears to us in whatever form we worship him, like a Wishfulfilling Gem which appears in any form we wish it to assume.[49] Śiva, the source of all the powers, becomes manifest through them and is worshipped in various ways, according to the form we conceive Him to have.[50] Yet, as Bhaṭṭa Nārāyaṇa says:

> O Lord, even though You are seen and desired in various ways, You bestow the wonderful (*citra*) fruit of Supreme Reality in its entirety.[51]

The names and forms of God may vary but ultimately all the forms in which the Deity may appear, or names that it may assume, are expressions of the radiant pulsation of man's own consciousness (*svātmasaṃvit-sphuraṇa*). Ultimately the most authentic form of God and the object of worship is the Self.[52] Maheśvarānanda asks: "Abandoning their own consciousness, what lifeless [object] should they worship?"[53]

Again:

> Those Who meditate on other deities abandoning attention to their own nature [although] possessing great wealth, go begging. And even when they have begged [their food, still remain] hungry.[54]

In reality, both the worshipper and the worshipped, the bound and the released, are Śiva:

> May Śiva Who has penetrated and become one with me, worship Himself thus by means of His own power that He may Himself reveal His own nature.[55]

The basis of Śaṅkara's divinity is His Spanda nature. Spanda converts the cold, impersonal absolute of monistic Vedānta into Śaṅkara, the warm, worshipful absolute of Kashmiri Śaivism. An impersonal absolute is unsatisfactory on metaphysical grounds, and fails to satisfy man's deepest need for devotion and grace. Kṣemarāja quotes Bhaṭṭa

Nāyaka as saying:

> O Lord, how fruitful can this neuter Brahman be without the beautiful female of Your devotion which makes of You a person?[56]

Through its divine power the Self assumes the form of a deity man can contemplate and venerate, even though Śiva, the pure subject, can never in fact be an object of meditation (*adhyeya*). Until we realise our true identity with Śaṅkara, He is worshipped and conceived to be a reality alien to ourselves. While we are in the realm of creation, He too is a creation or mode or appearing of the absolute, manifest to us in meditation, through His freedom as an eternal, omniscient being.[57] There is no gulf between the created and the uncreated creator:

> Nothing in reality, although an object of knowledge, ceases to be Śiva: this is the reason why meditation [on this or that aspect] of reality bestows its fruit.[58]

The world of the senses and mind appears to the Well Awakened (*suprabuddha*) as a theophany, an eternal revealing of God in His creation. The Doctrine of Vibration declares that "there is no state in word, meaning or thought, either at the beginning, middle or end, that is not Śiva."[59] To utter any word is, in reality, to intone a sacred formula.[60] Every act is a part of Śiva's eternal cosmic liturgy, every movement of the body a ritual gesture (*mudrā*), and every thought, God's thought.

> By what path are You not attainable? What words do not speak of You? In which meditation are You not an object of contemplation? What indeed are You not, O Lord?[61]

Spandaśakti, which accounts for the appearing of all things, is also the means by which Deity in its many varied forms appears to man. Kṣemarāja concludes:

> The ultimate object of worship of any theistic school differs not from the Spanda principle. The diversity of meditation is due solely to the absolute freedom of Spanda.[62]

Śaṅkara is not only the supreme object of devotion; as the static polarity of the absolute, He is the inner reality which holds together its outer manifestations.[63] Phenomena are patterns of cognitions projected onto the surface of self-luminous Śiva-consciousness. There they become apparent, directly revealed to consciousness according to their manifest form. Śiva is accordingly symbolized as the ground or surface of awareness, smooth and even like a screen (*samabhittitalopama*).[64] Inscribed on this screen (*kuḍya*) are the countless manifest forms which appear within it rendering it as diverse and beautiful as a fossil ammonite (*śālagrāma*).[65] Śiva is the sacred ground upon which the cosmic *maṇḍala* is drawn, the absolute surface of inscription which bears the mark (*cihna*) of the universe. Abhinava writes:

> The variety of this world can only be manifest if the Highest Lord, Who is essentially the pure light of consciousness, exists; just as a surface is necessary for a picture. If external objects were perceived in isolation then, because 'blue' and 'yellow', etc., are self-confined and the perceptions [we have of them] refer to their objects alone and so are insentient, mute and dumb in relation to one another . . . how would it be possible to be aware that an object is variegated? But just as depths and elevations can be represented by lines on a smooth wall, and we perceive [a female figure and think], 'she has a deep navel and upraised breasts', similarly it is possible to be aware of differences in the variegated (contents of experience) only if all the diverse perceptions are connected together on the one wall of the universal light of consciousness.[66]

Śiva is the perfect artist Who, without need of canvas or brush, paints the world pictures. The instant He imagines it, it appears spontaneously, perfect in every respect. The colours He uses are the varying shades and gradations of His own Spanda energy and the medium His own consciousness. The universe is coloured with the dye of its own nature (*svabhāva*) by the power of Śiva's consciousness (*citi*).[67] Rājānaka Rāma says:

> Homage to Him Who paints the picture of the Three Worlds, thereby displaying in full evidence His amazing genius (*pratibhā*); to Śambhu Who is beautiful with the hundreds of appearances laid out by the brush of His own unique, subtle and pure energy.[68]

Analogously, at the microcosmic level, all the cognitions and emotions, etc., which make up the individual personality form the outward flow of essentially introverted consciousness. They are specific pulsations (*viśeṣaspanda*) or aspects of the universal pulsation (*sāmānyaspanda*) of pure 'I' consciousness. At the lower level, within the domain of Māyā, they represent the play in the fettered soul of the three primary qualities (*guṇas*) or 'feeling-tones' which permeate to varying degrees his daily experience. These are: 1) *Sattva*—the quality of goodness and luminosity which accompanies blissful experience both aesthetic and spiritual. 2) *Rajas*—the passion or agitation which oscillates between the extremes of 'light' and 'darkness' and characterises inherently painful experiences. 3) *Tamas*—the torpor and delusion which accompany states of inertia and ignorance.[69] The liberated soul recognises that these three are the natural and uncreated powers of pure consciousness. For him they are manifest respectively as: 1) Śaṅkara's power of knowledge (*jñāna*)—the light of consciousness (*prakāśa*); 2) the power of action (*kriyā*)—the reflective awareness of consciousness (*vimarśa*); 3) the power of Māyā—which does not mean here the world of diversity, but the initial subtle distinction which appears between subject and object in pure consciousness.[70]

On the lower level, the power of awareness (*citiśakti*) is disturbed from its self-absorption and begins to generate thought forms (*vikalpa*) within itself. Consciousness devolves and becomes the thinking mind (*citta*).[71] Śaṅkara assumes the form of a human personality (*māyāpramātṛ*) residing in a world of limitations and diversity.[72] His consciousness is extroverted and generates out of itself a subtle body (*puryaṣṭaka*) consisting of the three components of the inner organ of mentation (*antaḥkaraṇa*)[73] and the five subtle essences (*tanmātra*) of taste, touch, smell, sound and sight. Residing in this subtle body, consciousness transmigrates from one physical organism to the next and is seemingly affected by *Sattva, Rajas* and *Tamas*. The higher stage represents a state of introversion when the subtle body, with its transient emotions and cognitions, is withdrawn into 'I' consciousness and dissolves away.[74] Śaṅkara is both these aspects simultaneously. Kṣemarāja criticises the Mīmāṃsaka who believes that the Self is pure being alone, only accidentally associated with transient perception. He explains that this is true only of the functions of the subtle body (*puryaṣṭaka*) when experienced as independent of consciousness.[75] According to the Doctrine of Vibration, the momentary, transient nature of the object, whether mental or physical,[76] does not affect the eternal stability of Śaṅkara, the Self. The Fully Awakened (*suprabuddha*) recognises this truth, while the unenlightened are always caught in the outward flow of events. The Fully Awakened yogi identifies himself with Śaṅkara, the universal (*sāmānya*) Spanda nature, and experiences the universal flow of consciousness in all the opposites. The unenlightened, however, who wrongly identifies himself with the body, is caught by his fascination for the individual pulses of emanation, dispersed and separated from each other by the tension of the opposites.

> Thus, these particular pulsations are to be totally avoided; they are present in the body, etc., which is other than the Self and arise by mistaking [the body, etc.,] for the Self. [The particular pulsations of consciousness] are the fields of sensory operation (*viṣaya*) of the phenomenal (*māyīya*) subject. Each is distinct from the others as on-going fluxes (*pravāha*) of perceptions (*pratyaya*) of the type (*guṇa*) 'I' am happy' or 'I am sad', which are the causes of transmigratory existence.[77]

However, these perceptions can in no way 'be an obstacle for the enlightened'.[78] Right and wrong, pleasure and pain, merge and all distinctions disappear in the universal vibration of Śiva's consciousness. Thus we read in the *Stanzas on Vibration:*

> The streams of the pulsation (*spanda*) of the qualities and the other [principles][79] are grounded in the universal vibration [of consciousness] and so attain to being; therefore they can never obstruct the enlightened. Yet for those whose intuition slumbers [these vibrations of consciousness] tend to disrupt their own state of being (*svasthiti*) casting them down onto the terrible path of transmigration so hard to cross.[80]

The universal vibration of consciousness understood as Śiva's perfect egoity is contrasted with the fettered soul's conceived notion of himself as the body. The latter's ego is a thought-construct (*pratyaya*) and hence limited and artificial. It consists of particular pulsations of consciousness. Śaṅkara's ego consciousness, on the contrary, is complete and integral (*pūrṇa*). Reflecting on Himself, He is aware that "I am pure consciousness and bliss; I am infinite and absolutely free."[81] Immersed in this contemplative state (*turīya*), Śiva delights in the awareness "the universe in all its diverse aspects arises out of Me, it rests within Me and once it disappears, nothing remains [apart from Me]."[82] Thus, this self-awareness is the universal Spanda of consciousness.

Rājānaka Rāma explains that the alert yogi in the course of his meditative practice gains an insight, by Śiva's grace, into the manner in which the particular pulsations (*viśeṣaspanda*) of his consciousness arise with their consequent effects. He constantly exerts himself to experience the pure universal vibration of his authentic 'I' consciousness and so free himself of the disturbing influence (*kṣobha*) the pulsations have on him.[83] He is always on the alert to discern universal Spanda.[84] Thus reflecting on his own nature as the pure awareness that 'I am' (*ahaṃ*), he distinguishes between the particular and generic vibration of consciousness. While the unawakened is constantly subject to the ups and downs of these individual pulses of consciousness, the awakened, on the contrary, turns even more resolutely to his true nature whenever he observes their activity within himself. Thus, for him, they serve as a means to liberation.

Śaṅkara is the ground of both the particular and universal aspect of Spanda. Through the discrimination (*viveka*) born of the intuition (*pratibhā*) of the universal pulsation of 'I-ness', contemplative souls discover Him to be their own pure subjectivity (*upalabdhṛtā*) which, as the source of all the individual pulsations of consciousness, is their ultimate reality (*paramārtha*) beyond all subject-object distinctions.[85] Reality cannot be discovered if we think of it as a 'something' of which we are ignorant but may come to know through practice. Reality is an experience—the experience of the fully enlightened.

The Nature of Śakti

Inherent in Śiva is His infinite power. Essentially one with Him, His power represents the freedom of His absolute nature *from* the limitations of the finite, and the freedom *to* assume the form of the finite while abiding as the infinite. Freedom from limitations implies the capacity to become manifest in countless diverse forms.[86] Ultimately, it is Śiva's freedom alone which unfolds everywhere as all things.[87] The universe exists by virtue of His power which is at once the universe itself and the energy which brings it into being.[88] Thus Abhinava says:

> The Lord is free. His freedom expresses itself in various ways. It reduces multiplicity into unity by inwardly uniting it and of one it makes many. . . . He is therefore described as the knowing and acting subject, perfectly free in all His activities and all-powerful; this [freedom] alone is the essential nature of consciousness.[89]

This freedom is also the inherent nature of the Self—man's authentic identity. Perceiving nothing but itself in all things, the Self requires no external aid in order to manifest itself in the sphere of objectivity. The ego, confined to the physical body and fashioned by the thought-constructs generated by a form of consciousness whose focus of attention is (apparently) outside itself, is not free. It is a 'non-self' dependent on outer objectivity. However, even in this condition destitute of power (*śakti-daridra*) the fettered, individualised ego-consciousness partakes of the autonomy of the pure conscious Self. One's own authentic nature (*svabhāva*) is independent of objectivity and so must necessarily objectivise itself for the world to become manifest without impinging on its freedom.[90] Thus the perfect autonomy of the Self is also its universal creativity. Absolute independence implies more than a transcendental, autonomous state of aloofness. It requires that this autonomy be creative. This is the freedom which is Śiva's power to do 'that which is most difficult' (*atidurghaṭakāritva*). His capacity to accomplish that which would be logically impossible (*virodhate*) in the domain of the empirical (*māyā*), governed by the principles of natural law (*niyati*). In order for Śiva to manifest as the diverse universe, He must deny His infinite nature and appear as finite entities and "what could be more difficult than to negate the light of consciousness just when it is shining in full?"[91] Thus, negation or limitation is a power of the absolute. Śakti is the principle of negation through which Śiva conceals His own undivided nature and becomes diverse.[92]

As the source of diversity, Śakti is the absolute's creative power of Māyā. Due to Māyāśakti, an initial contrast emerges within universal consciousness between the conscious (*cit*—subject) and the unconscious (*acit*—object). This split goes on to develop into the innumerable secondary distinctions which obtain between specific particulars.[93] The one power made manifest in this way appears to be diverse due to the diverse forms of awareness the subject has of the many names and forms of the object.[94] There is no object or event that does not disclose the presence of Śakti. "The universe," says the *Śivasūtra*, "is the aggregate of [Śiva's] powers."[95] Each power is a means, channel or outlet (*mukha*) through which Śiva, though formless (*anaṃśa*) and uncreated, becomes manifest in a particular form.[96] The very Being (*sattā*) of an entity consists essentially of its capacity to function (*arthakriyā*) within the economy of consciousness.[97] All things are endowed with Śakti in the form of their causal or pragmatic efficacy (*kāraṇasāmārthya*). It is on the basis of an entity's causal efficacy that we say that it is what it is and not anything else. Thus, there are innumerable powers in every object. Although these powers cannot be known directly, they are inferred from their effects.

Change is the coming to prominence of one power at the expense of another. When a jar, for example, comes into being, the pragmatic efficacy of the clay ball is superseded by that of the clay jar.[98] In this way the abiding fullness (*pūrṇatā*) of the one universal power, in a sense, alters as one aspect 'expands' and comes to the fore, while another 'contracts' or recedes into the background.[99] Śakti is, in this sense, in a state of perpetual pulsation (*spanda*), expanding and contracting, assuming now this, now that form. Thus, this one power appears to be many due to the diverse results of its activity.[100] Although reality is one, it performs many functions. Various aspects of the one universal potency appear in each individual entity as its specific functions and so the ignorant wrongly assume them to be divided from one another.[101] The enlightened, however, discover the universe to be power and thus undivided and at one with Śiva, their authentic nature as the possessor of power.[102]

Thus, Śakti is both immanent when actively giving rise to its effects, and transcendent when considered to be the source of its many powers. Spanda is both the universal vibration of energy (*sāmānyaspanda*) and its particular pulsations (*viśeṣaspanda*). Every power is like a pane of coloured glass through which the light of the absolute shines and assumes the form of the sparkling variegations of the manifest universe. The principal forms of power can be classified into three basic categories according to the sphere in which they operate, namely:

1) The Sphere of Śiva-Consciousness. The powers here include: a) *Śiva's Divine Attributes.* These divine attributes are five: omnipresence, eternality, freedom of will, omniscience and omnipotence. They correspond to Śiva's powers of consciousness, bliss, will, knowledge and action.

b) *Śiva's Cosmic Functions.* These cosmic functions are also five and are implemented by Śiva's five powers to create, maintain, destroy, conceal Himself and grace by revealing Himself.

c) *Śiva's Creative Energies.* The principal creative power in the sphere of manifestation is Śiva's power of Māyā, which is an aspect of His power of action. Other aspects of His power of action are *Nirmāṇaśakti*, the power to fashion particular entities out of His own undifferentiated consciousness, and *Kālaśakti*, the power of time through which Śiva creates the temporal order and hence the universe of change and becoming.[103]

2) The Sphere of Cognitive Consciousness. The preceding sphere can be said to have two aspects—inner and outer. The former corresponds to Śiva's divine attributes and the latter to His cosmic functions and creative energies. Similarly, at this level, the inner aspect is mental in which operate the power of cognition and memory along with the power to differentiate individual perceptions. The outer aspect corresponds to the powers of the senses.

3) The Sphere of Individualised Consciousness. In the individualised consciousness sphere the power of consciousness operates through the individual subjects and objects it engenders. The inner aspect corresponds to the many experiencing subjects, all of which are forms of the power of self-awareness.[104] In addition, we have the waking and other states which, as modalities of consciousness, are also powers. Again, there are the forces which help to elevate the soul and develop his consciousness to a more expanded state as well as those that, on the contrary, restrict it. To the outer aspect of individualised consciousness corresponds external objectivity, which includes the categories of existence, worlds and cosmic forces that bind them into a coherent whole. Belonging to all three spheres both in their inner and outer aspects is the power of speech. At the highest level it is the pure awareness Śiva has of His own nature. In the lower spheres it is the silent inner speech of thought as well as the manifest articulate speech of daily life. Thus, Śakti manifests as everything that can be denoted by speech as well as every form of speech.

These three spheres correspond to three aspects of Śakti: Supreme (*Parā*), Middling (*Parāparā*) and Lower (*Aparā*). Worshipped as three goddesses in the Trika school, this Triad is one of the most essentially defining features of this form of Śaivism and its earlier prototypes in the Āgamas. Kṣemarāja sees in this Triad aspects or phases of Spanda.[105] Accordingly, we turn now to a brief description of these three important energies.

The Supreme Power (Parā śakti). This energy operates on the Supreme Summit of Being (*parakāṣṭhā*). There consciousness reflects upon itself as the universal ego (*pūrṇāhantā*), which is the ultimate ground of all things[106] and abode of rest,[107] where everything is one and beyond all relative distinctions.[108] Knowledge and action, unsullied by their objects, abide here as Light and awareness. At this level, awareness (*vimarśa*) includes the Light of consciousness (*prakāśa*) and they are one.[109] Consciousness and its content merge like water in the sea or a flame in fire.[110] We can distinguish between two aspects of this energy corresponding to two aspects of the supreme state:

i) The first aspect is the supreme power unsullied by the products of its activity. This is the pure freedom of consciousness. It is the pure intention (*icchāmātra*) through which the absolute affirms its absolute Being unconditioned by the cosmic Totality generated by it. As such, it is the primordial vibration (*ādyaspanda*) of consciousness free of all restrictions on its activity. It generates and contains within itself the innumerable Benevolent (*aghora*) powers of consciousness that bestow the fruits of realisation to the enlightened yogi.[111]

ii) The purely transcendental state of the first aspect turns to immanence when this will is disturbed and aroused out of its quiescent state. The emanation of Totality dawns on the horizon of consciousness as its potential goal and the will to existence spontaneously presents itself as the exertive force that actuates it. It now acts as the Lordship (*īśikā*) of consciousness which governs the universe held within it. For the awakened yogi it operates as the actuality of a conscious exertion to make the oneness of the absolute apparent. Thus it sets into operation all its Benevolent (*aghora*) powers to guide the yogi's way along the path to realisation.[112]

The Middling Power (Parāparā śakti). The Intermediate level is that of unity-in-difference, between the lower level of the awareness of division (*bhedadṛṣṭi*) and that of unity (*abhedadṛṣṭi*) at the summit of consciousness. Here the universe is experienced within consciousness as one with it while maintaining itself distinct from it, like a reflection in a mirror. The form awareness assumes here is 'I [am] this [universe]' (*ahamidam*).[113] Subject and object are equal in status; they are distinct but not divided and experienced as the two aspects of awareness, namely, knowledge and action.[114]

This level is the point of contact between the absolute and its manifestations. It is the sphere of relatedness. Practical life is based on the relationship between immanence and transcendence and that between the elements of diversity.[115] Thus the energy which operates at this level is also the basis of all empirically definable experience.[116] By the power of awareness in this intermediate state we can make contact with the undivided unity of pure consciousness while we are on the level of diversity. However, the power of awareness operating here can also generate the Fierce (*ghora*) energies of consciousness that block the path to liberation by engendering attachment to the fruits of action, whether good or bad. If through this power the yogi realises the oneness of consciousness and its manifestations, he is elevated, but if he fails to do so, this same power throws him down. Thus the Intermediate power plays a dual role by illumining both the 'Pure Path' to liberation and the 'Impure Path' of bondage.[117] This ambiguity reflects the paradoxical nature of the absolute's knowledge of the universe it has willed into existence, as either one with it or separate from it. From the point of view of the absolute these two are complementary modes of experience, but from the point of view of the relative, knowledge of difference is binding, while knowledge of unity is liberating.

The Inferior Power (Aparā śakti). This energy operates in the Root (*mūla*) of consciousness where objectivity predominates,[118] and the inner awareness (*jñāna*) of the Self takes second place to outer activity.[119] This is the level of diversity where the beauty of the world picture, charming with its many details, is fully displayed:

> The lower (*aparā*) level corresponds to the extension of relative distinctions (*bheda*) which, like a [fine crop] of tender sprouts, are born of the potency of the Supreme Lord's contemplation (*vimarśa*) of His transcendental Light. It is the illusion of daily life (*vibhrama*) embossed with this cosmic multiplicity, pleasantly various like a work of art.[120]

Limitations which the Sun of consciousness imposes on itself shroud it like dark storm clouds. Subjective awareness (*ahaṃvimarśa*) contracts, conditioned by the body in which it has taken up residence and perceives particulars (both individual subjects and objects) as cut off from one another and from itself. Even so, the awareness it has of its own nature abides as the Lower power, pulsing and brilliant like a streak of lightning.[121] For those ignorant of its true nature this power operates as Māyā and generates the 'Extremely Fierce' (*ghoratara*) energies of consciousness that lay hold of the soul and throw him down to its lower levels.[122] However, to one who experiences the infinite consciousness of his own nature and Māyā as its eternal freedom, it bestows both yogic power (*siddhi*) and liberation (*mukti*).[123] The *Stanzas on Vibration* explain:

> This, Śiva's power of action, is binding when residing in the fettered soul (*paśuvartinī*); [but], when [its true nature] is understood and it is set on its own path it bestows success in Yoga (*siddhi*).[124]

According to the Doctrine of Vibration, the soul is liberated by recognising that 'the whole universe is the result of the activity of the [Spanda] principle.'[125] Conversely, by being ignorant of this he is bound.[126] Failing to contemplate his own Spanda nature, its activity functions as this Lower power and engenders gross action.[127] This breaks up the unity of his consciousness,[128] splitting up and obscuring it by the tension between the contrasting responses to what he seeks to acquire (*upādeya*) or give up (*heya*).[129] The universal act of self-awareness (*pūrṇāhantā*) assumes the form of a 'drop of egoity' (*ahantāvipruṭ*) which animates the gross and subtle body.[130] In this way *Aparā śakti* pervades the vital forces (*jīvakalā*) operating in the body.[131] Once the ignorance of Māyā has been overcome, the yogi recognises his oneness with Śiva by the power of his own self-awareness (*svasaṃvedana*). He ascends to the plane of the Well Awakened and, having achieved all that is to be achieved (*kṛtakṛtya*), attains both the supreme perfection (*siddhi*) of the realisation of his own Lordship and the lower perfections (*aparasiddhi*) of all the yogic powers (*vibhūti*) that accompany it. He recognises that even his lower embodied awareness is Parā, the Supreme Goddess Who contemplates the pure non-dual consciousness which is the innate nature of all things, and the Light of the Supreme Lord.[132] Pervading Śiva, this power pervades the universe. The yogi thus experiences Śiva-consciousness and cosmic consciousness simultaneously and this power is then said to be 'set on its own Path'.[133] In other words, it resides in one's own Śiva-nature, on the plane of absolute unity (*atyantābhedadaśā*) where awareness no longer moves to any other object (*viṣaya*). The Lower is then one with the Supreme power through which all things are experienced in their true universal (*sāmānya*) nature as pure consciousness.[134]

The harmonious union (*sāmarasya*) of these three planes are Bhairava's supreme glory, the radiance of the fullness of His power (*pūrṇaśakti*)[135] which fills the entire universe. Together, this triad constitutes the Deity's universal experience (*bhogya*). By sharing in it the yogi comes to realise the unsullied bliss of the absolute (*anuttarānanda*), the supreme form of Spanda.[136]

V

Śakti Cakra: The Wheel of Energies

As we have seen, the ceaseless flow of consciousness perpetually generates new forms within it as some of its powers come to the fore and become manifestly active, while others abide in a potential state within it. In this way novel patterns of energy spontaneously form on the surface of consciousness through its inherent activity, as do waves on the surface of the sea.[1] The arising and subsiding of each wave of cosmic manifestation is marked by a regular sequence (*krama*) of metaphysical events. Following one after another in recurrent cycles, each sequence is aptly symbolised by a rotating wheel (*śakticakra*), the spokes of which are the aspects of the divine creative energy of consciousness brought into play as the wheel revolves. Thus these Wheels collectively represent the primal form or 'archetype-field structure' of all experience. They are infinite in number and the number of spokes in each can vary from one to infinity in accord with the diversity of the configurations of power which form at each stage along the cycle of cosmic manifestation. Scripture says:

> These powers become diverse, increasing or decreasing in number, etc., in accord with the divine will (*svātantrya*). In this way, Bhairava becomes manifest as the 'Solitary Hero', as the couple (*yāmala*), as three, four, five, six, seven, eight, nine, ten, eleven powers, as the Lord of the great Wheel of twelve, a thousand or infinite spokes. [Thus He] ultimately unfolds as the master, endowed with all power, of the Wheel of the All.[2]

Like the circles of light produced by a whirling firebrand (*alāṭacakra*), the cycles of divine creative activity manifest as a single Act. As each Wheel rotates, one power after another becomes active, taking over from the one that went before it and blending into the one that follows. The flow of the energy of consciousness moves round the circle in harmony with the rhythm of its pulsation. Thus the Wheels of Energy are the vibrant radiance of Bhairava, the light of consciousness.[3] They represent the plenitude (*pūrṇatā*) of the absolute. Kṣemarāja explains that: "the universe is established and exists because its manifest form is one with the inner Light of the Lord. Hence it is said to be the Wheel of Energies.[4]

The Doctrine of Vibration teaches that there is an essential identity between the inner world of the subject and the outer world of the object.[5] The universe is equally the outer physical world and the inner world of mind and body.[6] Thus the emanation of these Wheels corresponds to the creation of both these worlds.[7] Accordingly, Kṣemarāja explains that the many deities well known to those learned in Āgamic lore, grouped and worshipped in circles, represent the biological components of the body and the transient moods, thoughts, etc., of the mind.[8] Śaṅkara is the Lord of the Wheel (*cakreśa*) and hence of both the macro- and microcosm. He is the 'source of the power of the Wheel of Energies'.[9] The Wheels of power unfold within Śiva's infinite consciousness, evolving as they do to higher degrees of complexity, and then once more dissolve into the undivided unity of His consciousness. They are generated and withdrawn in harmony with the evolution and involution of Śiva's Spanda energy. This expands and contracts at the transcendental level, beyond the categories of existence (*tattva*), generating as it does so, all these powers.[10] Abhinava explains:

> [We can see the many colours] white, red and yellow of the peacock's feathers when they are unfurled, but not when they are folded together. Similarly, if the Lord of the Wheel does not unfold [His powers, He] merges with [His own nature] full of subtle consciousness. He manifests variously through the unfolding and contraction [of His power]. Thus by the contraction of one [aspect] and through the unfolding of another [He] appears in [many] forms ranging from the single spoked Wheel to the Wheel of a thousand spokes.[11]

To witness this expansion and contraction and to worship its diverse aspects as Goddesses seated in the circles generated by this activity and recognised to be one's own authentic nature, is to worship the Supreme Lord in the fullness of mystic absorption (*turīya*).[12] Each Wheel rotates, radiant with the light of consciousness, in a space or spiritual sky (*vyoman*) of its own. Pure consciousness (*saṃvid*) is the universal space or Great Sky (*mahāvyoman*)[13] which embraces all the spiritual extensions which make room for the unfolding of every configuration of experience. Called the 'Sky of Śiva' (*śivavyoman*), the 'Abode of Brahman' (*brahmasthāna*) and the 'Abode of the Self' (*ātmasthāna*), it is at once Bhairava and the supreme form of Śakti (*parākuṇḍalinī*),[14] equally consciousness and its contents. In a sense everything, including consciousness, is empty. As Abhinava says:

> The [dawn] sky, though one, appears radiant white, red and blue, and the clouds accordingly seem various; so pure, free consciousness shines brilliantly with its countless forms, though they are nothing at all.[15]

Śakti represents the all-encompassing fullness (*pūrṇatā*) of the absolute, the ever-shifting power of awareness actively manifesting as the Circle of Totality (*viśvacakra*). Śiva is the Void (*śūnyatā*) of absolute consciousness—its supportless (*nirālamba*) and thought-free (*nirvikalpa*) nature. Integral and free, Śiva, the abode of the Void, dissolves everything into Himself and brings all things into being.[16] Fullness pours into emptiness and emptiness pervades fullness. Penetrating suddenly into the fullness of consciousness, all things are at once made part of its absolute and undefinable nature. "[For the yogi who] penetrates into the non-dual Void," teaches the *Vijñānabhairava*, "his true nature (*ātman*) is there made manifest."[17] The Void actively assimilates all diversity. In the pure subject the flux of objective perceptions dissolves away. The external personality merges in the supreme subject and the seed of all future diversification is destroyed, thereby freeing the yogi of all causal and *karmic* necessity: "Well concealed, and attainable only with great effort, is the subtle Void, the chief root of liberation".[18]

To experience this emptiness, the yogi must penetrate into the initial instant of perception (*prāthamikālocana*) when he directly perceives the object and no dichotomyzing thoughts have yet arisen in his mind. In this way he finds the centre (*madhyamapada*) between one thought and the next or between two perceptions.[19] In the Heart of his own consciousness, apparent in the Centre, he experiences the initial expansion (*unmeṣa*) of awareness at its most intense, just as it is about to blossom into the diversity of thought.[20] All objectivity is then suddenly dissipated and the yogi shares in the extraordinary sense of wonder (*camatkāra*) the Lord of Consciousness Himself experiences when he perceives the ideal universe within Himself on the point of emergence. Through this sudden eruption into reality, brought about by a supreme act of grace, the yogi is instantly absorbed in the fully expanded state of the Great Void (*mahāśūnya*).[21] He then moves freely, without obstruction or effort, in the Sky of Consciousness (*cidākāśa*) beyond time and space, at one with the power of awareness which wanders there in its infinite freedom. When all supports have fallen away, the yogi experiences the Void of the primal vibration (*spanda*) of the absolute as a single, undivided mass of consciousness (*cidekaghana*). The rays of the Wheels of his powers, both physical and mental, are drawn into the vibrating emptiness and the yogi is plunged in the direct actuality of the Present. He thus frees himself from the tyranny of the flow of time from the past to the future.

> Having checked the rays of one's own Wheel of Energies and drunk the incomparable nectar [of self-realisation], one remains fully satisfied in the [eternal] present, unconditioned by the two times [of past and future].[22]

Merged in the incessant systole and diastole of the Heart of consciousness, the yogi is no longer a victim of time but its master. He is the conqueror of time, one 'who delights in the relish of devouring time' (*kālagrāsarasika*) and assimilating it into his own eternal consciousness:

> [For the yogi] past and future are not different from the present; it is the present itself which becomes divided by the past and the future. When they no longer exist, the present also ceases to exist. The yogi, resting even for an instant is this ocean of consciousness, intent on devouring time, becomes instantly a 'Wanderer in the Sky' (*khecara*) [and is liberated].[23]

According to the *Svacchandabhairavatantra*, there are various degrees of Voidness. The yogi must traverse them all if his extroverted consciousness is to be brought completely to rest in its innate nature. The unchanging (*akrama*) Goddess of Consciousness, the embodiment of mystic absorption (*turīya*), then appears within the Great Pervasion (*mahāvyāpti*) of the Supreme Void.[24] This, the Void beyond all degrees of emptiness is called *'Fullness' (aśūnya—literally, the 'non-void')*. It is described as the compact mass of consciousness and bliss which is the pure dynamic Being (*sattāmātra*) of both the existent and the non-existent.[25] It absorbs all the levels of Voidness and contains them all, pervading them as does oil sesame seeds.[26] The 'Void beyond Mind' which precedes it is the transcendental experience of Śiva. If the yogi manages to rise beyond this transcendental emptiness, he attains the highest Void which is that of the supreme form of Śiva (*paramaśiva*). Here he experiences a state of transcendence in immanence and immanence in transcendence.[27] Inner and outer become one in the unifying experience of undivided consciousness. Voidness dissolves into Voidness until the yogi reaches the highest level of undifferentiated consciousness. Free of thought, beyond all distinctions of immanence and transcendence, Śiva and Śakti,[28] he attains the supreme place of rest (*viśrāntisthāna*).

> When, by means of this practice, the unfolding universe dissolves away in the Void and all that qualifies it in the Sky, and when this Void [itself] dissolves away [like a drop of water in the sea], the Good (*anāmāya*) alone abides. This, O Brahmin, is the essence of the true teachings.[29]

In one of the few places where the author of the *Stanzas on Vibration* takes time to indulge in polemics, he points out that the Voidness (*śūnyatā*) of the vibrating power (*spanda*) of consciousness, manifest when all diversity disappears, should not be confused with an empty 'nothing'. The universe of diversity is not annihilated, but recognised to be one. It is void in the sense that it is universally manifest and hence has no distinguishing features. Eternal and free of the contraries, it cannot be contrasted with anything else.[30] Intuited as the throb of one's own awareness, it is never known objectively and hence is essentially undefinable.[31] Although it is said to be the destruction of all objectivity, the Void is not a state of 'non-being' (*abhāva*). Kṣemarāja quotes the *Svacchandatantra* as saying:

> The non-void is described as the Void while the latter is nothing at all. O Goddess, that is considered to be nothing wherein all phenomena (*bhāva*) are destroyed [by losing their phenomenal nature].[32]

There can be no place anywhere in experience where we can discover that which is not. The light of consciousness illumines even that which we understand to be non-existent.[33] Being and non-being are merely conceived distinctions; both are qualities superimposed on that which is presented directly to consciousness. The absence or non-existence of an object in a particular place is just as much a positive reality as is its presence. Both the perception of its presence as well as its absence are equally apparent to consciousness.[34]

Although the non-dualist Śaiva agrees with the Buddhist who maintains that the true nature of things is essentially unspecifiable (*anirdeśya*), he does not agree that all determination of the emptiness of ultimate reality is an error. Kṣemarāja explains that the highest level of Voidness is the emptiness of reflective awareness, the pure undifferentiated pulsation of the power of consciousness, grounded in the consciousness and bliss of the Self—the Supreme Lord (*parameśvara*) of the universe.[35] If the Buddhist denies the existence of a perceiving subjectivity, how can he say that he has experienced emptiness? An experience of Voidness devoid of the awareness of Self is, from this point of view, little better than that of deep sleep (*suṣupti*). But even then a total loss of all subjective awareness is impossible. Even in deep sleep, or in certain states of contemplative absorption accompanied by ego-loss, some subjective awareness must persist. It would be foolish to believe, say the *Stanzas on Vibration*, that the subject ceases to exist in these states just because the effort normally directed towards perceiving his object ceases.[36] Once we have fallen deeply asleep there would be no way we could wake up if the subject who directs the movement of awareness out to the objective world ceased to exist. Moreover, if ego-loss is an experience, there must be someone who experiences it.[37] When we awake from deep sleep, we remember that we were sleeping; we can recall that something happened although we do not know what it was. We could not therefore have been totally unconscious.[38]

Moreover, any state liable to subsequent recall as an event in the past cannot be ultimate. The experience of 'I am' (*aham*) pervades all possible states whether they be the deeper ones of contemplative absorption (*samādhi*) or those closer to the surface consciousness (*vyutthāna*) of the waking state. The supreme state is uncreated (*akṛtrima*) and full of consciousness and action[39] while all the lower states are transitory (*kādācitka*) and creations of the higher. The emptiness of ego-loss experienced in certain types of absorption are liable to subsequent recall and are therefore transitory, artificial states which must be transcended to achieve the uncreated voidness of pure 'I' consciousness which, because it is always present, can never be recollected.[40] Far from being the ultimate reality, the emptiness of ego-loss can be an obstacle in the way of attaining the supreme realisation.[41] It separates the lower levels of consciousness based on subject-object distinctions from the higher level of pure 'I' consciousness, the fullness (*aśūnya*) of the empty (*śūnya*). Unlike the lower void of ego-loss, the Supreme Sky (*paravyoman*) of 'I' consciousness is brimming over with countless power of which Śiva is the master. Thus Śiva, Whose body is pure consciousness (*vijñānadeha*),[42] is the Lord of the Wheel of Energies, each of which represent aspects of His divine majesty, the power of His sovereignty (*aiśvarya*) and freedom (*svātantrya*). As His Wheel of Energies revolves, the universe is created and destroyed[43] manifesting in this way His power. The Liberated, at one with Śiva, share in His freedom while those ignorant of their true identity are caught in the movement of this Wheel and so bound to the recurrent round of birth and death:[44]

> Happy is the child who sucks at its mother's breast; it is the same breast it fed from in a former life. The husband takes his pleasure in his wife's belly, he was conceived there in the past!
>
> He who was the father is today the son and that son, when tomorrow comes, will be father in his turn.
>
> Such is the flow of *Saṃsāra:* men are like buckets around a waterwheel![45]

We experience this creation and destruction, this ceaseless coming and going, as binding only if we fail to recognise that everything abides within the light of consciousness.[46] If we realise that all this is merely the play of the power of consciousness—the rotation of the Wheel of Energies—the world no longer appears to us to be *Saṃsāra.* Abhinava exclaims:

> It is Śiva Himself, of unimpeded will and pellucid consciousness, Who is even [now] sparkling in my heart. It is His highest Śakti Herself Who is ever playing at the edge of my senses. The entire world glows at one with that bliss [of 'I-ness']. Indeed, I know not what the word *'Saṃsāra'* refers to.[47]

In our failure to contemplate the Lordship of our own nature, consciousness generates thought forms (*vikalpa*) which rise and fall as the Wheel of Energies rotates and we are caught in the seemingly endless wandering from birth to birth. Bhagavatotpala quotes *Nāradasaṃgraha* as saying: "all thought is *saṃsāra*, there is no bondage except thought."[48] Trapped by thought on the periphery of the movement of the Wheel, we lose hold of the inwardly unchanging nature of reality and are entangled in the fickle, transient and diverse nature of its outward appearance.[49] Conversely, when through an act of self-awareness, the restless movement of the mind (*citta*) is quelled and thought turns in on itself, the yogi realises the true nature of *Saṃsāra* to be the Wheel of Energies and is no longer bound, even in the midst of the change and diversity of the world.

> Worthy of attainment is that reality in which the yogi, brilliant with the rays of [his] consciousness fully formed, is established. [It is] the fully evident arising of an experience free of worldly bonds (*bhavavandhyodaya*). [It takes place] even while the Self, the radiance of one's own conscious nature, the internal senses which aid it, the group of external senses which depend on it for their activity, taste and the other objects of

the senses, are [all] fully active.[50]

Although the Wheels of Energies are innumerable, just as the aspects of Śaṅkara's ever emergent power of awareness are beyond number (*kalanā*),[51] only a few are important in the Doctrine of Vibration. According to the Krama doctrine adopted by Kṣemarāja in his commentary on the *Stanzas*, foremost among them is a cycle of twelve phases. It represents the twelve aspects of *'Kālasaṅkarṣiṇī'* (The Attractress of Time), the Goddess of Consciousness. Technically called 'the Wheel of the Absolute' (*anuttaracakra*), all the other Wheels emerge from it and are all eventually dissolved in it.[52] Subject, means of knowledge, object and pure cognitive awareness (*pramiti*) are symbolised by Wheels containing eight, twelve, sixteen and four elements respectively. The twelve-spoked Wheel thus represents the cognitive cycle (*pramāṇa-cakra*) and is symbolised by the sun which passes through the twelve signs of the zodiac in the course of a year.[53]

This Wheel represents, amongst other things, the twelve senses, that is, the intellect (*buddhi*) and mind (*manas*) together with the five organs of knowledge (*jñānendriya*) and the five organs of action (*karmendriya*).[54] It also represents the twelve vowels of the Sanskrit alphabet (excluding ṛ, ṝ, ḷ, ḹ,), symbolising the processes and forces operating directly within Śiva-consciousness (rather than Śakti, the universe, which is symbolised by the consonants).[55] Again, the twelve phases represent the three goddesses Parā, Parāparā and Aparā, each subject to a cycle of arising (*sṛṣṭi*), persistence (*sthiti*) and withdrawal (*saṃhāra*), together with the manifestation of their own undefinable nature (*anākhya*). As phases in the cognitive cycle, the twelve powers are worshipped as twelve Kālīs, normally divided into three groups of four. They are the subject, the means of knowledge and the object, each appearing in the process of emergence, persistence, withdrawal and an undefinable state (*anākhya*) beyond them.[56] According to Kṣemarāja, this cycle gives rise to a four-fold cycle of cosmic creation and destruction consisting of:

1) The initial exertion (*udyoga*) that arises within the body of the absolute that leads to its transformation into the universe.
2) The actual manifestation (*avabhāsana*) of the universe within the absolute.
3) The relishing (*carvaṇa*) or reflective awareness of the appearing of the universe within consciousness.
4) The destruction (*vilāpana*) or withdrawal of the universe back into the absolute when it resumes its pristine form as the radiant, Undefinable power (*anākhyaśakti*) of pure consciousness.[57]

This is just one possible way of analysing the Wheel's motion. In fact, it unfolds in many ways, both sequentially and instantaneously, assimilating into itself as it does so the subject, object, means of knowledge and resultant cognitive awareness. The yogi can, by close attention (*avadhāna*), observe the movement or Spanda of this Wheel in the course of each act of cognition, as it moves from the centre or 'Heart' (*hṛdaya*) of pure consciousness out to the periphery, where it becomes manifest as sense objects. In this way the yogi comes to realise that all is contained within, and generated through, the cycle of consciousness (*saṃviccakra*). Every sound, taste, smell—anything he then perceives—occasions in him a profound state of contemplative absorption. Abhinava describes the sequence (*krama*) of events in the process of this realisation as follows:

> This Wheel of the Absolute (*anuttaracakra*) flows out from the Heart throught the void of the eyes, etc., onto each sense object. The rays of this Wheel progressively engender the Fire [of the subject], Moon [of the object] and Sun [of the means of knowledge], in [each phase] of the destruction, creation and persistence of the external world. In this way [the yogi] should contemplate [how everything] in the field of sound, etc., becomes one with this Wheel as it falls upon it along the path of the voidness of the sense of hearing, etc.. This Wheel, which is all things, like a universal monarch, [is followed by its vassals, the senses] wherever it falls in this [all-embracing] process. In this way the Cosmic Path (*adhvan*) [of emanation] spontaneously merges with the great Wheel of Bhairava and [His] surrounding [goddesses] of consciousness. Then, even though the universe has merged [into it] leaving behind nothing but its faint latent trace, contemplate this great whirling Wheel as the outpouring (*ucchalattā*) of one's own nature. When all the fuel [of objectivity] is consumed [in the fire of the Wheel] and its latent traces are destroyed, contemplate the Wheel on the verge of extinction, in the process of extinction [and finally as totally] extinct. In this way, by this meditation, the universe dissolves into the Wheel and this into consciousness, which finally shines forth void of all objects. The nature of consciousness is such, however, that there is again a new creation, for such [is the activity of the] Goddess of Consciousness (*cinmaheśvarī*). He who every instant dissolves the universe thus into his own consciousness and then emits it is eternally identified with Bhairava.[58]

Abhinava adds that this process is common, in its basic form, to all the meditations leading to the realisation of the absolute (*anuttara*).[59] Moreover, the yogi can meditate on other Wheels apart from this one and still be graced with the same fruits.[60] To be successful, however, he must identify with the Lord of the Wheel Who resides in its centre as the pure 'I' consciousness, which is the impelling force (*anuprāṇitva*) behind the emanation and movement of its powers. Kṣemarāja refers to Him as the 'Churning Bhairava' (*manthānabhairava*) because 'He engenders the creation, etc., of all things [by arousing] and churning His own power.'[61] Śiva churns and whirls the energies around Himself, creating and destroying the universe through the pulsation (*spanda*) of His universal will[62] while He abides unmoving (*acala*) in the Heart—the centre of the Wheel.

> He, Śiva, the One of unmeasured (*akalita*) greatness pulsing and self-established, measures out (*kalayati*) in the Heart, the universe from Earth to Sadāśiva, and by diverse conjunctions [of aspects of His nature], emanates the wonderful sport of emission and withdrawal.[63]

In the centre, Śiva is free in the greatness of the Wheel: He is not a slave of its operations.[64] Fully Awakened, He sees and contemplates its movement and effects in all of life's daily activities. The individual soul, bound by the Wheel of the world and of the body, is liberated the instant he discriminates between himself as the embodied and the 'body-world' he lives in.[65] By experiencing the entire universe ranging from Earth, the grossest, to Śiva, the subtlest, he recognises that he is Śiva,[66] the pure 'I' consciousness which eternally delights in the play of the Wheel.

> Śambhu triumphs [over all] by the glory of [His] incomparable and undivided Bliss. He, like a newly wedded husband, constantly gazes at His beloved power Who, although inwardly undivided, dances in many ways outside [Her] own nature, [Her] diverse forms and seemingly new aspects conceived in the varied light of thought.[67]

Sharing in Śiva's experience of Śakti we participate in His Lordship and are free to create and destroy the subtle body of the mind and sensations (*puryaṣṭaka*) and so become the Lord of the Wheel. The *Stanzas on Vibration* declare:

> But when [the mind of the fettered] is firmly established in one place, then generated and withdrawn [by him at will], his state becomes that of the [universal] subject. Thus he becomes the Lord of the Wheel.[68]

Kṣemarāja, in his *Heart of Recognition* (*Pratyabhijñāhṛdaya*), explains where the 'one place' the yogi should fix his attention is found:

> Then, by becoming absorbed in the integral 'I-ness' which is the bliss of the light of consciousness and the power of the Great Mantra, [the yogi] achieves mastery of the circle of the deities of his own consciousness who engender perpetually the emanation and withdrawal of all things.[69]

To become Lord of the Wheel and be liberated, the yogi must become one with the absolute (*anuttara*), identified with the power residing in the space of the Heart of consciousness. The yogi who grasps the true nature of the absolute need not know or practice anything else, not even contemplation of the Wheel of Energies.[70] The yogi who is unable to merge directly with the absolute is instructed to penetrate the Centre of the Wheel by contemplating its universal activity and concentrate on the great whirling Wheel as the vibration of his own nature.[71] Through the power of the Great Mantra—'I' (*aham*)—the yogi must vibrate the circle of powers, thus saturating the rays of his own consciousness with the plenitude of self-awareness. Whatever he perceives is then filled with the pulsation (*spanda*) of the light of his self-realisation:

> [The yogi experiences] stability, satisfaction and merger in the Light to the degree in which consciousness deploys itself and progressively covers objectivity. [He experiences] there the vibration which allows him to realise the supreme freedom everywhere pervaded by this essence.[72]

The unfolding of the Wheel of Energies confers upon the yogi the enjoyment (*bhoga*) and bliss (*ānanda*) of cosmic consciousness. When the Wheel contracts, the yogi's individuality fuses with pure consciousness and he experiences its unconditioned freedom (*svātantrya*). In these two movements yogic powers (*siddhi*) are conferred by the particular waves of energy (*viśeṣaspanda*) of the universal vibration (*sāmānyaspanda*) of consciousness which is the source of liberation (*mokṣa*). Mastery over all things and the realisation of the oneness of consciousness are thus achieved by discovering oneself to be the Lord of the Wheel (*cakreśvaratvasiddhi*). This liberating realisation issues from a state of uninterrupted absorption in the vibration (*spanda*) of consciousness both in the ecstasy of contemplation 'with the eyes closed' (*nimīlanasamādhi*), and when the yogi has risen out of it (*vyutthāna*), to regain the more normal waking consciousness which for him is transformed into a state of contemplation 'with the eyes open' (*unmīlanasamādhi*). Thus, whether his eyes are open when awake, or closed when sleeping or meditating, the yogi merges with the pulsation of consciousness which moves like a fire-stick between these two poles generating in him the brilliance of enlightened consciousness[73] and he is liberated while still residing in the body:

> If [the yogi] resides without a break for three hours in his own nature which shines once [and forever], is free of diversity and is absorbed in contemplation, the mothers Brāhmī, etc., and the mistresses of yoga realised by practice centred on that Wheel together with the Heroes, Aghora, etc., the Lords of the Heroes and the nine-fold god, etc., all become fully manifest and the perfections (*siddhi*), which are the powers generated by practising [attention to the movement of] that Wheel, are attained. These [powers] possess Bhairava's energy. The yogi becomes powerful through it and by virtue of the Śākinī energies associated with it, various according to [their] diverse forms ranging from Khecarī onwards. All these liberate him through this very body itself and [bestow upon him] Supreme Perfection (*paramasiddhi*) [in the practice of yoga which is the realisation of his immanence everywhere] in the cosmic order ranging from Earth to Śiva.[74]

Thus for the enlightened yogi, the power (*prabhava*) of the Wheel of Energies is the Light (*prabhā*) which illumines his mind and the divine breath of the spirit which blows (*vāti*) within him as pure—'I-ness'. It impels his every act and perception. Presiding over and sanctifying his mind and body, it brings all things to rest within his own nature.[75] Again, it bestows upon the yogi "the ability to ascend in terms of his own essential nature to ever higher levels by foresaking the lower ones."[76] The yogi penetrates into the Great Light which is his free, undivided nature through the divine rays of his consciousness gathered together in the Wheel of Energies.[77] The Wheel is thus the source of the spiritual power the yogi enjoys when he achieves the object of his meditation through grace and his purified intuition.[78] But as Kṣemarāja is quick to point out:

> It is only a few who, [blessed with] the wealth of absolute contemplation (*anuttarasamādhi*), ascend intuitively (*dhiṣaṇā*) into the light of Śaṅkara which is their own true nature and lordship of the Wheel of consciousness; others, afflicted by embodied egoity, do not do so.[79]

The Wheel of Energies can function in two opposite ways. It can either be the source of bondage for those deluded by Māyā, or else represent the powers the enlightened achieve through yogic practice.[80] The same forces which bind and condition man can also lead him to the higher levels of enlightenment. That which binds the ignorant sets free the man of wisdom.[81] We shall see how this works in the following account of the Wheels of Energies contemplated in the Spanda tradition as presented by Kṣemarāja.

The Wheel of Vāmeśvarī

Again borrowing from Krama doctrine, Kṣemarāja explains that the pure universal pulsation of consciousness (*sāmānyaspanda*) is manifest in five cycles or pulses of power (*viśeṣaspanda*) represented by five concentric circles. These circles symbolise the states of individualised consciousness ranging from the subtlest, most internal and subjective to the grossest, most external and objective. Four of these groups of energies[82] serve as a link between absolute, unmanifest consciousness and the realm of manifestation. They are:

1) the circle of *Khecarī* energies which constitute the individual subject,

2) the circle of *Gocarī* energies which are the powers of the inner organ of mentation (*antaḥkaraṇa*),

3) the circle of *Dikcarī* energies which are the powers of the senses, and

4) the circle of *Bhūcarī* energies which represent the outer objects of the senses.

5) In the centre of these four circles is the fifth—the circle of pure consciousness. It represents the absolute as cosmic motion transfigured into the inner revolving power of pure consciousness. The centre of the fifth circle is empty. In the Void of the Centre the power of awareness (*cicchakti*) is 'established on the thought-free plane of the Supreme Lord's inner nature'.[83]

This power wanders in the void of the absolute, the sacred space which abides for the divine eternity before the cosmogonic split between subject and object occurs. It is the primordial outpouring (*ullāsa*) of the undivided awareness of universal consciousness within the 'own nature' (*svarūpa*) of all things and within which all spatially perceived diversity (*diṣyamānabheda*) emerges. This power is the Supreme Goddess Who acts as the root-consciousness and ground of sensory perception. She personifies the powers of the internal and external senses as well as their objects, both inner emotive states, thoughts, etc., and outer physical sensations. In Her wanderings in the Sky of Consciousness (*cidākāśa*) She perceives all things. When the split emerges within consciousness between subject and object and they are perceived as a multitude of diverse entities,

She is the source of the positive and negative responses of the perceiver to the perceived.[84] These responses are implemented by the four circles which evolve out of Her as aspects of Her nature when this split occurs. Hence this Goddess is called 'Vyomavāmeśvarī',[85] 'Vyomeśvarī' or simply 'Vāmeśvarī.[86] She is the Goddess (*īśvarī*) Who resides in the Sky (*vyoman*) and emits, spits out or vomits (Sanskrit root *Vam*) the universe of personal experience out of the universal experience of the absolute, much as a person suffering from cholera vomits out everything in his stomach.[87] She is the fullness (*pūrṇatā*) of pure consciousness and the source of the other limited forms of awareness manifest as Her four circles of powers.[88] She personifies the pure subjectivity which operates in all individual subjects and becomes manifest at the instant of complete realisation.[89] Kṣemarāja explicitly identifies Vāmeśvarī with the Spanda principle[90] that brings about the extending perception (*prathā*) of the Triad of powers, Supreme (*parā*), Middling (*parāparā*) and Inferior (*aparā*). Thus She impels every form of emanation at all levels of manifestation.[91]

As Her name 'Vāmā' (meaning 'left', 'perverse' or 'contrary') indicates, She accounts for a reversal or, more precisely, a 'double-reversal' within the absolute. For the unenlightened She is the source of diversity and, as such, She is the potential cause of bondage—the 'reverse' of Śiva's state of unity and freedom. For the enlightened She is the power of awareness which 'runs counter to the normal course of transmigratory existence'.[92] For them, Vāmā represents the spiritual energy (*kuṇḍalinī*) latent in man when it awakens and illumines his consciousness.[93] Her powers: "lay hold of, and throw down from a great height the essence of diversity and bestow the perfect oneness (*abheda*) of unity in the midst of multiplicity (*bhedābheda*)."[94] The fettered soul is caught in the force of the downward rush of the flux of emanation from the undivided (*abheda*) level to that of division (*bheda*). The enlightened soul, however, merges in the current which flows from the level of diversity to that of unity.

The Circle of Khecarī Energies. The previous level was the sphere of the universal subject; this level is the sphere of the individual subject. While the former represents the experience of the oneness of pure consciousness enjoyed by the enlightened, this circle represents the powers which accompany this realisation. The powers of Khecarī are the very essence of the expansion of consciousness and bliss. They are the attributes of consciousness when it is in its most expanded, unconditioned state. These are five: omnipotence, omniscience, perfect completeness, freedom from natural law and eternality. At the level of the pure individual subjectivity which emerges when consciousness limits itself prior to any contact with the subjective sphere, these same powers function as the five obscuring coverings (*kañcuka*) which limit the five divine attributes of consciousness. These are:

> The power of limited action (*kalāśakti*),
> the power of limited knowledge (*vidyāśakti*),
> the power of attachment (*rāgaśakti*),
> the power of natural law (*niyatiśakti*), and
> the power of time (*kālaśakti*).

The Circle of Gocarī Energies. The word *'go'*, Kṣemarāja tells us, means 'speech'. Accordingly, the three powers which operate in this sphere are the primal energies of the mind (*antaḥkaraṇa*) said to constitute the subtle, inner discourse (*saṃjalpa*) of thought. For the unenlightened these energies function via the intellect (*buddhi*), ego (*ahaṃkāra*) and mind (*manas*) as the powers to determine distinction (*bhedaniścaya*), to identify the Self with diversified objectivity (*bhedābhimāna*) and to form thought-constructs centred on diversity (*bhedavikalpa*), respectively. For those who enjoy a state of grace, they give rise to pure determinate awareness in the intellect (i.e., the direct experience of unity); pure self-arrogation in the ego (i.e., the reflective awareness that 'I am Śiva'), and pure intent in the mind (i.e., the synthesis of diversity into a unified whole).

The Circle of Dikcarī Energies. Moving further out we reach the sphere of the ten senses (five of knowledge and five of action), symbolised by the ten directions (*dik*). Through these sensory powers the unenlightened perceive only multiplicity. When these same powers have been purified and energized by Śiva's grace, the awakened yogi perceives through them Śiva's pure unity revealed in the diversity of sensations.[95]

The Circle of Bhūcarī Energies. This is the outermost circle—the sphere of objectivity—'Earth' (*bhū*). The energies operating in this sphere manifest as the five objects of the senses: form, taste, sound, smell and touch. The enlightened experience their consonant harmony (*tanmaya*) with the senses and so their ultimate identity with consciousness. These powers 'are manifest as the body of the light of consciousness for the awakened, while they display limitation everywhere to others.'[96]

The Wheel of the Senses

Sensory activity is the most tangible expression of the power of consciousness to know and act. The physical organs of sight and hearing, for example, are merely 'doors' (*dvāra*) or channels through which this power flows; they do not in themselves account for the sensory perception of light and sound.[97] They are merely the locii (*golaka*) of particular aspects of the pervasive power of universal consciousness to know all things in all possible ways. Kṣemarāja explains that the Lord of Consciousness operates the body and senses of each individual by His own power of Māyā.[98] The senses are instruments of the power of awareness projected out of consciousness through this same power.[99] Thus the perceptions and activities of the countless living beings in the universe function as the senses of the Supreme Lord of Consciousness.[100] They are aspects of His power of awareness impelled by His Spanda energy to activity. Thus the *Stanzas on Vibration* teach:

> That principle should be examined with effort and respect because this, its uncreated freedom, prevails everywhere. By virtue of it the senses, along with the inner circle, [although] unconscious, behave as if conscious in themselves, move towards their objects, rest [there] and withdraw [from them].[101]

The senses are figuratively arranged in two concentric circles. The outer circle consists of the ten senses: five of knowledge (*jñānendriya*) and five of action (*karmendriya*). The inner circle is the inner organ of mentation (*antaḥkaraṇa*).[102] It consists of the intellect (*buddhi*), ego (*ahaṃkāra*) and mind (*manas*). The Doctrine of Vibration stresses that Spanda can be experienced through the operation of the senses. By practice and Śiva's grace, the yogi attains a state of alert awareness. He then ranks amongst the Awakened (*prabuddha*). Awakened, he can perceive Spanda as the vibration of consciousness that animates the body and is the impulse which drives the senses. By attending carefully to this vibration he experiences the unity between himself, Śiva (Who is universal consciousness) and the world of objects and perceptions. At first he experiences this only occasionally, but once this experience becomes permanent, he is Fully Awakened (*suprabuddha*) and, as such, liberated. To understand how this works, we turn now to a description of the senses.

The Intellect (buddhi). The individual soul divested of all sensation and thought reposes in a state of deep sleep in union with the primordial substance (*prakṛti*) from which the objective world (including the psycho-physical organism) is generated. The substance of all that can be perceived objectively in any form, this primordial matter is understood to be a power of consciousness technically called Śāmbhavīśakti.[103] This energy is roused to activity by consciousness personified as the god Svatantreśa, otherwise known as Ananta.[104] The equilibrium (*sāmarasya*) of its three qualities (*guṇa*) of *Sattva, Rajas,* and *Tamas* is then disturbed (*prakṣubdha*) and the lower principles are generated from them. The first principle to emerge is the intellect.[105] Experience at this level is like that of waking from sleep. For a moment we are not clearly aware even of ourselves but merely register that things exist around us and that we are waking up. Similarly, the intellect is free of both the sense of ego and the determinative mental activity of the mind. Thus the images that appear in the intellect are apprehended directly, its function being merely to illumine the products of sensory and mental activity[106] projected onto it where their existence (*sattā*) is registered.

The Ego (ahaṃkāra). The emergence of the ego marks the next stage in the process through which we come to know ourselves as individuals and the world about us. The ego's function is to appropriate and personalise experience—to link it together as 'my own'. It arises from the mistaken notion that the light of consciousness reflected in the intellect and coloured by objectively perceived phenomena is the true nature of the Self.[107] Thus, the personal ego falsely identifies the Self with that which is not the Self and vice versa.[108] The individual soul is bound by this mistake in identity which functions not only in relation to the subtle, inner operations of the intellect, but also in relation to gross, physical objects.

> 'I am wealthy', 'I am thin', 'I delight in the senses', 'I am content', 'I breathe', (and when in deep sleep) 'I am empty': egoity (*asmitā*) is observable on these six levels.[109]

The ego which forms a part of the inner mental organ should not be confused with the pure egoity (*ahaṃbhāva*) of consciousness. 'I' consciousness is of two kinds. One is pure and is Śiva, the light of consciousness reposing in itself.[110] The other is a product of Māyā. The pure ego rests on pure consciousness and the impure ego on outer objective forms.

> [Universal] 'I' consciousness rests on freedom whose primary characteristic is perfect autonomy. It is without any break, like an inward consent (*antarabhyupagamakalpa*). It is the Self which abides as the living being whose nature is the essence of the light of consciousness, pure and unsullied by any association with the body, etc. It is [perfectly real] and not a thought-construct.[111]

False identification conditions this pure egoity (*ahantā*), limiting it to the psycho-physical organism. It is imperfect (*apūrṇa*) and hemmed in on every side by the limitations imposed upon it by its physical and mental environment. Pure egoity is uncreated (*akṛtrima*) and free. The individual ego is a creation (*kṛtakatva*) imagined into existence (*kalpita*) by pure 'I' consciousness.[112] Even so, there is in fact only one ego which operates within different parameters. The pure ego functions at the universal level of cosmic subjectivity (*viśva-pramātṛtā*) and the impure ego at the individual level of the Māyā-subject. By recognising that 'I' (*aham*) is Śiva and that this ego is not that of the fettered soul (*paśu*), we realise our identity with Śiva and are liberated. We must stick to the abiding conviction that our authentic ego and Śaṅkara are identical.[113] To have an ego is not in itself harmful or bad:

> O Supreme Lord, although I have understood that pride is vain, even so, if I do not measure [the expanse] of my own nature by the pride of thinking, 'I am made of You', all joy comes to nought.[114]

This pure ego is Spandaśakti. It manifests as the individual ego which transmits the impulse (*saṃrambha*) of consciousness that activates the vital breaths[115] animating the mind and body. According to Kṣemarāja the Doctrine of Vibration teaches:

> Anointed by a drop of the nectar (*rasa*) of egoity even the unconscious becomes conscious. Thus this reality, infusing consciousness into them, renders both the senses and the conceived subject (*kalpita-pramātṛ*), falsely assumed to be the impelling force (*prerakatva*) behind their activity, capable of performing their functions. Thus [the individual soul] falsely assumes that he impels the senses to action.[116]

The individual ego is the source of all the other senses. As uninterrupted self-awareness, it is called the Sun of Knowledge. Around the sun of the ego rotate the twelve suns of the other senses. They emerge from it and are drawn back into it just as, according to Śaiva cosmography, the twelve suns, corresponding to the signs of the zodiac, emerge from and return to the thirteenth sun.[117] Thus the function of the ego is the self-arrogation of experience through the identification it engenders between consciousness and the senses which are its instruments of knowledge and action. Although those ignorant of the authentic identity of the ego are bound by its operations, it is nonetheless an essential component of individualised consciousness. Directing its sensory and mental activity, it reflects in the microcosm the supremity of the universal ego that is the source and master of all that takes place in the domain of manifestation.

Mind (manas). The ego full of the brilliance of *sattva* is the source of the mind (*manas*) and the five organs of knowledge (*jñānendriya*). Mind (*manas*) is the instrument through which consciousness fashions specific, clearly defined mental representations of the world of sensations, which pours into the inner mental organ through the channels of the outer senses and is reflected in the intellect. Like a chisel which cuts away the unwanted stone from a block of marble to reveal the image contained within it, mind (*manas*) excludes all the sensations not immediately useful to the perceiver and focuses his attention onto those that are. Without mind (*manas*) our field of awareness would be flooded with thousands of indiscernible sensations. It would be impossible to follow a sequence of events or go about any task without succumbing to a thousand distractions. A faint sound heard in the distance would be registered with the same intensity of awareness as the music we were listening to in a concert hall.

Manas selects and isolates specific sensations from the mass reflected in the intellect. This sensation is then compared with similar sensations perceived in the past, the latent traces of which are stored in the intellect and named according to the prevailing linguistic convention (*saṅketa*). The two sensations—one in the past, the other in the present—are held together by the continuity of awareness between these two moments and so we come to recognise that the two sensations belong to the same class and *manas* is able to form a discursive representation (*vikalpa*) of the sensation perceived. *Manas* thus not only analyses and dissociates individual sensations from each other, but also synthesises a set of sensations into a single whole.[118] For example, a series of discrete sensations occurring in successive moments is grouped together by *manas* in the notion of action or in the notion of relation in general. The basis of this determinative activity (*anuvyavasāya*) is unity-in-difference (*bhedābheda*) and its function, the structured ordering of sensations.[119]

Manas (in the normal states of waking and dreaming) is always moving (*cañcala*) from one sensation to the next. Unlike the external organs of knowledge, *manas* is not confined to a specific field of operation (*viṣaya*). It can equally well apprehend sound, taste, smell, etc., and thus relate them to one another to form a single, coherent picture of the world of physical objects. As no activity is possible in the absence of a will to act, *manas* is said to be full of will (*icchā*) or desire to move on to, and process, different sensations. It is driven to its task by the ego's incessant seeking to appropriate and assimilate experience. The pure sensation clothed in thought and differentiated from other sensations by *manas* and personalised by the ego (*ahaṃkāra*) is then presented to the intellect, where it becomes known to consciousness.

Maheśvarānanda, explaining the process of perception and the function of the inner mental organ, compares its three constituent elements to waves (*kallola*) which form in the ocean of the Heart (*hṛdaya*) of consciousness. As they rise out of the Heart of pure 'I' consciousness, they carry with them some of its egoity and spill it out onto the object of perception. The 'thisness' (*idantā*) of objectivity is drawn into intimate relationship with the 'I-ness' of subjectivity. The three senses of the inner mental organ "drag 'thisness' there [into the ocean of the Heart] and project 'I-ness' out here [onto the object of perception]."[120] There is a movement (*spanda*) of awareness in two directions—from inner to outer and outer to inner. This movement free of temporal distinctions,[121] is a great wave (*mahātaraṅga*) of the ocean of consciousness. From this great wave originate the smaller waves which are the movements of the outer senses, just as ripples or eddies follow in the wake of large waves.[122] Thus the power of the Heart of consciousness emanates out to the outer world and back, vibrating as it moves. Although the entire process of perception constitutes a single event, Maheśvarānanda analyses the pulsation of the Heart into three phases as follows.

> *Primal vibration* (*ādyaspanda*). This is the initial throb of awareness that pulses in the subject. It corresponds to the tendency (*aunmukhya*) inherent in the power of consciousness to expand out into universal manifestation.
> *Intense vibration* (*parispanda*). This is the universal vibration of consciousness that reveals itself in the outpouring of awareness that takes place during each act of perception.
> *Vibrating radiance* (*sphurattā*). In the final phase of perception it matures into a fully formed cognition which is imprinted on consciousness through the pulsing and illuminating activity of the senses. The five-fold universe of sound, taste, touch, smell and sight now becomes

fully manifest,[123] brilliant with the radiance of consciousness.

We move on now to examine the nature and function of the ten outer senses.

The Outer Senses. All of manifest creation can be divided into two primary categories, namely, conscious and unconscious manifestations (*cid-* and *acidābhāsas*)—sentient beings and inert objects.[124] The ability to know and act is the very life (*jīvana*) of sentient beings,[125] and their knowledge and action are most tangibly externally manifest through the functions of the senses. Coupled with the limited power of knowledge, the power of limited action (*kalāśakti*) constitutes the conditioned agency which operates through the inner mental organ, impelling[126] and guiding the functions of the senses, linking together the stream of data coming in through the organs of perception and the outgoing responses through the organs of action.[127]

The Organs of Knowledge. According to Spanda doctrine, the five organs of perception—the senses of taste, touch, smell, hearing and sight—are aspects of the radiant pulsation (*sphurattā*) of consciousness. Each of these five senses is confined to its own locus (*golaka*) in the body, situated where it can pick up the maximum amount of information in the most efficient way.[128] Like a lamp set inside a perforated jar, the light of consciousness radiates through the senses, freely limiting itself so that each one is confined to its own specific field of operation (*viṣaya*). The Kashmiri Śaivite rejects the view that the sources of the senses are the gross physical elements. He contends that they are the products of the ego (*ahaṃkāra*) brilliant with the lustre of *Sattva*,[129] insofar as all sense perception is accompanied by 'I' consciousness. The notions: 'I hear', 'I see' or 'I smell', etc., are always attended by the ego.[130] As we have seen, from the Kashmiri Śaiva point of view, perception is an activity as well as a state of awareness. Knowledge and action are two interdependent categories; they are never found apart.[131] As instruments of the act of perception, the senses require the conscious agency of the ego. In the absence of an agent who implements their activity, we would have to posit the existence of another instrument to perform this function and there would be no reason why that too should not require a third and so on, leading to an infinite regress.[132]

However, from the point of view of a phenomenology of sensory perception, the ego alone does not fully account for the existential being of the senses. The senses can have no real existence as such, without the objects with which they are correlated. Thus, along with the senses, the ego, full of the inertia of *Tamas*,[133] generates the pure sensations (*tanmātra*) of taste, touch, smell, etc., corresponding to each sense organ. In this way the essential elements of sensory perception, namely, the perceiving ego, the senses and the perceived sensation are accounted for by the activity of the sentient subject.

The Organs of Action. The organs of action presuppose the existence of the organs of perception. They are generated from the ego as instruments to implement its responses to the sensations coming in through them. While the activity of the organs of action is accompanied by bodily movement, the activity of the organs of perception is not.[134] Although bodily movement is essentially one, it is differentiated into five categories according to the diverse conceptions we form of its nature.[135] Handling, picking up or grasping is the activity of the hand. Excretion is the activity of the excretory organs. Locomotion is the activity of the feet and emission that of the sexual organ. These four are said to correspond to the outer actions of appropriation (*ādāna*), rejection (*hāna*), both[136] and neither.[137] The fifth action is speech; it is internal and hence does not belong to any of these four categories. Although each organ of knowledge is invariably associated with only one specific locus, this is not the case with the organs of action. A lame man can move about from place to place without the use of his feet and we can pick up things with parts of the body other than the hands.[138]

To conclude: the inner and outer senses are aspects of the vibration of consciousness and, as such, are the channels through which consciousness becomes manifest as the world of perceptions. Together they are said to be 'the vibration of the glory of consciousness'.[139] Through this vibration the yogi catches a glimpse of the wonder of the Divine, brilliantly manifest in its creation. By its Light, he ultimately realises Śiva's ubiquity as all things and that this is, in fact, his own presence everywhere.

VI

The Divine Body and the Sacred Circle of the Senses

The yogi seeking enlightenment must undergo a complete conversion or reversal (*parāvṛtti*) of perspective. To know as man knows is the very essence of bondage;[1] freedom is to know reality as God knows it. The seeker then finds himself in a new existential situation in which he recognises his own authentic Being by being as God is. This is achieved by a pure and intense act of self-awareness in which the old mode of understanding reality is dropped in favour of a new and deeper knowledge of oneself as unlimited, infinite consciousness. This change in perspective discloses a new dimension of experience. In the moment of realisation, man and the world reveal themselves as an ontophany in which consciousness of Being coincides with the worship of Being as the sacred. The realisation of Being is fused with participation in the Holy. The sacred ontophany of manifestation is realised in the wonder (*camatkāra*) inspired by the theophanic vision. To see the world with God's eyes is to witness the eternal worship of His Being. The organ of vision is the sacred circle of the senses and the abode of its operation, the Divine Body.

True monism (*parādvaya*), as we have seen, requires that each part be the Whole, that the Wholeness of totality be manifest in every aspect of its fullness.[2] Every existent thing is sacred and enshrines the divine cosmos in the fullness of its participation in Being. The human body, in a particularly special way, is the epitome of the universe; it is the pure vessel of pure consciousness.[3] Pervaded by consciousness, the body partakes of the sacred character of the absolute. Consecrated by the divine presence within it, it is the temple of God,[4] the sacred place of sacrifice and worship. We do not experience our consciousness as something external to the body, like a blanket or an outer garment.[5] In the same way, the universe, with all that we perceive, is an intimate extension of our own pure conscious being.[6] Abhinava writes:

> Thus, one should think of the body as full of all the Paths (*adhvan*) [to enlightenment and cosmic emanation]. Variegated by the workings of time, it is the abode of all the movements of time and space. The body seen in this way is all the gods, and must therefore be the object of contemplation, veneration and sacrifice. He who penetrates into it finds liberation.[7]

Everything is a part of God's Divine Body—the sacred cosmos in which God's blissful activities are made manifest through the workings of natural law (*niyati*).[8] The presence of 'I' consciousness in the body is revealed by the movement of its limbs; the presence of God in His Cosmic Body is seen in the movement of the universe.

> Just as the ego (*asmitā*) in the body flings apart the two lifeless arms by a mere act of will, so [the universal ego] in the universe [rends asunder] mountains by its power.[9]

Similarly, the yogi who perceives that all things are like the limbs of his own body (*svāṅgakalpa*) plunges in the divine awareness that: 'I am this [universe]' (*aham-idam*). Bondage is a false identification with the physical body and liberation a true identification with the cosmic body. Thus the split between subject and object is healed and the yogi perceives reality everywhere, as an undivided unity (*avibhakta*) in which inner and outer blend together like the juices in a peacock's egg.[10]

Each level of consciousness corresponds to a degree of spiritual attainment. At each stage of ascent along the 'living ladder of consciousness'[11] the yogi achieves a higher degree of mastery over the cosmic processes taking place within his own universal consciousness. With each degree of empowerment, he penetrates into a fresh dimension of experience. In the theosophical language of the Tantras, he is said to become the lord of a higher world-order (*bhuvana*). He possesses a different 'space' in the pure extension of conscious Being and lives in this world in a body suited to his new existential situation.[12] At the

Paraśiva level his body is the universe, the sum total of all spiritual extensions and world-orders. In a sense, however, because Śiva does not confront any reality outside Himself, He has no body at all. His body is a body of Consciousness (*vijñānadeha*), the sacred image (*mūrti*) of His manifest form.[13] This is the Supreme Body (*paradeha*), the greatest of all bodies[14] radiant with the infinite vitality (*Ojas*), fecund power (*vīrya*), strength (*bala*) and divine vibration (*spanda*)[15] of the supreme state of subjectivity (*parapramātṛbhāva*) it enshrines. This Divine Body (*divyadeha*) is entirely spiritual and no longer belongs to matter. It is the Body of Power (*śāktadeha*), the universe of energy replete with the five principle powers of consciousness, bliss, will, knowledge and action.[16] In failing to contemplate the Cosmic Body of the Self, we fail to experience the sacred festival (*utsava*) of the external manifestation of the glory of its pure Spanda nature (*vibhūtispanda*).[17] We must rid ourselves of the false notion that the body is in any way impure.[18] We must recognise that it is pure consciousness alone and give up the fruitless quest for satisfaction in objects we fail to realise are part of our own Cosmic Body.

> Once the tendency (*aunmukhya*) [to see external] objects ceases and limitation is destroyed, what remains in the body apart from the nectar (*rasa*) of Śiva's Bliss? [Thus] seeing and worshipping the body night and day as replete with [all] the categories of existence and full of the nectar of Śiva's Bliss, [the yogi] becomes identified with Śiva. Established in that holy image (*liṅga*), content to rest in [his] cosmic body, [the yogi] does not aspire to any outer Liṅga, [to make any] vows, [travel to] the sacred sites or practise [external] disciplines.[19]

To attain this pure body of consciousness or, to be more precise, to recognise our own body to be it, we must first purge ourselves of the lower states of embodied consciousness. We must unite the knot of ignorance which binds us and leads us to suppose that the psycho-physical organism, with all the subtler bodies contained in it, is our true body. When this false identification is overcome, consciousness, which formerly seemed contracted, now presents itself in its true, fully expanded (*vikasita*) form. The individual ego merges in the pervasive, universal ego, just as the space in a broken jar merges with the space around it.[20] The yogi then realises that the Spanda energy of this authentic egoity does all things and that he, the individual, is the agent in this sense alone. Thus the action of the wise, free of false identification with the physical body, entails no *Karma* and they are liberated.[21]

The false identification of the ego with the physical body conditions the power of awareness (*citiśakti*) by generating thought-forms (*vikalpa*) based on the notion of that a difference exists (*bheda*) between the embodied subject and the extra-corporeal object. These thought-constructs constitute the lower order of embodied subjectivity and, to all intents and purposes, its body. The yogi transmutes thought back into its original form as the light of consciousness by burning it in the sacred fire of consciousness (*cidāgni*) inflamed by the contemplative awareness that: "It is I, the Great Lord, Who, as pure consciousness, always shine thus as all things".[22] This inner awareness is the divine radiance (*sphurattā*) of the rapture of the supreme ego.[23] It is pure Spanda energy, the secret power of Mantra (*mantravīrya*) which burns away the false identification with the body and with it the body of thought.[24] This is the true fire sacrifice in which, as the *Aphorisms of Śiva* declare, this body is the oblation.[25]

External rites are of no avail if their inner significance is not understood and their symbolic function does not correspond to an inner activity within consciousness. The inner conscious processes (*vāsanākrama*) corresponding to the outer ritual activity (*pūjākrama*) must be understood and mastered. Whether outer rites are actually performed or not makes no difference from this point of view. In reality, all of life's activities are part of the great sacrificial rite (*mahāyāga*) eternally enacted by universal consciousness within itself, to itself. In this rite, the sacrificial fire is the Great Void (*mahāśūnya*), the supreme reality (*paratattva*) entirely devoid of all division (*bheda*) and beyond the emptiness of insentience. The sacrificial ladle is awareness (*cetanā*) and the offering is the entire outer universe of diversity, including the gross elements, senses, objects, world-orders and categories of existence, together with the inner world of mind (*manas*) and thought.[26] All division between subject and object is burnt away and everything made one with the fire of consciousness. Abhinava explains:

> Oblation is effortlessly offered in the fire of [Śiva's] intensely flaming consciousness by offering fully all of the great seed of internally and externally created duality (*bheda*).[27]

The fuel offered in the fire of this supernal (*alaukika*) and eternal sacrifice is the forest of duality, and death is the sacrificial victim (*mahāpaśu*).[28] We must rid ourselves of all attachment, of all sense of 'me' and 'mine', however painful this may be, and thus acquire a new, transfigured body, not made of matter but of the spiritual essence of consciousness. In the chilling words of the Tantras:

> O Goddess, by eating the body of the beloved, a relative, close friend, benefactor or dear one, one must fly upwards with the Maiden of the Sky, [the power of consciousness].[29]

What this verse means is that the embodied subjectivity (*deha-pramātṛtā*) must be assimilated into consciousness so that the disturbing thought-constructs engendered by it may no longer agitate it. Then the yogi spontaneously recognises the highest level of Spanda's power within himself.[30] All duality is burnt away and consciousness rests tranquil, firmly fixed (*dhruva*) and free of the waves of cosmic manifestation (*nistaraṅga*). Nothing remains of the yogi's unenlightened individuality and he shares in the pure contemplative absorption consciousness itself enjoys. Thus, no longer identifying himself with the body, he recognises his true nature to be the vibrant power of Spanda, personified as the goddess Bhairavī, and so unites with Bhairava, the Great Light of consciousness.[31]

The first vibration (*spanda*) or wave of activity that rises spontaneously out of this state of tranquility (*viśrānti*) is the immaculate body (*mūrti*) of consciousness.[32] Pure, undifferentiated Śiva-consciousness unfolds in this way as the universe and displays its true nature.[33] The yogi united with Śiva witnesses the emanation of Śiva's cosmic body as the creation of his own perfected, divine body. This pure emanation (*śuddhasṛṣṭi*) confirms the yogi's state to be that of Bhairavī.[34] In this state the yogi experiences the identity (*sāmarasya*) of unity and diversity in the oneness of his pure Spanda nature. This unity for the fettered soul corresponds to the unfolding of his Śiva-nature; diversity, the unfolding of Māyā.[35] The enlightened yogi, identified with Śiva, resides in Śiva's abode located in the centre between the two sides of this expansion. In this way he experiences the bliss of the emergence[36] of consciousness within his spiritual cosmic body.

In the centre of his body, the yogi contemplates the power of his own consciousness (*citi*), the radiant Fire of Time where all the categories of existence are burnt away. The perfected yogi (*siddha*) thinks his physical body to be hardly more than a corpse—mere dead matter, like all the other objects he perceives within his cosmic body. The universe appears to him to be a vast cremation ground strewn with the lifeless 'corpses' of phenomena. He makes the Vow of a Hero (*vīravrata*) to see all things, however disgusting or attractive, with an equal eye,[37] aware that they are all manifestations of consciousness. He carries in one hand the sacred staff (*khaṭvāṅga*) of awareness with which he smashes the body of his own ego to pieces. In the other hand, he bears the skull bowl of the portions of the universe which appear in the purview of his senses, white with the light of consciousness. From this bowl he drinks the wine of the essence (*rasa*) of the universe.[38] Absorbed in the contemplation of the fire of his own consciousness (*citi*), he enters the cremation ground of his own body, terrible with the funeral pyres (*citi*) in which all the latent traces of his past actions (*krama*) are burnt to ashes.[39] Abhinava writes:

> "[The body] is the support of all the gods, the cremation ground frightening with the pyre [of consciousness, *citi*, which destroys all things]. Attended by siddhas and yoginīs, it is their awesome (*mahā-raudra*) playground wherein all embodied forms (*vigraha*) come to an end. Full of the countless pyres [of the senses] and pervaded by the halos of their rays, the flux of the darkness [of duality] is destroyed and, free of all thought-constructs, it is the sole abode of bliss. Entering this [body], the cremation ground of emptiness—who does not achieve perfection?"[40]

All Tantric traditions, including those of Kashmiri Śaivism, teach that the senses, along with the body, should be venerated as manifestations of the sacred power of consciousness which emits them as the sun does its rays.[41] Accordingly, the senses can be personified and worshipped as deities that surround and attend upon the god (or goddess) who is their master. According to Kṣemarāja, although the senses and their presiding deities do not in fact differ, the Spanda teachings distinguish between them. The physical senses are merely the external expansion (*vijṛmbha*) of the body of consciousness (*vijñānadeha*) which belongs to the deities of the senses. The Supreme Lord and inner master of the Circle (*cakradevatā*) is the universal subject (*mahāpramātṛ*) Who, endowed with the sacred power of the senses, is seated in the Heart of consciousness within the sacred abode (*pīṭha*) of the body,[42] and there playfully rotates the wheels of their powers.[43]

The forms and names ascribed to the deities of the senses vary considerably in different traditions and even in different Tantras belonging to the same tradition. The reason for this, according to Abhinava, is largely due to the ritual context in which they are venerated and the functions ascribed to them. The activities of the senses are altered by the emotions generated by consciousness, and so the character of their presiding deities changes accordingly. Thus, in rites performed in anger with the aim of killing an enemy, the deities are represented in a wrathful (*raudra*) attitude. Rites intended to bring peace and prosperity are attended by deities of a peaceful (*saumya*) disposition.[44]

The original rites described in the Tantras have no place in the yogic teachings of the Spanda school; even so, the esoteric philosophy (*rahasyadṛṣṭi*) at the root of their symbolic significance has been retained. This makes sense because the spiritual, cosmic body is more 'internal' than the lower-order body through which the rites are performed. It is one with the universal consciousness residing in the Centre, the pulsing Heart (*hṛdaya*) of pure 'I' consciousness, the 'great abode of the universe'[45] in which everything rests[46] and which gives life and being to all things. Jayaratha quotes:

> Although [the Light] pervades all the body and senses, even so, its supreme abode is the core of the Lotus of the Heart.[47]

This same inwardness is shared by the sacred circle of the senses of this Divine Body. It is the inner circle of the goddesses of the senses (*karaṇadevatā*). Kṣemarāja, expounding the Doctrine of Vibration, says that they are the "circle of the rays of the glory of the Self" which presides over and gives life to the outer circle of the physical senses.[48] In his "Hymn to the Circle of Deities in the Body" (*Dehasthadevatācakrastotra*), Abhinava describes the goddesses of the senses. Although this hymn belongs to the Krama tradition, not to Spanda, it is clear that Kṣemarāja understood the nature of these divine powers essentially in the way Abhinava describes them here. He portrays the goddesses of the senses as seated on the petals of the lotus of the Heart arrayed around the Divine Couple, Ānandabhairava and Ānandabhairavī, Who are in the calix. The goddesses move restlessly hither and thither in search of the most pleasing sensations to offer in worship to the Couple in the Centre. Abhinava begins by saluting Gaṇeśa and Vaṭuka, the inhaled and exhaled breaths (*apāna* and *prāṇa*). He then praises Ānandabhairava, the true teacher (*sadguru*) Who is the yogi's attentive awareness (*avadhāna*) that illumines Śiva's Path—the universe—by the power of His intellect (*dhī*). Meanwhile His consort, Ānandabhairavī, playfully gives rise (*udaya*) to the universe, manifests it (*avabhāsana*) and relishes its pure conscious nature (*carvaṇa*). Around them are Brahmāṇī, the intellect (*buddhi*), who offers the flowers of certainty (*niścaya*); Śāmbhavī, the ego (*ahaṃkāra*), who offers the flowers of egoity; Kaumārī, the mind (*manas*) who offers her flowers of thought (*vikalpa*); Vaiṣṇavī, the ear, offering sounds; Vārāhī, the skin, offering tactile sensations; Indrāṇī, sight, offering forms; Cāmuṇḍā, the tongue, offering tastes; and Mahālakṣmī, the nose, who offers smell. After rendering homage to the Self, replete with all the categories of existence, Abhinava concludes with the words:

> I venerate in this way the circle of deities eternally active (*satatodita*) in my own body, ever present in all beings and the essence of the radiant pulsation of experience (*sphuradanubhava*).[49]

At the lower level of consciousness, the physical senses are hardly more than unconscious instruments of perception. They are extroverted and operate in relation to external objects. At the higher level, when 'the island of embodied consciousness' has been destroyed and submerged into the ocean of pure consciousness, the senses perceive reality in a new, timeless mode.[50] They are introverted in the sense that they are recognised to be spiritual forces operating within sacred consciousness. Plunged in Bhairava's Great Light, the senses are divinised and their activity leads the yogi to the higher reaches of consciousness even as they perceive their objects. The senses thus illumine the yogi after having themselves been illumined by Śiva and he realises in this way that the senses are the pure Spanda energy of consciousness which perceives the Divine manifest as sensations.

Śiva manifests His freedom in the joy (*āhlāda*) he feels as the subject who perceives the world through the pulsing activity of the senses. He sports in the garden of His universe delighting in the five flowers of smell, taste, sight, touch and sound.[51] At the same time Śiva rests in His own nature. The repose He thus enjoys is the source of His bliss and the foundation of His freedom. Embracing the diversity of things in the oneness of His nature, Śiva is content. The yogi must seek to imitate Śiva, the archetype of Fully Awakened (*suprabuddha*) consciousness. The yogi's experience conforms to Śiva's blissfully unifying vision to the degree in which he succeeds in maintaining a state of authentic self-awareness. The perfected yogi is always established in himself, reflecting on his true and uncreated (*akṛtrima*) nature. But although self-absorbed, he is never abstracted from the world. In fact, by being constantly mindful of himself, he sees and hears with greater clarity and understanding, and, with his senses and mind thus actively in touch with the world, his meditation matures and becomes perfect.

The Spanda teachings, accordingly, instruct the yogi to observe the movement of the senses, mindful that their activity is an extension of the activity of Śiva—the universal consciousness which is the yogi's true nature.[52] In this way he comes to recognise himself to be full of the Spanda energy which impels the operation of the senses.[53] Sensations of all sorts thus ultimately lead him to recognise himself to be the pervasive experience of the Great Light (*mahāprakāśa*) of consciousness, filling both his individual subjectivity and his environment.[54] Consequently, although many spiritual paths seek to curb and discipline the senses, seeing in them one of the principle sources of bondage (*saṃsāra*), the Spanda teachings, and Kashmiri Śaivism in general, maintain, on the contrary, that they can serve both initially as a means to self-realisation and, ultimately, are the very bliss of liberation itself.[55] Utpaladeva, the great exponent of the philosophy of recognition, repeatedly dwells on this theme in his hymns to Śiva. Realising his authentic Śiva-nature and thus inspired by the spirit of the highest form of devotion (*parabhakti*), Utpaladeva exclaims:

> May the outpourings of the activity of my senses fall on their respective objects. May I, O Lord, never be so rash as to lose, even for a moment, the joy of my oneness with You, however slightly.[56]

The yogi can take pleasure in sense objects; indeed he is specifically instructed to do so,[57] if he maintains an awakened, mindful attitude (*prabuddhabhāva*) and does not just blindly follow his natural inclinations as does an animal with a bare minimum of self-awareness. The pleasure we derive from physical objects is, in reality, the repose we enjoy when the activity of the mind is momentarily arrested and delights one-pointedly in the source of pleasure. All pleasure, in other words, is essentially spiritual. It is a state the subject experiences and not a property of the object. It is 'a drop from the ocean of Śiva's bliss',[58] a small wave or pulse in the universal vibration of consciousness. The yogi must fix his attention on the source of pleasure, freeing his mind of all disturbing thoughts and so make the transition to a state of awareness in which his personal concerns are transcended in the pervasive experience of consciousness. This yogi is no hedonist. He is free of the false notion that the body is the Self and so does not crave for the pleasures of the senses, although he does make use of them as spring-boards to project him beyond the realms of physical, transitory objectivity into the eternal sphere of consciousness.

If the connection between 'worldly' pleasure and spiritual bliss is strong, the link between aesthetic experience and the rapturous delight (*camatkāra*) of consciousness is even more so. Sweet song, a pleasing picture, the sight of a beautiful woman, all these are full of a 'juice' (*rasa*) which the senses relish or 'taste' and which, like food, feeds consciousness with delight and wonder (*camatkāra*). The senses are the organs of this 'tasting' (*āsvadana, rasanā*) and a state of aroused consciousness is the fruit. Abhinava writes:

> Once one has overcome distraction, the pleasure one enjoys

> through the sentiments of love, etc., expressed in poetry or drama, for example, differs from the pleasure derived from sense objects. This is because [one gains access to it] by the removal of such obstacles as the anticipation of possible personal gain. So, once freed of these impediments, the experience (*pratīti*) is one of 'relishing' (*rasanā*), 'tasting' (*carvaṇa*) or 'contentment' (*nivṛti*) and is, in fact, repose in the cognising subjectivity. It is right to describe it in these terms because the Heart, that is, self-awareness (*parāmarśa*) is [in this experience] the predominant factor. Although the *Prakāśa* aspect, centred on the object, is also present, the sensitivity [on the part of the subject] to its aesthetic quality (*sahṛdayatā*) is a result of ignoring [this objective aspect]. . . . When one tastes sweet or other juices (*rasa*), contact with the object of sense represents an obstacle [to the blissful experience of its purely pleasurable potential]. Similarly, in the case of poetry and drama, etc., although there may be no such obstacles, their latent traces continue to be perceived. Even then, however, by removing the partial obstruction that arises in that way [we] gain attentive Hearts and that is supreme bliss.[59]

Changes occasioned in the powers of the senses in contact with the aesthetic object represent a shift of awareness from the surface consciousness of mundane experience to deeper levels. Here the fragmentation of the surface is resolved in the fullness of the vibration of 'I' consciousness in the centre of the circle of sensory energies. The senses initially resonate, as it were, in consonance with the aesthetic object, penetrating and mingling with it so completely, that the boundary between sensation and appreciative awareness dissolves away, leaving a state of unity (*tanmayībhāva*) which pervades both the senses and the aesthetic object. This leads to a heightened state of introversion (*antaḥpraveśa*) in which the aesthetic object is experienced with such intimacy and sense of direct contact that it is no longer felt to be external. It is submerged (*nimajjana*) in the field of awareness, filling it so completely with the aesthetic delight (*rasa*) it arouses, that the subject loses all sense of his individuality. Consciousness, now freed from the restrictions of the narrow confines of individual subjectivity, spontaneously expands to finally delight in the untrammelled outpouring (*ucchalanā*) of his own pulsation (*spandana, vighūrṇana*) as the pure appreciative subjectivity.[60]

Whatever enters the field of awareness through the channels of the senses and mind affects the perceiving subject and brings him to life, as it were, as the centre of awareness in the world of perceptions. The influx of sensations is a stream of energy which 'feeds' the vibrant power of consciousness much as the vital breath vitalises the limbs of the body. Spanda is this dynamically effective character of consciousness—its vitality (*vīrya*) and fecund power (*ojas*) apparent as the beauty (*kāntatā*) of all its manifestations.[61] The arousal or intensification of this power is the most essential, indeed the basic, element of all aesthetic experience. The sound of pleasing music, the smell of incense, a gentle caress, etc., can all arouse the subject from a state of inattentive indifference (*mādhyasthya*) and stimulate the Heart of consciousness to pulsate more intensely with the subtle movement of awareness and bliss.[62] This movement, or arousal of the vitality of consciousness (*vīryakṣobha*), is the unfolding of the power of awareness (*śāktasphāra*) which inspires the aesthete with wonder (*camatkāra*) and delight (*ānanda*). It creates for him a new world of beauty, the creation of which, at its most intense and sublime level, coincides with the creation of an entire universe of experience, generated by the constantly renewed emissive power (*visargaśakti*) of consciousness. None other than the subtle transcendental movement of Bhairava's awareness in all its fullness, this 'arousal of vitality' (*vīryakṣobha*) is the ecstatic experience of the outpouring of His powers of freedom and bliss.[63] The yogi, fully centred on the aesthetic object, his thoughts and senses stilled, becomes one with it and consciousness turns in on itself to realise its eternal, pulsing (*spanda*) nature as a divine aesthetic continuum, vibrant with vitality (*vīrya*).[64]

Wonder is the essence of life. To be incapable of wonder is to be as dead and insensitive as a stone. We live and enjoy the vitality (*vīrya*) of consciousness to the degree in which we are sensitive to the beauty of things around us. Each aesthetic experience, had with mindfulness and a disciplined intention directed towards heightening our general level of aesthetic sensitivity, brings us a little closer to the sustained wonder of the pulsation (*spanda*) of consciousness which permeates all experience. The yogi at first practices to penetrate into this state of wonder through the medium of objects more easily pleasing and then, as he makes progress, he learns to discern that same sense of wonder in himself even when confronted with the foulest of things or in times of great trouble and pain.

The whole of life with all its events and our reactions to them is the unfolding drama of cosmic manifestation staged by the creative genius (*pratibhā*) of consciousness. Śiva is the seer, the poet (*kavi*) Who writes the plot and is, at the same time, the Self who plays all the roles[65] on the stage of the mind[66] with the senses as the spectators.[67] The three moments during which the plot is introduced, runs its course and is concluded correspond to the creation, persistence and destruction of Śiva's universal creation.[68] The perfected yogi shares in Śiva's delight and experiences all things as full of the varied sentiments (*rasa*) which they, at once Śiva and His wonderful creation, can impart to a receptive consciousness. The delight the yogi takes in the things about him transcends the pleasures of the hedonist or even those of the most refined aesthete. For although all aesthetic experience is a glimpse into a different, supernal (*alaukika*) order of reality, the yogi alone can maintain this awareness constantly. The moment of aesthetic delight is for him both the result and the essence of an attitude which can ony be adequately described as religious. Utpaladeva writes:

> How wonderful it is that although only one sound, that is, Śiva's name, is always on the tips of their tongues, yet [His] devotees can taste the ineffable relish of all the objects of the senses![69]

For the yogi the pleasing, beautiful objects from which he derives so much strength and satisfaction are sacred manifestations of consciousness offered to the Lord of consciousness in worship.[70] When recognised to be one with 'Brahman's Abode', whatever brings pleasure to the mind through the workings of the senses is an aid to worship.[71] This is what the yogi offers in the Sacred Festival (*mahotsva*) of non-dual worship (*advayapūjā*), plunged in the inebriating experience of Cosmic Bliss (*jagadānanda*). Again Utpaladeva exclaims:

> Drunk am I by drinking the wine of the Elixir of Immortality (*rasāyana*) which is Your worship, perpetually flowing through the channels of the senses from the goblets, full [to overflowing], of all existing things.[72]

At the lower, contracted (*saṃkucita*) level of consciousness, the senses are expressions of the limited powers of knowledge and action (*vidyā-* and *kalā-śakti*) of the fettered soul. At the higher, expanded (*vikasita*) level of consciousness, the senses express the pure awareness (*bodha*) and freedom (*svātantrya*) of the absolute. These higher, empowered senses make the entire universe one with consciousness the instant they behold it in the purview of their universal activity.[73] These higher, divinised senses are the deities of the sensory powers said to reside in the inner circle located within the circle of the physical senses. In this way the divine senses are symbolised as being more internal (i.e., closer to consciousness) than the physical senses. Their function is of a higher order, serving as the organs of Śiva's omniscience and omnipotence. They are not 'senses' in the normal sense of the word. Yogarāja illustrates this point by quoting the Śaiva *Śvetāśvataropaniṣad:*

Seeming to possess the quality (*guṇa*) of all the
senses, It is devoid of all the senses; . . .

Without foot or hand, He is swift and a seizer!
He sees without eye, He hears without ear!
He knows whate'er is to be known; Him there is
none who knows!
Men call Him the Great Primeval Person.[74]

The outer circle of the physical senses goes through three phases during the act of perception.

1) The initial outpouring of sensory activity (*pravṛtti*). This phase corresponds to the initial unfolding of the senses towards their object when they 'face' it and the subject is intent (*unmukha*) on its perception.

2) The initial phase intensified or stabilized (*sthiti*). At this stage the senses are actively affected by their object which they now clearly perceive and which abides at one with their field of awareness (*gṛhītārthaviśrāntyavasthā*).

3) When their operation reaches a fruitful conclusion, the object is abandoned and sensory activity merges with the undifferentiated awareness of pure consciousness and so comes to a halt.[75]

At the higher level of consciousness, when the outer circle of the physical senses is recognised to be one with the inner circle of goddesses, these three moments of perception are seen to correspond to the three moments of creation, persistence and destruction. As Kṣemarāja says:

Even when the Supreme Lord resides in the body, He effects the creation and destruction of the five-fold universe of form [taste, touch, smell and sound] by the expansion (*unmīlana*) and contraction (*nimīlana*) of the senses.[76]

When the wheel of sensory energies contracts, it returns to its Centre, the Heart of consciousness where it reposes, to then expand from it. Then the Heart, like a vast lake full to overflowing, again pours the currents of sensory activity out into the external world.[77] Thus:

The channels of the senses by which the yogi enjoys the pleasure of the objects of sense are those through which he fills the three worlds with the consciousness emitted from his own Heart.[78]

The senses are outer, subsidiary cycles of conscious energy (*anucakra*), revolving around the core or primary cycle (*mukhyacakra*) of pure consciousness. They scintillate with the diversity of sensations and resonate in the field of their awareness like the feathers of a peacock unfurled and folded back in the ecstasy of its dance.[79] Ultimately it is Śiva Himself Who, for His own pleasure,[80] extends and withdraws them,[81] not the individual soul. The outward movement of the senses is the creative flow of consciousness from the subject who, like an ocean, is the source of the waves of their activity and the final resting place of the flow of the rivers of sensations and thought-forms that unfold through the arising of the power of each of the senses.[82] The *Stanzas on Vibration* declare:

> Indeed the individual soul does not activate the impulse of the will [which directs the body's activity] by himself alone but through his contact with [his] own [inner] strength (*bala*) made in such a way that he identifies with it [thus acquiring its power].[83]

The close contact between the senses and universal consciousness vitalises them and sets them in motion. They share in the properties of consciousness, just as a heated iron ball can burn, cook or give out light.[84] Spanda doctrine does not agree with the Sāṃkhya view that the individual soul (*puruṣa*) alone stimulates activity in the objective sphere (*prakṛti*) by the contact he makes with it. The soul can do this only because universal consciousness animates him. Moreover, consciousness, which has the power to impel this activity, cannot itself be inactive as the Sāṃkhya maintains. The influence it has on lifeless matter implies an active exertion.[85] This activity is the subtle, inner outpouring of the Self (*svātmocchalattā*) within the Self. Outside the confines of time and space, in the centre of the circle of the senses, this inner activity initiates the expansion (*prasara*) of the flow of conscious energy. As the pure exertion (*udyoga, udyama*) of Being (*bhāva*), it is the source of the initial unfolding (*unmeṣa*) of Becoming.[86] Kṣemarāja explains:

> [By] 'exertion' (*udyama*) is [meant] the emergence of the supreme [level of] intuition (*pratibhā*) which is the sudden outpouring of the [immanent and transcendental] unfolding of the reflective awareness of pure consciousness.[87]

The direct, intuition (*pratibhā*) of reality, free of thought-constructs, is the supreme power (*parāśakti*) of consciousness. The yogi can gain this pure intuitive awareness by grasping the initial expansion (*unmeṣa*) of consciousness which engenders the emergence of thought and the activity of the senses. It can be discovered in the subtle Centre, between one thought and the next. The *Stanzas on Vibration* teach:

> The expansion of consciousness that takes place when one is engaged in a single thought should be known to be the source from whence another arises. One should experience that for oneself![88]

This does not mean that the unfolding expansion of consciousness (*unmeṣa*) is an intermittent, transitory occurrence.[89] As the source of all thought, including the notions of past, present and future,[90] it stands outside the confines of time. Consciousness is in a state of perpetual expansion. It is an ever developing process, a tiny part of which we observe as the flow of events around us and the thoughts and feelings within us. The totality of this process can never be grasped objectively. Objectivity is a state of fragmentation (*bheda*) in which discrete elements are discernible and mutually distinguished as individual, specifically definable entities. It is the realm within which thought and language operate. To grasp reality in its completeness, we must go beyond the partial representations of thought and speech. To experience the primordial source and basis of all things, we must pierce through the outer periphery of thought and plunge into the Centre, to discover the instant in which thought, and with it, the sense of diversity, initially emerges. Kṣemarāja cites a practice from the *Vijñānabhairava* through which the yogi can achieve this state of awareness:

> Checking [the movement of] attention (*cit*) once it has quit its object, it must not [be allowed] to move to any other; contemplation (*bhāvanā*) then blossoms forth by [experiencing] the state in the centre between them (*tanmadhyabhāva*).[91]

Left unattended and undisciplined, awareness spontaneously shifts from one object of thought to the next. The transition from one to the other entails a movement through a state of pure indeterminate (*nirvikalpa*) awareness divested of all thought-forms and perceptions. The yogi who succeeds in checking the movement of his attention, experiences within himself the subsidence of thought into the emptiness of the Centre which unfolds full of the powerful pulsation of consciousness within which all objectivity merges and becomes one[92] in the transcendental outpouring (*lokottarollāsa*) of its aesthetic rapture.[93]

Turning in on himself, the yogi must exert his power of awareness to discern the vitality of his own blissful Spanda nature. Just as a distant object becomes more clearly visible by exerting an effort to perceive it, in the same way, through practice, the yogi's own Spanda nature becomes progressively more evident to him.[94] The effort the yogi exerts to free himself of ignorance is essentially one with the force of awareness that impels the senses and mind. This inner exertion is the basis of every means to liberation. Ultimately bestowing the bliss of self-realisation, it carries the yogi along the path to salvation with all its twists and turns like wind which blows a cloth in various directions.[95] As the basis and ultimate goal of all yogic practice, this exertion is the pure wonder (*camatkāra*) inspired by the realisation of the essential identity of consciousness (*cit*) and being (*sat*).[96] As such it is the divine radiance (*sphurattā*) of the Heart of one's own consciousness[97] where the powers of will, knowledge and action merge in the harmony (*sāmarasya*) of bliss.[98] Thus the highest form of worship (*varivasyā*) is the contemplation of the inner strength (*bala*) or universal exertion of one's own true nature.[99]

> "One should examine [that reality]," says Kṣemarāja, "with the exertion which is Bhairava's nature and is true service (*sevana*) to the integral inner nature [of all things] and the unfolding of the activity of one's own vitality (*ojas*) which withdraws all duality [back into consciousness]."[100]

Mindful of the eternal joy (*āhlāda*) of his inner strength, the yogi must give up all desire for the fleeting moments of petty pleasure (*kṣaṇikasukhalava*)[101] he may glean from outer objects. He must even give up the desire to achieve enlightenment and a reality (*tattva*) which can never be realised through a personal act of will.[102] In short, he must die to himself in an act of profound faith (*śraddhā*) and adoration (*ādara*) to find rest in the supreme reality free from the binding dichotomy of means and objectives (*upeyopāyabhāva*)—the reality of his perfected effort. The yogi, now full of devotion for this reality unfolding within himself and the universe (*antarmukhatattva*), merges into it and, by achieving the pure consciousness and bliss (*cidānanda*) of the power (*bala*) of his own nature, achieves oneness.[103]

The yogi is firmly established in his true nature by recognising the creative unfolding (*unmeṣa*) of consciousness through which he is able to know all things, whether in the present, past or future.[104] Master of the vitality which gives life to his mind and body, he can strengthen it directly without need of food or drink,[105] or quit it at will to vivify that of another.[106] Experiencing the eternal satisfaction of his own uncreated nature,[107] the yogi is freed of disease and the infirmities of old age.[108] Inspired by this vitality, he has the inner strength to overcome the severest hardships and obstacles in the way of his ultimate goal.[109] The *Stanzas on Vibration* explain:

> Lassitude ravages the body and this arises from ignorance but if this is eliminated by an expansion of consciousness (*unmeṣa*), how can [ignorance], deprived of its cause, continue to exist?[110]

Doubt (*śaṅkā*) is the source of every spiritual ailment.[111] A man in doubt about his true nature, and the path to follow by which he may come to realise it, is constantly overcome by difficulties.[112] "Due to ignorance" teaches the *Sarvācāratantra*, "the deluded man is in doubt and thus [suffers the cycle] of birth and death."[113] Caught between conflicting alternatives, the mind shifts from one to the other becoming more entangled in its own thoughts as it does so. Doubt thus contracts consciousness[114] sullying it with the turbulence of confused thinking.[115] At once both the root of "the ancient tree of transmigration" and the first sprout of its seed,[116] doubt deprives man of the innate bliss (*sahajānanda*) of his own nature.[117] Like a thief it steals away the wealth of true knowledge and reduces man to an imagined state of poverty in which he feels hemmed in on all sides by constraints and limitations.[118] Ignorance and its sister, doubt, are the essence of all impurities (*mala*) which sully consciousness. To the degree in which the yogi is cured of this ailment, namely, the lassitude (*glāni*) of doubt, his true nature becomes manifest, just as raw gold when heated is freed from dross. When the yogi recognises the all-powerful expansion (*unmeṣa*) of his consciousness, he is projected beyond the realm of relative distinctions between virtue and vice. Thus overcoming all doubt as to what he should or should not do, he penetrates into the pulsing Heart of Bhairava's consciousness.[119] As the *Stanzas on Vibration* say:

> An individual who [though] desirous of doing various things [but] is incapable of doing them due to his innate impurity, [experiences] the Supreme state when the disruption (*kṣobha*) [of his ego] ceases. Then [the soul realises] that his [true] uncreated nature is [universal] agency and perceiving subjectivity and so he knows and does whatever [he] desires.[120]

The individual soul is a combination of conscious (*cit*) and unconscious (*acit*) elements[121] brought together when he allows the power of his authentic nature to be obscured by his own impurity. This impurity is three-fold. The first is technically called the 'Impurity of Individuality' (*āṇavamala*). Due to this impurity, the individual soul fails to recognise his all-embracing fullness (*pūrṇatā*) and is disturbed by his craving for experience (*bhoga*) based on the unreasoned assumption that he is incomplete (*apūrṇa*) and in need of something outside himself.[122] Thus it manifests as desire or attachment (*rāga*).[123] At the same time it is primordial ignorance, 'the cause of the sprout of transmigration'.[124] As such, it works in two ways. Firstly, it deprives individual consciousness of freedom. The yogi affected by this impurity is incapable of entering or emerging out of the states of contemplation as he wishes. Secondly, this impurity renders the individual unconscious of his freedom, which for the yogi means that he is liable to lose consciousness of his true nature when he is not in a state of contemplative absorption.[125]

The second impurity is called the 'Impurity of Māyā' (*māyīyamala*). This comes into operation when consciousness has been contracted by the Impurity of Individuality. It limits the power of knowledge operating in the individual soul through the inner and outer organs of perception.[126] Due to this impurity he perceives diversity everywhere.[127] Finally, the third impurity, that of *Karma*, comes into play when the individual, deprived of the freedom and knowledge of unconditioned consciousness, acts in his limited way prompted by desires and fears for his personal gain. Disturbed by these three impurities the soul cannot find rest in himself. When he manages, however, to overcome their disturbing influence, he experiences the pure vibration (*spanda*) of consciousness and through this recognition realises his essentially omnipotent and omniscient nature.

In order to do this the yogi must first discover universal consciousness within himself. Secondly, he must learn to recognise his own Spanda energy operating in the outer world. In the first stage, the power which flows through the channels of the senses and mind is withdrawn into itself (*śaktisaṃkoca*) through a powerful, one-pointed act of introspection.[128] If the yogi is successful, he comes to perceive the totality of existence reflected in his mind (*citta*) and pervaded by the light of consciousness. Thus he enjoys the inner bliss of contemplative absorption with his eyes closed (*nimīlanasamādhi*). As Bhairava instructs the goddess:

> Merging the senses in the centre, between the upper and lower lotuses [of the Heart], in the void of the Heart, with mind unwavering,

O Fair One, attain the Supreme Bliss.[129]

The restriction imposed on the exertion (*udyama*) of the senses by the confining perception of outer objectivity is thus overcome and the senses move freely in the 'Sky of the Heart of Consciousness'.[130] Like fuel in a fire, diversity is burnt to ashes and fused with the pure energy of one's own nature.

> All things deposited in the fire of the belly of one's own consciousness, suddenly (*haṭhataḥ*) abandoning all distinctions, feed it with their own power. When the diversity which divides things is dissolved away by this violent digestion (*haṭhapāka*), the deities of consciousness [i.e., the senses] devour the universe transformed [by this process] into the nectar [of 'I']. Once they are satisfied, they rest at one with the God (*deva*) Bhairava Who is the fullness of one's own nature and the Sky of Consciousness which, solitary, rests in the Heart.[131]

The yogi is now absorbed in the unfolding (*unmeṣa*) of consciousness and becomes one with its universal vibration.[132] The 'Great Expansion' (*mahāvikāsa*) of the yogi's consciousness unfolds as he penetrates and becomes one with the pure Being (*sattā*) of Bhairava[133] and thus enjoys the bliss (*bhoga*) of simultaneously making all things one with consciousness, 'savouring' their essence and 'protecting' or securing their place and function within the economy of the Whole.[134] The yogi experiences consciousness expansion both inwardly and externally. When all things are absorbed in the introverted unity of his consciousness, it emits itself into itself freely without succession or division. In this way his consciousness also unfolds throughout the external world mediated by the senses divinised by the grace of his inner realisation and he perceives its transcendental nature immanentalise into the activities of the universe. His senses open up fully in an instant as the power hidden within consciousness expands out from it.[135] The state of absorption 'with the eyes closed' (*nimīlanasamādhi*) thus leads spontaneously to a state of absorption 'with the eyes open' (*unmīlanasamādhi*) and vice versa. The yogi, with the greatest respect and devotion for the reality now unfolding before him, must learn to unite these two forms of absorption and experience the underlying unity of his consciousness which pervades both simultaneously from the Centre between them. Kṣemarāja explains:

> By [the practice] of introverted and extroverted absorption and by being firmly fixed in the Centre which pervades both simultaneously,

> having laid hold of the fire-stick (*araṇi*) of their two-fold emanation (*visarga*) with all thought fallen away, the circle of the senses expands instantaneously.[136]

The activity of the senses is now unconditioned by time and space; free of all obstacles, they function perfectly. They unfold to fill the entire universe with the power of their awareness and thereby withdraw into their pure and undivided source—the omnipresent Lord they perceive in all things. This state of simultaneous expansion (*vikāsa*) and contraction (*saṃkoca*) beyond both outward and inner movement is technically called Bhairavīmudrā. The experience of this attitude (*mudrā*) of awareness takes place thus:

> [If] you project the vision and all the other powers [of the senses] simultaneously everywhere onto their respective objects by the power of awareness, while remaining firmly established in the centre like a pillar of gold, you [will] shine as the One, the foundation of the universe.[137]

The One is the Lord of the Centre Who manifests all the deities of the inner circle as the essence of His pure awareness (*svasaṃvittisāra*) together with the outer circle of the physical senses.[138] The power of awareness thus manifests itself on two levels simultaneously. It functions at the microcosmic level as the power of sensory awareness which apprehends specific objects in the field of individualised, embodied awareness. At the macrocosmic level it functions as the divine power of sensory awareness which apprehends the universal, cosmic object in the field of universal consciousness. Through the practice of Bhairavīmudrā these two aspects are experienced together in the blissful realisation that results from the union of the inner and outer states of absorption.[139] Thus, nothing that appears before him is any longer confined within the ridged structures of thought and, supportless, he becomes inwardly absorbed in Śiva's consciousness.[140] Kṣemarāja quotes an unknown Tantra as saying:

> With one's aim inside while gazing outside, eyes neither opening nor closing—this is Bhairava's Mudrā kept secret in all the Tantras.[141]

During the initial instant of perception, 'I' consciousness is manifestly apparent and the yogi, participating in its plenitude, observes the outer world without being attached to any particular or singling it out from any other, like a man who observes a city from a high mountain peak.[142] He sees the outer world reflected within his consciousness free of thought-constructs and so 'stamps' the outer on the inner while absorbing the object and means of knowledge in the pure subject which grasps them as the expansion of his own nature.[143] Kṣemarāja says:

> By penetrating into *Bhairavīmudrā*, the yogi observes the vast totality of beings rising from, and dissolving into, the Sky [of consciousness], like a series of reflections appearing and disappearing inside a mirror.[144]

Through the practice of *Bhairavīmudrā* the yogi realises that he is the substratum consciousness (*adhiṣṭhātṛ*)[145] which both underlies and is the essence of all things. He discovers that phenomena have no independent existence apart from him and so are, in this sense, void. At the same time, he realises that because all things are consciousness, they are far from unreal. He views the outer world yet sees it not. Beyond both Voidness and Non-voidness he penetrates into the Supreme Abode (*paraṃ padam*) of Śiva's consciousness.[146]

> [The powers of the senses] endowed with the attributes of the Great Union [between subject and object] whose form is the awakening of man's spiritual potential (*kuṇḍalinī*), fill [with consciousness] the outer clatter of diversity (*bhedaḍambara*) born of its intense power and are then established in the unobscured abode of the void of consciousness to shine [there] eternally. Thus residing beyond Being and Non-being, the sole protector of the unity which is tranquil and expanding [consciousness], whose glory is all-embracing and form unobscured, is called *Bhairavīmudrā*.[147]

Through the practice of *Bhairavīmudrā*, the yogi unites the universal vibration of 'I' consciousness with the individual pulsation of objectivised 'this' consciousness. The two aspects of consciousness are now in a state of equilibrium like the two pans of an evenly weighed balance[148] and the yogi experiences the pure knowledge (*śuddhavidyā*) that: 'I alone am all things'. Thus becoming the master of the Wheel of Energies he is free, like Śiva, to create and destroy.[149]

> When [the yogi] is well established, without wavering, solely in the integral egoity of his authentic nature, the Spanda principle, and is absorbed in contemplation (*samāviṣṭa*), he becomes one with it

> (*tanmaya*). Then . . . dissolving and creating the universe by means of his introverted and extroverted absorption, he destroys and creates all things out of Śaṅkara, his innate nature. [Thus] he assumes the state of the universal experiencer and having absorbed all that is to be experienced from [the grossest level]—Earth—to (the subtlest)—Śiva—he reaches the state of the supreme subject by progressively recognising [his identity with Him].[150]

Thus, introverted and extroverted absorption both lead to the recognition of the pulsation (*spanda*) of one's own consciousness.[151] At the level of consciousness corresponding to Śiva's basic state (*śāṃbhavāvasthā*), the alternation from inner to outer is instantaneously resolved into the vibration of His nature. When the yogi finally comes to be constantly aware of this reality, his enlightenment is full and perfect.[152] Freed of all means (*anupāya*) and delighting in the power of his bliss (*ānandaśakti*), he knows and does whatever he pleases. The yogi seeking self-realisation must acquire mastery over this movement. Kṣemarāja stresses that the Doctrine of Vibration teaches that liberation can only be achieved by first withdrawing all sense activity in introverted contemplation (*nimīlanasamādhi*) to then experience the 'Great Expansion' (*mahāvikāsa*) of consciousness while recognising this to be a spontaneous process within it.[153] This is done through the practice of *Kramamudrā*. A passage from the now lost *Kramasūtra* explains:

> Although the adept's attention [may be] outwardly directed, he enjoys contemplative absorption through the introverted aspect of *Kramamudrā*. Initially he turns inward from the outside world and [then] from within [himself] he exits into the outer world under the influence of his absorption. Thus the sequence (*krama*) in this attitude (*mudrā*) [ranges through] both inner and outer.[154]

The yogi must pervade the surface level of awareness (*vyutthāna*) with the same bliss he experiences plunging into the depths of contemplative absorption (*samādhi*). Submerging himself and emerging repeatedly from *samādhi*, he eventually recognises that the unity of consciousness pervades both states:

> The best of yogi's, who has achieved a state of complete absorption even when risen from meditation, [inwardly] vibrating like a drunkard in blissful inebriation from the after-effects of the nectar of contemplation, sees all things dissolving in the Sky of Consciousness like a cloud in the autumn sky. He plunges repeatedly within himself

> and becomes aware of his identity with consciousness by the practice of introverted contemplation. Thus even when he is said to have risen from absorption, he is one with [his] experience of it.[155]

Kṣemarāja goes on to explain that this practice is called *'Mudrā'* because it both fills the adept with bliss (*mud*) and is itself the bliss of consciousness. Moreover, it dissolves away (*dra*) all bondage and 'stamps' the universe of experience with the seal (*mudrā*) of the fourth state (*turīya*) of enlightened consciousness beyond, and including, the three states of waking, dreaming and deep sleep. It is called *'Krama'* because it is the root source of all emanation and all other conscious processes which succeed one another in ordered sequence (*krama*) and is, at the same time, their successive (*krama*) appearance as well.[156]

By the practice of *Kramamudrā* the opposites fuse and Śiva and Śakti unite. They yogi comes to experience the simultaneous pervasion of all the lower, grosser categories of existence by the higher and the presence of the lower in the higher. Commencing his practice in a low form of *Bhairavīmudrā*, the yogi conjoins the outer with the inner; then, in *Kramamudrā*, he fills both the outer with the inner and the inner with the outer. When he achieves perfection in this two-fold movement, he attains to the highest form of *Bhairavīmudrā* in which the two merge completely in the experience of the absolute (*anuttara*), free of all differentiation and polarities. If he fails to maintain awareness of this state, he again falls into *Kramamudrā* until he has finally completely merged all the highest states in the lower and the lower in the higher. He then no longer needs to resort to any means (*anupāya*) to achieve liberation. All he says or does, anything he perceives or thinks, instantly occasions in him the highest level of consciousness. Thus the fruit of *Bhairavīmudrā* is the wonder (*camatkāra*) or amazement (*vismaya*) that overcomes the yogi when he reaches the plane of union (*yogabhūmikā*),[157] where all opposites merge in the radiance of the Great Light of consciousness. The *Stanzas on Vibration* teach:

> How can one who, as if astonished, beholds his own nature as that which sustains [the existence of everything] be subject to this painful round of transmigration (*kusṛti*)?[158]

The yogi, recognising his true nature to be the supreme subject, is astonished to suddenly discover that the individual he thought he was, caught up in the trammels of thought and living in a world enmeshed in the web of time and space, does not really exist at all.[159] He experiences a 'turning about' (*parāvṛtti*) in the deepest seat of consciousness as he penetrates his true nature. The sudden eruption of this intuition (*pratibhā*) arouses in him a cry of amazement as he transcends all thought-constructs and, perfectly absorbed in his own nature, is liberated.

VII

The Path to Liberation

Essentially, Spanda doctrine is concerned with two matters. The first is to impart to those who are fit to receive the teachings a deeper understanding of the ultimate goal of life (*upeya*). When we have understood what truly benefits us and is worth attaining and what, on the contrary, is of no real value but stands in the way of this attainment, we can begin to make progress towards our goal. This is Spanda doctrine's second concern, namely, to show the way in which we can develop spiritually through Śiva's grace and the right application of the means to realisation that it teaches. When both these aspects of the teaching have been correctly understood and applied, the Spanda yogi achieves a clear and permanent realisation of his goal and is liberated, thus fulfilling the ultimate aim of the teaching. The Doctrine of Vibration is not meant for the spiritually dull. It is not for the worldly whose consciousness, clouded by ignorance, is as if dreaming, even during the waking state of daily life, the dream of its own thought-constructs.[1] The teachings are meant for those who are awake (*prabuddha*), those who, full of faith and reverence, are always alert and intent on discerning the true nature of ultimate reality.

This reality is understood in three basic ways. The first is purely transcendental. The *Stanzas* choose this aspect as the one which formally defines it most specifically. Ultimate reality transcends all the opposites, including subject and object. This does not mean, however, that it is an unconscious void,[2] a mere absence of all existence. In fact, this negative characterisation of reality (which includes also a denial of all that is unconscious) implies a positive immanence in which the opposites are united in the oneness of pure consciousness that is equally Śiva and Spanda, His universal activity. These two seemingly contrasting aspects are reconciled in the third, namely, reality understood as the essential nature of all things. Although universal and everywhere the same, it is understood to be the essential and specific nature of each existent as its 'own nature' (*svabhāva*). In the case of the individual soul it is even more specific, more personal as his own 'own nature' (*svasvabhāva*). Belonging to none other than oneself it is the pure subjectivity who perceives, experiences, enjoys, reflects, thinks and senses as well as being the conscious agent who creates every possible form of experience in all the states of consciousness.[3] The liberating knowledge of reality thus corresponds to our regaining possession of ourselves (*svātmagraha*). We must lay hold of ourselves and abide in our authentic nature. Reality coincides with our own most fundamental state of being (*svasthiti*), free of all contrasts and contradictions. Once we have overcome the negative forces that arise from our ignorance and prevent us from abiding in ourselves, we are liberated. To do this, we must penetrate through the pulsing fluctuations of objectively experienced states and perceptions at the surface level of consciousness and gain insight into the timeless rhythm of our own nature manifest in the universal arising and falling away of all things. We are not freed of the trammels of perpetual change by setting it aside; on the contrary, we must gain insight into the recurrent cycles of creation, persistence and destruction, or else be bound by our ignorance.[4]

This spiritual ignorance consists essentially of our contracted state of consciousness and so can only be effectively countered by expanding it[5] to reveal our own authentic nature as this expanded state itself, which is the universal vibration (*sāmānyaspanda*) of consciousness. The Spanda yogi treads the Path of Consciousness Expansion. The movement from the contracted to the expanded state marks the transition from ignorance to understanding, from the dispersion and incompleteness of a form of consciousness entirely centred on an objectively perceived and discursively represented reality to a direct, intuitive awareness of the unity and integral wholeness of our own absolute Spanda nature. Along the way to this supreme realisation consciousness develops, as veil after veil is lifted, until it becomes full and perfect in the absolute which encompasses within itself all possible formats of experience. As Abhinava says:

> [This realisation] is the supreme limit of plenitude and as such there can be no higher attainment. Any [other] attainment [we can] conceive issues from a state that falls short of [this] perfection. Once [this] uncreated fullness has been attained, pray tell, what other fruit can there be [beyond it]?[6]

The fettered soul's contracted state of consciousness binds him because he is deprived thereby of the subtle, intuitive insight into the underlying unity of existence and his attention is focused instead on its gross, outer diversity easily apparent to everybody, however restricted his consciousness may be.[7] However, although the fettered soul in this state is ignorant of this unity, this does not mean that his knowledge of diversity is false. Ignorance entails a form of knowledge which, although quite correct, is binding.[8] We are not absolutely ignorant of reality for if we were we would be totally unconscious. Spiritual ignorance is always linked with some degree of consciousness. Those subject to the round of birth and death are not inert clods of earth.[9] Thus, although ignorance obscures consciousness, it is wrong to think of it, as dualist Śaivites do, in terms of a defiling impurity that shrouds it like a cloth covering a jar.[10] Spiritual ignorance can be nothing but consciousness itself, albeit in a limited state. Śiva, Who is universal consciousness, is the innate nature of both its contracted and expanded states,[11] both of which are forms of knowledge, namely:

1) Supreme Knowledge (*parajñāna*) defined as the revelation of one's own innate nature as the one reality which is the Being of all things.[12]

2) Inferior Knowledge (*aparajñāna*) which Jayaratha explains results from the mental activity (*vyāpāra*) of the individual subject whose consciousness is contracted. It consists of the mental representations (*vikalpa*) he forms of himself and his object, of the type 'I know this'.[13] The lower knowledge obscures the higher and binds the soul by breaking up his direct, pervasive awareness of his own pure consciousness nature, free of mental representation.[14] The *Stanzas on Vibration* teach:

> Operating in the field of the subtle elements, the arising of mental representation marks the disappearance of the flavour of the supreme nectar of immortality; due to this [man] forfeits his freedom.[15]

As we have already seen,[16] three factors are necessary for perception and thought to be possible, namely, the perceiving subject, the means of knowledge and the object perceived. Rājānaka Rāma, in his commentary on the *Stanza* cited above, explains at length that these three factors correspond to three major divisions in the lower thirty-one categories of existence, namely:

> 1) *The object.* This consists essentially of the five primary sensations which are the subtle elements (*tanmātra*) of smell, taste, sight, touch and sound along with the five gross elements—earth, water, fire, air and ether—of which these sensations are the perceivable qualities.

2) *The means of knowledge.* This consists of the senses and the inner mental organ.

3) *The subject.* At this level, the subject is the individual soul (*puruṣa*) whose consciousness is contracted by the five obscuring coverings (*kañcukas*) of limited knowledge and action, attachment, natural law and time along with Māyā, their source.

All these categories belong to the Impure Creation (*aśuddhasṛṣṭi*), which is the sphere of Māyā where the lower order of knowledge operates and subject and object are divided. Above them are five more categories which belong to the Pure Creation (*śuddhasṛṣṭi*) where subject and object are still united. The highest of those categories are Śiva and Śakti. Combined they represent the state of pure 'I' consciousness and its sentient subjectivity (*upalabdhṛtā*), respectively. The next category is called Sadāśiva. Here faint traces of objectivity appear in the pervasive, undivided consciousness of Śiva and Śakti. Consciousness, now full of the power of knowledge (*jñānaśakti*), views the All in a state of withdrawal (*nimeṣa*), shining within, and at one with its own nature. 'I' consciousness predominates over 'this' consciousness which it encompasses in the awareness that: 'I am this [universe]' (*aham-idam*). Next comes the category *'Īśvara'* corresponding to the awareness: 'this (universe) is me' (*idam-aham*). 'This' consciousness takes the upperhand over 'I' consciousness and unfolds externally full of the creative power of action (*kriyāśakti*). The All now becomes more clearly manifest as an independent reality. It is still experienced as one with consciousness but is no longer fully merged within it. Finally, when both subjective and objective aspects share an equal status in the two-fold awareness that: 'I am this (universe) and this (universe) is me (*ahamidam-idamaham*)', Pure Knowledge (*śuddhavidyā*), the last of these categories, emerges.

The pure categories are the experience of the impure categories when they are recognised to be one with consciousness. They are experienced within the domain of the pure universal subject the enlightened yogi realises himself to be. Mental representations (*vikalpa*) emerge from this pure awareness and subside into it in consonance with the rhythm of the emanation and withdrawal of the lower categories. Impelled by the universal will, this movement is spontaneous and free. Free of all hopes and fears the enlightened yogi sees all things as part of this eternal cosmic game, played in harmony with the blissful rhythm of his own sportive nature at one with all things. *The Stanzas on Vibration* teach:

> Everything arises [out of] the individual soul and he is all things. Being aware of them, he perceives his identity [with them]. Therefore

> there is no state in the thoughts of words or [their] meanings that is not Śiva. It is the enjoyer alone who always and everywhere abides as the object of enjoyment. Or, constantly attentive, and perceiving the entire universe as play, he who has this awareness (*saṃvitti*) is undoubtedly liberated in this very life.[17]

According to the Doctrine of Vibration, only liberation in this life (*jīvanmukti*) is authentic liberation.[18] Liberation after death (*videha-mukti*) in some form of disembodied state free of all perceptions and notions of the world of diversity is not the ultimate goal. Kṣemarāja stresses that liberation is only possible by realising one's own identity with the whole universe, however difficult this may be.[19] Similarly, he maintains that the suspension of all mental and sensory activity, which takes place in the introverted absorption of contemplation with the eyes closed (*nimīlanasamādhi*) that leads to identification with transcendent consciousness is complemented and fulfilled by the cosmic vision had through the expansion of consciousness that takes place in contemplative absorption with the eyes open (*unmīlanasamādhi*).[20] Consequently, Kṣemarāja explains that the first of the three sections, into which he divides the *Stanzas*, deals with the former mode of contemplation and the second section with the latter. Significantly, the last *Stanza* of the second section ends with the declaration that 'this is the initiation that bestows Śiva's true nature'.[21] In other words, this realisation, attained through the expanding consciousness of contemplation with the eyes open, initiates the yogi into the liberated state, which is identification with Śiva whose body is the universe.[22]

In order to attain this expanded state of liberated consciousness, the yogi must find a spiritual guide because the Master (*guru*) is the means to realisation.[23] The Master is for his disciple Śiva Himself for it is he who through his initiation, teaching and grace, reveals the secret power of spiritual discipline.[24] Instructing in the purport of scripture he does more than simply explain its meaning: he transmits the realisation it can bestow. The Master is at one with Śiva's divine power through which he enlightens his disciple. It is this power that matters and makes the Master a true spiritual guide,[25] just as it was this same power that led the disciple to him in his quest for the path that leads to the tranquility that can only be found 'in the abode beyond mind'.[26] The Master is the ferry that transports the disciple over the ocean of thought[27]—if, that is, the disciple is ready. The disciple must be 'awake' (*prabuddha*),[28] attending carefully to the pulse of consciousness. This alert state of wakefulness is at once the keen sensitivity of insight as well as the receptivity of one who has no other goal to pursue except enlightenment.

The highest, most perfect relationship the disciple can have with his Master is such as it is with Śiva Himself: one of identity. The exchange that takes place between them is an internal dialogue within universal consciousness, their common identity (*svabhāva*). Limiting itself to a point source (*aṇu*) and obscured by the thought-constructs born of doubt and ignorance, consciousness assumes the guise of the disciple who seeks to attain the expanded fullness of his Master's consciousness.[29] The Master, on the other hand, embodies the aspect of consciousness which responds to the inquiring consciousness of his disciple.[30] Free of the notions of 'self' and 'other', when the disciple is liberated by his grace, it is the Master who in reality liberates himself.[31]

Although Kṣemarāja assures us that the Master can by himself enlighten his disciple by the initiation he imparts to him[32] and the other means (*yukti*)[33] he adopts, even so, he is not the only guide on the path. Apart from the Master there is scripture and, above all, one's own personal experience,[34] because, as Abhinava says:

> The knowledge [acquired] by gradually [coming to understand the meaning of] the scriptures and following the Master [who knows them] leads, [when] confirmed for oneself, to the realisation of one's own identity with Bhairava.[35]

It is important to know the scriptures. God reveals Himself through them; they are one of the forms in which He is directly apparent in this world.[36] They teach man what is worth attaining and what should be avoided[37] and so like a boat convey him across the ocean of profane existence (*saṃsāra*) to the other shore where God's true nature is revealed to him.[38] However, the study of the scriptures is of value only if accompanied by the spiritual knowledge that results from personal experience. Maheśvarānanda writes:

> Being well versed in the nature of Deity is one thing, but being well versed in the sacred scripture is another, just as the peace of that Abode is one thing and what worldly people experience is another.[39]

Vasugupta, who found the *Śivasūtra*, knew the means to realisation (*yukti*) as well as the scriptures and had fully experienced the one ultimate reality. Therefore, Kṣemarāja declares him to be amongst the best of teachers.[40] The *Stanzas on Vibration* (that Kṣemarāja attributes to Vasugupta) accordingly transmit the secrets of the *Śivasūtra* in accord with scripture, sound reasoning and personal experience.[41] The latter is particularly important for the Spanda yogi; he is not interested in wasting his time in useless discussion about the experience of consciousness expansion and its fruits, for that can only be known for oneself.[42] The yogi can achieve this experience either through faith in the Master or personal insight (*svapratyayataḥ*) acquired by unswerving devotion to God. Kṣemarāja accordingly quotes a passage from the *Bhagavadgītā* where Kṛṣṇa says:

> Those I deem to be the best yogis who fix their thoughts on Me and serve Me, ever integrated [in themselves], filled with the highest faith.[43]

But while the yogi's development depends on faith and personal experience of the higher states of consciousness, he can, and must, strengthen his conviction in the light of reason. When reason (*upapatti*) and direct insight (*upalabdhi*) work together, they serve as a means to liberation. Reason alone cannot help us, but when it is based on an intuitive insight of fundamental principles along with a direct experience of reality, error is eradicated and the yogi is freed.[44] In this way the Awakened yogi realizes his inherent spiritual power (*svabala*) with which he exerts himself to distinguish between the motions of individualised consciousness and the universal vibration (*sāmānyaspanda*) of the collective consciousness that is their ultimate ground and firm foundation.[45] Thus, although the doctrine taught in the *Stanzas on Vibration* accords with scripture,[46] it is supported by reason and above all by personal experience. Thus, for example, the seventeenth *Stanza* describes the difference in the manner in which the Well Awakened and the unawakened experience their own nature (*ātmopalambha*),[47] while the eighteenth describes the experience of the Well Awakened in the three states of waking, dreaming and deep sleep.[48] Indeed, Rājānaka Rāma, one of the commentators, explains that the first sixteen *Stanzas* establish on the basis of personal experience (*svānubhava*) that one's own true nature is independent of the body.[49] Similarly, the remaining *Stanzas* also discuss the direct experience of one's own nature, but this time as the unity of all things. This direct experience, in its diverse aspects, is both the means by which the yogi develops his consciousness as well as his ultimate goal.

Spanda practice is based solely on the processes inherent in the act of awareness and hence on the self-evident (*svataḥsiddha*) fact of being conscious. Even so, this does not mean that sound argument is useless. Right reasoning clears the understanding of false notions; it uproots, as it were, the tree of duality.[50] Leading the pilgrim on the path of truth along the right road of the highest doctrine, it protects him from falling to lower views. As such, it is the best limb of Yoga and, indeed, the only truly effective one.[51] Right reasoning is based on, and ultimately blossoms fully into, the Pure Knowledge (*śuddhavidyā*) that: 'I am this universe and this universe is me'.[52] In this way argument not only sustains doctrine but also leads to the firm conviction that results in, and essentially is, the recognition of one's own authentic identity as Śiva.

All those who have commented on the *Stanzas on Vibration*, particularly Kṣemarāja, are concerned to establish on a sound logical basis that the intuitive awareness of one's own inherent existence is valid. The Doctrine of Vibration seeks to show the Awakened yogi the way in which he can make the experience of his own pure subjectivity, the pulse of consciousness, permanent. It therefore concerns the experiencing subject most intimately. This is true of the philosophy of Recognition of the Pratyabhijñā school as well. However, the liberating recognition of one's own authentic identity that it teaches allows for no intermediary between it and the lower states of consciousness. The yogi must grasp reality directly in an instant. This is only possible through a firm conviction of the Self's supreme identity, and argument in the philosophy of Recognition serves a key role to instil this conviction in him. The Doctrine of Vibration, on the other hand, chalks out a path to this recognition through the experience of Spanda based on practice (*abhyāsa*),[53] and so argument plays a secondary role. Thus, although Kṣemarāja insists that an understanding of the philosophy of Recognition is essential for the Spanda yogi, he excuses himself with the 'tender hearted' who prefer the intimacy of a personal experience of Śiva and His Spanda nature, rather than the intricacies of philosophy. Accordingly, when his discussion begins to seem too long and complex he refers his reader to the Pratyabhijñā to find there the arguments which establish the permanent existence of the Self.[54] His need to philosophise and refute possible objections is not however entirely his own. As he himself points out, the author of the *Stanzas on Vibration* similarly takes time, at least in one place, to do the same even though philosophy is clearly not his main concern.[55] Let us return now then to that which does concern Spanda doctrine directly, namely, practice.

The Means to Realisation

As a sequel to this book we will publish a translation of the *Stanzas on Vibration* along with a number of hitherto untranslated commentaries. In that work we will present an analysis of the practices and doctrines taught in the *Stanzas* to show how commentators have interpreted and extended them further by their own contributions drawn from various sources. Therefore, in order to avoid unnecessary repetition, we conclude this volume with a brief exposition of the basic principles underlying Spanda practice framed in the wider context of Kashmiri Śaivism as a whole. We are aided in this task by Abhinavagupta's brilliant synthesis of Śaiva Tantra into Trika doctrine presented by him in the *Light of the Tantras* (*Tantrāloka*). There, he divides all practice into four basic categories which he calls the 'Four-fold Knowledge' (*jñānacatuṣka*).[56] These four categories are exemplified by the many means to realisation presented in the course of his systematic exposition of the Śaiva ritual, cosmography, theology, metaphysics and Yoga that he incorporates into Trika.

Abhinavagupta himself realised the highest levels of consciousness through this 'Four-fold Knowledge' taught him by his Trika teacher, Śambhunātha.[57] This great yogi taught Abhinavagupta much about the rituals and practices of the Śaiva Tantras known in Kashmir, particularly the *Mālinīvijayottaratantra* upon which the *Light of the Tantras* is avowedly based. Even so, Śambhunātha was not himself a native of Kashmir but, coming from outside, probably brought with him new interpretations of the Tantras which contributed to the further development of the Tantric schools of Kashmiri Śaivism.[58] Thus, although three of the four categories of practice are defined in the *Mālinīvijaya*, there is no evidence to suggest that they were known, or in any way extensively applied as categories of interpretation, by anyone before Abhinavagupta. They do, nonetheless, characterise remarkably well the forms of practice outlined in Kashmiri Śaiva works that precede him.[59] This is particularly true of the *Śivasūtra* and, consequently, of the *Stanzas on Vibration* which is closely related to it.[60] Significantly, only Kṣemarāja finds these categories of practice exemplified in these works. As he was a direct disciple of Abhinava, this should not surprise us. Again, that other writers do not do so indicates nothing more than the fact that they lived before Abhinava and so had no knowledge of them. It does not mean that they are not applicable to Spanda practice. Indeed, Kṣemarāja makes an important contribution to a deeper understanding of it by locating it in this wider context. Significantly, he calls the three sections of the *Śivasūtra* 'Expansions of Consciousness' (*unmeṣa*). Although this is one of many possible ways of naming sections or chapters of a Sanskrit work,[61] clearly what Kṣemarāja is implying is that each section of the *Śivasūtra* deals with one of the three basic formats of practice that leads to consciousness expansion.[62] Thus although the Spanda texts themselves do not attempt to present a universal typology of spiritual discipline, Spanda practice can be, and has been, characterised in terms of these basic types which we shall now outline.

Abhinavagupta calls each category of practice a 'means to realisation' (*upāya*). This does not imply that there is just one means to realisation belonging to each category, but rather that all forms of spiritual discipline are based on one or other of these principles. Once we have understood clearly what these principles are, we can identify the categories to which any given practice belongs. Kashmiri Śaivism does not reject any form of spiritual discipline which genuinely elevates consciousness. It is, in a sense, a science of spirituality which allows for the possibility that any discipline may be effective, although some may be more so than others. While no limit is set on the number of possible means to realisation the yogi may adopt, he should dedicate himself to the means most proximate to the reality he seeks to know.[63] Accordingly, the Master first instructs in the highest means and then tries lower ones if he fails to liberate his disciple. Thus the first section of the *Śivasūtra*, according to Kṣemarāja, deals with the Divine Means (*śāmbhavopāya*), which is the highest of the three.[64] The second section is concerned with the Empowered Means (*śāktopāya*) and the last with the Individual Means (*āṇavopāya*), which is the lowest. Again, although the *Mālinīvijayatantra* defines the lowest means first, when Abhinava quotes from it, he starts from the highest. He also explains them individually in this order in separate chapters of his *Light of the Tantras.* Developing in different ways from differing initial states, the three types of practice lead to corresponding forms of mystical absorption (*samāveśa*) that, although fundamentally identical, are distinguished on this basis and defined accordingly as follows:

> The Divine (*śāmbhava*) form of mystical absorption is said to be that which is born of an intense awakening of consciousness [brought about by the Master in the disciple][65] free of all thought-constructs.
>
> 'Empowered' (*śākta*) is the name given here to the mystical absorption attained by pondering mindfully (*cetasā*) on reality [directly], unmediated [by other means, be it] the recitation of Mantra (*uccāra*) [or anything else].
>
> The absorption attained by the recitation of Mantra, postures of the body (*karaṇa*), meditation, the mystical letters (*varṇa*) and the formation of supports (*sthānaprakalpanā*) is rightly called 'Individual' (*āṇava*).[66]

Basically, these definitions characterise the three categories of practice in the following manner:

The Divine Means (śāmbhavopāya). This means functions within the undivided realm of Śiva's pure consciousness which, free of all thought-constructs, is the universal subject Who contains within Himself all objectivity. Practising this means the yogi is carried to the supreme level of consciousness by a powerful and direct awareness of reality awakened in him by Śiva's grace through which he attains identity with Śiva without resorting to any form of meditation.[67]

The Empowered Means (śāktopāya). The practices belonging to this means are all internal. They function within the mental sphere (*cetas*) by reconverting thought (*vikalpa*) back into the pure consciousness which is its source and essence. Practice here is centred on the flux of perception (*pramāṇa*) through which the cyclic activity of the powers of the senses and mind merge with the cycle of universal consciousness (*saṃviccakra*).

The Individual Means (āṇavopāya). This means operates in the individual soul's (*aṇu*) sphere of consciousness. Any spiritual discipline which involves the recitation of Mantras, posturing of the body, meditation on a particular divine or cosmic form and concentration on a fixed point, either within the body or outside it, belongs to this category. This Means, like the Empowered Means, is concerned with the purification of thought (*vikalpasaṃskāra*), which in this case is achieved through the contemplative absorption that results from a meditative awareness sustained by objective supports. These, ranging from subtle to gross, may be centred in the intellect, vital breath and body or external physical objects. Included, therefore, in this means are all forms of outer ritual.

It is in the sphere of Śiva's power that a distinction arises between Him as the goal and the means to attain to Him (*upeyopāyabhāva*). It is here also that Śiva freely chooses to create the many means to realisation[68] as aspects of His power which reveal the freedom of His universal consciousness. Thus, corresponding to the four basic categories of practice, there are four basic aspects of Śiva's power. Ranging from the highest to lowest, these are the powers of bliss, will, knowledge and action. Again, these means operate on the three levels of Śiva's universal manifestation while the fourth means—*Anupāya*—is transcendental. These levels are the Supreme (*para*), Middling (*parāpara*) and Inferior (*apara*), which correspond to the perception of unity (*abheda*), unity-in-diversity (*bhedābheda*) and multiplicity (*bheda*).[69] According to Trika doctrine these levels correspond to those of Śiva, Śakti and the individual soul (*nara*) respectively.

We can also distinguish between types of practice according to the manner in which they develop. Thus, some reach their goal instantly without any intervening stages (*akrama*) through an intense act of will. Other practices develop in parallel with the cognitive processes operating within consciousness which are, as we have seen, explicable only in terms of a succession of simultaneously experienced metaphysical events. Based on a direct intuition of reality which, although immediate, matures progressively as the factors which obscure it are removed, these practices are both direct as well as successive (*kramākrama*). Finally, there are those practices that develop progressively as consciousness unfolds in successive stages (*krama*). The three categories of practice can be distinguished in this way because they are each related to different phases in the cognitive cycle. Each act of perception starts with a direct intuition of objectivity in its most generic form through the initial awareness the subject has of himself. He then defines his specific object by dividing it off from all others to analyse it part by part through a series of mental representations of a discursive order confined to the object previously determined[70] by the subject's direct intuitive awareness. This intuition, independent of thought and objectivity[71] and hence free of all gradations (*tāratamya*), is the form of awareness the yogi who practices the Divine Means (*śāmbhavopāya*) exercises. It is the consciousness of the subject free of all thought-constructs (*avikalpa*), comparable to the initial certainty we have that two and two equals four without need of further analysis. Practising the Empowered Means (*śāktopāya*) the yogi links together the discrete parts with the whole, that is, himself as the subject with his object, through the flux of the means of knowledge (*pramāṇa*) which flows between them. It is like adding two and two together. The Individual Means (*āṇavopāya*) deals with the diversity and relative distinctions between particulars. It is like counting one to four to arrive at the answer we intuited originally. Thus although the means are diverse and correspond to different levels of consciousness, this does not affect their ultimate goal.[72] By practising any one of these means we can achieve both liberation and all the yogic powers (*siddhi*) which issue from the perfection of practice.[73] Every means is, from this point of view, the supreme means. Abhinava explains:

> Although the causes may be various, the result, that is, the destruction, disappearance and removal of impurity (*mala*) and the power which determines it, is nevertheless one, just as a jar can be destroyed [in various ways].[74]

Although the principal categories of practice are three (not counting *anupāya*), these are again divisible into innumerable secondary varieties to suit the level of consciousness and capacity of each aspirant. If the yogi fails to achieve absorption by practising one means, he must appeal to others. Thus, for example, while practising the Empowered Means (*śāktopāya*) he may sometimes need to resort to practices belonging to the Individual Means (*āṇavopāya*). Thus, the three means become six if we add those mediated by others. This number is again multiplied by two according to whether they reach completion or not and again by two according to whether practice is blocked by extrinsic factors or progresses smoothly. The number of means thus becomes twenty-four. As the possible impediments to progress are countless, the means to overcome them are equally so; in actual fact there is no end to the number of means that may need to be applied by different people in various circumstances.[75] The means we adopt is not, however, a matter of personal choice. Reality reveals itself to the degree in which ignorance is removed and this, in a sense, takes place independently of our efforts. Śiva manifests His true nature as He chooses, whether in all its fullness at once, or successively, part by part.[76] The yogi, in order to make progress, must be empowered by the grace of Śiva's enlightened consciousness. When permeated by the power of Śiva's grace (*śaktipāta*), the powers of will, knowledge and action operating through the means to realisation are directed to a complete and unwavering insight into the true nature of reality. Then the yogi discovers that the pure knowledge (*pramitibhāva*) of universal consciousness inwardly manifests as every act of will and each perception, and outwardly as action. This realisation is consciousness free of all means (*anupāya-saṃvitti*). Although there is nothing more for the yogi to do at this level, the flow of awareness in this state is a sort of means—a 'No-means means'—a 'Pathless Path', to which we now turn our attention.

For a tabular arrangement of this material, see table 1.

No-Means (Anupāya)

It is possible to penetrate into supreme consciousness directly without the mediation of any means.[77] In fact, all means ultimately lead to the practice of 'No-means' for it is the direct experience reality has of itself as the uninterrupted awareness (*aviratānuttarajñāpti*)[78] the yogi acquires when he penetrates into his true nature. 'No practice' is the only practice which conforms fully to reality.[79] Consciousness is ever revealed; it cannot be sullied by anything outside it. Nothing can be added or subtracted from its fullness. Those who are ignorant of this fact fall to the lower levels of consciousness and so have to practice.[80] When the uninterrupted consciousness and bliss, the subtle inner nature of all things, are submerged below the horizon of awareness by the power of ignorance we lose sight of our own authentic identity and experience it as if it were distant from us, like a goal to be attained. But as Abhinava explains:

Table 1 The Means to Realisation

Means	Metaphysical Category	Format of Experience	Manner of Development	Mode of Perception	Phase of Perception	Existential Status	Power	Level
No-means (*Anupāya*)	Anuttara (the absolute)	Undefinable	Beyond succession and non-succession (*Kramākramātīta*)	Pure Awareness	Pure Consciousness (*Pramiti*)	Beyond subject and object	Bliss (*Ānanda*)	Beyond transcendence and immanence (*Parātīta*)
The Divine Means (*Śāmbhavopāya*)	Śiva	Unity (*Abheda*)	Non-succession (*Akrama*)	Immediate Perception	Subject (*Pramātṛ*)	I	Will (*Icchā*)	Supreme (*Para*)
The Empowered Means (*Śāktopāya*)	Śakti	Unity-in-diversity (*Bhedābheda*)	Non-succession cum succession (*Kramākrama*)	Synthetic Perception	Means of knowledge (*Prāmāṇa*)	You	Knowledge (*Jñāna*)	Middling (*Parāpara*)
The Individual Means (*Āṇavopāya*)	Nara (the individual soul)	Diversity (*Bheda*)	Succession (*Krama*)	Analytic Perception	Object (*Prameya*)	He, She, It	Action (*Kriyā*)	Inferior (*Apara*)

> Those who are purified by this supremely real consciousness firmly affirmed within them become well established on the path of the absolute (*anuttara*) and are not bound by practice.[81]

In fact, there is nothing we can do to free ourselves.[82] All forms of practice, whether internal or external, depend on consciousness and so cannot serve as a means to realise it.[83] He who seeks to discover this reality by practice is like a man who tries to see the sun by the light of a firefly.[84] Those who are in the realms of 'No-means' (*anupāya*) recognise that the light of consciousness shines as all things. All the opposites merge and their seeming contradiction is resolved. Liberation and bondage become synonymous just as the words 'jar' and 'pot' indicate the same object.[85] No-means (*anupāya*) is the experience of the absolute (*anuttara*) beyond both transcendence and immanence (*Śiva* and *Śakti*). Undefinable and mysterious, it is neither existent (*sat*) nor non-existent (*asat*), neither is it both nor neither.[86]

> Not grounded in anything, this [Light] is not energy, the Great Goddess; nor is it God, the power-holder, because it is not the foundation of anything. It is not an object of meditation because there is none who meditates, nor is it he who meditates because there is nothing to meditate on. It is not an object of worship because there is none to worship it, nor is it the worshipper because there is nothing to worship. This all-pervasive [reality] is not Mantra, not that which is expressed by Mantra, nor he who utters it. This [reality], the Great God (*maheśvara*), is not initiation, the initiator or the initiated.[87]

To all intents and purposes *Anupāya* is liberation itself. It is the eternal fullness of consciousness, which is already liberated before we even begin to practice (*ādimukta*). Those who reach this level of practice do not need to exert themselves at all to grasp reality everywhere constantly present.[88] *Anupāya* is the way of bliss (*ānandopāya*); it is the untroubled rest within one's own nature (*svātmaviśrānti*) experienced when the recognition dawns that it is this which appears as all things. At that instant the powers of will, knowledge and action merge into the bliss of consciousness:

> In this way, even supreme knowledge, divested of all means, rests in the power of bliss said to be [the presence] of the absolute here [in every moment of experience].[89]

Thus there are two levels of *Anupāya*. At the higher level nothing can be said about it. It is literally the reality which cannot be described in any way (*anākhya*) or approached by any means. To this level belong those rare, highly spiritual souls who are born fully enlightened and come into the world to show others the way to attain their liberated state. For them *Anupāya* literally means that they do not need to practice at all. Most yogis, however, have to prepare themselves for this state and when they are ready achieve instant access to it through the practice of *Anupāya* as the most subtle means possible (*sūkṣmopāya*). The adept whose consciousness has been purified and made fully receptive to instruction needs to be taught this practice just once for it to mature in an instant to the fullness of perfect enlightenment. When the disciple is truly fit to receive the teachings and be liberated,[90] all the Master needs to do is to tell him that he shines by the light of Śiva's consciousness and that his true nature is the entire universe.[91] Thus:

> When the Master utters [his instructions] with words intent on the thoughtless, [the disciple] is liberated there and then, and all that remains [of his former state] is the machine [of the body].[92]

When such a disciple sits before his Master, all he has to do is to gaze at him and be aware of his elevated state to feel the fragrance (*vāsanā*) of the Master's transcendental consciousness extending spontaneously within him. Abhinava explains:

> So gracious is he that, by transferring his own nature to those whose consciousness is pure, they became one with him at his [mere] sight.[93]

If the disciple does not possess the strength of awareness to allow the Master to infuse this consciousness into him directly in this way while his eyes are open, he is instructed to close them. The Master then bestows upon him a vision of former perfected yogis (*siddha*) while the disciple is in a state of contemplation with his eyes closed (*nimīlanasamādhi*). Through the vision of these perfected yogis (*siddhadarśana*)[94] he recognises their level of consciousness and so experiences it within himself. The disciple's consciousness thus suddenly expands within him like the violent and rapid spread of poison through the body (*bhujaṅgagaralavat*). He thus becomes one with his Master in the unifying bliss of universal consciousness and so, whether his eyes are open or closed, continues to enjoy the same state constantly.

Although it is possible to catch glimpses of the highest reality in advanced states of contemplation before attaining perfect enlightenment, these states, however long they last, are transitory (*kādācitka*) and when they end the vision of the absolute ceases with them. The highest realisation, however, persists in all states of consciousness. It happens once and need never occur again. A passage from a lost Tantra declares: "the Self shines forth but once, it is full [of all things] and can nowhere be unmanifest."[95] All spiritual discipline culminates in this moment of realisation. Accordingly, Abhinava stresses that the goal of all the means to realisation, even the Individual Means, is this absolute consciousness.

Finally, it is worth noting that although Abhinava affirms that the teachings concerning *Anupāya* are found in the *Siddhayogeśvarīmata* and the *Mālinīvijaya*, both of which, according to Abhinava, are major Tantras of the Trika school, it is in the theology of the school of Recognition that it is best exemplified. Abhinava himself refers to Somānanda, the founder of this school, as teaching it and alludes to the following passage in the *Vision of Śiva* to support his own exposition:

> When Śiva, Who is everywhere present, is known just once through the firm insight born of right knowledge (*pramāṇa*), the scripture and the Master's words, no means [to realisation] serves any purpose and even contemplation (*bhāvanā*) [is of no further use].[96]

Anupāya is therefore, according to Abhinavagupta, the recognition of one's own authentic Śiva-nature, which all the higher Tantric traditions teach is the ultimate realisation. This is also true of the Doctrine of Vibration whose precedents are clearly traceable to these same traditions. Thus, although the *Stanzas* themselves never refer directly to enlightenment as an experience of recognition, there can be little doubt that Spanda practice leads to this same realisation. Accordingly, commentators stress that we realise the vibration of consciousness by *recognising* its activity and that liberation depends on the recognition of this as one's own nature.[97] Kṣemarāja describes what happens in this moment of Recognition according to the Doctrine of Vibration thus:

> At the end of countless rebirths, the yogi's [psycho-physical] activity [which issues from ignorance] is suddenly interrupted by the recognition of his own transcendent nature, full of a novel and supreme bliss. He is like one struck with awe and in this attitude of astonishment (*vismaya-mudrā*) achieves the Great Expansion [of consciousness] (*mahāvikāsa*). Thus he, the best of yogis, whose true nature has been revealed [to him] is well established [at the highest level of consciousness], which he grasps firmly and his hold upon it never slackens. Thus he is no longer subject to

profane existence (*pravṛtti*), the abhorrent and continuing round of birth and death, which inspires fear in all living beings, because its cause, his own impurity, no longer exists.[98]

The Divine Means (Śāmbhavopāya)

In *Anupāya* the yogi does not need to deal with the world of diversity at all; only Paramaśiva exists there. Beyond both immanence and transcendence, He has nothing to do with the world of practice and realisation. *Anupāya* is the experience of the undefinable (*anākhya*) light of consciousness, which is the pure bliss beyond even the supreme state (*parātīta*) of *Śivatattva.* At a slightly lower level, corresponding to the Divine Means, a subtle distinction emerges between the goal and the Path. The yogi now practises within the domain of the outpouring of the power of consciousness. From this level he penetrates directly into the universal egoity of pure consciousness by the subtle exertion (*udyama*) of its freedom (*svātantrya*) and reflective awareness. The yogi who practises the Divine Means is not concerned with any partial aspect of reality but centers his attention directly on its abounding plenitude. Hence this means is based on Śiva's own state (*śāmbhavāvasthā*) in which only the power of freedom operates as the pure Being (*sattā*) or essence of all the other powers. This state is the light of consciousness which, free of all thought-forms, is the basis of all practice.[99] The yogi who recognises that pure consciousness, free of thought-constructs (*nirvikalpa*), is his basic state, can practice in any way he chooses; even the most common Mantra will lead him directly to the highest state. Thus the forms of contemplative absorption, empowered (*śākta*) and individual (*āṇava*), that are the fruits of the other means to realisation both attain maturity in this same undifferentiated awareness. This awareness is the pure ego manifest at the initial moment of perception (*prāthamikālocana*), when the power of the will to perceive is activated. It is the subtle state of consciousness that reveals the presence and nature of its object directly:

> That which shines and is directly grasped in the first moment of perception while it is still free of differentiated representations and reflects upon itself is [the basis of the Divine Means] said to be the will. Just as an object appears directly to one whose eyes are open without the intervention of any mental cogitation (*anusaṃdhāna*), so, for some, does Śiva's nature.[100]

The movement of awareness at this level of practice attains its goal quickly. While consciousness is heightened progressively in the other Means, here it expands freely to the higher levels, unconfined by any intruding thought-constructs. The Divine Means is a 'thoughtless thought', a 'processless process', that occurs at the juncture between Being and Becoming. Abhinava explains:

> When the Heart [of consciousness] is pure and [free of thought-constructs], it harbours the light which illumines the radiant, primordial plane (*prāgrabhūmi*) together with all the categories of existence. [The yogi] then realises through it his identity with Śiva Who is pure consciousness.[101]

The yogi must catch the initial moment of awareness (*ādiparāmarśa*) just when perception begins. He must not move on from the first pure sensation of the object but return to its original source in his own 'I' consciousness. Observing in this way the objective field of consciousness without labouring to distinguish particulars, the yogi penetrates into his own subjectivity which, vacuous and divested of all outer supports (*nirālamba*), is not directed anywhere outside itself (*ananyamukha-prekṣin*). Here he can lay hold of the power inherent in his own consciousness through which he discerns the true nature of whatever appears before him. Thus the *Stanzas on Vibration* teach:

> Just as an object, which is not seen clearly at first even when the mind attends to it carefully, becomes later fully evident when observed with the effort exerted through one's own [inherent] strength (*svabala*), in the same way, when [the yogi] lays hold of that same power, then whatever [he perceives manifests to him] quickly according to its true nature, whatever be its form, locus, time or state.[102]

Thus, although the practice of this Divine Means starts by catching hold of the will in the first moment of awareness, it also concerns the second and third moments in which the means of knowledge and the object are made manifest. When practice at this level proceeds smoothly and without interruption, the three powers of will, knowledge and action fuse into the Trident (*triśūla*) of power, which is the subject free of all obscuration (*nirañjana*),[103] at one with the power of action in its most powerful and evident form. The Kaula schools call this state the stainless (*nirañjanatattva*). Equated in the Spanda tradition with the dawning of the vibration of consciousness (*spandodaya*), it is the enlightenment the Spanda yogi seeks.

Many practices taught in the *Stanzas on Vibration* belong to the Divine Means. Spanda practice is based on the experience of Spanda which, as we have seen, is defined as the intent (*aunmukhya*) of consciousness, unrestricted to any specific object and hence free of thought-constructs.[104] Spanda can therefore be experienced directly when a powerful intention develops within consciousness, whatever be its ultimate goal or cause. We have already noted that intense anger, joy, grief or confusion are such occasions.[105] Similarly, the yogi can make contact with the omnipotent will, which he as Śiva possesses, through intense prayer. Directing his entire attention to Śiva, the Benefactor of the world, entreating Him fervently and without break, his will merges with Śiva's universal will, which is the source of every impulse and perception. As he looks about him, the yogi realises that it is Śiva Himself, the universal consciousness and the yogi's authentic identity, Who ordains his every action, thought and perception. Thus the yogi's cognitive intent on his object coincides with the universal will to make that object known to him, whether the yogi be awake or dreaming. He is thus no longer like the worldly man who cannot dream as he wishes and is forced to experience whatever spontaneously happens in these states of consciousness.[106]

Ultimately the yogi manages, by Śiva's grace, to maintain a constant awareness of his own pure perceptive consciousness (*upalabdhṛtā*) divested of all obscuring thought-constructs in deep sleep as well as in the contemplative state (*turīya*) beyond it. When he rises to the higher levels of contemplation in which the breath is suspended and all sensory and mental activity ceases, the yogi who manages to sustain this pure, undifferentiated awareness does not succumb to sleep as do less developed yogis. Perfection in the practice of the Divine Means thus coincides with the goal of Spanda practice, namely, a constant, alert attention to the perceiving subjectivity which persists unchanged in every state of consciousness both as the perceiver and agent of all that it experiences.

Another important Spanda practice belonging to this means is Centering. The Spanda yogi seeks to find the Centre (*madhya*) between one cognition and the next, for it is there that he discovers the expansion (*unmeṣa*) of consciousness free of thought-constructs from whence all differentiated perceptions (*vikalpa*) emerge.[107] Abhinava explains that this pure awareness is called:

> . . . the expansion (*unmeṣa*) of [consciousness] or the creative intuition (*pratibhā*) [experienced] in the interval which divides two [moments] of differentiated perception (*vikalpa*). It is here that they arise and disappear. The *Śāstras* and *Āgamas* proclaim with reasoned argument that it is free of thought-constructs (*nirvikalpa*) and precedes

all mental representations of any object. None can deny that a gap exists between perceptions insofar as two moments of thought are invariably divided. This [gap] is the undifferentiated unity of all the countless manifestations.[108]

Similarly, in the outer more objective sphere, where change consists of the alterations in the configurations of manifest appearances (*ābhāsa*), the transition from one to another corresponds to a phase of pure luminosity that marks the beginning of one form and the end of another.[109] The world of manifestation and differentiated perceptions (*vikalpa*) thus extends from one Centre to the next. Although it is never in fact divorced from the subject who resides there, the ignorant fail to grasp this fact and so, cut off from the Centre, the world of objectivity becomes for them the sphere of Māyā.[110] Bhagavatotpala quotes the *Light of Consciousness* (*Saṃvitprakāśa*):

This ever pure experience (*śuddhānubhava*) is variegated by each form [revealed within it]; even so it remains unstained (*nirmala*) when moving to another. Just as a cloth which is naturally white, once dyed, cannot change colour without [first] becoming white again, similarly the pure power of awareness, (*citi*) once coloured by form, is pure [again] at the Centre where that form is abandoned and from whence it proceeds to another.[111]

In his *Essence of Vibration* (*Spandasaṃdoha*), Kṣemarāja explains that the rise and fall of every individual perception in the field of awareness is a specific pulsation of consciousness. From the point of view of the object, the expansion (*unmeṣa*) of this pulse is represented by the initial desire to perceive (*didṛkṣā*) a particular object, while the contracted (*nimeṣa*) phase is the withdrawal of attention from the object previously perceived. From the point of view of the perceiving subjectivity, the phases are reversed, so that the initial desire to perceive marks the contraction (*nimeṣa*) of subjective consciousness while the falling away of the previous perception is its expansion (*unmeṣa*). At the higher level, where these two phases are experienced within consciousness, they represent the state of the categories of Īśvara ('this universe is me') and Sadāśiva ('I am this universe'). Utpaladeva says:

Expansion (*unmeṣa*), which is in the external manifestation [of objectivity], is Īśvaratattva while contraction (*nimeṣa*), which is in the internal manifestation [of subjectivity], is Sadāśiva.[112]

At this level all the powers of consciousness fuse and both phases are manifest as part of one reality. This unity is in fact apparent to everybody at each moment. However, within the domain of Māyā, which is the sphere of differentiated perceptions (*vikalpa*), it is clearly manifest only at the juncture (*madhya*) between two cognitions.[113] In this Centre resides the void (*kha*) of consciousness (free of thought-constructs) which, divested of diversity, digests into itself all the psycho-physical processes that give life to the multiplicity of perceptions. The yogi moves from the particular vibrations of consciousness at its periphery to the universal throb of the Heart in the Centre. As Abhinava explains:

> The self-reflective awareness in the Heart of pure consciousness, present at the beginning and end of each perception, within which the entire universe is dissolved away without residue, is called in the scriptures, the universal vibration of consciousness (*sāmānyaspanda*) and is the outpouring (*uccalana*) [of awareness] within one's own nature.[114]

All the categories of existence (*tattvas*) are united in the Heart of the Centre where the life-giving elixir of Śiva's consciousness floods one's own inner nature. To reside in the Centre is to abide by the law of totality (*grāmadharma*) in a state which transcends the workings of the mind (*unmanā*).

> Consciousness (*jñāna*) with Light as its support, residing in the Centre between being and non-being is known as the act of abiding in one's own abode as the perceiving subjectivity (*draṣṭṛtva*) free of all obscuration. That which has been purified by pure awareness (*śuddhavijñāna*) is called the transcendent (*viviktavastu*), said to be the mode of being (*vṛtti*) of the law of totality (*grāmadharma*) through which everything is easily attainable.[115]

The power in the Centre (*madhyaśakti*) is the eternal Present. Beyond time it is the source of both past and future. To be established there is to abide without a break in Rāma, the supreme enjoyer, in every action of one's life.

> Rāma is Śiva, the supreme cause Who pervades the fourteen aspects which embrace the entire universe of experience, namely, moving, standing, dreaming, waking, the opening and closing of the eyes, running, jumping, exertion, knowledge [born] of the power of the senses, the [three] aspects of the mind, living beings, names and all kinds of actions.[116]

By developing an awareness of the Centre, the yogi experiences the bliss of consciousness.[117] Through this gap he plunges into introverted absorption (*nimīlanasamādhi*) and then emerges again to pervade the field of awareness between Centres and so experience the Cosmic Bliss (*jagadānanda*) of the universal vibration of consciousness.[118] He then recognises that this state pervades every aspect of experience. In this way the yogi's consciousness is no longer afflicted by the power which obscures it, hemming the Centre in on both sides with thought-constructs that seemingly deprive it of its fullness. As he realises directly his pure conscious nature as the universal ego free of all mental representations, it expands out to embrace all things within itself. Thus the realisation the Divine Means leads to, and is directly based upon, is that this pure ego is in all things just as all things are within it.

In the Spanda tradition, as recorded in the *Stanzas on Vibration*, no such ego is recognised.[119] Man's authentic nature is, however, understood in personal terms as every individual's own 'own nature' (*svasvabhāva*) which is Śiva, the universal vibration of pure subjectivity (*upalabdhṛtā*). It is not surprising, therefore, that later commentators found these two conceptions to be essentially the same and accordingly identified one's own inner nature with the pure ego. This came as a natural development in Spanda doctrine not only for this reason but also because the universal ego is experienced as the inner dynamics of absolute consciousness. To conclude our summarial exposition of the Divine Means, which is centred on the direct experience of this pure ego (and hence on Spanda in this form), we turn now to a brief description of its inner, cyclic activity. We shall do this by examining Abhinava's esoteric exegesis of the symbolic significance of the word 'AHAṂ', which in Sanskrit means 'I', and symbolises by its form the ego's dynamic nature.

The objective world of perceptions is, as we have seen, essentially a chain of thought-constructs (*prapañca*) closely linked to one another and woven into the fabric of diversity (*vicitratā*). This thought (*vikalpa*) is a form of speech (*vāc*) uttered internally by the mind (*citta*), which is itself an outpouring of consciousness. Consciousness also, in its turn, resounds with the silent, supreme form of speech (*parā vāc*) which is the reflective awareness through which it expresses itself to itself. Consequently, the fifty letters of the Sanskrit alphabet, which are the smallest phonemic units into which speech can be analysed, are symbolic of the principal elements of the activity of consciousness. Letters come together to generate words and words go on to form sentences. In the same way the fifty phases in the cycle of consciousness represent, in the realms of denoted meaning (*vācya*), the sum total of its universal activity (*kriyā*) corresponding to the principal forces (*kalā*) which come together to form the metaphysical categories of experience, which in their turn appear in the grossest, most explicitly 'articulate' form as the one hundred and eighteen world-systems (*bhuvana*).

'A', the first letter of both AHAṂ and the Sanskrit alphabet, is the point of departure or initial emergence of all the other letters and hence denotes *Anuttara*—the absolute. 'Ha', is the final letter of the alphabet and represents the point of completion when all the letters have emerged. It represents the state in which all the elements of experience, in the domains of both inner consciousness and outer unconsciousness, are fully displayed. It is also the generative, emission (*visarga*) which, like the breath, casts the inner into the outer, and draws what is outside inward. The two letters 'A' and 'Ha' thus represent Śiva, the transcendental source and Śakti, His cosmic outpouring that flows back into Him. The combined 'A-Ha' contains within itself all the letters of the alphabet—every phase of consciousness, both transcendental and universal. (For a graphic representation of this analysis, see figure 1.)

Ṃ, the final letter of AHAṂ, is written as a dot placed above the letter which precedes it. It comes at the end of the vowel series and before the consonants and so is called *'anusvāra'* (lit. 'that which follows the vowels') and also *'bindu'* (lit. 'dot,' 'drop,' 'point' or 'zero'). While the consonant 'M' symbolises the individual soul (*puruṣa*), *'bindu'* represents the subtle vibration of 'I', which is the life force (*jīvakalā*) and essence of the soul's subjectivity manifest at the transcendental, supra-mental level (*unmanā*).[120] It is the zero-point in the centre between the series of negative numbers, in this case the vowels which represent the processes happening internally within Śiva, and the series of positive numbers—the consonants which symbolise the processes happening externally within Śakti.

Bindu, as a point without area, symbolises the non-finite nature of the pure awareness (*pramitibhāva*) of AHAṂ. It is the pivot around which the cycle of energies from 'A' to 'Ha' rotates, the Void in the centre from which all the powers emanate and into which they collapse. As such, it is the supreme power of action which holds subject, object and means of knowledge together in a potential state in the one Light that shines as all three[121] containing them in its repose[122] (*viśrānti*). *Bindu* is the 'knower' (*jñātṛ*), who is essentially consciousness that, though omniscient, does not manifest its intelligence, like a man who knows the scriptures but having no occasion to explain them to others silently bears this knowledge within himself. As such, it symbolises the union of Śiva and Śakti (*śivaśakti-mithunapiṇḍa*)[123] in a state of heightened potency in which they have not yet divided to generate the world of diversity. It stands, in other words, at the threshold of differentiation in the stream of emanation still contained within Śiva.

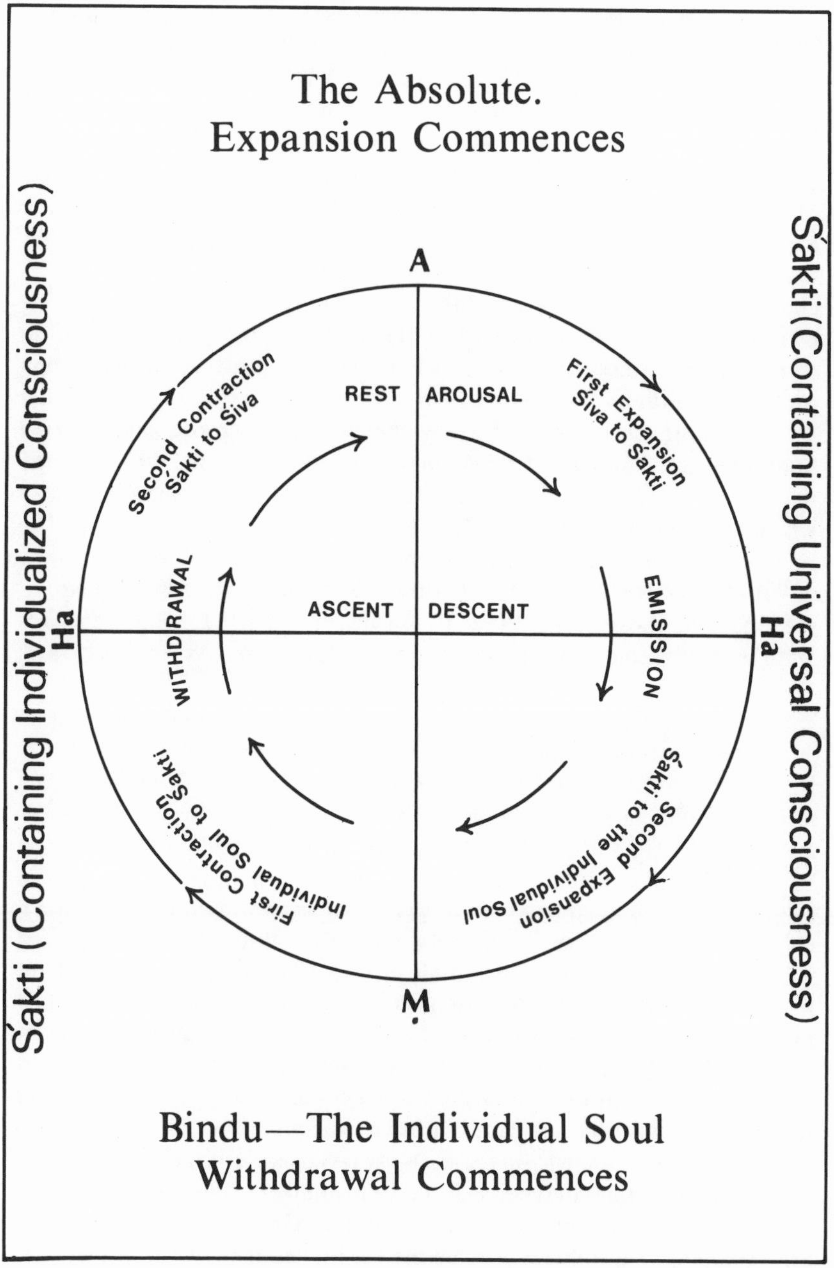

The Absolute.
Expansion Commences
A
Ha
Ha
Ṃ
REST
AROUSAL
ASCENT
DESCENT
WITHDRAWAL
EMISSION
First Expansion
Śiva to Śakti
Second Expansion
Śakti to the Individual Soul
First Contraction
Individual Soul to Śakti
Second Contraction
Śakti to Śiva
Śakti (Containing Universal Consciousness)
Śakti (Containing Individualized Consciousness)
Bindu—The Individual Soul
Withdrawal Commences

Figure 1

> Then, to the degree in which that which is to be accomplished by the power of action residing within it [as a potential] penetrates into the absolute, it appears initially as *bindu*, which is the light of pure consciousness.[124]

When outer objectivity is reabsorbed into its transcendent source, *bindu* is the point into which all the manifest powers of consciousness are gathered and fused together. The universal potency of all the letters is thus contained in *bindu* which, as the reflective awareness of supreme 'I' consciousness,[125] gives them all life. Thus *bindu* also marks the beginning of Śiva's internal movement back to the undifferentiated absolute and so stands at the threshold of both emission and absorption without being involved in either.

The three aspects of AHAṂ together constitute a movement from the undifferentiated source of transcendental consciousness—'A'—through the expansion or emission of its power—'Ha'—to the subject—'Ṃ'—which contains and makes manifest the entire universe of experience. The reverse of this movement, that of withdrawal (*saṃhāra*), is represented by Ṃ-Ha-A. AHAṂ and Ṃ-Ha-A alternate in the rotation (*ghūrṇana*) of the reflective awareness of 'I' consciousness as immanent Śakti emerges from transcendental Śiva to then merge back into Him. As Abhinava says:

> The universe rests within Śakti and She on the plane of the absolute (*anuttara*) and this again within Śakti . . . for the universe shines within consciousness and [consciousness shines] there [within the universe by the power of] consciousness. These three poles, forming a couple and merging, make up the one supreme nature of Bhairava Whose essence is AHAṂ.[126]

At the microcosmic level, 'A' represents the initial moment when the subject begins to rise out of himself to view the object. The movement from 'A' to 'Ha' marks the emergence of sensation within the field of awareness, which is represented by the fifty letters of the alphabet symbolic of the fifty aspects of the flux of consciousness leading to objectified perception. 'Ṃ' is the subject who, resting content within himself when he has perceived his object, merges through the inner flow of awareness into 'A', the absolute. Then from the absolute (A) its emission (Ha) flows back into the pure subject (Ṃ) set to perceive his object. Thus all the cycles of creation and destruction are contained within AHAṂ through which they are experienced simultaneously as the spontaneous play of the absolute. The yogi who recognises this recurrent pulse of awareness to be the movement of his own consciousness merges his limited ego with the universal ego. Thus he realises that its power to create, sustain and destroy all things is his own inner strength (*svabala*) that he exerts effortlessly in the same state of mystical absorption (*turīya*) in universal consciousness that the absolute itself enjoys. In this way he shares in the three-fold awareness Śiva Himself has of His own nature which Abhinava describes as follows:

> 'I make the universe manifest within myself in the Sky of Consciousness. I, who am the universe, am its creator!'—this awareness is the way in which one becomes Bhairava. 'All of manifest creation (*ṣaḍadhvan*) is reflected within me, I cause it to persist'—this awareness is the way in which one becomes the universe. 'The universe dissolves within me. I who am the flame of the [one] great and eternal fire of consciousness'—seeing thus one achieves peace.[127]

The experience of the liberated thus coincides with the realisation of their own divine nature which, through its power, rules and guides the cosmic order. Thus this attainment (*siddhi*), which is liberation itself, is in the Doctrine of Vibration technically called 'Mastery over the Wheel of Energies' (*cakreśvaratvasiddhi*) because the liberated soul, identified with Śiva, now governs, as does Śiva, the cycle of the powers that bring about the creation and destruction of all things.[128]

The Empowered Means (Śāktopāya)

All the practices taught in the *Stanzas on Vibration* are internal. Whenever ritual is mentioned, it is invariably interpreted in terms of the dynamics of the inner processes the yogi experiences and implements in the course of his yogic practice. The Doctrine of Vibration, Kṣemarāja affirms,[129] is concerned entirely with these inner disciplines centred, as it is, in one way or another, on consciousness or, at least, on the inner activity of the mind. Thus the Empowered Means which, like the other categories we have discussed, is entirely internal, includes an important part of Spanda practice. Spanda practice belonging to the Divine Means centres on one's own inherent nature (*svasvabhāva*) as Śiva, the universal perceiver and agent, that belonging to the Empowered Means on His power. Instead of arriving directly at the all-embracing emptiness of subjective consciousness, the yogi practising the Empowered Means realises his true nature through the fullness of its energy. Practising the Divine Means, the yogi plunges, as it were, straight into the fire of consciousness; practising the

Empowered Means he merges with its rays. Either way the yogi is centred equally on ultimate reality. The power of consciousness is no less absolute than its possessor. To make this point Abhinava quotes the *Mātaṅga-tantra:*

> This reality consists of the rays of [Śiva's] power and is variously said to be the abode of the Lord's manifestation . . . That same [power] illumined [by Śiva] is itself also luminous, unshaken and unmoving. That very [power] is the supreme state, subtle, omnipresent, the nectar of immortality, free of obscuration, peaceful, yearning for pure Being alone (*vastumātra*) and devoid of beginning and end. Perfectly pure, it is said to be the body [of ultimate reality].[130]

The yogi concentrates on the powers operating in all of life's activities as particular pulsations (*viśeṣaspanda*) in the universal rhythm (*sāmānyaspanda*) of the power of consciousness. In this way he rises progressively from the particular to the universal until he reaches pure Being (*sattā*), the greatest of all universals (*mahāsāmānya*) and the highest form of Śiva's power. Thus the creative power of Māyā, manifest through countless lesser powers, no longer causes the yogi to stray from Śiva's consciousness but becomes the means through which it can be realised[131] in the illuminating brilliance (*sphurattā*) which is Śiva's pure Being. Thus by discovering the true nature of Śakti, the yogi realises himself to be Śiva, its possessor Who consists of all its countless powers. Thus practise belonging to this Means leads to the same pure consciousness free of thought-constructs realised through the Divine Means. Although the ultimate realisation is instantaneous, the yogi rises to it gradually by freeing his consciousness of the limitations imposed upon it by thought. Abhinava explains:

> The same occurs in the Empowered Means [as does in the Divine]. At the discursive level of consciousness (*vaikalpikībhūmi*) [where the Empowered Means functions] knowledge and action, although evident, are, for the reasons explained previously, contracted. A blazing energy [is revealed within] the one who dedicates himself to removing the burden of this contraction. [This energy eventually] brings about the inner manifestation (*antarābhāsa*) of pure consciousness he seeks.[132]

Consciousness is individualised and its power of knowledge and action contracted by the thought-constructs born of ignorance. The arising of these mental representations, as the *Stanzas on Vibration* say, deprives the soul of its freedom and immortal life.[133] The practise of the

Empowered Means is meant to free the fettered soul of this constriction on his consciousness. It operates within the mental sphere (*cetas*)[134] and is designed to purify thought (*vikalpasaṃskāra*) in order to reveal the pure consciousness which is its ground and ultimate source. Thus, the Empowered Means is concerned with the second instant of perception, during which the subject forms mental representations of his object. Thought functions on the basis of an awareness of relative distinctions between specific particulars, distinguishing them from one another and thus seemingly fragmenting the essential unity of reality.[135] The vibrant vitality of consciousness, universally manifest, is clouded like a mirror by a child's breath[136] and the soul is deprived of the liberating intuition of the one reality free of thought-constructs (*nirvikalpa*). Abhinava writes:

> The [fettered soul] is like a dancing girl who although wishing to leave the dancehall is collared by the doorkeeper of thought and thrown back onto the stage of Māyā.[137]

All thought is centred on objectivity and hence dislodges awareness from the plenitude of pure subjective consciousness. Thus, to regain the original state of rest (*viśrānti*) consciousness enjoys, the yogi must rid himself of thought. As thought-forms decrease, pure, thought-free awareness is strengthened[138] until the yogi is fully established in a state in which the relative distinctions (*bheda*) conceived between entities dissolve away. Everything appears to him as pure Being (*sattāmātra*)[139] and the entire universe shines before him pervaded by Śiva's radiance.[140] His intuitive faculty (*mati*) thus purified, the yogi gains both the perfections (*siddhi*) of yogic practice and liberation (*mukti*). His consciousness is now like a well-polished mirror which reflects everything he desires and grants it to him.[141] Abhinava writes:

> Just as a man who has been ill for a long time forgets his past pain completely when he regains his health, absorbed as he is in the ease of his present condition, so too those who are grounded in pure awareness free of thought-constructs are no longer conscious of their previous [fettered] state. Consciousness, the sole truly existent reality, free of thought-constructs is made fully and evidently manifest by eliminating these differentiated perceptions. The wise man should therefore exert himself to attend closely to this [state of awareness].[142]

The thought-constructs generated within consciousness do not in reality affect it at all. They can neither break up nor add anything to the Light which shines as all things.[143] They are in fact nothing but consciousness itself[144] which perceives, through its power of reflective awareness (*vimarśa*), the multitude of objects in diverse ways, and so assumes this form.[145] Although thought-constructs are mental representations of objects once seen or present, they are products of the power of consciousness and not of the objects they represent.[146] Thought is both analytic and synthetic;[147] it serves the useful purpose of separating individual elements of experience from others and linking together those that appear to be distinct from one another so that they can be better understood.[148] It does not consist merely of false mental constructs projected onto reality that need to be wholly rejected. Thought obscures consciousness and distracts it only when it appears in the form of doubt, vacillating between alternatives.[149] Once this conflicting duality (*dvaitādhivāsa*)[150] is eliminated, thought is purified and rests in itself as the 'thought-less thought' of pure consciousness.[151] By gradually eliminating the multitude of conflicting notions that agitate him, the yogi ultimately achieves the certainty (*niścaya*) corresponding to a direct awareness of his own divine nature.[152] Abhinava explains:

> Thought is in reality none other than pure consciousness. Even so, it serves as a means to liberation for the individual soul (*aṇu*) only when it takes the form of certainty (*niścaya*).[153]

The yogi must eliminate every doubt and misguided notion that leads him to believe himself to be other than Śiva. By developing the thought: 'I am Śiva', it ultimately affirms itself directly as a pure awareness beyond thought without any intervening mental representations. Abhinava says:

> Just as the man who thinks intensely that he is a sinner becomes such, just so one who thinks himself to be Śiva, and none other than He, becomes Śiva. This certainty (*dārḍhya*), which penetrates and affirms itself in our thoughts, coincides with an awareness free of thought-constructs engendered by a series of differentiated mental representations, the object of which is our identity with Śiva.[154]

As thought is gradually purified, it becomes progressively clearer until its object becomes maximally apparent (*sphuṭatama*).[155] The stream of perceptive consciousness (*pramāṇa*) progressively reveals each aspect of its object which, thus affirming itself with increasing clarity, reveals its ultimate nature. The yogi reflects repeatedly upon it as the object of his realisation and loving devotion, for all that is perceptible and need be known (*jñeya*) is Śiva alone. As Abhinava says:

> What should we say of those who before they are satisfied have to see their beloved again and again, caress her and think about her for a long time?[156]

The yogi practising the Empowered Means is initiated into the Great Sacrificial Rite (*mahāyāga*), eternally enacted at the interface between the inner and outer aspects of consciousness, by a direct infusion of awareness from his master who is the embodiment and outer symbol of the yogi's enlightened identity.[157] The rite begins with ritual bathing (*snāna*) which is in this case the immersion of the body of thought in the white ashes of the cosmic fuel of duality, burnt in the fire of consciousness.[158] The yogi then goes on to worship (*pūjā*) by uniting all that is pleasing to the senses in the oneness of consciousness.[159] The ritual formula (*mantra*) he recites is the eternal resonance of the awareness which is the pulsation of the Heart of his own consciousness.[160] Repetition (*japa*) of the formula is every activity, perception, breath or thought which arises within him while plunged in the universal awareness of his true nature.[161] The mental image he visualises meditating (*dhyāna*) on the Deity in the course of the rite, is whatever the yogi spontaneously imagines and contemplates as the outpouring of the universal creativity of consciousness.[162] Ritual gesture (*mudrā*) is whatever bodily posture the yogi may assume when, fully absorbed in consciousness, he moves, staggering about (*ghūrṇita*) as it were, drunk with the wine of self-realisation.[163] Oblation is performed by offering with devotion and awareness all the sensations which flow in through the channels of the senses to the fire of his subjectivity, which is thus inflamed (*uddīpita*) and makes all things one with itself.[164]

The outer ritual which commences in the sphere of the Individual Means thus leads naturally to the inner rite of the Empowered Means. When the yogi's practise (*abhyāsa*) reaches fruition, the rite merges with the spontaneous activity of consciousness. This is fullness (*pūrṇatā*), the completion and reunification of the forces within consciousness which, through the power of ignorance, were formerly dispersed and divided.

> "Just as a horse driven here and there", writes Abhinava, "over plains, hills and dales follows the will of its rider, so also consciousness, driven by various expedients (*bhaṅgi*), quiescent or terrific, abandoning duality, becomes Bhairava. Just as by looking repeatedly at one's own face in a mirror one comes to know that it is the same [as the image reflected], so also, [one sees] in the mirror of mental representations of meditation (*dhyāna*), ritual (*pūjā*) and worship (*arcā*) one's own Self as Bhairava and so quickly identifies with Him. This identification is the realisation that takes place in the absolute (*anuttara*)."[165]

By ridding himself of the relative distinctions engendered by thought, the yogi practising the Empowered Means, illumined by the power of self-awareness of Pure Knowledge (*śuddhavidyā*), transcends the distinction between right and wrong, purity and impurity. He is led to the conviction that the pure consciousness, which is his true nature, is unaffected by whatever action he may do, whether conventionally accepted as good or bad. Abhinava quotes the *Mālinīvijaya* as saying:

> All here is enjoined and all prohibited. This alone, O Lord of the gods, is here prescribed as obligatory, namely that the mind be firmly applied to the true reality. It matters little how this is achieved. He whose mind is firmly established in [this] reality, even if he eats poison, is as little affected by it as are lotus petals by water.[166]

Impurity is a state of seeming separation from consciousness.[167] The yogi who has freed himself of all false notions comes to realise that the true nature of consciousness can never be sullied or limited by any object appearing within it.[168] This is the realisation the ancient sages achieved through a direct intuition of reality free of intruding thought-constructs (*avikalpabhāva*), but kept secret in order not to confuse the worldly.[169] Similarly, in reality nobody is ever bound. It is ignorance to believe bondage exists and to contrast it with a conceived state of liberation.[170] If the Self is one with Śiva, how can it be either bound or released?[171] Nothing essentially distinguishes those who are bound from those who are free.[172] The difference between their states is merely conceptual.[173] Pure consciousness abides free of all such distinctions. Thus Bhagavatotpala, in his commentary on the *Stanzas*, repeatedly stresses that thought-constructs obscure consciousness and misguide the individual soul.[174] Those who are bound are convinced that they are dull witted, conditioned by *Karma*, sullied by their sin and helplessly impelled to action by some power beyond their control. He who manages to counter this conviction with its opposite achieves freedom.[175] He who considers himself to be free is free indeed, while he who thinks himself bound remains so. Thus at the highest level of realisation, as Abhinava says:

> Nothing new is achieved nor is that which in reality is unmanifest, revealed—[only] the idea is eradicated that the luminous being shines not.[176]

Nothing is impure, all is perfect, including Māyā and the diversity it engenders. To say that illusion exists and that ignorance must be eradicated implies that it has a separate existence apart from consciousness. If this is so, it has as little reality as the shadow of a shadow, but if not,then it must be consciousness itself. Thus, as Kallaṭa says, bondage, the binder and the bound are in fact one.[177] It is Śiva Himself Who freely obscures His own nature. Śiva binds Himself by Himself.[178] Concealing and revealing Himself, Śiva plays His timeless game.

At the Divine (*śāmbhava*) level of pure Śiva-consciousness, the Spanda yogi directly lays hold of the power inherent in his own conscious nature (*svabala*) which gives life to the psycho-physical organism and impels the senses and mind to action.[179] In this way every thought-construct, and with it the ego, is instantly annulled in the immediacy of the pure subjectivity that remains unaltered throughout every perception and state of consciousness. The same takes place at the Empowered level by attending to the recurrent activity—Spanda—of the subject, that is, the flux of awareness through the cyclic movement of the powers of consciousness.[180] By attending (*avadhāna*) to this movement the thought-constructs that emerge and subside in the course of perception are seen to be part of this universal process, and, in this way purified, are no longer binding. Thus, Kṣemarāja says that the Spanda teachings are concerned most directly with the Empowered Means.[181] The yogi who is always alert to discern the pulse of Spanda quickly realises his own authentic state of being (*nijaṃ bhāvam*).[182] He is then truly awake, not only literally, but also in the deeper sense that he is awake to his authentic nature, its power and activity. When attention (*avadhāna*) slackens, this movement takes place unconsciously and so the thought-constructs and perceptions generated through it appear to take on an autonomous existence of their own, just as happens when we dream.[183] The spontaneity of the movement that travels between subject and object and holds them together in the pure awareness of the universal subject's identity with his cosmic object devolves into the creative activity of waking and dreaming. Man, in other words, becomes a victim of his states of consciousness and the contents that they, by their very nature, generate within themselves.[184]

The Spanda teachings are not only concerned with the structure of thought and its functions, but also with the powers and properties of its vehicle, namely, speech. Speech issues out of consciousness, develops into thought to then become articulated sound. A focal point of Spanda doctrine is thus the role speech plays in the formation of thought-constructs and their purification. Although this takes place at all levels of practise below the Divine (*śāmbhava*), the Spanda teachings, meant as they are for advanced yogis, ignore the outer forms of spiritual discipline to concentrate on practise in the Empowered (*śākta*) psychic sphere (*cetas*) and what lies beyond it where speech is the pure inner awareness (*vimarśa*) of the light of consciousness. The Doctrine of Vibration identifies this, the highest level of speech (*parā vāc*), with the universal pulse of consciousness that resounds spontaneously within it as the inner flow of its own undifferentiated awareness.[185] Beyond the realms of language, it is the transcendental consciousness in which all language is rooted and pervades all that language denotes as its essential being. Utpaladeva writes:

> The Supreme Voice is consciousness. It is self-awareness spontaneously arisen, the highest freedom and sovereignty of the Supreme Lord. That pulsing radiance (*sphurattā*) is pure Being, unqualified by time and space. As the essence [of all things] it is said to be the Heart of the Supreme Lord.[186]

When the intention arises within consciousness to discern its own brilliance manifest in the world of denotations and denoted meanings, speech turns from the supreme transcendental level to that of immanence and assumes the form of a pure intuitive awareness (*pratibhā*) which perceives and comprehends its universal manifestation. This is the voice of intuition (*paśyantī*), which grasps the meaning inherent inwardly in all words and externally in all that they denote. Analogous to the non-discursive, instinctual knowledge animals possess, it is a pure generic perception not yet formed into language in which the act of denotation, its object and that which denotes it are indistinguishable. Illumined by the voice of intuition birds migrate in their due seasons, the cock crows at dawn and young mammals suck at the breast.[187] Infants similarly reflect and respond instinctively to their environment by virtue of this intuitive sense[188] and through it come to grasp the link between words and the objects they denote. As they learn to speak, they begin to form concepts and so the next two levels of speech develop. One is the outer corporeal speech (*vaikharī*) and the other the subtler, inner discourse (*antaḥ-saṃjalpa*) of thought that forms at the intermediate level (*madhyama*) where the ratiocinating mind stands between the higher levels of intuition and its outer verbal expression. In this way the development of speech in infancy reflects its progressive actualisation in every spoken word. A hymn to the Goddess quoted by Bhagavatotpala describes this process well:

> Therefore, O Supreme Goddess, the highest form of speech should be worshipped as the [universal] cause that establishes the existence of all things by insight (*niścaya*) into their nature (*artha*) brought about by their manifestation through the superimposition [of verbal designations].
>
> O Mother, insight into the true nature [of things] is nothing but the

act of intent of that [same speech], apart from which [speech itself and all that it expresses] could not attain to its own nature. Again, in that state [speech] is said to be the light of one's own nature. Free of division and succession it is attainable [only] by the yogi.

Then from the state of intent, O Śivā, speech [assumes] the nature of thought as the radiant pulse (*sphuraṇa*) of desire to speak of that which is in the domain of words. Then consisting of words, it bears a clearly expressed meaning, for if [speech] were not such, meaning could not be understood.[189]

Personal experience clearly proves that thought is invariably associated with speech.[190] Thought is a function of language. Through it we communicate to ourselves a mental image of the world about us and can construct complex ideas about ourselves. Language is the fabric from which our world of ideas is woven. Mental representation which orders the influx of sensation and presents us with a meaningful, picture of the world, memory, the elaboration of ideas and the shifting tides of emotion are all intimately connected with language and through it to the consciousness which underlies them. To think of language as nothing more than a system of denotation based on a commonly accepted convention (*saṅketa*) fails to fully account for its inherent power to convey meaning (*vācakaśakti*). In order to learn the convention we must be born with an innate ability to grasp meaning, and this ability is not itself learned nor found anywhere within the domain of convention. Lacking this ability we would be caught in an infinitely expanding system of denotation in which each element pointed to some other within it, without ever coming to rest anywhere. Unless we can couple the word 'jar' with the object it denotes, explaining that the word 'pot' is a synonym of the word 'jar' would leave us none the wiser.[191] The connection between word and meaning is only explicable if we postulate that it is an inherent property of the power of awareness to link one with the other. Language must be grounded in the pure cognitive awareness (*pramā*) of consciousness which stands beyond, and yet illumines, the sphere of experience we define and understand through the medium of language. As Abhinava says:

Someone may hear another person speak, but if his awareness (*pramā*) is obscured, he is unable to rise, unconscious as he is, to the level of the experiencing subject [who understands] what has been said. He only grasps the outer successive (sound) of what the other person says and thus can only repeat it as would a parrot. An understanding of its meaning presupposes that he has caught hold of his own power of awareness (*pramā*) by attaining the autonomy [of the conscious, universal subject].[192]

Outer, articulate speech consists of a series of ordered phonemic elements produced and combined by the vocal organs to form meaningful words. In order for this to be possible, these elements must also be grounded in consciousness (*pramā*). The articulated phonemes are merely outer, gross manifestations of the phonemic energies (*varṇagrāma*) held in a potential state within consciousness. This 'mass of sounds' (*śabdarāśi*) is the light of consciousness (*prakāśa*) which makes the universe manifest and contains all things within itself. In other words, it is the totality of consciousness expressed as the collective awareness symbolised by all the letters corresponding to the introverted subjectivity of Śiva Himself. The power through which this potential actualises itself into speech and the world of denotation is technically called '*Mātṛkā*'. It is the reflective awareness (*vimarśa*) and radiance (*sphurattā*) of the supreme subject—the 'mass of sounds' (*śabdarāśi*)—and the undivided wonder Śiva experiences when He contemplates the universe He gathers up into Himself in the form of countless words (*vācaka*) and their meanings (*vācya*).[193] *Mātṛkāśakti* is manifest in the second movement of consciousness after the primal vibration of the pure luminosity of the 'mass of sounds', as the state of pure potency which arises when its unsullied subjectivity begins to turn away from itself and is associated with faint traces of objectivity (*āmṛśya-cchāyā*).[194] *Mātṛkā* contains within itself the various aspects of objectivity that, although not yet manifest, are ready to issue forth. Thus this power, at one with Śiva, is called '*Mātṛkā*' because she is the mother (*mātṛkā*) of the universe that she contains within herself as does a pregnant woman her child.[195]

The circle of the powers of *Mātṛkā* (*mātṛkācakra*) consists of the phonemic energies contained in AHAM, the universal ego.[196] When grasped in its entirety at its source, these energies elevate the consciousness of the enlightened, but when split up and dispersed give rise to the obscuring forces (*kalā*) which lead the ignorant away from realisation. The fettered soul is ignorant of the pure egoity that is the source of speech and so it generates, through its powers, the many thought-constructs that deprive him of the awareness of unity and obscure Śiva's universal activity.[197] The *Stanzas on Vibration* declare:

> He who is deprived of his power by the forces of obscuration (*kalā*) and a victim of the powers arising from the mass of sounds (*śabdarāśi*) is called the fettered soul.[198] The powers [of speech] are always ready to obscure his true nature as no mental representation can arise that is not penetrated by speech.[199]

The rays of phonemic energies emanate from the light of Śiva, the 'mass of sounds' (*śabdarāśi*) in eight groups. They constitute the powers of the inner mental organ and the five senses, figuratively arranged in a circle around the sacred shrine (*pīṭha*) of *Mātṛkāśakti* who manifests externally as the body.[200] The eight classes and the names of the deities presiding over them are as follows:[201]

Gutturals	Brāhmaṇī	Intellect (*buddhi*)
Palatals	Māheśvarī	Ego (*ahaṅkāra*)
Cerebrals	Kaumārī	Mind (*manas*)
Dentals	Nārāyaṇī	Hearing
Labials	Vārāhī	Touch
Semivowels	Aindrī	Sight
Sibilants	Cāmuṇḍā	Taste
Vowels	Mahālakṣmī	Smell

The yogi who grasps the true nature of the power of *Mātṛkā* and its phonemic forces is liberated[202] by recognising that the activity of the senses and the discursive representations of the mind are in fact emanations of universal consciousness. Conversely, when ignorant, he is affected by its power in its multiple negative aspects known as *'Mahāghora'* ('greatly terrible') and, unable to rest within himself free of the sense of diversity, he is constantly disturbed by the flux of extroverted perceptions.[203] Abhinava explains:

> When the [phonemic energies] are not known to be [emanations of the Lord] they conceal the wonder (*camatkāra*) of consciousness which is the one essential non-discursive awareness [present throughout perception] and even in discursive thought. They obscure it with thought-constructs constituted by the diverse configurations of phonemes and syllables which [although also] a form of the deity [are no longer benevolent but] most terrible. Inducing doubt and fear, they engender the fettered soul's state, bound by the shackles of transmigration. . . . But once their true nature is understood correctly in this way, they bestow freedom in this very life. . . . This knowledge of their intimate being [at one with the absolute] consists of this, namely, that even in the midst of all these fluctuations, free at their inception of discursive representations, thought-constructs do not conjoin [individualised consciousness] with the wheel of energies consisting of the totality of phonemes, even though [these constructs] are coloured by the many diverse words generated by the aggregate of phonemes.[204]

Language has a powerful effect on us. A few words we may hear or read can inspire us with joy, fear or sadness, and the constant inner dialogue of thought arouses intense feelings within us. This power hidden in language, which binds us through the thought-constructs it generates, can also be used to free us of them by channeling it through Mantra. Mantric practice begins at the Individual (*āṇava*) level where Mantras are recited in consonance with the rising and falling away of the breath. In this way they are charged with the vibration (*spanda*) of consciousness and, in their turn, make consciousness vibrate. Serving as a means to concentration, they free the mind of discursive representations.[205] The word 'Mantra' is thus traditionally said to derive from the words *'manana'* and *'trāṇa'*. *'Manana'* literally means 'reflection'. In this context it denotes the continuous thought or awareness of Mantra which is universal, omniscient consciousness (*viśvavijñāna*). *'Trāṇam'* means to 'save' and Mantra 'saves' us by freeing the mind from the bondage of transmigration.[206] Mantras thus serve to generate a higher level of consciousness by a process of *'manana'* which the texts describe as 'a progressive heightening of the reflective awareness which is the aesthetic rapture that threads through each state of being'.[207] As Maheśvarānanda puts it:

> Reflection (*manana*) on one's own omnipresent consciousness (*nijavibhava*) and protection from the fear of one's own limitations is the undefinable intuition (*anubhūti*) which has absorbed all dualistic thoughts and is the meaning of Mantra.[208]

Although Mantras may convey an intelligible meaning, they are not bound to a convention (*saṅketa*) as is common speech. The 'language' of Mantras is not concerned with external objects. It is language directed inward, deriving its energy from the supreme power of consciousness into which it ultimately involutes, transcending the outer and reverting to the inner. The Mantra, like the visualised image of a deity, is a symbol which, precisely because it has no assigned connotation as has the literal sign we use in propositions, is capable of being understood in more significant ways, so that its meanings are fraught with vital and sentient experience. The Mantra opens a new avenue of thought which becomes truer to itself than does any other type of thinking which has found its limits in devitalised symbols or signs that can be used to signify anything without themselves being significant. "Mantras are pure," writes Rājānaka Rāma, "in the sense that they are not tainted by a conventionally accepted meaning (*vācya*) and transcend the usual form of awareness created by reflection on the phonemes [conjoined to form words]."[209]

The essence of Mantra is an experience entirely free of objective relations. It is the pure power of awareness directed at its own nature and thus free of objectivity and eternal.[210] It frees us of the desire to attend to things temporal by redirecting attention to the heart of consciousness which thus assimilates thought back into itself and stills the agitation (*kṣobha*) occasioned by object-centred awareness.[211] In this way the yogi rises from the partial perceptions individualised by thought, to the universal perception free of thought-constructs. By remembering (*smaraṇa*) and rightly enunciating the Mantra, he attains a level of reflective awareness in which all things are experienced as one with his own nature.[212] Thus Mantra has meaning and serves a purpose (*artha*) to the degree in which it is possible to intuit through it the power of consciousness which gives it, and all things, being. The outer forms of the Mantra are expressions of the powers experienced inwardly.[213] At root, the Mantra represents the pure signification of all possible sentences and words relating to the world of particulars. It enshrines a form of undivided, non-discursive intuition necessarily represented in parts (as the phonemic body of the Mantra) but whose full significance is transcendental and includes all possible forms of verbal expression.[214] The yogi who repeats his Mantra undistractedly achieves the power to understand the ultimate significance of the formula he is repeating. Thus understood, it awakens in him a state of contemplative absorption at the Empowered (*śākta*) level in which he experiences the pulsing power of consciousness that emits from itself, in progressively grosser stages, thoughts and articulated words along with their meaning. Abhinava writes:

> A waterwheel moves a series of machines connected to it and can set them into operation by the force of its unified impulse. In the same way, by the power of the one continuous act of awareness (*anusaṃdhāna*) which corresponds to the incessant arising of Mantra, the deities of all Mantras, at one with them, become automatically (*ayatnāt*) propitious.[215]

The recitation of Mantra starts at the Individual level in consonance with the movement of the vital breath. To be effective, however, the Mantra and its component syllables and words must resonate with the force of awareness. They must be energised with the pulsation (*spanda*) of consciousness and so penetrate into the absorption of the Empowered level of practice. At that level the pure thought of the Mantra gradually takes over from the impure and dispersed thought of the world of objects, wrongly perceived to be severed from consciousness and so leads the adept to the Divine level where the ultimate source of its power resides.[216] This vitality is Spanda, the universal pulse (*sāmānyaspanda*) of awareness residing in the heart of consciousness at the supreme level of speech (*parā vāc*) as all-embracing 'I' consciousness.[217] 'I' consciousness (*AHAṂ*) is the Great Mantra eternally manifest as the wonder inspired by the light of consciousness. The Mantra AHAṂ which gives life to every living being contains all the powers of the letters within itself; giving rise to the entire universe, it is present at the very beginning of manifestation where it is established in pure consciousness free of time and space.[218] Kṣemarāja explains:

> All-embracing 'I-ness' (*pūrṇāhantā*) is the mistress of all the letters from [the first] 'A' to [the last] 'Kṣa' which, as the absolute (*anuttara*) power of unstruck sound (*anāhata*), it contains and encapsulates. Thus it is a pure immutable awareness even though it has absorbed into itself every cycle of creation and destruction in the play of the Wheel of Energies constituting the unfolding cosmic order (*ṣaḍadhvan*) of countless words and all they denote. It is the supreme level of speech, the great unspoken Mantra which, eternally manifest, is the life of all beings. Here [in the Spanda school] it is called the vibration of the Lord because it unfolds pulsating within one's own being as does the movement of this divine universe.[219]

Mantric energy is not to be sought in the actual sound or form of the Mantra directly. The ordering of its phonemic constituents (*varṇa-sanniveśa*) is merely a channel through which the yogi can tap the energy of his own consciousness. The Mantra should be recited with the full force of awareness. It can only be effective when associated with the adept's consciousness.[220] The Mantra and the reciter of Mantra must be rooted in the one conscious reality, otherwise the Mantra can bear no fruit.[221] As Rājānaka Rāma puts it, Mantras are a mere flux of phonemic sounds, powerless to bend even a blade of grass unless the adept makes contact with Śiva's plane of oneness.[222] The imperishable power of awareness he attains thus is the very life of Mantras; without it they are as fruitless as autumn clouds.[223] Through this power consciousness emanates and withdraws the countless Mantras[224] to gratify the wishes of each adept and bestow upon him the well-deserved fruits of his practice. Mantras are thus full of the knowledge and action[225] they derive from the Spanda energy of universal consciousness through which they are empowered to perform their function.[226] The vitality of Spanda is the ground of all Mantras. It is the power by which they emerge from the emptiness of consciousness and are drawn back into it, along with the adept's mind, when they cease to exist as articulate sound.[227] They are Śiva Himself, one with the universal vibration of consciousness through which they are created and in which they lead the yogi to union with Śiva. The awakened realise that the power hidden in Mantras is the vibration of Śiva's pure subjectivity (*upalabdhṛtā-*

mātra) which is both the transcendental inner nature of all things and the immanent awareness that threads through (*anusyūta*) all the planes of consciousness.[228] Rājānaka Rāma explains:

> The vitality of Mantra (*mantravīrya*) is Śiva's power, the undivided reality of Mantra and mind (*cetas*) both when they arise and when they fall away. It emerges from Śiva both as Mantra and as the adept's mind (*citta*) in the form of phonemes and thought-constructs (*saṅkalpa*). The Mantric power manifest [this way] is capable of producing only limited (*niyata*) results for those yogis who have not come in contact with the power of their own nature. However, when the yogi achieves a firm insight into his authentic identity, all Mantras can do all things [for him] because he knows how they arise and fall away.[229]

So while Mantra at the Divine level of practice (*śāmbhavopāya*) is the silent consciousness of 'I', at the Empowered and Individual levels it serves as a means to purify thought.[230] It leads the adept in stages along the rungs of the ladder of consciousness, ascending which he abandons the lower stages of conditioned awareness to reach the highest state of Śiva-hood, dense with the light of consciousness.[231] Thus the supreme form of Mantric energy destroys the obstacles to enlightenment set up by impure thought and establishes individual consciousness in the true universal thought of pure Being.[232] Filled with this energy Mantras are like rays that emanate from the all-consuming fire of consciousness, depriving thought-constructs of their essence.[233]

The aesthetic rapture (*camatkāra*) the yogi experiences increases to the degree in which the uncreated reality of this pure awareness (*pramā*) abounds[234] and the power of his intuition is heightened as the conventions of the day to day, spoken language are immersed and absorbed in the supernal (*amāyīya*) energy of the phonemes of the Mantra.[235] The mind of the adept is freed of the constraints imposed upon its attention (*abhisaṃdhyupādhi*) and so, free of thought-constructs, merges with the silence of consciousness together with the Mantra.[236] The *Stanzas on Vibration* declare:

> Seizing that strength (*bala*), Mantras, endowed with the power of omniscience, perform their functions, as do the senses of the embodied. It is there alone that they, quiescent and stainless, dissolve along with the adept's mind and so partake of Śiva's nature.[237]

At this stage any thought the yogi may conceive is vibrant and full of energy because, having thus absorbed all objectivity into itself, his mind is one with Mantra.[238] So although in the beginning individual Mantras may effectively correspond to distinct levels of consciousness and stages in the cosmic process, once the yogi has ascended through the planes of power by merging with the vibration of the Mantras at each level, he emerges into a state where he enjoys a direct awareness of his own nature. Śiva's power, which determines the nature and function of all things, (*niyatiśakti*) is transcended and the yogi's own mind, discovered to be the source and essence of all Mantras, can now implement any one of them to achieve anything he wishes, including liberation.[239]

The Individual Means (Āṇavopāya)

As Kṣemarāja points out, none of the practices taught in the *Stanzas on Vibration* belong to the Individual Means[240] and so it does not, strictly speaking, concern Spanda doctrine, if that is, we consider the *Stanzas* to be the basic text of the Spanda school.[241] From Kṣemarāja's point of view, however, the third section of the *Aphorisms of Śiva* (*Śivasūtra*), which is both the last and most extensive, is largely an exposition of this category of practice.[242] The *Stanzas* and *Aphorisms* have been traditionally linked together and so, even though we feel that they should be distinguished insofar as the *Stanzas* rather than the *Aphorisms* teach the Doctrine of Vibration as such, we are nonetheless justified in referring to the *Aphorisms* as its major source. Our exposition of the Individual Means will therefore be largely based on Kṣemarāja's interpretation of the third section of *Aphorisms* and we will present it, as he does, as an exposition of a possible mystical journey of individualised (*āṇava*) consciousness to realisation. We follow Kṣemarāja because he understood the practise taught in the *Aphorisms* in these terms, thereby not only illustrating for us how it fits into this scheme but also how he understood the basic categories of practice and their relationship to one another.

According to Kṣemarāja, the first *Aphorism* of each section of the *Śivasūtra* characterises the condition and nature of the Self at the corresponding three levels of practice. In other words, they indicate the yogi's basic state at each level in terms of his self-identification. This identification corresponds to his existential condition as a degree of self-realisation in the process leading to the authentic self-awareness of the liberated. The very first *Aphorism* starts directly with this, the highest state, by declaring that the Self is pure, dynamic and universal consciousness (*caitanya*).[243] This is true for the yogi who has awakened to his authentic nature at the Divine (*śāmbhava*) level of being. At the

Individual (*āṇava*) level, however, the situation has changed. In this sphere of consciousness the intermediate processes of discernment, analysis and classification of perceptions, which bridge the gap in the flow of awareness from the universal subject to a specific object of knowledge, appear to take over the status of the perceiving subjectivity which underlies them. The universal Self recedes into the background as a pure, undefinable awareness, and the individual ego, consisting of the perceptions, thoughts and emotions generated by the contact between the universal perceiver and the perceived, emerges in the juncture between them. Thus at this level, as the *Aphorisms* say, the Self is the mind.[244] This is the Self which moves (*atati*) from one state of being to another, from one body to the next carrying with it subtle traces left behind by its sensory and mental activity. Together these are said to constitute, and be caused by, the subtle body technically called the 'City of Eight' (*puryaṣṭaka*) with which consciousness is identified and due to which it is subject to the constant alterations of pleasure, pain and inertia. The *Stanzas* teach:

> [The soul] is bound by the City of Eight (*puryaṣṭaka*) that resides in the mind, intellect and ego and consists of the arising of the [five] subtle elements [of sensory perception]. He helplessly suffers worldly pleasure and pain (*bhoga*) which consists of the arising of mental representations born of that [City of Eight] and so its existence subjects him to transmigration.[245]

Whereas consciousness itself is the subject who practises the Divine Means (*Śāmbhavopāya*), the subject who practises the Individual Means is the mind. Unlike the Empowered Means, however, the mind is not directed inwards onto itself. At the Empowered level, enlivened by the direct intuition (*pratibhā*) consciousness has of its own nature, mind ceases to function merely in the paradigmatic, formative manner which gives rise to mental representations, but operates instead as the subtle introverted activity of reflective awareness (*vimarśa*), the power of consciousness (*śakti*).[246] This activity, as we have seen, is the essence of Mantra[247] which, independent of the senses, is no longer restricted in any way. At the Individual level, however, the creative powers of consciousness reflected through the extroverted mind are greatly attenuated. All that remains is the power to form thought-constructs and make determined resolutions (*saṅkalpa*) which go on to issue through the body into outer action to make the private creations of the mind apparent to others.[248]

The Individual Means, therefore, deals with the objectively perceived contents of consciousness and hence with the individual subject as a composite aggregate of objective elements, ranging from the subtle life force (*prāṇa*) to the physical body[249] and its outer environment. The practices belonging to this Means are thus of two types. One is concerned with the individual subject who resides in, and as, the psycho-physical organism; the other with external reality.[250] What this implies essentially is that practice at this level is not concerned as much with the will or cognitive consciousness as are the other two Means, but with the power of action applied, in the context of the practice taught in the *Aphorisms*, to the spiritual activity of Yoga. According to Kṣemarāja, the Individual Means culminates in the Empowered state and hence leads to the levels of practice beyond it.[251] This is possible because, despite their differences, there is an essential similarity between them. The aim of both the Individual and Empowered Means is to purify the discursive representations of differentiated perceptions (*vikalpasaṃskāra*)[252] and so lead the yogi to the expanded (*vikasita*) consciousness of the Divine (*śāmbhava*) state. The other levels of practice therefore both sustain and complement it. The activity of individual consciousness can be fully perfected only when it operates through the flow of the conative and cognitive powers which together constitute the pure activity of universal consciousness beyond all means (*anupāya*).

In fact, according to Kṣemarāja, all three soteriological types function together in various ways, their corresponding states representing dimensions of the same experience. For example, the upsurge of consciousness (*udyama*) which is the supreme, illuminating intuition (*parapratibhā*) of the Divine state (*śāmbhavāvastha*)[253] is concomitant with the gathering together of all the powers of consciousness in the Empowered state.[254] The Divine Means, in other words, leads to the experience of Power (*śakti*) which in its turn, when fully affirmed, marks the attainment of a permanent contemplative consciousness (*turīyātīta*) at the Divine level which persists unaltered in every state of consciousness. Consequently, Kṣemarāja concludes his exposition of the first section of the *Aphorisms* which exemplifies, according to him, the Divine Means, by saying:

> Thus we have explained the first expansion which starts with [the Aphorism] 'the Self is pure dynamic consciousness' and expounds the nature of the realisation (*prathana*) attained through the Divine Means. It is the intuitive insight (*samāpatti*) of Bhairava's nature which is, as we have said, the upsurge of consciousness that quells all bondage, namely, the ignorance of that freedom which makes it manifest. Transforming all things into the nectar of one's own innate bliss, it bestows every yogic accomplishment (*siddhi*) including mystic absorption in the vitality of Mantra, the highest of them all. Accordingly, we have, in the course of this exposition, explained the nature of *Śakti* in order to show that the

Divine nature (*śāmbhavarūpa*) possesses [every] power.[255]

Another way in which the Means are related to one another is illustrated by the recurrence of the same Aphorism in different sections of the *Śivasūtra* which indicates, according to Kṣemarāja, that the same practice belongs to more than one Means. Both times this happens, the *Aphorism* appears first in the section dealing with the Divine Means and then recurs in that concerned with the Individual Means.[256] In one case, Kṣemarāja tells us this is because practice at the Divine level requires no effort whereas at the Individual level, the yogi must exert himself to achieve the same state that at the Divine level dawns spontaneously.[257] At the Empowered level also, as the *Śivasūtra* says, 'effort achieves the goal'.[258] Here, however, because as the Empowered Means is, according to Kṣemarāja, predominantly concerned with the contemplation (*anusaṃdhi*) of the vitality of Mantra,[259] the effort exerted is that required to bring the practice of Mantra to fulfillment. It is, as Kṣemarāja says, 'the spontaneous effort exerted to grasp the initial expansion of intention to apply oneself to the contemplation [of Mantra]. It is this exertion which wins the favour of the gods of Mantra and identifies the adept with them.'[260]

The second case of the same practice being taught in different sections of the *Aphorisms* concerns the realisation of the Fourth State of contemplative consciousness (*turīya*) in the other three states of waking, dreaming and deep sleep. At the Divine level this takes place by 'violently digesting' (*haṭhapāka*) the three states in the Fourth. At the Individual level the Fourth state is first experienced at the junctures between the other three states and then induced gradually to spread out from these Centres to pervade the other states like oil extending slowly through a piece of cloth.[261] The difference in this case between the level of practice is not only that at the Divine level it reaches fulfillment spontaneously, but it is also sudden and complete, leading directly to the liberated state of consciousness Beyond the Fourth (*turīyātīta*).[262] At the Individual level, however, practice is gradual and even when the yogi manages to rise to states of contemplation, he must take care not to fall to lower levels of consciousness. Indeed, until the yogi attains the sudden and direct realisation of perfect enlightenment, whatever be his state of consciousness or level of practice, he is bound to rise and fall because his contemplative state is necessarily transitory (*kadācitka*) however long it may last.

The yogi is more prone to these ups and downs the lower his basic state of consciousness. Consequently, the last section of the *Śivasūtra* repeatedly instructs the yogi not only how to rise to higher levels of consciousness and maintain them, but also in what way he is liable to fall from them and how to regain them.[263] Kṣemarāja stresses that the rise from one level of consciousness to another is marked by the transition from a lower Means to a higher. Conversely, a fall from the higher level to the lower entails practice of a lower Means. The measure of the yogi's level of consciousness, and that which sustains him in it allowing him to progress further, is his *attentiveness* (*avadhāna*) to the higher realities he experiences in the more elevated states. Thus the last *Aphorism* of the second section of the *Śivasūtra* warns the yogi that if his pure awareness (*śuddhavidyā*) of his oneness with all things slackens, he will fall from his awakened state to dream the dream of thought-constructs.[264] From Kṣemarāja's point of view this means that the negligent yogi must now resort to the Individual Means described in the next section to return to his former, higher Empowered practice in which he experiences this oneness.[265]

Kṣemarāja expounds practice at the Individual level, as he sees it in the *Aphorisms*, as extending from one Means to the next. For example, practice at the Individual level diverts the flow of the vital breath (*prāṇa*) from its more usual course and induces it to enter the Central Channel (*suṣumnā*) along which it rises as a pure conscious energy (technically called '*kuṇḍalinī*'). This leads the yogi to the Empowered state in which he enjoys the pure awareness of unity. If he manages to make it truly his own and it becomes his basic state of being, he enters the Divine plane (*śāmbhavapada*) of identity with Śiva.[266] The Individual Means is both a point of departure to higher levels of practice and the level to which the yogi returns if he falls. Thus although the practices taught in the last section of the *Aphorisms* may belong to any one of the three Means, they are collectively treated as part of the Individual Means because they start from it and because it is the yogi's abiding standby if he falls.[267]

Let us turn now to the basic practice at the Individual level, as Kṣemarāja understands it. This is essentially Yoga. According to the Classical Yoga system taught by Patañjali in the *Aphorisms of Yoga* (*Yogasūtra*), Yoga is defined as 'the quelling of the fluctuations of the mind' (*cittavṛttinirodha*).[268] The aim is to sever the spiritual essence of the Person (*puruṣa*) from the defiling materiality of Nature (*prakṛti*), even though the word 'Yoga' means to 'unite' or 'yoke together.' Here, however, Yoga combines both union and cessation. It is the act (*kriyā*) of removing the latent traces (*vāsanā*) of differentiated perceptions (*vikalpa*) born of the impurities (*mala*) which contract consciousness.[269] This is achieved by uniting all the elements of experience (*tattva*) together in the wholeness of the activity of consciousness. As Jayaratha explains:

> 'The [wise] consider Yoga to be the union of one thing with another,'[270] thus, in accord with this dictum, Yoga is the [act] of uniting [all] the metaphysical principles together within consciousness. . . .[271]

Kṣemarāja seeks initially to establish the best form of Yoga for the yogi to practice at the Individual level. His sources are two Tantras he knew well and considered to be amongst the most important, namely, *The Tantra of* (*Śiva's Third*) *Eye* (*Netratantra*) and *The Tantra of the Liberated Bhairava* (*Svacchandabhairavatantra*). The basic model is that of the Eight-limbed Yoga (*aṣṭāṅga*) taught by Patañjali which consists of:

> 1) The five restraints (*yama*), namely, abstention from violence (*ahiṃsā*), falsehood (*satya*), dishonesty (*asteya*), sexual intercourse (*brahmacarya*) and desire for more than the essential (*aparigraha*).[272]
> 2) The five disciplines (*niyama*), namely, cleanliness (*śauca*), contentment (*santoṣa*), austerity (*tapas*), study (*svādhyāya*) and reverence for God (*Īśvarapraṇidhāna*).[273]
> 3) Posturing of the body (*āsana*) in a manner conducive to the practice of meditation and physical health.[274]
> 4) Regulation of the breath (*prāṇāyāma*).[275]
> 5) Withdrawal of the senses from their objects (*pratyāhāra*).[276]
> 6) Focusing of attention (*dhāraṇā*).[277]
> 7) Meditation (*dhyāna*), that is, steady, uninterrupted concentration.[278]
> 8) Contemplation (*samādhi*).

Kṣemarāja rejects Patañjali's system because he believes it to be a form of Yoga that can, at best, lead only to limited yogic attainments (*mitasiddhi*).[279] In the *Netratantra*, however, Śiva teaches a different, higher form of the Eight Limbs of Yoga which lead to perfect penetration into the supreme, transcendental principle[280] of which the *Netratantra* says:

> Speech cannot express, nor the eye see, the ears hear, or the nose smell, the tongue taste, the skin touch or the mind conceive that which is eternal. Free of all colour and flavour, endowed with all colours and flavours, it is beyond the senses and cannot be objectively perceived. O goddess, those yogis who attain it become immortal gods! By great practice and supreme dispassion . . . one attains Śiva, the supreme imperishable, eternal and unchanging reality.[281]

A necessary preliminary of all Tantric Yoga is a process technically called the 'purification of the elements' (*bhūtaśuddhi*), through which the body is homologized with the macrocosm and so made a fit vessel for the pure, conscious presence of the Deity within it. Kṣemarāja equates this with the meditation (*dhyāna*) which, according to the *Mālinīvijayatantra*, characterises the Individual Means.[282] In order to practice this meditation the yogi must visualise the dissolving away of all the forces in the body.[283] There are two ways in which this can be done. The first is called 'the contemplation of dissolution' (*layabhāvanā*). Through it the progressive differentiation of consciousness from its causal, pre-cosmic form to its phenomenal manifestation is reversed. As the *Vijñānabhairava* teaches: "One should meditate on the All in the form of the Paths of the world-orders etc. considered in their gross, subtle and supreme forms until, at the end, the mind dissolves away."[284]

Mediated by consciousness, the macrocosm rests in the microcosm which is emitted along with it successively in the emptiness of the individual subject, vital breaths, mind, psychic nerves (*nāḍī*), senses and external body.[285] The yogi reproduces this process by visualising the totality of reality including the world-systems, metaphysical principles and cosmic forces along with the Mantras, letters and syllables which represent them, as arising successively throughout the psycho-physical body so as to constitute it. Deployed in this way they form the Cosmic Path along which the yogi ascends, absorbing as he does so, the lower elements into the higher, thus strengthening and extending his unifying awareness (*anusaṃdhāna*) of the configuration of the Path. Thus, moving from the gross elements constituting the outer physical body, to pure sensations (*tanmātra*), then to the senses and mind back to their primordial source, the yogi rises from the embodied subjectivity of the waking state to the Fourth State (*turīya*) of contemplation where he is one with the pervasive intent which initiates the creative vision of consciousness. Abhinava writes:

> Once [the yogi] has known [this] Path in its completeness, he must then dissolve it into the deities who sustain it and these successively into the body, breath, mind [and emptiness] as before, and all these into his own consciousness. Once this is full and an object of constant worship, it destroys, like the fire at the end of time, the ocean of transmigration.[286]

Thus, the second method Kṣemarāja teaches to dissolve away the diversity of sensory, mental and physical energies into the unity of consciousness is a meditation on the Fire of Consciousness (*dahacintā*) which the yogi visualises as burning away all division. At the Divine level (*śāmbhavopāya*) the yogi witnesses the sudden and violent withdrawal of all objectivity into the pure ego (*aham*), like the pouring of fuel into a raging fire.[287] He does not need to visualise this process but merely attend to it with a passive, receptive attitude. At the Individual level the yogi must exert his imagination to induce this process and so rise to the Divine level through the Empowered. The *Vijñānabhairava* teaches:

> Visualise the fortress [of your body] burning with the Fire of Time (*kālāgni*) risen from the Abode of Time; then at the end peace manifests.[288]

The Fire of Time (*kālāgni*) resides underneath the hell worlds at the bottom of the Cosmic Egg (*brahmāṇḍa*). It issues from Ananta—a form of Śiva who presides over the lower regions. He floats on a boat in the causal waters supporting the Egg, his mind all the while fixed on Bhairava. The flames of the Fire of Time rise up to the hell-worlds heating them intensely[289] and radiate its energy throughout the universe. At the end of each period of creation the flames rise higher and destroy the old cosmic order to make room for a new one.[290] At the microcosmic level the yogi reproduces this process by mentally placing the letters of the alphabet, in the prescribed order, on the limbs of his body starting from the left toe to the top of the head. As his attention progresses upwards, he visualises the Fire of Time moving with it in such a way that his bodily consciousness, together with the universe of differentiated perceptions, is gradually burnt away leaving in its place the white ashes of the undivided light of consciousness.

Kṣemarāja considers this meditation (*dhyāna*) to be a limb of a programme of yogic practice at the Individual level[291] of which the remaining limbs are as follows:[292]

Posture (Āsana). The yogi fixes his attention on the centre between the inhaled and exhaled breath, absorbing in this way the flux of his awareness into the unfolding power of knowledge which rises initially as the upward flowing breath (*udānaprāṇa*) in the Central Channel (*suṣumnā*) between the other two breaths. The *Prāṇic* aspect of this flow disappears as it moves upward and the yogi experiences the spontaneous rise of the omniscience of consciousness within himself. The mind reverts back to its original, pervasive conscious nature and understands the infinite fact of Śiva's omnipresence. This is the firm seat (*āsana*) upon which the yogi sits to practice.

Regulation of the Breath (Prāṇāyāma). To regulate the movement of the breath, the yogi must first cleanse the right and left channels of the ascending and descending breath by blocking the left nostril while exhaling and the right while inhaling a few times. This ensures that the movement of the breath is firm and evenly distributed. Next, without attempting to control it in any way, he attends to the flow of his breathing. As the mind becomes steadier and in closer harmony with the rhythm of its movement, the duration of each inhalation and exhalation gradually alters until they become equal. At this stage they unite and merge in the upward flowing current of vitality in the Central Channel (*Suṣumnā*). This is when true Prāṇāyāma begins. The yogi's mind pure and tranquil, he returns, as it were, to a prenatal state and the external breathing cycle is internalised, so that it no longer moves through the lungs but passes directly to the universal source of vitality. The yogi, now at the Empowered level of practice, experiences this movement as travelling from the Heart centre upwards to a point distant twelve fingers above the head where it merges in the void of consciousness. Free of its outer gross form, the breath moves freely through the Central Channel and soon transcends even this subtle movement to become one with the supreme vibration of consciousness. In this way, the yogi's breathing becomes one with the spontaneous rise and fall of energy from the bosom of the absolute. Abhinava quotes the *Tantra of the Line of Heroes* (*Vīrāvalītantra*) as saying:

> When, by constantly merging the mind in Śiva, Who is the pure conscious nature, the Sun and Moon [of the two breaths] have dissolved away and the Sun of Life, which is one's own consciousness, has reached the twelve-finger space, this is termed liberation. Breath control [at this stage] serves no useful purpose. Breath control which merely inflicts pain on the body is not to be practised. He who knows this secret is both himself liberated and liberates others.[293]

Focusing of Attention (Dhāraṇā). Attention is fixed on the psychic centres in the body corresponding to the five gross elements. In this way the vital breath is successively directed to these centres from the Heart of consciousness to refresh and stimulate their activity. First it moves to the Earth centre in the throat which regulates the firmness of the bones and flesh of the body; then to the Water centre in the glottis responsible for the balance of the bodily fluids. After this it travels to the navel which is the Fire centre dealing with digestion and anabolesis and catabolesis in general. It then moves to the Wind centre in the toe of the left foot which governs the movement of gases to and from the cells via the circulatory system. When the yogi has thus achieved control over these forces, the breath rises from the Heart to the top of the head and he becomes master of the Ether element and so attains every yogic power.[294]

Meditation (Dhyāna). The highest form of meditation stills the flux of the qualities (*guṇa*) and induces the mind into a state of contemplative absorption. The object of this meditation is the supreme and pervasive divinity of the pure subject whose true nature is known to none but himself alone (*svasaṃvedya*). The yogi attains him by merging into the constant flow of awareness that streams into the Light which illumines his own nature.

Contemplation (Samādhi). The yogi rises to the level of contemplation when the awareness he has of himself and the things around him become one and he realises his own identity with Śiva, the sole reality.[295]

The aim of this Yoga in all its phases is to achieve the Fourth State of consciousness (*turīya*) beyond the three states of waking, dreaming and deep sleep and to then ultimately reach the liberated state Beyond the Fourth (*turīyātīta*). These five states correspond to: (a) Śiva's activity (*vyāpāra*), that is, His power of action; (b) Śiva's Lordship (*adhipātya*), which is His power of knowledge; (c) the absence of these two, which corresponds to Śiva's power of will; (d) His exertion (*prerakatva*), which contains all the cycles of creation and destruction and, (e) the rest Śiva enjoys in His own nature, which is His power of consciousness.[296] The first three states, when divorced from the last two, belong to the sphere of transmigratory existence. The Fourth and Beyond the Fourth on the other hand are higher, supramundane (*alaukika*) states of consciousness in which the yogi enjoys bliss and repose (*viśrānti*) in his own nature by penetrating (*samāveśa*) into the universal consciousness of the Self, through which he ultimately becomes liberated (*jīvanmukta*). Beyond the Fourth is the state of awareness Paramaśiva Himself enjoys when duality has entirely disappeared and everything is realised to be one with consciousness. The Fourth is the state of awareness of the yogi who, catching hold of the pure subjectivity (*upalabdhṛtā*) flowing through the lower three states, is still actively eliminating his sense of duality. While the former is the supreme subject as 'I' consciousness (*aham*), the latter is the pure awareness (*pramā*) or 'I-ness' (*ahantā*) of the subject which encompasses the lower states, giving them life and uniting them together.[297] As such, the Fourth State is the reflective awareness of one's own nature shining in all three states at one with them.[298] The fact that we recall that we slept well is proof that this state of consciousness persists even in deep sleep. Indeed, if the flow of *Turīya* could somehow be brought to a halt, all the other states of consciousness would come to an end in the absence of the pure subjectivity which makes them, and their contents, manifest.[299] The states of waking, dreaming and deep sleep correspond to the form of awareness consciousness assumes when it it predominantly manifest as the object, means of knowledge and individual subject, respectively. *Turīya* is the pure awareness (*pramā*) that both transcends them and merges them all into itself.[300] As such, it appears as the triad of deed, means and agent in the pure act (*vyāpāra*) of consciousness unsullied by any outer reality.[301] Abhinava explains:

> (*Turīya*) transcends the three aspects of 'form', 'sight' and 'I' consisting as it does of the pure act of 'seeing'; therefore any means [by which this state could be realised] has merely a [provisional] instrumental value. It is, in other words, pure subjectivity of the nature of absolute freedom, independent of all external means. This is the state of consciousness called *Turīya*, luminous with its own light.[302]

Turīya is thus not just a psychological state but the supreme creative power (*parā śakti*) of consciousness, the Goddess (*saṃviddevī*) Who generates and withdraws the entire universe of subject, object and means of knowledge. In the *Heart of Recognition* Kṣemarāja explains:

> Whenever the extroverted [conscious] nature rests within itself, external objectivity is withdrawn [and consciousness] is established in the inner abode of peace which threads through the flux of awareness in every [externally] emanated [state]. Thus *Turīyā*, the Goddess of Consciousness, is the union of creation, persistence and destruction. She emanates every individual [cycle] of creation and withdraws it. Eternally full [of all things] and [yet] void [of diversity] She is both and yet neither, shining radiantly as non-successive [consciousness] alone.[303]

The yogi is fully absorbed in this state of consciousness and takes possession of its power when he is able to rise from contemplation (*samādhi*) carrying with him the abiding awareness of Turīya throughout his waking, dreaming and deep sleep. When he achieves this constantly, he continues to experience these states individually, but they no longer obscure the insight (*pratibhā*) he has acquired because he realises that they are all aspects of the bliss of Turīya. Thus, while the common man calls this state the 'Fourth' (*turīya*) because he cannot experience it directly and knows only that it is beyond the other three, the yogi calls it 'Beyond Form' (*rūpātīta*) because it transcends the detachment of the state of deep sleep which, devoid of objective content, is the naked 'form' of the individual subject tending towards the fullness of consciousness. Those who are on the path of knowledge (*jñānin*) call it the 'Whole' (*pracaya*) because, in this state, they see the entire universe gathered together in one place.[304] 'Supra-mental Awareness' (*manonmanā*) is the name given to the experience of Turīya in the waking state. The yogi in this state moves and lives in the world of waking experience free of all disturbing thoughts while abiding in the transcendental silence beyond the activities of the mind. 'Infinite' is the name of the experience of Turīya while dreaming because, free of the limitations imposed upon the body by time and space, the yogi enjoys the unlimited expanse of the Self. When *Turīya* is experienced in deep sleep, the yogi's state is called 'All things' (*sarvārtha*) because in it he discovers his freedom from limitations in this, the most contracted state of human consciousness. The yogi who manages to maintain *Turīya*-consciousness comes to experience the three states of waking, dreaming and deep sleep as the constant flow of the bliss of consciousness in which all traces of the relative distinction between these states and their contents is eradicated.[305] Following the stream of *Turīya* to its highest level (*parā kāṣṭhā*), he reaches the state Beyond the Fourth (*turīyātīta*), which is the universal consciousness (*caitanya*) of the Self. Here the yogi comes to rest within his own nature. Plunged in the vast, waveless ocean of the consciousness and bliss (*cidānanda*) of the state Beyond the Fourth, the yogi becomes Śiva,[306] the Free One (*svacchanda*), and thus wanders freely, practising the Yoga of Freedom.[307]

Kṣemarāja equates the Fourth State with the pure (*śuddha*), innate (*sahaja*) knowledge that one's own conscious nature is all things. It is the Supra-mental State (*unmanā*) in which Śiva's pervasive presence is experienced[308] once the Yoga practised at the Individual level attains fruition at the Empowered.[309] What the yogi must do, once consciousness is elevated to grasp the Fourth State, is make it constant. He must forcefully lay hold of it within himself and not release his grip until it becomes permanent. Then he travels 'Beyond the Fourth' to enlightenment.[310] Before this ultimate attainment the yogi inevitably falls. The forces operating within consciousness that limit and obscure it throw him down whenever they possibly can. The only way the yogi can defend himself against them is to maintain a constant attentive awareness of the Fourth State.[311] He falls when he is distracted but when he attends carefully to his pure conscious nature, he realises that every aspect of his state of being, including the forces that lead him astray, are one with the pulsing flux of his own consciousness and so cannot affect him.

These powers, which are the energies of *Mātṛkā* we have already discussed, are not the only obstacles the yogi must overcome. He must, for example, also resist the temptation to rest content with the miraculous yogic powers (*siddhi*) he acquires in the course of his spiritual development. Again to do this he must practice Yoga. Similarly, in order to pervade the Fourth State gradually through the other states in the manner proper to practice at the Individual level, the method is the same. He must practise the higher yoga of the Tantras which, turning his mind inwards and freeing it from discursive representations, allows him to penetrate into the Supreme Principle.[312] Once the yogi has attained this contemplative state, his main problem is to make it permanent. In the introverted state the gross external movement of the breath is suspended and with it the activity of the intellect, mind, individualised consciousness, powers of the senses and the ego.[313] When the yogi rises out of this state, he is liable to fall again into the lower order of creation generated by Māyā if he does not maintain his awareness of the higher reality he has experienced and allows his awakened, illumined insight to be obscured by the dream-like vision of thought-constructs.[314] Naturally, the yogi must rise out of the introverted condition of suspension. It is inherent in the very nature of reality that it should move out of itself.[315] Pure, universal consciousness initially transforms itself into the vital breath[316] charged with the impression (*vāsanā*) of the power of awareness attained through introversion. By attending to the pulse (*spanda*) of the breath as it moves out of the absolute, the yogi can develop an intuitive sense of the inherent unity of all he will perceive in the mental and physical spheres created by the outpouring of consciousness. In this way he realises that his own nature is everywhere present in all he perceives and that all things thus reside within him. Blessed with this insight his consciousness remains free and unlimited even at the individual level where the breath, mind, senses and body are active.

If the yogi fails to do this, he finds himself once again beset by the strictures of his embodied existence and must, as before, try to pervade all his other states of consciousness with the aesthetic delight (*rasa*) and wonder (*camatkāra*) of the Fourth State he experienced in contemplation. Again this means that he must strengthen his pure, empowered awareness that his universal nature manifests as all things.[317] In this way he discovers Śiva's presence in every sphere of individualised consciousness ranging from the breath to outer objectivity. The yogi's mind then becomes tranquil and undistracted because wherever it may wander, the yogi perceives only Śiva, his authentic nature.[318] Consciousness is thus freed of all external referents and the yogi's subjectivity is purified of all identification with the body or anything else that belongs to the objective sphere. The yogi then becomes detached from the opposites of pleasure and pain and is transcendentally free (*kevalin*).[319]

The yogi is again, however, liable to fall if he allows himself to get entangled in the play of opposites. This fall is more serious than the others because, although he is caught by the confining restrictions of individualised consciousness as before, he is now also affected by karma. Fleeing from pain in the pursuit of pleasure he is bound to act (*karma*) to minimise one and maximise the other and so is thrown down to the lowest level of embodied subjectivity (*sakala*). In order to regain his lost state, he must ascend gradually, by Śiva's grace, from one order of subjectivity to the next and so free himself progressively of the limitations of the lower levels to gain the greater freedom and expansion of the higher. As he progresses, the objective sphere also evolves from the grossest perceptions of physical objects outside the lowest order to subjectivity, through to the subtler inner, mental perceptions to finally reach the order of subjectivity that contains objectivity within itself and is free to externalise it at will.[320]

The degree to which this process develops depends, as before, on the yogi's awareness of the Fourth State. In consonance with the general principle that the remedy should suit the defect, the yogi is instructed to seek this higher state of consciousness in the wonder (*camatkāra*) or delight (*ānanda*) he feels in moments of intense physical pleasure. At first he experiences this subtle consciousness for an instant in the subjective sphere. If he manages to catch hold of it, it becomes more intense as the cognitive and objective spheres are also gradually pervaded and vitalised by it. Occasions for this practice are, for example, the sense of satisfaction one feels after a good meal or the aesthetic delight one experiences when listening to good music or the pleasure of sexual union with the Tantric consort or even solitary sexual excitation. In these moments of delight the yogi can penetrate momentarily into his own authentic Śiva-nature (*śambhavāveśa*) through the empowered contact (*śāktasparśa*)[321] he makes with it in the freedom of the pure subjectivity of the Fourth State.[322] If the yogi develops his awareness of this higher level of consciousness and maintains it, he eventually experiences it constantly.[323]

Clearly, what prevents the yogi from attending to his state of consciousness rather than the circumstances which induce it is the craving for pleasure (*abhilāṣa*) born of ignorance—the source of every impurity which clouds consciousness. Craving directs the yogi's attention towards outer, worldly things and so he is caught in the net of thought-constructs.[324] To free himself of his worldly desires and reverse this binding extroversion, the yogi must eradicate its cause. To be freed of all the ups and downs of the path and no longer be tormented by the possibility of a fall, the yogi must see reality perfectly and completely. This insight is itself liberation and the moment it dawns the yogi is instantly freed. This sudden realisation is the goal of Tantric Yoga.

Accordingly the Tantra declares: "He who perceives reality directly, even for the brief moment it takes to blink, is liberated that very instant and never reborn again."[325]

Although the yogi's body and mind continue to function as before, they are like mere outer coverings[326] which contain, but do not obscure, the mighty, universal consciousness which operates through them. The yogi's body is the universe, the senses the energies that vitalise it, his mind Mantra, the rhythm of his breath the pulse of time and his inner nature pure, dynamic consciousness. Raised above all practice, and hence all possibility of falling to lower levels, the yogi realises that he has always been free[327] and that his journey through the dark land of Māyā was nothing but a dream, a construct of his own imagination.

ABBREVIATIONS

A.P.S.	Ajaḍapramātṛsiddhi
Bh.G.	Bhagavadgītā
Bhā.	Bhāskarī
B.P.	Bodhapañcadāśikā
Br.Sū.	Brahmasūtra
Bṛ.Up.	Bṛhadāraṇyakopaniṣid
C.G.C.	Cidgaganacandrikā
Chān.Up.	Chāndogyopaniṣad
Ī.P.	Īśvarapratyabhijñā
Ī.P.v.	Īśvarapratyabhijñāvimarśinī
Ī.P.V.V.	Īśvarapratyabhijñāvivṛtivimarśinī
K.K.V.	Kāmakalāvilāsa
K.S.T.S.	Kashmir Series of Texts and Studies
K.J.N.	Kaulajñānanirṇaya
Kena Up.	Kenopaniṣad
K.N.P.	Kramanayapradīpikā
L.S.	Lalitāsahasranāmastotra
L.V.	Lallāvākyāni
L.Ā.S.	Luptāgamasaṃgraha
M.P.	Mahānayaprakāśa
M.M.	Mahārthamañjarī
M.U.V.	Mahopadeśaviṃśatikā
M.V.	Mālinīvijayatantra
M.V.V.	Mālinīvijayavārtika
Mā.Kā.	Māṇḍūkyakārikā
Mu.Up.	Muṇḍakopaniṣad
N.A.	National Archives
N.T.	Netratantra

N.T.U.	Netratantroddyota
N.P.	Nīlamatapurāṇa
Pañcast.	Pañcastavī
P.C.	Paramārthacarcā
P.P.	Paryantapañcāśikā
P.S.	Paramārthasāra
Parāpra	Parāpraveśikā
P.T.	Parātriṃśikā
P.T.L.V.	Parātriṃśikālaghuvṛtti
P.T.V.	Parātriṃśikāvivaraṇa
Pr.Hṛ.	Pratyabhijñāhṛdaya
R.T.	Rājataraṅgiṇī
R.S.O.	Ricerche e Studi Orientali
Ṣ.C.N.	Ṣaccakranirūpaṇa
Śā.Dṛ.	Śāktadṛṣṭi
Sām.P.	Sāmbapañcāśikā
Sām.Kā.	Sāṃkhyakārikā
Ś.B.	Śaṅkarabhāṣya on the Brahmasūtra
Ś.Dṛ.	Śivadṛṣṭi
Ś.St.	Śivastotra
Ś.Sū.	Śivasūtra
Ś.Sū.vā.	Śivasūtravārtika
Ś.Sū.vi.	Śivasūtravimarśinī
Sv.T.	Svacchandabhairavatantra
Sv.Up.	Śvetāśvataropaniṣad
Sp.Kā.	Spandakārikā
Sp.Kā.vi.	Spandakārikāvivṛti
Sp.Nir.	Spandanirṇaya
Sp.Pra.	Spandapradīpikā
Sp.Sam.	Spandasaṃdoha
St.Ci.	Stavacintāmaṇi
T.U.	Taittirīyāraṇyakopaniṣad
T.Ā.	Tantrāloka
T.Sā.	Tantrasāra
Vā.P.	Vākyapadīya
V.R.	Varivasyārahasya
V.B.	Vijñānabhairava
V.P.P.	Virūpākṣapañcāśikā
Y.Sū.	Yogasūtra
Y.Hṛ.	Yoginīhṛdaya

NOTES

INTRODUCTION

1. A. H. Francke and E. W. Thomas, *The Chronicles of Ladhak and Minor Chronicles* (*Antiquities of Indian Tibet*) Part 2, Asiatic Society of India, New Imperial Series, (Calcutta: 1926), vol. L, pp. 39-40.

2. G. Tucci, *La Via dello Svat*, (Bari: 1963), pp. 16, 97.

3. L. Nadou, *Les Buddhistes Kaśmiriens au Moyen Âge* (Paris: Presses Universitaires de France, 1968), p. 38. The reader is referred to this book for a detailed account of Buddhism in Kashmir.

4. See *Introduction to the Pāñcarātra and the Ahirbudhnya Saṃhitā* by F. Otto Schrader, Adyar Library Series, 2nd ed. (Adyar: 1973), p. 20ff.

5. Yāmunācārya is the earliest Śrīvaiṣṇava author whose works have come down to us. He lived in South India about the middle of the tenth century and was the teacher of Rāmānuja's teacher. He is credited with having written a work, now lost, called *Authoritativeness of the Kashmiri Āgama*. This work is said to have established the revealed character (*apauruṣeyatva*) of the Ekāyana branch of the White Yajur Veda which Pāñcarātrins claim is the original source of their Āgamic literature. (See M. Narasimhacharya, *Contributions of Yāmuna to Viśiṣṭādvaita* (Madras: M. Rangacharya Memorial Trust, 1971), p. 12. For Yāmuna's date see ibid. pp. 10-11) The origins of the Pāñcarātra were, therefore, it seems, linked by Yāmunācārya with the Kashmiri Āgamas and the Ekāyana. Recently discovered material confirms that the Ekāyana was known in Kashmir before the eleventh century. Bhagavatotpala (who probably belongs to the eleventh or tenth century) frequently quotes a work called *Saṃvitprakāśa* in his commentary on the *Stanzas on Vibration* (Sp.Pra. pp. 85, 87, 89, 95-6, 99, 100 and 112). (For abbreviations see pp. 219-220.) At least two incomplete manuscripts of this work are still extant. One is deposited in the research Centre in Srinagar responsible for the K.S.T.S.. A copy of this manuscript was kindly given to me by Professor R. Gnoli. Another manuscript which is less complete is MS no. C4003 deposited in the Central Library of Banaras Hindu University. A verse at the end of the first chapter reads:

ekāyane prasṛtasya kaśmīreṣu dvijanmanaḥ
kṛtir vāmanadattasya seyaṃ bhagavadāśrayā (fol. 6b).

We can gather from these lines that the author of this work was Vāmanadatta who was a Kashmiri Brahmin belonging to the Ekāyana. It is significant that this author should be quoted so extensively by Bhagavatotpala who was himself a Kashmiri Vaiṣṇava Brahmin by descent even though he was a Śaivite. It shows the close affinity between certain forms of Vaiṣṇavism in Kashmir with monistic Śaivism. Bhagavatotpala's is the oldest work so far recovered anywhere which quotes Vaiṣṇava Āgamic sources. There can be no doubt, therefore, that Kashmir was an important centre of Tantric Vaiṣṇavism (the Pāñcarātra) at a relatively early date.

6. Kalhaṇa wrote the introduction to his *Chronicles* in 1148-49 A.D. and completed his work the following year. See R.T. Intro. p. 6; also ibid., verse 1/52 and 8/3404.

7. Stein, the editor of the *Rājataraṅgiṇī*, writes: "It is characteristic that the Kashmir tradition knows the great Aśoka both as a founder of *vihāras* and *stūpas* and as a fervent worshipper at the ancient Śaiva shrines." R.T., Intro. p. 9, fn. 25. See R.T. 1/102ff. and 1/1055ff.

8. For a more detailed treatment of the Śaiva canon, the reader is referred to the author's *The Canon of The Śaivāgama* (Albany: SUNY Press, 1987).

9. For their names and brief details, see the introduction by Filliozat to the *Rauravāgama*, vol. 1 (Pondichery: 1961) pp. v-xv.

10. For the inscriptional and textual references which support this account see *Śaivism in Early Mediaeval India as Known from Archaeological Sources* by V. S. Pathak in Bhāratī: Bulletin of the College of Indology, no. 3 (1959-60). Also Rohan A. Dunuwila, *Śaiva Siddhānta Theology* (Delhi: M. Banarsidass, 1985), p. 34ff.

11. See *Gli Āgama Scivaiti nell'India Settentrionale* by R. Gnoli in *Indologica Tourinensia*, vol. I (Torino: 1973), pp. 61-9. Also, for an account of these Kashmiri Siddhāntins and their work, see K. C. Pandey, *Bhāskarī*, vol. 3. The Princess of Wales Sarasvati Bhavan Texts no. 84 (Lucknow: 1954), Intro. p. lxvi ff.

12. The term "Kashmiri Śaivism" can be misleading. The monistic Śaivism we generally indicate by this term was not the only form of Śaivism in Kashmir, nor was it entirely confined to Kashmir. Scholars first came to know of the existence of a distinct form of Śaiva theology prevalent in Kashmir when the fourteenth century work by Mādhavācārya, the *Sarvadarśanasaṃgraha*, came out in the *Bibliotheca Indica* series in 1858 edited by Īśvaracandra Vidyāsāgar. In 1877 G. Bühler published a general account of the works of non-dualist Kashmiri Śaiva authors in his *Detailed Report of a Tour in Search of Sanskrit Manuscripts Made in Kashmir* (extra number of the *Journal of the Bombay Branch of the Royal Asiatic Society, 1877*). J. C. Chatterjee, the first director of the research centre in Srinagar responsible for the editing and publication of the Kashmir Series of Texts and Studies, in his book *Kashmir Shaivaism* (Srinagar, 1914), was the first to refer to the monistic Śaivism elaborated by Kashmiri authors from about the middle of the ninth century, and preserved in the works later published in the series as 'Kashmir

Shaivaism'. He did so simply in order to "distinguish it from the other forms of Shaivaism known and still practised in different parts of India." (Ibid., p. 1). This term has since been generally adopted by scholars, even though we nowhere come across it in the works of these authors who simply considered themselves to be Śaivites expounding Āgamic Śaivism (*Śaivaśāsana*) from a non-dualist standpoint with no emphasis on anything peculiarly Kashmiri about it.

13. We suppose that this is so because Tantras of this class are hardly quoted by Kashmiri Śaiva authors. Moreover, the passages from Tantras they quote relating to the Śaivāgamic canon tend to omit these two groups indicating, possibly, that this tendency was not only confined to Kashmir. Practically the only Tantra that belongs to these groups that is quoted is the *Kriyākalottara* (N.T.U., vol. 2, pp. 148, 151, 157-8 and 196-9). A manuscript of this Tantra is preserved in Nepal dated Nepal Saṃvat 304, i.e., 1148 A.D. (N.A., no. 3/392). See the catalogue *Bṛhatsūcipatram*, Part IV Tantra, vol. 1, compiled by Buddhisāgara Śarmā, Vīrapustakālaya, Kathmandu, 1964, pp. 96-8. In the passage quoted from the beginning of this Tantra the Goddess asks Kārttikeya a number of questions. She says that she has not yet heard the *Gāruḍatantra* and would like to do so along with the *Bhūtatantra* and *Mantravāda*. She wishes thereby to learn the characteristic features of snakes and those of other kindred species such as scorpions. She also wants to know about the planets and their (evil) influences and about the potentially malevolent spirits such as Yakṣas, Rākṣasas, Piśācas and Śākinīs. Other matters are the evil planetary influences that take possession of children and trouble pregnant women.

14. *The Vīṇāśikhatantra: A Śaiva Tantra of the Left Current* edited with an introduction and a translation by Teun Goudriaan (Delhi: Motilal Banarsidass, 1985).

15. A description of Tumburu, found in the (unedited) *Jayadrathayāmala* is recorded in *The Canon of The Śaivāgama*, part 1 fn. 181.

16. Goudriaan, Intro. p. 25.

17. For a more detailed account refer to Goudriaan, Intro. pp. 24-30.

18. According to the first etymology, Bhairava's name is derived from the roots *'Bhṛ'*, meaning to sustain and nourish, and *'Ru'*, to shout.

19. From the roots *'Bhī'*, 'fear' and *'Av'*, 'protect'.

20. From *'Bhi-rava'*, 'a cry (for help born) of the fear of transmigration in the hearts of those who invoke Him'. The form 'Bhairava' thus means 'He who is born from this cry'.

21. The word 'Bhairava' is here derived from *'Bhā'*, meaning 'star' and the root *'Īr'*, to push, impel, or move. Together they form the word *'Bhera'* understood to mean time. The last syllable—*'Va'*—is interpreted as a derivative of the root *'Vai'*, to exhaust. Thus the *'Bheravas'* are those who exhaust (*vayanti*) time, while Bhairava (derived from *Bherava*) is their inner nature.

22. According to his interpretation 'Bhairava' is a compound referring to those powers 'whose shouting instils fear', while Bhairava is their Lord.

23. T.Ā., 1/96-100a.

24. *'Mahākāla'* means both the 'Great Black One' and the 'Great Time'. Bhairava is well known to Kashmiri Śaivism as the eternity of all-destroying and

universally creative time. Similarly in the Buddhist Tantric tradition, time is an important representation of Emptiness. *'Kal'* is, by coincidence, both an Indo-European root meaning 'time' and a non-Aryan root meaning 'black' or 'dark blue'. For a discussion and references see *Myth, Cult and Symbols in Śākta Hinduism* by Wendell C. Beane (Leiden: E. J. Brill, 1977), pp. 81-4.

25. For accounts of the mythical origins of the gods we must generally turn, not to the Tantras, but to the Purāṇas and Vedic literature. Although we do come across mythological material in the Tantras, myths concern them little and only indirectly. They focus on ritual and all that concerns its execution and ultimately its symbolic meaning. For the beheading of Brahmā, why it took place and Bhairava's origin see *Asceticism and Eroticism in the Mythology of Siva* by Wendy Doniger O'Flaherty (Oxford: Oxford University Press, 1973), pp. 123-7.

26. Ś. Sū., 1/5.

27. The *Pāśupatasūtra* and an old commentary have been translated into English under the title *The Pāśupatasūtram with Pañcārthabhāṣya of Kauṇḍinya* by Haripada Chakraborti (Calcutta: Academic Publishers, 1970).

28. For an interesting account of Śaiva sects such as these and their Pāśupata affiliations drawn mostly from inscriptions and literary sources see *The Kāpālikas and Kālāmukhas: Two Lost Śaivite Sects* by David N. Lorenzen (Berkeley: University of California Press, 1972).

29. Jayaratha in his commentary on the *Tantrāloka* (vol. XIb, p. 4) quotes fragments from Āgamic sources in which the term 'Kula' is defined. These are as follows: "Kula is the supreme power." "The nature of the arising and falling away (of all things) is consciousness, therefore that is said to be Kula." "Kula is pure consciousness present in the innate nature (*svabhāva* of all things) and is the universal cause." "O Best of Women, Kula is subtle, all-pervasive and the agent of all things." "O Goddess, Kula is the Lord of all things, is all things and is established in all things. That brilliant energy (*tejas*) is supremely terrible . . ." "Know that Kula, everywhere present, is vitality in the sphere of power." "Kula is supreme bliss." "Kula is indeed one's own innate nature" and "Kula is said to be the body". Abhinavagupta explains what Kula is in his *Parātriṃśikātattvavivaraṇa*, p. 61 ff. This work has been translated into Italian by R. Gnoli: *Il commento di Abhinavagupta alla Parātriṃśikā* Serie Orientale Roma vol. 58 (Rome, 1985). See also T.Ā., 29/111b ff. for an extensive exposition of the relationship between Akula and Kula, i.e., Śiva/Bhairava and His power.

30. K. C. Pandey was the first to identify these three periods of Abhinavagupta's work. See K. C. Pandey *Abhinavagupta, an Historical and Philosophical Study*, 2nd ed. (Varanasi: Chowkhamba, 1963), p. 191.

31. T.Ā, 37/58. Abhinava had great respect for his father whom he considered to be the greatest of his teachers (T.Ā., 1/12, M.V.V. 1/5) and a fully realised soul who knew the deepest meaning of the scriptures (T.Ā., 1/12).

32. Ibid., 37/56-7.

33. Ibid., 37/63.

34. Ibid., 37/64.

35. Ibid., 37/65.

36. Ibid., 37/70.

37. See the *Gurunāthaparāmarśa* by Madhurāja, K.S.T.S. no. 85, edited by P. N. Pushp, 1960, verse 18. The same work was edited by V. Raghavan from a South Indian MS. Although substantially the same, the order of the verses does not quite tally. See *Gurunāthaparāmarśa* in *Abhinavagupta and his Works* by R. Raghavan (Varanasi: Chowkhambha Orientalia, 1981), pp. 3-16. In this edition the verse referred to above corresponds to verse 20. See Pandey, pp. 20 ff. for a detailed account of Madhurāja's work.

38. T.Ā., 1/14.

39. K. C. Pandey did not wish to consider the Trika a separate system, nor did he succumb to the view prevalent in Kashmir nowadays, and supported by the writings of J. C. Chatterjee and others, that Trika is Kashmiri Śaivism in toto. In fact, as Pandey rightly remarks, 'Trika' stands for "the entire Śaiva thought as presented by (Abhinava) in his *Tantrāloka.*" (Pandey, p. 295). Even so, although Abhinava certainly contributed enormously to enstating Trika in the Kashmiri Śaiva milieu (and in so doing practically created a Trika system of his own), it is clearly an equally exaggerated view to simply ignore it as a distinct system (as Pandey has done) as it is to identify it wholesale with all of Kashmiri Śaivism.

40. T.Ā., vol. 1, p. 236.

41. For references and discussion about this Tantra see my *Translations from the Spanda Tradition of Kashmiri Śaivism* (Albany, State University of New York Press forthcoming).

42. The Triad is referred to in Sp.Pra., p. 91; it is not, however, certain that this work pre-dates Abhinavagupta. See *Translations.*

43. For a historical survey of the Krama system represented in the works of Kashmiri Śaiva authors, see *The Krama Tantricism of Kashmir* by Navjivan Rastogi (Delhi: Motilal Banarsidass, 1979). Also the relevant chapters on Krama and Kula in K. C. Pandey's *Abhinavagupta.*

44. See *The Canon of the Śaivāgama* for an account of the relationship between Krama, Trika, Kula and the Śaivāgama. This work pretends to do little more than present a broad outline of this, as yet, hardly researched area. Hopefully this preliminary study will be followed soon by more extensive work in this field.

45. See Pandey p. 491 ff.

46. As an example of the close relationship between the Trika and Kula one can cite Abhinava's treatment of the Kaula element in the *Parātriṃśikā.* This brief tract drawn from the *Rudrayāmala* deals with what Abhinava defines as the path of Anuttara—the absolute. This path, he asserts, is that of the Kaulika (See Pandey, p. 46) and indeed the text is so thoroughly couched in Kaula terminology that some scholars hold the view that it belongs to the Kaula tradition (see, for example Dvivedi in L.Ā.S., vol 2, p. 39). Abhinava, however, calls it the '*Trikasūtra*' because it expounds in brief the basic principles (*prameya*) of the Trika system (T.Ā., 12/15). Again, the text along with Abhinava's commentary, is called *Anuttaraprakriyā* (T.Ā., VI, p. 249) which reminds us of the name Abhinava gives to Trika, namely *Anuttaratrikakula.*

47. Jayaratha writes:

> In this way Trika, the sixth, includes all the dualist and other scriptures which issue from Īśa, Vāma and Aghora, the Supreme Lord's (faces), because it is the abode in which the three goddesses, Parā, etc. reside. As the saying goes:
>
> 'Just as scent (pervades a) flower, oil the sesame seed, life the body and flavour water, just so Kula is (everywhere) present in all scriptures.'
>
> May [Trika] accordingly, flood [all doctrines] with the nectar of Supreme Unity (*paramādvaya*) that it may serve as the means to realize the supreme state. (T.Ā., I, p. 45).

We said above (in fn. 39) that it is a wrong to identify Kashmiri Śaivism with Trika as some scholars have done. If they were the same, Trika would have no independent identity either as an Āgamic or Kashmiri Śaiva school. This is not the case. Let us start with Trika's Āgamic identity. Jayaratha quotes a passage which follows a long series of references from the *Śrīkaṇṭhīyasaṃhitā* suggesting that it is possibly drawn from the same Tantra. This passage states:

> "The three powers [reside], in due order, in the [Tantras] of the Upper Face [Īśāna, i.e., the Siddhānta], the left [i.e., the Vāmatantras] and the right [i.e., the Bhairavatantras]. Starting from the lower to the supreme, *Trika* encompasses them all." (T.Ā., I, p. 46)

Trika 'contains' all the Tantric teachings in the sense that it was originally an oral tradition that explained their ultimate purport in Trika terms. Jayaratha consequently appeals to the authority of the tradition handed down by the Tantric masters to support Trika's contentions. In this way he tacitly agrees that there is no scriptural authority for it. He does, however, stress that Trika is an independent school and quotes (the *Śrīkaṇṭhīya*?) accordingly as saying: "Trika doctrine is in this way dispersed amongst [the scriptures] variously. It resides in the Master's house because it is handed down by tradition (*sampradāya-krama*)." (Ibid).

Abhinava himself seems to support the view that Trika is predominantly an oral tradition when he says: "The teachings of the Lord are divided into ten, eighteen and sixty-four (Tantras) the essence of which are the Trika teachings (*Trikaśāstra*) and of these the *Mālinīvijaya*. Therefore, at the command of the Master, we will explain all that is contained here [in these scriptures particularly] that which sages not belonging to any spiritual lineage (*sampradāya*) have failed to observe." (T.Ā., 1/18-19). Although Abhinava takes the *Mālinīvijayatantra* as the prime authority for his Trika, this Tantra nowhere refers to Trika as an independent school, much less to itself as a Trikatantra. Even so, it most certainly deals with specifically Trika matters, such as the Mantric system centred on the Trika goddesses Parā, Parāparā and Aparā. See R. Gnoli, *Luce delle Sacre Scritture* (*Tantrāloka*) *di Abhinavagupta* (Torino: Classici Utet, 1972), pp. 715-30. In the footnotes to his translation of chapter 30 of the T.Ā. he notes all the parallel passages in the M.V. which deal with the mantras of these goddesses and their consorts.

It seems, therefore, that Trika was not originally fully defined in the Āgamas as an independent school even when the elements of Trika ritual, etc. had already developed. However, there can be no doubt that it did become an independent school(s) not only in the oral tradition but also in the Āgamas prior to Abhinava. We know this from references to Trika in Āgamic sources. *The Essence of Trika* (*Trikasāra*), a lost Tantra predating Abhinava, clearly belonged to this school (Ś.Sū.vā., p. 31; for other references to this Tantra see L.Ā.S., II, pp. 39-40). But whatever Trika's identity and character may have been before Abhinava's time, there can be no doubt that he considers it to have had an independent identity both in the Āgamic context and in terms of other Kashmiri Śaiva schools. Thus he says: "Many are the manuals in use in the many and diverse traditions, yet for the rituals of the *Anuttaratrika* there is not one to be seen." (T.Ā., 1/14). To make up for this deficiency he wrote his *Light of the Tantras.*

If Trika is not Kashmiri Śaivism, then what do we mean when we say that Trika is 'the culmination of the entire Śaivāgamic tradition and encompasses it'? We are referring here to an exegetical method which we find exemplified not only in Abhinava's Trika but also in other Hindu traditions and even outside them. Dunuwila, who refers to this same method in the context of the Śaivasiddhānta, describes it as follows: "What we have here is a structured theology of Comparative Religion, on the 'gradationist' model, which establishes a hierarchy of systems, the lowest being the furthest away from the truth, and the highest the most near to it, if not identical with it. This model is common in Christian and Islamic theologies." (Dunuwila, p. 47). The higher truth contains the lower truth, but this does not mean that they have no separate identity. Trika can be, and is, an independent school although it contains, from its own point of view, all others.

48. Abhinava thus refers to the *Bhairavakulatantra* as saying: "The master who knows the supreme principle, although consecrated on the path of the Vāma (Tantras), needs to be further initiated, first into the Bhairava (Tantras), then into those of Kula, Kaula and (finally) Trika." (T.Ā., comm. 13/302). Again he says that: "according to the venerable *Bhairavakula*, only the master who has been thoroughly purified by the five initiations and has crossed over the lower currents (of the Āgamas) is established in Trika doctrine." (T.Ā., VIII, p. 182).

49. T.Ā., 15/319.

50. See Pandey, pp. 297-8.

51. See T.Ā., I, p. 236.

52. That Kalhaṇa was a Śaivite is clear from the fact that he begins every chapter of his work with a verse of praise dedicated to Ardhanarīśvara, the hermaphrodite union of Śiva and Pārvatī.

53. R.T., 5/66.

54. T.Ā., 35/43-4.

55. R.T., 7/279 and 7/283; see also 7/295 ff. 7/253 and 7/712.

56. T.Ā., 37/44.

57. It appears that Kṣemendra tells us in one of his works that he learnt poetics from Abhinavagupta. Although not all scholars agree about this,

there can be no doubt that he heard Abhinavagupta lecture on poetics and respected him as his elder. See Pandey, pp. 153-6 and *Minor Works of Kṣemendra* edited by E. V. V. Raghavacarya and D. G. Padhye (Hyderabad, 1961) Intro. p. 1 ff.

58. "Satire has been deftly utilised by three well-known writers, Daṇḍin, Somadeva and Kṣemendra in Sanskrit with the pious motive of reforming the administrative machinery and the degenerating antisocial elements in the country." (Ibid., p. 7.) Kṣemendra himself states more than once that he wrote his satires not merely for their own sake, but also to inspire social reform and an upliftment of moral values. (Ibid.)

59. *Narmamālā*, 3/14b-17. *Minor Works of Kṣemendra* p. 337.

60. *Deśopadeśa*, 8/11-13. *Minor Works of Kṣemendra* p. 299.

61. This took place during the reign of King Yaśaskara (939-48 A.D.) at his instigation for he wished to "exercise control over the caste and over the condition of life (*varṇāśramadharma*) of his subjects" R.T., 6/108-12.

62. The work is called *Śrīpīṭhadvādaśikā* and has been edited, although not yet published, by Mr. G. S. Sanderson who gave me this information.

63. See *Yaśastilaka and Indian Culture* by K. K. Handiqui (Sholapur, 1949) p. 205, fn. 7. Another Jaina writer, Yaśaḥpāla (author of the *Moharājaparājaya* written in the twelfth century) creates a Kaula in his play who says that one should eat meat daily and drink heavily because the religion he teaches allows free scope to one's desires (Ibid., p. 204). This reference proves that this form of Śaivism was known in South India in the twelfth century. According to Somadeva's account of *Trikamata* practice, the initiate, after eating meat and drinking wine, should worship Śiva by offering him wine in the company of a female partner seated on his lap. The worshipper is to identify himself with Śiva and his consort with Pārvatī (ibid., p. 204). Again, we are told that a young prince called Māradatta considered his body to be divine, like one initiated into Trika doctrine (ibid. p. 43).

64. Ī.P., 3/2/2.

65. Ibid., 3/2/3.

66. Ibid., 4/2/2.

67. Ś.Dṛ., 7/109-123.

68. The legendary sage Durvāsas is intimately related to Śiva according to both the Purāṇas and Āgamas. According to the *Brahmāṇḍapurāṇa* the circumstances that attended his birth are as follows. Once a quarrel arose between Brahmā and Śiva. Śiva became very angry and his appearance became so frightening that the gods fled in terror. Pārvatī, his wife, also frightened by him, exclaimed "durvāsaṃ bhavati me," meaning: "it has become impossible for me to live with you!" Śiva realised that his anger was the cause of useless suffering and deposited it in the belly of Anusūyā from whom was born the sage Durvāsas. Durvāsas is therefore considered to be an aspect (*aṃśa*) of Śiva. (See Vettam Mani, *Purāṇic Encyclopaedia* [Delhi: Motilal Banarsidass, 1954], pp. 256-7 for this and other myths relating to Durvāsas). Commonly

portrayed as a devout Śaivite in the Purāṇas, Durvāsas is also particularly associated with the Śaivāgamas. According to the *Harivaṃśa*, Kṛṣṇa was taught the sixty-four monistic Āgamas by Durvāsas who is the revealer of them in the Kali age (Pandey, p. 63). The Siddhānta also venerates Durvāsas and would like to identify him with Āmardaka, although he sometimes figures as his predecessor (Dunuwila, pp. 35, 43).

69. The Śaivāgama, according to Abhinava, is divided into two major currents (*pravāha*); one originates from Lākulīśa, the other from Śrīkaṇṭha. The latter consists of the five streams (*srotas*) which constitute the majority of the Śaivāgama. T.Ā., 36/13b-17.

70. J. C. Chatterjee quotes it at length, as a part of Jayaratha's commentary on the *Light of the Tantras* in a variant form that can only be partly traced in the printed edition. *Kashmir Shaivaism*, p. 6, fn. 1.

71. nikhilaśaivaśāstropaniṣatsārabhūtasya ṣaḍardhakramavijñānasya (Ibid.).

72. T.Ā., 36/11-12.

73. teṣu mateṣu praśastam advayārthaviṣayakaṃ trikākhyamataṃ traiyambakasampradāyakaṃ sarvaśreṣṭhaṃ praśasyate. *Kashmir Shaivaism*, p. 6, fn. 1.

74. *Kashmir Shaivaism*, p. 17. See fn. 42 above. Pandey writes:

> "We know that the word 'Trika' is used for the philosophy presented in the monistic Śaivāgamas, revealed to humanity by Durvāsas, through his mind-born son, Tryambaka, at the behest of Śrīkaṇṭha." (Pandey, p. 599) He refers to Jayaratha (T.Ā., I, p. 28) who "speaks of the system, introduced to humanity through the descendents of Tryambaka as *'ṣaḍardhakramavijñāna'*." He concludes, "it is, therefore, indisputable that the word 'Trika' is used for the Pratyabhijñā system also." (Ibid., p. 600)

75. Pandey, p. 135-6.

76. Ibid., p. 137.

77. Ī.P., 4/2/1.

78. R. K. Kaw, *The Doctrine of Recognition* (Hoshiarpur: 1967), p. 4.

79. The philosophy of the Siddhānta was right from its inception concerned to establish the validity of our daily experience that the world is real. Accordingly, Sadyojyoti, the earliest Siddhāntin whose works are still extant "never condemns perception, inference and the other modes of knowledge as illusory. His respect for the objective witness is as high as that for the most revered revelation." Sadyojyoti "tries, with great success, to prove the existence of everything whether secular or otherwise by such methods as are intelligible to all." (The *Nareśvaraparīkṣā* of Sadyojyoti with commentary by Rāmakaṇṭha, K.S.T.S., XLV, edited by Madhusūdana Kaula Śāstrī 1926, Introduction p. 11.)

Sivaraman writes: "Śaiva Siddhanta approaches the reality of God in a different spirit. The theory of the illusoriness of the world is not a necessary formulation of religious consciousness, which is alive to the reality of God more as the 'Absolute Thou' than as being in general negatively implied by phenomena."

K. Sivaraman *Śaivism in Philosophical Perspective* (Varanasi: Motilal Banarsidass, 1973), p. 66. The phenomenology of perception requires the authentic existence of the perceived world. This is the *a priori* basis for any discussion about its possible nature. Expressing the Siddhānta's view Sivaraman writes: "But before showing the significant truth about the world's existence in time, it has to be acknowledged that the world *is*. The world must exist. The most formal statement we seem capable of making about the 'world' involving a minimum of theory is that the world intelligible to our understanding is *qua* intelligible an existent, in whatever sense the term 'world' is understood." (Ibid., p. 56). The Siddhānta theologian is particularly concerned to prove the existence of a real world so that he can establish the existence of God Who is its cause (ibid., p. 69).

80. Sadyojyoti writes:

> Now, because the nature of consciousness is experience-as-such (*anubhava*), it is right to equate it with direct perception. Therefore the object immediately in front of us in the field of (this pure) experience is devoid of non-being. One should know this, namely, that there is a clearly evident distinction between consciousness and its object. The form of the first is experience while the latter is that which is experienced. (*Nareśvaraparīkṣā*, 1/8-9).

81. See *The Kashmiri Śaiva Response to the Buddhist Challenge* by Dyczkowski, lecture delivered at the Seventh World Buddhist Conference, Bologna, forthcoming.

82. In the first section of the *Nareśvaraparīkṣā*, Sadyojyoti seeks to establish the existence of the individual soul as both perceiver and agent. His chief opponent here is the Buddhist. According to Madhusūdana Kaula: "the Buddhists receive a severe thrashing at the hands of our author and are defeated in their arguments more systematically and more directly than any other school." Ibid., Intro., p. 12.

83. Sadyojyoti writes: "Therefore, although an object may change to some extent, it is perceived to be inherently stable because it is recognised [to be the same at all times]." Ibid., 1/34. In the absence of recognition, says Sadyojyoti, language would not be possible. If when we hear sounds, we can distinguish and recognise phonemic components within them and link them together as words that convey a meaning (again sensed through recognition), we have language. Ibid., 3/35-41.

84. Ś.Dṛ., 4/118 ff.

85. Ś.Sū.vi., pp. 2-3. The reader is referred to the bibliography for bibliographical notes on these texts and their edition.

86. See bibliography.

87. R.T., 5/66.

88. See my *Translations from the Spanda Tradition of Kashmiri Śaivism* (Albany: State University of New York Press, forthcoming).

89. See bibliography.

90. See my *Translations from the Spanda Tradition of Kashmiri Śaivism*

(Albany: SUNY Press, forthcoming).

91. Sp.Nir., p. 33.

92. K. C. Pandey does not therefore consider Spanda to be an independent system or school in its own right, but rather says that "the *Spandakārikā* is simply an amplification of the fundamental principles of Śaivaism as aphoristically given in the *Śivasūtra*" (Pandey, p. 155). From another point of view K. C. Pandey sees in the *Stanzas* mere dogmatic statements of the fundamental principles of what he defines as the Spanda branch of the Pratyabhijñā (ibid., p. 294). All the Kashmiri commentators on the *Stanzas*, however, consider it to represent an independent tradition, while the South Indian Mādhavācārya in his enumeration of the works of the Pratyabhijñā in the *Sarvadarśanasaṃgraha* does not include Spanda works. Although Pandey is reluctant to concede to the view that Spanda is an independent branch of Kashmiri Śaivism, he does treat it as such when dealing with the *Śivasūtra, Spandakārikā* and their commentaries.

There are evident differences of opinion on this point. Thus J. C. Chatterjee criticises Bühler for saying that the Spanda- and Pratyabhijñā-śāstra are two different systems, insisting that the term *'śāstra'* means here simply 'treatise' and not system. He believes that these works all belong to Trika (See *Kashmir Shaivaism*, p. 7, fn. 1). Dr. Kaw follows Chatterjee's classification verbatim. Pt. Madhusūdana Kaula also agrees (preface to the I.P.v., I, p. 1). Dvivedi maintains that Spanda is an independent branch of Kashmiri Śaivism; however, he identifies Trika with the Pratyabhijñā (L.Ā.S., II, p. 11) and so cannot think of Spanda as part of Trika without identifying it with the Pratyabhijñā even though he does not want to do this. Although it is true that the *Spandakārikā* is by no means as philosophical as the works of the Pratyabhijñā and is particularly concerned with doctrine rather than argument, it does present its own views and doctrines in a terminology clearly distinguishable from the Pratyabhijñā.

93. śivopaniṣatsaṃgraharūpāṇi śivasūtrāṇi (Ś.Sū.vi., p. 2): Kṣemarāja writes in the concluding verses of his commentary:

> "This is a commentary on the *Aphorisms of Śiva*, expounded in order to penetrate Śiva's secret doctrine and beautiful in its agreement with the scriptures and the Spanda [teachings]. To sever the bondage of phenomenal existence (*bhava*), may the pious savour this lucid [commentary], the *Śivasūtravimarśinī*, full of the flavour of the essence of the nectar that flows ever anew from the teachings of Śiva's secret doctrine." (Ibid., p. 70).

94. According to Kṣemarāja, Śiva graced Vasugupta by revealing the *Aphorisms* to him so that the secret tradition might not be lost in a world given over to dualism (Ś.Sū.vi., p. 1). Similarly, non-dualist Śaivism is characterized by Somānanda in his *Śivadṛṣṭi* as a 'secret doctrine' (*rahasyaṃ śāstram*) in danger of being lost in the Kali age. (Ś.Dṛ., p. 220).

95. The term 'system' is one that has been in general use since the earliest studies in Kashmiri Śaivism. Bühler, as far back as 1877, made free use of the term. Later writers regularly referred to the major schools they discerned within

Kashmiri Śaivism as 'systems'. Pandey makes explicit what he means by this term when he says that "these 'systems' are fundamentally distinct from one another. Each has a different history, a distinct line of teachers, a set of books in which it is propounded and a different conception of the ultimate reality" (Pandey, p. 295). The term 'system' is, however, problematic if we analyse Kashmir Śaiva sources on these lines. It is not really possible to think of the Siddhāntāgamas, for example, as collectively concerned with a single theological standpoint or with the same ritual programmes in all their details. There are unmistakeable resemblances between Āgamas, but the differences are equally notable. The same is particularly true of the Āgamas belonging to the other groups. Thus, according to Abhinava, it is part of the Śaiva teacher's job to find uniformity and consistency (*ekavākyatā*) in the scriptures. These Kashmiris have, in their own brilliant way, sought and found such uniformity in the form of the Tantric systems which they have constructed from the raw and disordered material of the original sources. In this they do nothing new but participate, develop and extend a process apparent in the scriptures themselves.

96. Ś.Dṛ., 6/9. The other schools of Vedānta Somānanda refers to here are the *citrabrahmavādins*, who hold that Brahman assumes the diverse forms of the universe of objects, and the *nānātmavādins*, who attributed plurality to the Self (ibid., 6/3). Another school of Vedānta maintained that the Self, or Brahman, is the material cause (*upādānarūpa*) of the universe (ibid., 6/8). There were also the *ātmavādins* who argued that the Self, that is, the individual soul, is the absolute, and the *netivādins* who disagreed with them (ibid., 6/9). The *sphuliṅgātmavādins* maintained that individual souls are related to Brahman as sparks are to a fire. The *pratibimbavādins* held that the Self is a reflection of Brahman (ibid., 6/11). One school of Vedānta declared that the Self is different in different bodies and that plurality (*bheda*) is inherent in the world, while another school maintained that although individual embodied souls do differ, they are in essence one with Brahman, just as waves are one with the sea (ibid., 6/13).

97. The discovery of manuscripts of the *Light of Consciousness* (*Saṃvitprakāśa*) by Vāmanadatta (see above fn. 5) has brought to our notice an entirely new field of research, namely, monistic Kashmiri Vaiṣṇavism. There appears to have been a number of works written by Kashmiri Vaiṣṇavas which present basic Vaiṣṇava tenets found in the Pāñcarātra and elsewhere in terms of an idealistic monism very similar to that of Kashmiri Śaivism. Apart from the *Saṃvitprakāśa* we know that the *Discernment of the Six Attributes* (*Ṣāḍguṇyaviveka*) and the *Essence of Ultimate Reality* (*Paramārthasāra*) were monistic Vaiṣṇava works. These and other such works were well known to Kashmiri Śaivas and influenced them. The quotations from Bhāskara's lost *Kakṣyāstotra* clearly show signs of monistic Vaiṣṇava influence (see Sp.Pra., p. 103). Abhinava himself refers to Vāmanadatta with respect as his elder and teacher (or predecessor, T.Ā., 5/155). Bhagavatotpala's commentary on the *Stanzas on Vibration* is particularly important from this point of view. In this work he clearly attempts an extensive integration of monistic Vaiṣṇavism with Spanda doctrine and hence with Kashmiri Śaivism. For a fuller treatment of these matters the reader

is referred to the *Translations*.

98. See below chapter 3.

99. See Sp.Kā.vi., p. 29.

100. Sp.Nir., p. 5.

101. It is a notable fact that these terms, so important in the technical vocabulary of the Pratyabhijñā, are not at all common in the Śaivāgamas, although the concepts they denote are represented there. Consequently, these terms do not belong to the terminology of the Tantric systems syncretized into Kashmiri Śaivism, at least as far as we can gather from the sources quoted by these Kashmiri authors themselves. As examples of the uncommon occurrence of the term *'vimarśa'* we can cite the *Kālīkūla:* "The supreme power of the Lord of the gods Whose nature is supreme consciousness is reflective awareness (*vimarśa*) endowed with omniscient knowledge" (quoted in N.T.U., I, p. 21, and also in Ś.Sū.vi., p. 55). Abhinava refers to the *Gamatantra* which says: "The deity of mantra is considered to reflective awareness (*vimarśa*) co-extensive in being with the Great Consciousness." (T.Ā., X., p. 117). These two are virtually the only references quoted from the Āgamas where this term occurs.

102. Śv.Up., 6/14 quoted by Bhaṭṭānanda on p. 51 of his commentary on the *Vijñānabhairava* edited by Mukundarāma Śāstrī K.S.T.S. No. 8 (Bombay: 1918).

103. Ī.P., 1/5/11.

104. Ī.P., 1/1/4.

105. Ś.Dṛ., 1/1.

106. Sp.Kā., 28-9.

107. Ibid., 10.

108. Ibid., 5.

109. Utpaladeva writes that "repose in one's own essential nature (*svasvarūpa*) is the reflective awareness (*vimarśa*) that 'I am'" (A.P.S., v. 15). One might say that Utpaladeva is here explaining, in Pratyabhijñā terms, that the Spanda doctrine of 'establishment in one's own essential nature' (*svasvarūpasthiti*) implies that this, the liberated condition, is that of the pure ego-identity.

110. Pandey says: "the books, for instance, which include the word 'Spanda' in their titles, deal with what is referred to as 'Caitanya' or 'Vimarśa' (consciousness) in the *Śiva Sūtra* and *Īśvara Pratyabhijñā Kārikā* respectively.... They are mere dogmatic statements of the fundamental principles of the Spanda branch of the Pratyabhijñā." (Pandey, pp. 293-4).

111. Ī.P.v., I, p. 208.

112. Sp.Kā.vi., p. 1.

113. Thus Dr. Rastogi, for example, in his book *The Krama Tantricism of Kashmir* discusses the Spanda school because he finds that Spanda doctrine is, like Krama, Śākta. This, he believes, links them vitally together. He says:

> It has been frequently repeated that the Spanda system is nearest to the Krama for its unmistakeable emphasis on the dynamic aspect of reality which technically passes under the name of Śakti or Spanda or Vimarśa. If this be granted, the *Spandakārikā* must propound

a system that is Śākta in nature (p. 116).

114. T.Ā., 4/122b-181b.
115. T.Ā., 1/168-70 where M.V., 2/21-3 is quoted.

CHAPTER I

1. Cf. Chān.Up., 4/6/4.
2. K. Potter, *Presuppositions of India's Philosophies* (Westport: Greenwood Press, 1977), p. 3.
3. Sāṃ.Kā., v. 21.
4. Ibid., v. 59.
5. Ibid., v. 62.
6. Bṛ.Up., 2/3/6.
7. Sp.Saṃ., p. 24.
8. Br.Sū., 3/2/23.
9. Bṛ.Up., 2/4/14.
10. Kena Up., 1/3.
11. Ś.B., 3/2/17.
12. Bh.G., 2/20.
13. When we refer to 'Vedānta' in this work we mean both the Advaita Vedānta developed by Śaṅkara and, by extension, other forms of Vedānta of the same type.
14. Mā.Kā., 4/13.
15. Mā.Kā., 3/21, 4/7.
16. Ś.B., 1/1/1.
17. Whenever we refer to 'Śaivism' or 'Śaiva absolutism' we mean Kashmiri Śaivism as a whole. Although a number of conceptions of the absolute are distinguishable in Kashmiri Śaiva works, we are not concerned here with these differences but will, for our present purpose, treat them collectively as aspects of a single fundamental concept, the nucleus of which is its dynamic—Spanda—character.
18. L. N. Sharma, *Kashmir Śaivism* (Varanasi: Bhāratīya Vidyā Prakāśana, 1972), p. 9.
19. K.Ā., 1/110.
20. M.V.V., 1/628.
21. *Samvidullāsa*, quoted in M.M., p. 75.
22. T.Ā., 2/18.
23. G. Kaviraj, *Bhāratīya Saṃskṛti aur Sādhanā*, vol. 1 (Patna: 1963), p. 5.
24. Throughout this work the appellation 'Śaiva' refers to monistic Kashmiri Śaivism unless otherwise specified.
25. T.Ā., 1/136.
26. Ibid., 6/9-10.
27. As an example we can quote the following verse from one of Utpaladeva's *Hymns* (Ś.St., 16/30) also quoted by Rājānaka Rāma in his commentary on the

Stanzas on Vibration (Sp.Kā.vi., p. 8): "O Lord of All! Your supreme [transcendent] lordship triumphs for it Lords over nothing. Just so is Your lower [immanent] Lordship by virtue of which this universe is not such as it appears to be."

28. Kṣemarāja, commenting on the verse quoted in the previous footnote, explains that it is not the universe (considered as an independent reality) which manifests but God as all the categories of existence. In this sense it is quite real. He quotes Utpaladeva as saying: "In this way all these physical objects (*jaḍa*) which in themselves are as if unreal are [the forms] of the Light [of the absolute] alone. The Light alone exists, [manifesting] its own nature both as itself and as [everything] else." (A.P.S., 13). At Śiva's supreme level all that manifests is Śiva alone and so there is no world apart from Him. Śiva's lower level of sovereignty corresponds to the states of *Sadāśiva* and *Īśvara* in which the universe is manifest within consciousness. It does not, therefore, appear as it does now to the ignorant, to whom it manifests as separate from consciousness (Ś.St., p. 270).

29. T.Ā., 6/9-10.

30. Abhinava writes: "How can any aspect [of reality] be manifest within the Light [of the absolute] if it is not that same Light? If it shines there within it, no duality between them is possible. If it does not, how can one say that it has any existence (*vastutā*)? Thus it makes no sense to say that the Light has any particular form." (T.Ā., 2/20-3).

31. S. Dasgupta, *History of Indian Philosophy* vol. 1 (Cambridge: Cambridge University Press, 1969), p. 443.

32. Mā.Kā., 3/44.

33. *'Navamārga'* or 'New Way' is an expression Utpaladeva has coined to refer to his systematization of the Pratyabhijñā in the *Stanzas on the Recognition of God* as taught originally by Somānanda, his teacher. Ī.P., 4/1/1.

34. T.Ā., 32/1-2.

35. Cf. G. Kaviraj, *Tāntrik Vāṅgmaya meṃ Śākta Dṛṣṭi* (Patna: Bihāra Rāṣṭrabhāṣā Pariṣad, 1963), Chap. 6.

36. M.V.V., 1/240.

37. Ibid., 1/241-2.

38. Ibid., 1/245.

39. Ibid., 2/100-2.

40. Ibid., 1/262a.

41. T.Ā. comm. 3/72a, sṛṣṭavyānārūṣitecchāmātrarūpā; cf. M.V.V., 1/248.

42. T.Ā., comm. 4/257b-8a.

43. Cf. B. N. Pandit, *Kāśmīra Śaiva Darśana* (Jammu: Ranavīr Kendriya Sanskṛt Vidyāpīṭha, 1973), p. 7.

44. M.V.V., 1/180-2.

45. Abhinava writes: "if daily life which is useful for everybody, everywhere and at all times were not real then we know of nothing else which is real." Ī.P.v., II, p. 59.

46. T.Ā., 4/254.

47. M.V.V., 1/629-31.

48. Sp.Kā.vi., p. 163.

49. See M.M., pp. 44-7, particularly p. 47.
50. Ibid., p. 46.
51. M.V.V., 1/123-4a.
52. M.M., p. 47.
53. Ibid.
54. Pr.Hṛ., sū. 8, tadbhūmikāḥ sarvadarśanasthitayaḥ; M.M., p. 12.
55. M.M., p. 11.
56. Ī.P.V.V., I, p. 12.
57. M.M., p. 12.
58. Ibid., p. 38, yā cit sattaiva sā proktā sā sattaiva ciducyate.
59. Ibid., p. 34.
60. T.Ā., 6/15; see also comm., Ī.P., I/6/4-5.
61. Ś.Dṛ., 4/7a, 4/29.
62. Ibid., 5/1-4a.
63. M.V.V., 1/88.
64. Sām.Pañ., p. 49.
65. T.Ā., 3/4.
66. M.M., pp. 4-5, svātmasaṃvitsphurattāmātrasvarūpeti prakāśa eva viśvopāsyā devatetyāpatitam.
67. Sp.Pra., p. 104.
68. Pr.Hṛ., pp. 27-8.
69. Pr.Hṛ., p. 63.
70. Sp.Nir., p. 3.
71. Ś.B. (Gambhīrānanda's trans.), p. 142.
72. Ibid., p. 344.
73. Sv.T., vol. 1, p. 57.
74. See L. Silburn, *Vijñānabhairava*, (Paris: E. de Boccard, 1961) p. 12; also Pandey, p. 331.
75. K.N.P., p. 4.
76. P.T.v., p. 134.
77. Ś.St., 10/12.
78. Ś.Dṛ., pp. 129-30; *Anuttarāṣṭikā*, v. 7-8.
79. T.Ā. comm. 3/21, vol. 2, pp. 29-30.
80. Ī.P., 1/8/7.
81. T.Ā., comm. 3/9, vol. 2, p. 11, saṃvitsaṃlagnameva hi viśvaṃ saṃvedyate.
82. Ś.Dṛ., comm. 4/31.
83. Ī.P.V.V., I., pp. 4-5; cf. Sp.Nir., p. 10 and Ī.P., comm. 1/5/9.
84. Ī.P., comm. 1/5/12.
85. T.Ā., comm. 10/89-91a.
86. *Ucchuṣmabhairavatantra*, quoted in Ś.Sū.vi., p. 4.
87. M.V.V., 1/427a.
88. Ī.P.V.V., II, p. 78.
89. T.Ā., comm. 1/136b.
90. M.V.V., 1/720.
91. Ī.P.V.V., II, p. 159.

92. Ibid.
93. Ī.P.V.V., I., p. 52.
94. M.V.V., 1/430.
95. Ī.P., I., p. 95, paraprakāśanātmakanijarūpaprakāśanam eva hi svaprakāśatvaṃ jñānasya bhaṇyate.
96. sahopalambhaniyamād abhedo nīlataddhiyoḥ iti vijñānākāramātraṃ nīlādi prasādhayituṃ nirūpitam.
Ī.P.V.V., II, p. 78; cf. B.B., p. 4, T.Ā. comm. 3/123; also ibid., comm. 3/57.
97. Sp.Pra., p. 89.
98. See Pr.Hṛ., p. 52; Sp.Saṃ., pp. 11-12.
99. Quoted from the *Kālikākrama* in comm. T.Ā., 5/80; comm. T.Ā., 3/57. Attributed to the *Devikākrama* in M.M., pp. 9-10.
100. *Vijñāptimātratāsiddhi*, v. 1.
101. Sp.Nir., p. 10.
102. M.M., v. 25; P.S., v. 26.
103. Sv.T., 4/233.
104. M.M., p. 53.
105. Ś.Dṛ., 5/34; 5/105-6.
106. Ibid., 5/16.
107. Ibid., 5/104.
108. Ibid., 5/109.
109. Ś.Dṛ., 5/105-6.
110. M.V.V., 1/764.
111. Ibid., 1/747.
112. Ibid., 1/768 and 1/762-3.
113. M.M., p. 79.
114. M.M., p. 44.
115. Pandey, Intro. to *Bhāskarī* III, p. cc.
116. 'Kashmiri Śaivism', J. Rudrappa, *Quarterly Journal of the Mythic Society* vol. 45, no. 3 (Bangalore: 1955), p. 29.
117. Pandey, Intro. to *Bhāskarī*, III, p. cc.
118. R. K. Kaw, *The Doctrine of Recognition* (Hoshiarpur: Viśveśvarānanda Institute, 1967), p. 358.
119. T.Ā., 3/93b, yo 'nuttaraḥ paraḥ spando . . . .
120. Ī.P.v., I, p. 209, bhavanakartṛtā.
121. Ī.P., II, p. 71, ābhāsamātraṃ vastu.
122. Ī.P.V.V., I, p. 220, astitvaṃ prakāśamānatvam eva.
123. Sp.Nir., p. 12.
124. M.V.V., 1/219.
125. Ī.P.V.V., I, p. 10.
126. T.Ā., 10/82.
127. Quoted by L. M. Vail in *Heidegger and Ontological Difference*, Pennsylvania: Rider College, 1972, p. 10 from *Sein und Zeit*.
128. Ibid., p. 15.
129. *Sein und Zeit*, p. 36, quoted by L. M. Vail, p. 10.
130. Ī.P.v., comm. 2/2/7.

131. Ī.P.V.V., I., p. 292.
132. Quote from Divākaravatsa's *Vivekāñjana* in Ī.P.v., I., p. 10.
133. Ī.P., comm. 1/7/14.
134. T.Ā., 10/144.
135. Ī.P.V.V., I., p. 192.
136. M.M., p. 47.
137. Ī.P., v. II, p. 116.
138. Bhā., vol. 2, p. 63.
139. Ī.P.V.V., I, pp. 266-7; cf. P.T.v., p. 139 ff.
140. Ś.Dṛ., p. 7, parāvasthāyāṃ punaḥ pūrṇo 'hamityeva svasvabhāvaḥ prakāśate.
141. Quote in Sv.T., vol 2, p. 59; M.M., p. 65; cf. M.V.V., 1/658.
142. M.V.V., 1/641; cf. P.T.v., p. 140.
143. M.V.V., 1/1063-4.
144. P.T.v., pp. 136-7.
145. M.V.V., 1/131-2.
146. Ī.P.v., comm. 2/3/7.
147. Ibid.
148. Ī.P.v., comm. 2/3/3.
149. Ī.P.,v., comm. 2/3/1-2.
150. Ī.P.v., comm. 2/3/6.
151. Ī.P.v., I., pp. 329-30.
152. Ī.P.v., II, pp. 91-2.
153. Ī.P.v., I, p. 109.
154. Ī.P.V.V., II, p. 107.
155. Ī.P.v., I, p. 326.
156. Ī.P., 1/8/6 and comm.
157. Ī.P., 1/8/7.
158. Ī.P., 1/8/6.

CHAPTER II

1. Ī.P.V.V., II, p. 68: prakāśa eva arthasya ātmā; Ī.P.V.V., II, p. 69: arthasya ca prakāśamānatā anubhavarūpatā ātmā.
2. T.Ā., 3/2: yaḥ prakāśaḥ sa sarvasya prakāśatvaṃ prayacchati.
3. T.Ā., 8/3.
4. Sp.Kā.vi., p. 16.
5. T.Ā., comm. 5/59; Intro. comm. to Ī.P., 1/5/4-5; Ī.P.v., I, pp. 277-8.
6. M.M., pp. 132-3.
7. M.M., p. 10.
8. Pr.Hṛ., p. 26.
9. M.V.V., 1/62b-64.
10. Ī.P.V.V., II, p. 69: na tu asau prakāśamānatātmā prakāśo 'rthasya svarūpabhūto 'rthaśarīramagnaḥ.

11. Ī.P.v., I., p. 277.
12. T.Ā., 1/136b.
13. Sp.Kā., 2.
14. P.T.L.V., intro. verse.
15. M.M., v. 67, gūḍhād gūḍhataro bhavati sphuṭād api sphuṭatara eṣaḥ.
16. Ī.P.V.V., I, p. 5; Ś.Sū.vi., p. 2; M.V.V., 1/61; 1/419.
17. M.V.V., 1/69-70a.
18. M.M., p. 4; Y.Hṛ., p. 1.
19. Y.Hṛ., p. 65; M.M., v. 10.
20. V.P.P., v. 22; cf. B.P., v. 1 and P.T.L.V., p. 1; Y.Hṛ., 2/75.
21. P.T.V., p. 134.
22. *The Divine Names* by Dionysius the Areopagite, trans. C. E. Rolt. (London: 1937), pp. 79-80.
23. *Anuttarāṣṭika*, v. 4.
24. K. C. Bhattacarya, *Studies in Philosophy* vol. 2 (Calcutta: 1959), Intro., p. xiii.
25. M.M., p. 88, prakāśyate 'nena prameyajātam iti vyutpattyā prakāśaḥ pramāṇam ityartho bhavati.
26. Ī.P., I, p. 151.
27. Quote from Utpaladeva's commentary on his own *Ajaḍapramātṛsiddhi* in M.M., p. 133.
28. M.M., p. 76.
29. Ī.P.V.V., I, p. 710, *Saṃvitprakāśa* quoted in M.M. p. 20 and Sp.Pra. p. 114: jñānam iti hi jñātṛtaiva uktā.
30. M.M., p. 133; M.V.V., 1/433.
31. Ī.P., v. II, p. 66.
32. M.M., p. 76: puṭatvaṃ caiṣām aśeṣaviśvakroḍīkārasāmarthyāt.
33. T.Ā., 4/171-2; cf. P.S., comm. v. 4 and Ī.P., 2/1/8.
34. *Jñānagarbhastotra* quoted in Sp.Nir., p. 48.
35. Cf. Ī.P., 1/5/12 and Ī.P.v. I, p. 198.
36. V.R., comm. v. 3.
37. Y.Hṛ., p. 65; also T.Ā., comm. 3/2a.
38. T.Ā., 3/120-1.
39. Ibid.
40. See S. K. Saksena, *The Nature of Consciousness in Hindu Philosophy* Chowkhamba, (Benares: 1969), p. 73.
41. M.M., p. 30; T.Ā., 2/9; 17/20a-2a, 10/144-6a.
42. Sp.Kā. vi., p. 92; cf. P.S., v. 6 and comm.
43. Ī.P., v. II, p. 48.
44. Ī.P., vol. 1, p. 162; Ī.P.V.V., III, pp. 79-80.
45. Ī.P., v. I, p. 160.
46. Ī.P., 1/5/3.
47. Ī.P., v. I, p. 160.
48. T.Ā., 2/18.
49. Ibid., 2/20-1; T.Sā., pp. 5-6.
50. T.Ā., 3/101b-2a; M.V.V., 1/80.

51. T.Ā., 3/100b-1a.
52. Quoted in Ī.P., v. II, p. 177.
53. Ibid.
54. *Kāmikāgama*, quoted in T.Ā., 1/66; cf. P.S., v. 6.
55. T.Ā., 3/8.
56. Ī.P.V.V., I, p. 6.
57. Ī.P.v., II, p. 178; P.S., v. 12-3.
58. T.Sā., chap. 3.
59. T.Ā., 3/49.
60. Ibid., 3/37.
61. Ibid., 3/59.
62. Ibid., comm.
63. Ibid., 3/33.
64. Ibid., 3/34.
65. Ibid., 3/29.
66. Ibid., 3/58.
67. Ibid., comm. 3/1, svatantrād eti prakāśanakriyākartṛtvam.
68. Ibid., 3/11.
69. Ī.P.V.V., I, p. 9.
70. T.Ā., 3/3.
71. T.Ā., 4/138.
72. Sp.Nir., p. 3.
73. Ī.P.V.V., II, p. 69: arthasya ca prakāśamānatā anubhavarūpatā ātmā . . . arthasya yā prakāśamānatā sa prakāśo 'nubhavaḥ.
74. C. G. Jung, *Psychology and Religion: East and West*, vol. XI of the *Collected Works* (London: Routledge and Kegan Paul) pp. 1-2.
75. T.Sā., p. 12; cf. Ī.P.v., p. 338.
76. M.M., p. 34, evaṃ ca prakāśasya vimarśaḥ svabhāva ityaṅgīkāryam.
77. Ī.P., 1/5/11.
78. Ī.P.v., comm. 1/5/20.
79. Ī.P.v., I, p. 198.
80. Ibid.; T.Ā., comm. 4/172.
81. Cf. P.T.V., p. 136.
82. M.M., p. 67: vimarśākhyo yaḥ saṃrambhaḥ svāntaḥsphuratkriyāśaktisphārarūpaḥ . . .
83. Ibid.
84. Parāpra, pp. 1-2.
85. M.M., v. 12; ibid. p. 67.
86. Ī.P.V.V., I, pp. 5-6; Ī.P.v., I, p. 198.
87. Sp.Nir., p. 13, vastutastu etad vīryasāram evāśeṣam.
88. A.P.S., v. 15.
89. P.T.V., p. 75.
90. M.V.V., 1/381-2.
91. Ī.P.v., comm. 1/5/18.
92. Pandey, pp. 324-5.
93. Ī.P.v., II, pp. 223-4.

94. M.V.V., 1/88.
95. M.M., p. 40.
96. Ī.P.v., I, p. 338.
97. L. Silburn, M.M., p. 95.
98. Ī.P., 1/1/4.
99. Ī.P., 1/5/19.
100. Ibid. comm.; Ś.Dṛ., p. 12.
101. Ī.P.V.V., I, p. 5.
102. P.T.V., p. 130.
103. M.V.V., 1/625-6a.
104. M.M., v. 12.
105. Ī.P.V.V., II, p. 38: itthamābhāsasya vimarśa eva jīvitam iti tadbhedābhedakṛtaiva vastubhedābhedasthitiḥ | iha ca vimarśa aikyena eva.
106. Ī.P.v., I, p. 202.
107. Ibid.
108. Sp.Nir., pp. 31-2.
109. Ī.P.v., I., p. 205.
110. Sp.Nir., p. 66.

CHAPTER III

1. Ī.P.v. I, p. 43, fn. 79.
2. T.Ā., 4/122b-3a; cf. ibid., 4/147.
3. Sp.Kā., 16.
4. M.M., p. 110.
5. Ī.P., 1/8/8b.
6. T.Ā., 4/147.
7. Ī.P., 1/6/3-5; P.S., comm. v. 2.
8. M.V.V., 1/623.
9. P.S., p. 10.
10. Ibid. Ī.P.V.V., III, p. 318; Sp.Nir., p. 23; M.M., p. 44.
11. Ī.P., 2/1/8.
12. T.Ā., 3/141b.
13. Ī.P.V., II, p. 144.
14. Sp.Nir., p. 32.
15. Sp.Kā.vi., p. 50.
16. Sp.Nir., p. 32.
17. Ī.P.v., I, pp. 208-9.
18. P.T.V., p. 207.
19. Y.Hṛ., p. 15.
20. Ś.St., 20/9, quoted in Sp.Saṃ., p. 9.
21. Ī.P., 2/1/2.
22. Ś.Dṛ., pp. 10-11; ibid. p. 11, fn. 1.
23. T.Sā., p. 84: atra ceṣāṃ vāstavena pathā kramavandhyaiva sṛṣṭir

ityuktaṃ kramāvabhāso'pi cāstītyapi uktam eva.

24. Sp.Saṃ., p. 25; cf. T.Ā., comm. 4/179.
25. T.Ā., 10/220b-2.
26. Ī.P., 2/1/4a.
27. Ī.P.V.V., II, p. 318: sa eva cāpekṣāntareṇa yaugapadyam.
28. T.Ā., 9/17b.
29. Ī.P., 2/1/3.
30. M.V.V., 1/125-6a.
31. M.V.V., 1/419.
32. Sp.Saṃ., p. 8.
33. T.Ā., 4/179b-180a; cf. ibid. 29/80a and 10/224a.
34. Sp.Nir., p. 5.
35. T.Ā., 11/110.
36. Sp.Kā., 45.
37. Pr.Hṛ., comm. sū. 8; P.T.v., p. 165.
38. Sp.Nir., p. 10.
39. Śt.Ci., p. 1; T.Ā., 5/79.
40. Sp.Nir., pp. 3-4.
41. M.U.V., v. 9.
42. Ibid., v. 11.
43. Sp.Kā., 1; Sp.Nir., p. 5; M.M., p. 74; P.T.L.V., p. 2.
44. M.V.V., 1/260-1.
45. Sp.Saṃ., p. 4.
46. T.Ā., comm. 5/62.
47. Ī.P.V.V., I, p. 45.
48. Sp.Nir., p. 4.
49. M.M., p. 74.
50. Sp.Saṃ., pp. 5-6.
51. Sp.Nir., pp. 5-6.
52. Sp.Nir., p. 5.
53. e.g., Chān. Up. 3/14/18; "Verily, this whole world is Brahman. Tranquil, let one worship It as that from which he came forth, as that into which he will be dissolved, as that in which he breathes" (Hume's translation).
54. Mā.Kā., 2/27-8.
55. Ś.B., trans. pp. 327-8 (italics mine).
56. Bṛ.Up., 5/1/1.
57. Sp.Pra., p. 85.
58. Ī.P.V.V., I, p. 8.
59. Ibid., I., pp. 8-9.
60. Ibid., I, p. 145.
61. T.Ā., VI, p. 7: kāryakāraṇabhāvātmā tattvānāṃ pravibhāgo vaktavyaḥ . . .
62. Sp.Nir., p. 4.
63. P.T.V., pp. 135-6.
64. Cf. T.Ā., 4/167a.
65. See Chapter 7, p. 164.

66. Sp.Pra., p. 90.
67. Ī.P., comm. 1/5/14.
68. Ś.Dṛ., 1/19-22a.
69. P.T.V., p. 177.
70. Ś.Dṛ., 1/2; cf. also ibid., pp. 13-4; Sp.Pra., p. 90.
71. Ś.Dṛ., comm. 1/2.
72. Ś.Sū., 1/17 (Bhāskara's recension).
73. Ibid., comm.
74. Ś.Dṛ., comm. 1/3-4.
75. Sp.Pra., p. 88.
76. Sp.Nir., p. 6; Sp.Pra., p. 98; Sp.Saṃ., p. 6.
77. Ī.P., 2/4/21.
78. Ī.P.V.V., II, p. 233.
79. Ī.P.v., I., p. 193.
80. Ī.P.V.V., II, p. 234.
81. Ś.Dṛ., p. 17: karmāvacchinnanivṛtir aunmukhyam.
82. Ibid.: anavacchinnā nivṛtimātram ānandaśaktiḥ.
83. Ī.P.V.V., II, p. 355.
84. M.V.V., 1/214-5.
85. M.M., p. 75.
86. Sp.Saṃ., p. 7.
87. Ś.Dṛ., 1/7b-8.
88. Sp.Pra., p. 84.
89. Ś.Dṛ., p. 12 (footnote).
90. Sp.Kā.vi., p. 129.
91. Ś.Dṛ., 1/13b-5.
92. Ś.Dṛ., p. 11, fn. 1.
93. Ibid., p. 10, fn. 2.
94. Ibid., pp. 10-11.
95. Sp.Nir., p. 40; Pr.Hṛ., p. 79.
96. V.B., v. 71.
97. P.T.V., p. 42.
98. Sp.Kā., 22; cf. V.B., v. 101; ibid., v. 118.
99. Sp.Kā.vi., p. 73.
100. M.V.V., 1/367b-8a.
101. Sp.Kā.vi., pp. 73-4.
102. Ibid., p. 121.
103. T.Ā., 5/104b-5a.
104. Sp.Pra., p. 123.
105. Cf. Pr.Hṛ., sū. 20 and comm.
106. Cf. Sp.Kā., 29.
107. Sp.Pra., p. 123.
108. Sp.Nir., p. 64.
109. Sp.Kā.vi., p. 124.
110. T.Ā., II, pp. 85-6.
111. M.V.V., p. 26.

112. Ibid., 1/267.
113. Sp.Kā., 3.
114. Ī.P.v., I, p. 108.
115. Ī.P.V.V., I., p. 286: tatra ca yadaiśvaryaṃ svātantryaṃ sā jñānaśaktir iti.
116. Sp.Kā.vi., p. 7: nimeṣa prasṛtakriyāśaktitvāt svarūpasaṃkocarūpe jagataḥ udaya udbhavaḥ.
117. Ī.P.v., II, p. 136.
118. Ī.P., comm. 1/5/14.
119. Ś.Sū.vi., p. 2.
120. Ś.Dṛ., p. 148.
121. M.V.V., 1/344-a.
122. Ibid., 1/310b-11a.
123. T.Ā., 3/99a-100a.
124. Sp.Kā.vi., p. 4.
125. T.A., 1/314b-5a.
126. N.T., 21/39b-40a.

CHAPTER IV

1. O Three-eyed Lord! You contemplate Your pairs of opposites (*yuga*) such as Heaven and Earth, ocean and river, tree and forest, tone and microtone, internal and external, white (semen) and red (ovum), light and darkness, knowledge and action in [Your] extensive consciousness of both.
M.M., p. 72.
2. V.B., v. 18.
3. Ś.Dṛ., 3/7a.
4. Ibid., 3/2b-3.
5. Sp.Nir., p. 6.
6. P.P., v. 30.
7. T.Ā., 3/93b.
8. yāmalaṃ prasaraṃ sarvaṃ, ibid., comm. 3/67; also ibid., 3/68 and ibid., 29/49.
9. Ibid., comm. 28/322a.
10. Sp.Nir., p. 3.
11. T.Ā., 5/60-1a.
12. Ibid., comm..
13. Ibid., 29/116-7a.
14. Ibid., 29/119-20: My translation differs from Gnoli's who renders 'iti tathoditaṃ śāntam' as: 'tale e la descrizione della forma quiescente'. The context is the sexual union of Siddha and Yoginī through which they realise the union of opposites.
15. Ibid., 29/120-1.
16. M.M., v. 28.

17. *Saṃvidullāsa* quoted in M.M., p. 152.
18. P.T.V., p. 167.
19. K.K.V., p. 158.
20. Ibid., p. 156.
21. Ibid., v. 50.
22. Ibid., p. 153.
23. Ibid., p. 157.
24. Sp.Nir., p. 66. See Chapter 7 for a detailed description of this movement.
25. K.K.V., v. 5.
26. Ibid., v. 25.
27. Ibid., v. 50.
28. Sp.Kā., 1; Sp.Nir., p. 8.
29. Ibid., p. 19; cf. Sp.Pra., p. 108.
30. T.Ā., comm. 1/74; V.B., v. 20-1.
31. Sp.Pra., p. 85.
32. Sp.Kā., 29a.
33. Ī.P.v., I, p. 9.
34. śaṃ karoti iti saṃkaraḥ, Sp.Pra., p. 88; Sp.Kā.vi., p. 3; Sv.T., I., p. 9.
35. Sp.Pra., p. 85.
36. Ī.P.v. I., p. 17.
37. Sp.Nir., p. 3.
38. Sp.Pra., p. 88.
39. Ibid., p. 90.
40. Ś.St., 20/12, quoted in Sp.Nir., p. 19.
41. Sp.Pra., p. 84.
42. Sp.Nir., p. 3.
43. St.Ci., v. 69.
44. Ibid., v. 73.
45. A verse quoted from his own *stotra* by Kṣemarāja in comm., St.Ci., v. 34.
46. Ī.P.v., I, pp. 13-4.
47. Śt.Ci., v. 34.
48. Ibid., v. 33.
49. Sp.Pra., p. 85.
50. Sp.Pra. p. 92; M.M., p. 118 yad yad rūpaṃ kāmayate tat tad devatārūpaṃ bhavati.
51. St.Ci., v. 96.
52. M.M., pp. 3-4.
53. Ibid., p. 117.
54. Ibid., p. 118.
55. Ś.Dṛ., 1/1.
56. Sp.Nir., p. 18.
57. T.Ā., 1/73; Ī.P., comm. 1/5/16-17.
58. T.Ā., 10/120.
59. Sp.Nir., p. 48; cf. M.M., p. 155.
60. Ś.Sū., 3/27: kathā japaḥ.
61. St.Ci., v. 21.

62. Sp.Nir., p. 12.
63. Ibid., p. 15; Sp.Pra., p. 95; cf. Ī.P., comm. 2/2/3.
64. Ī.P., 2/3/15; Pr.Hṛ., sū. 2.
65. M.V.V., 1/1041; cf. 1/951-2; T.Ā., 11/97-9.
66. Ī.P., comm. 2/3/15-6.
67. M.V.V., 1/276-7.
68. Sp.Kā.vi., p. 8.
69. T.Ā., 9/221-2.
70. Sp.Nir., p. 36; Ī.P., 4/1/4.
71. Pr.Hṛ., sū. 5.
72. Ibid., sū. 6; Ś.Sū., 3/1.
73. See below chapter 5, fn. 102.
74. Sp.Nir., p. 16.
75. Ibid.
76. Sp.Kā.vi., p. 28.
77. Ibid., p. 64.
78. Sp.Kā., 19b.
79. Although Kṣemarāja glosses *'guṇādi'* (lit. 'qualities, etc.') as referring to the qualities of *Sattva, Rajas* and *Tamas*, Swami Laksmanjoo of Kashmir interprets *'guṇādi'* to mean the powers of the sense organs of knowledge and action (*karma-* and *jñānendriya*). According to this interpretation, what the verse means is that the generic vibration of universal consciousness can be realised by means of the particular pulsations of consciousness operating through the senses.
80. Sp.Kā., 19-20.
81. P.S., comm. v. 39.
82. T.Ā., 3/287a.
83. Sp.Kā.vi., pp. 66-7.
84. Sp.Kā., 1/21a.
85. Sp.Pra., p. 106.
86. T.Ā., 9/52b-3a.
87. Ī.P.V.V., II, p. 209.
88. Bhā., vol. 2, p. 208; cf. T.Ā., 4/171-2.
89. Ī.P.v., I, pp. 31-2.
90. Ī.P.v., comm. 1/5/15.
91. Ī.P., comm. 2/3/17.
92. P.S., comm. v. 4.
93. Sp.Kā.vi., p. 9; cf. Ī.P.V.V., II, p. 208; T.Ā. 4/171-2.
94. Ibid.
95. Ś.Sū., 3/30.
96. T.Ā., 1/74.
97. Cf. Ś.Dṛ., 4/1-3.
98. Ibid., comm.
99. Ī.P.V.V., I. p. 273; T.Ā., 10/163; cf. Ś.Dṛ., 4/2.
100. T.Ā., comm. 1/69: phalabhedād aropitabhedaḥ padārthātmā śakti.
101. Ī.P.V.V., I, p. 288.

102. Sp.Kā.vi., p. 12.
103. Ī.P.v., II, p. 43.
104. T.Ā., 1/78-81.
105. Sp.Nir., pp. 14-5.
106. M.M., p. 47.
107. T.Ā., comm. 1/2.
108. P.T.V., p. 130.
109. Ī.P.v., I., p. 338.
110. P.T.V., p. 133.
111. M.V., 3/33, quoted in T.Ā., 3/71b-2a and Sp.Nir., pp. 67-8.
112. T.Ā., 3/72b-3a.
113. Ī.P.v., comm. 1/8/10-11.
114. Ibid.
115. Ī.P.v., comm. 2/2/3.
116. M.M., p. 47.
117. T.Ā., 3/74b-5a.
118. Ī.P.v., comm. 1/8/10-11.
119. Ibid.
120. M.M., p. 47.
121. T.Ā., 1/3.
122. M.V., 3/31, quoted in Sp.Nir. p. 67.
123. T.Ā., 13/266-8a; Sp.Kā.vi., p. 133.
124. Sp.Kā., 48.
125. Sp.Nir., p. 72.
126. Intro., comm. in Sp.Nir. on Sp.Kā., v. 48.
127. Sp.Kā.vi., p. 144.
128. T.Ā., 13/269.
129. Sp.Nir., p. 72.
130. Ibid.
131. Quote from Kallaṭa's comm. in Sp.Kā.vi., p. 143.
132. Ibid.
133. Sp.Kā., 48.
134. Sp.Kā.vi., p. 152.
135. T.Ā., 3/192b-3a.
136. T.Ā., 3/93.

CHAPTER V

1. T.Ā., 5/102b-4a.
2. T.Ā., 1/109-12.
3. P.T.V., p. 35.
4. Sp.Nir., p. 6.
5. Sp.Saṃ., p. 14.
6. Ibid.

7. Śā.Dṛ., p. 182.
8. Sp.Saṃ., p. 22.
9. Sp.Kā., 1.
10. M.M., p. 38; T.Ā., 3/266-7.
11. M.V.V., 1/944-6.
12. M.M., p. 82.
13. An unknown Tantra Jayaratha quotes in T.Ā., p. 40 says: "The Supreme Sky is the King of Realities (*tattva*), the abode of contemplation, the contemplative absorption which pervades upward from the Centre [of consciousness]."
14. Ibid., 3/140.
15. M.V.V., 1/949.
16. V.B., pp. 110-1.
17. Ibid., v. 89.
18. S.C.N., v. 42.
19. Sp.Saṃ., p. 6; M.M., p. 50.
20. Cf. Sp.Kā., 41.
21. Ī.P.V.V., II, p. 63-4.
22. P.T.V., p. 35.
23. M.V.V., p. 16.
24. Pr.Hṛ., pp. 46-7.
25. Sv.T., vol. 2, pp. 185-94.
26. Ibid.
27. T.Ā., 11/21.
28. L.V., v. 40.
29. Ibid., v. 39.
30. Sp.Pra., p. 97.
31. *Ālokamālā* quoted in Sp.Nir., p. 28; Sp.Pra., p. 97.
32. Sv.T., 4/292 in Sp.Nir., p. 11.
33. Sp.Nir., p. 11; ibid., p. 27.
34. Ibid.
35. Ibid.
36. Sp.Kā., 15.
37. Sp.Nir., pp. 32-3.
38. Sp.Kā., 12.
39. Ibid., 10.
40. Ibid., 13.
41. Sp.Nir., p. 29: spandatattvasamāvivikṣūṇām api ca śithilībhūtaprayatnānāṃ śūnyam etad vighnabhūtam.
42. Kallaṭa's comm. on Sp.Kā., 1.
43. Pr.Hṛ., comm. sū. 20.
44. Ś.Dṛ., p. 6.
45. Yogatattva Up., 131-3.
46. Ī.P.V.V., I., p. 47.
47. Quoted in M.M., p. 24.
48. Sp.Pra., p. 88.
49. Ī.P.V.V., II, pp. 258-9.

50. M.V.V., 2/115; T.Ā., 5/127.
51. T.Ā., 5/37-40.
52. Ibid., 3/254.
53. Ibid., 4/146b.
54. See below.
55. T.Ā., 3/250b-1a.
56. Ibid., comm. 4/145.
57. Sp.Nir., p. 6.
58. T.Ā., 5/27b-36.
59. Ibid., 5/42.
60. Ibid., 5/37-8.
61. *Kramakeli* in M.M., p. 172; Sp.Nir., p. 6.
62. Kallaṭa's comm. on Sp.Kā., 1.
63. Sp.Saṃ., p. 1.
64. Sp.Nir., p. 7.
65. Sp.Kā.vi., p. 162.
66. Sp.Nir., p. 74.
67. Sp.Kā.vi., p. 164.
68. Sp.Kā., 51.
69. Pr.Hṛ., sū. 20.
70. Cf. P.T.V., p. 251.
71. T.Ā., 5/33.
72. P.T.L.V., p. 7.
73. Sp.Nir., p. 25.
74. P.T.L.V., p. 13.
75. Sp.Saṃ., p. 17.
76. Ibid., p. 18.
77. Ibid., p. 23.
78. Ibid., p. 17.
79. Ibid., p. 12.
80. Ibid., p. 20-1.
81. *Kulayukti* quoted in Sp.Pra., p. 86.
82. See Sp.Nir., p. 38.
83. M.M., p. 86.
84. P.T.V., pp. 39-40.
85. M.M., p. 86.
86. Sp.Nir., p. 37; Sp.Saṃ., p. 21.
87. M.M., p. 86; K. C. Pandey, p. 508.
88. P.P., v. 23.
89. T.Ā., 4/177b-8a.
90. Sp.Nir., p. 37.
91. Sp.Saṃ., p. 21.
92. Pr.Hṛ., p. 60.
93. L. Silburn, V.S., p. 75.
94. Sp.Saṃ., p. 20; cf. Sp.Nir., p. 28.
95. Sp.Saṃ., p. 20; Pr.Hṛ., p. 60-1.

96. Sp.Saṃ., p. 21.
97. Cf. Sp.Nir., p. 20; L.Ā.S., p. 63.
98. Sp.Nir., p. 46.
99. T.Ā., 9/244-5.
100. Ī.P. comm., 4/1/1/.
101. Sp.Kā., 6-7.
102. This is according to Kallaṭa's interpretation of this passage. Rājānaka Rāma and Bhagavatotpala agree with this view. Kṣemarāja, however, interprets the 'inner circle' to mean the presiding deities of the senses (see below) and expressly refutes the other commentators' interpretation. Kṣemarāja also rejects Abhinava's view (expressed in Ī.P.V.V., II, p. 301) that the 'inner circle' stands for the subtle body (*puryaṣṭaka*) which transmigrates at death. Sp.Nir., p. 20-1.
103. M.M., v. 20.
104. T.Ā., 9/225; M.V., 1/30.
105. T.Ā., 9/227.
106. Ibid., 9/228-9.
107. Ibid., 9/230.
108. T.Sā., p. 86.
109. V.P., v. 3.
110. A.P.S., v. 22b.
111. Ī.P.v., I., p. 239.
112. T.Ā., 9/231-2; T.Sā., p. 86.
113. T.Ā., 37/2; V.B., v. 109.
114. St.Ci., v. 37.
115. T.Ā., 9/231.
116. Sp.Nir., p. 22.
117. T.Ā., 4/160-3.
118. Ibid., 9/277.
119. See Ī.P., 2/2/3 and comm. T.Ā., 9/278-9.
120. M.M., v. 21.
121. Ibid., p. 61.
122. Ibid., p. 61.
123. Ibid., p. 84.
124. Ī.P.v., comm. 1/1/3.
125. Ī.P., 1/1/4.
126. T.Ā., comm. 9/246.
127. M.M., p. 62.
128. Ibid.
129. T.Ā., 9/234.
130. Ibid., 9/241.
131. Ibid., 9/249-50.
132. T.Ā., 9/242-3.
133. Ibid., 9/271-2.
134. M.M., p. 63.
135. T.Ā., 9/265b-8.

136. Walking entails abandoning one place and reaching another.

137. At the climax of sexual union the individual experiences the bliss and contentment of resting in his own nature and so neither seeks to procure nor abandon anything.

138. T.Ā., 9/256.

139. M.M., p. 61. This is also the name of a section of the *Stanzas on Vibration.*

CHAPTER VI

1. Ś.Sū., 1/2: jñānaṃ bandhaḥ.
2. Cf. T.Ā., 12/5; M.M., p. 73.
3. T.Ā., 4/119b-20a.
4. P.S., v. 74.
5. Ī.P.V.V., I., p. 43.
6. Ś.Sū., 1/14; M.M., p. 80: dṛśyaṃ śarīram.
7. T.Ā., 12/6-8.
8. M.M., p. 73.
9. V.P., v. 6.
10. Ś.Sū.vi., p. 15.
11. Ī.P.V.V., II, pp. 135-6.
12. T.Ā., 9/161b-4a.
13. Ś.Sū.vā., p. 5; Sp.Kā.vi., p. 10.
14. Ś.Sū.vā., pp. 37-8.
15. T.Ā., 6/62; M.M., v. 29.
16. Ś.Sū.vā., p. 23.
17. M.M., p. 74.
18. T.Ā., 4/119.
19. Ibid., 15/284b-7a.
20. P.S., comm. v. 60.
21. Ibid., comm. v. 67.
22. Ibid., comm. v. 68.
23. Ibid., comm. v. 76.
24. T.Ā., 15/234b-6.
25. Ś.Śu., 2/8.
26. V.B., v. 149.
27. P.S., v. 76.
28. Ibid., comm.
29. Quoted in Ś.Sū.vi., p. 33.
30. Sp.Kā., 9 and comm. by Kṣemarāja.
31. T.Ā., IX, pp. 129-30.
32. Ibid., 15/238.
33. Ibid., 15/265.
34. Ibid., comm. 15/261.

35. Ibid., 15/267b-8a.
36. Ibid., 15/167.
37. Ibid., 12/12.
38. P.S., v. 79-80.
39. Cf. ibid., v. 61-2.
40. T.Ā., 29/183-5.
41. P.T.V., p. 42.
42. M.M., v. 34.
43. P.S., v. 47-50.
44. P.T.V., p. 42.
45. Ś.Sū.vā by Varadarāja, 1/77b.
46. P.T.V., p. 61.
47. T.Ā., comm. 5/20.
48. Sp.Nir., p. 20; Sp.Saṃ., p. 15.
49. See Pandey (appendix C), pp. 952-3.
50. P.S., comm. v. 51; Sp.Kā.vi., p. 40.
51. M.M., v. 24.
52. Sp.Nir., p. 20.
53. Ibid., p. 20.
54. M.M., pp. 7-8.
55. M.M., p. 14.
56. Ś.St., 8/5 quoted in Sp.Nir., p. 21.
57. V.B., v. 74.
58. St.Ci., v. 61.
59. Ī.P.V.V., II, p. 178-9.
60. T.Ā., 10/160-1.
61. Ibid., 3/229b.
62. Ibid., 3/209b-10.
63. P.T.V., pp. 45-52.
64. T.Ā., 3/229.
65. Ś.Sū., 3/9; cf. Ś.Dṛ., 1/37; M.M., v. 19.
66. Ś.Sū., 3/10.
67. Ibid., 3/11.
68. St.Ci., v. 59.
69. Ś.St., 1/20.
70. T.Ā., comm. 3/229.
71. Ibid., 4/120.
72. Ś.St., 13/8.
73. T.Ā., 5/83.
74. Śv.Up., 3/17a-19 (Hume's trans.).
75. Sp.Kā.vi., p. 34.
76. Sp.Nir., p. 8.
77. Ś.Sū., 1/22.
78. M.M., v. 63.
79. V.B., v. 32.
80. P.S., p. 47.

81. Sp.Saṃ., pp. 2-3.
82. Sp.Pra., p. 94; M.M., pp. 60-1.
83. Sp.Kā., 8.
84. Sp.Pra., p. 97.
85. M.M., pp. 56-7.
86. Ś.Sū.vā., p. 8.
87. Ibid.
88. Sp.Kā., 41.
89. Sp.Kā.vi., p. 116.
90. P.T.V., p. 108.
91. V.B., v. 62.
92. Sp.Nir., p. 62.
93. Ibid.
94. Sp.Kā., 36-7.
95. M.M., pp. 174-5.
96. Ibid., comm. v. 13.
97. Ibid., p. 106.
98. Ibid., p. 174.
99. Ibid., v. 42.
100. Sp.Nir., p. 19.
101. Sp.Kā.vi., p. 38.
102. Sp.Nir., p. 22.
103. Pr.Hṛ., sū. 15.
104. Kallaṭa, comm. Sp.Kā., 37.
105. Sp.Kā., 38.
106. Kallaṭa, comm. Sp.Kā., 6-7.
107. Sp.Kā.vi., p. 111.
108. Kallaṭa, comm. Sp.Kā., 38.
109. Sp.Nir., p. 59; Sp.Kā.vi., p. 110.
110. Sp.Kā., 40.
111. T.Ā., 12/24: śaṅkayā jāyate glāniḥ.
112. Ibid.
113. P.T.V., pp. 233-5.
114. T.Ā., 12/20.
115. Ibid.
116. P.T.V., p. 233.
117. Sp.Kā.vi., pp. 114-5.
118. Sp.Nir., p. 61.
119. P.T.V., p. 235.
120. Sp.Kā., 9-10.
121. T.Ā., 9/144b-5a.
122. Ibid., 9/62; P.T.V., p. 41.
123. Sp.Nir., p. 23.
124. M.V., 1/23.
125. Ī.P., 3/2/4.
126. Sp.Nir., p. 23.

127. Ī.P., 3/2/5: bhinnavedyaprathā.
128. Pr.Hṛ., p. 79.
129. V.B., v. 49.
130. C.G.C., v. 28.
131. T.Ā., 3/262-4.
132. P.Hṛ., p. 97: citsāmānyaspandabhūḥ unmeṣātmāvyākhyātavyā.
133. Sv.T., I., p. 14.
134. Ī.P.V.V., II., p. 25.
135. Pr.Hṛ., p. 79.
136. Sp.Nir., p. 25.
137. *Kakṣyāstotra* quoted in Pr.Hṛ., p. 80; M.M., p. 80.
138. Sp.Nir., p. 20.
139. M.M., p. 90.
140. Ibid.
141. Quoted in Sp.Nir., p. 25; M.M., p. 90.
142. Ī.P.v., II, p. 178; V.B., v. 60.
143. M.M., p. 91; Sp.Nir., p. 25; on Mudrā see T.Ā., XXXII; Pr.Hṛ., pp. 85-88.
144. Sp.Nir., p. 25.
145. Sp.Kā., 11.
146. T.Ā., 5/80b.
147. M.M., p. 91.
148. T.Ā., comm. 5/79.
149. Ś.Sū., 1/21; Pr.Hṛ., sū. 20 and comm.
150. Sp.Nir., p. 74.
151. Ibid., p. 44.
152. Ibid.
153. Ibid., pp. 25-6, p. 54.
154. Quoted in Pr.Hṛ., p. 86.
155. Pr.Hṛ., pp. 85-6.
156. Ibid., p. 88.
157. Ś.Sū., 1/12.
158. Sp.Kā., 11.
159. Sp.Nir., pp. 25-6.

CHAPTER VII

1. 'The waking state is knowledge'. 'Dreaming is the formation of thought-constructs.' Ś.Sū., 1/8-9. Kṣemarāja, commenting on these *Aphorisms* says: "the first moment of awareness (*jñāna*), free of the thought-constructs proper to the dreaming state, is waking. Again, those thought-constructs which [arise] there constitute dreaming." Ś.Sū.vi., p. 11.

2. Sp.Kā., 5: "That exists in the ultimate sense where there is neither pleasure nor pain, subject nor object, nor an absence of consciousness."

3. Sp.Pra., p. 111, 115; Sp.Kā., 10.
4. T.Ā., 6/68-9.
5. Ibid., 15/107-9a.
6. Ibid. 4/209b-10. This verse refers to the realisation of identity with Śiva in the absolute (*anuttara*) which Abhinava identifies with the supreme form of Spanda (ibid., 3/93b).
7. Ibid., comm. 4/94. Jayaratha says: "Bondage is defined as the spatial and other relative distinctions which pertain to the contracted condition consciousness freely assumes."
8. Ś.Sū., 1/2.; T.Ā., 1/26-30.
9. Ibid., 1/25.
10. Ibid., 9/71b-5a.
11. Pr.Hṛ., p. 32: Kṣemarāja writes: "If we reflect carefully on the nature of contraction [we discover that] because we experience it to be one with consciousness, even that is nothing but consciousness itself."
12. T.Ā., 1/141.
13. Ibid., comm. 5/9.
14. Ś.Sū.vā., p. 12, fn. 14.
15. Sp.Kā., 46.
16. See above pp. 63-4.
17. Sp.Kā., 28-30.
18. Sp.Pra., p. 88.
19. Sp.Nir., p. 49 and Jayadeva Singh's translation pp. 119-20.
20. Sp.Nir., p. 44.
21. Sp.Kā., 32.
22. Sp.Nir., p. 52.
23. Ś.Sū., 2/6.
24. See Kṣemarāja's commentary on Ś.Sū., 2/6.
25. Kṣemarāja says that the Supreme Goddess, the power of grace and the Master are equal. He quotes the *Mālinīvijayatantra* as saying: "That [power of grace] is called the Wheel of Energies said to be the Master's mouth" and the *Tantra of the Three-headed Bhairava* which says: "Higher than the Master is [his] power which resides in his mouth."
26. Ś.Sū.vā., p. 35.
27. Sp.Kā., 52.
28. Ibid., 44.
29. T.Ā., 1/253.
30. Ibid., 1/256.
31. Ibid., 1/234-5.
32. Sp.Nir., p. 52.
33. *'Yukti'* is a term which, in these works, means a number of things including 'reason', 'expedient', 'means', and in a more technical sense, a knowledge of the means to self-realisation. Thus the *Vijñānabhairava* teaches 112 such means. Kṣemarāja explains that "the word *'yukti'* indicates there [in the *Vijñānabhairava*] the knowledge of the 112 planes of yoga [taught therein]." Ś.Sū.vi., p. 121. For the usage of this term in this technical sense see V.B., v. 148.

Note also the names of two works quoted in Bhagavatotpala's commentary on the *Stanzas*, namely, *Tattvayukti* and *Kulayukti.*

34. *Kiraṇāgama* 1/9, 13b quoted in T.Ā., 4/41, 4/78, 13/162b. The *Niśācāratantra* says the same; see T.Ā., 4/78.

35. T.Ā., 4/77b-8a.

36. Sp.Pra., p. 84.

37. Ibid., p. 83.

38. Ibid., p. 84.

39. M.M., p. 6.

40. Sp.Nir., pp. 16-7: yuktyanubhavāgamajño rahasyagurupravaraḥ.

41. Sp.Nir., p. 2.

42. Sp.Kā., 42. Abhinava similarly says: "How can [the experience of] that which is our own consciousness be ever set to writing?" T.Ā., 29/126a.

43. Bh.G., 12/2, quoted in Sp.Nir., p. 49.

44. Sp.Pra., p. 115.

45. Sp.Kā.vi., p. 64.

46. Ś.Sū.vi., p. 70.

47. Sp.Nir., p. 33.

48. Ibid., p. 35.

49. Sp.Kā.vi., p. 55.

50. Sp.Nir., p. 49. Abhinava also says:

> The wise sever the very root of this tree of harmful multiplicity, so hard to fell (*durbheda*), with the axe of sound reasoning: such is our conviction. This [reasoning] the awakened call the contemplative actualisation of Being (*bhāvanā*), the wish-granting cow which renders evident even that which is beyond the sphere of desire.
> T.Ā., 4/13-4.

51. Ibid., 4/15-6.

52. Ibid., 4/39-40.

53. Sp.Kā. vṛtti, p. 31.

54. Sp.Nir., p. 16.

55. Ibid., p. 29 with reference to Sp.Kā., 12-13. 15.

56. T.Ā., 1/245. cf. T.Ā., 2/4: "The four-fold emergent (*udita*) nature of the All-pervasive Lord's consciousness should be known to be one's own nature itself, the eternally manifest (*nityodita*) Lord."

57. T.Ā., v. I, pp. 52-3. See above p. 12.

58. See above p. 12.

59. Good examples are the practices taught in the *Vijñānabhairava*, a text which certainly pre-dates Abhinava. Kṣemarāja, and later Śivopādhyāya, both indicate to which of these categories the practices taught in it belong.

60. We shall discuss the relation between the *Stanzas on Vibration* and the *Śivasūtra* in the companion volume of this work.

61. The nomenclature of the division into chapters in Sanskrit works in general is very varied and particularly well illustrated in the Tantras and related literature. Thus "there are *Paricchedas* "Sections", *Prakāśas* "Rays", *Ullāsas*

"Illuminations", *Taraṅgas* "Waves", and many others. A popular principle is that of adapting the term for "chapter" to the title of the whole work. Thus the *Mantraratnākara* and *Mantramahodadhi*, two "Oceans of Mantras" are divided into "Waves", the *Śivārcanacandrikā* "Moonlight of Śiva Worship" into "Rays", the *Saubhāgyakalpadruma* "Fabulous Tree of Delight" into *'Skandha'*, "Branches"; the *Bhuvaneśvarīkalpalatā* "Wish-granting Creeper of Bhuvaneśvarī" into *'Stabakas'*—Bunches of Flowers." Teun Goudriaan and Sanjukta Gupta, *Hindu Tantric and Śākta Literature*, A History of Indian Literature, edited by J. Gonda, vol. 2 fasc. 20 (Wiesbaden: Harrassowitz, 1981), p. 31.

62. See footnote 64 below.

63. T.Ā., 4/273.

64. We have said that there are four types of means to realisation. Although this is quite true from one point of view, the fourth and ultimate means is not one in the same sense as are the others. Considered to be the highest form of the Divine means (*śāmbhavopāya*, for which see below), it is the end of all practice and is accordingly called 'No-means' (*anupāya*). It is the uninterrupted consciousness the absolute has of its own nature (T.Ā., 2/1) spontaneously and completely realised in an instant. Thus *'Anupāya'* is the means (*upāya*) that concerns the absolute (*anuttara*) directly. This means is very important in Abhinavagupta's Trika which aims primarily at the realisation of *Anuttara*. The reader is referred to P.T.V., pp. 81-4 for the meanings Abhinava attributes to this term (see also Gnoli's translation, pp. 49-50). Abhinava does not quote scripture to define this Means. Possibly Abhinava intends to imply in this way that, insofar as no practice is involved here, it is essentially undefinable. For the same reason it is sometimes not counted amongst the means to realisation which are thus reduced to three.

65. According to Abhinava the word *'guruṇā'* can mean either 'by the Master' or 'intense'. We have put the former meaning in brackets because what is essential at this level of practice is that consciousness be intensely alert; it does not matter whether this takes place spontaneously or is induced.

66. T.Ā., 1/168-70 quoted from M.V., 2/21-3.

67. T.Ā., 1/178b-9a.

68. Ibid., 1/91.

69. Ibid., 1/241-3.

70. Ibid., 1/180b-1a.

71. Ibid., 1/182b-3a.

72. ibid., 1/144b, 1/165.

73. Ibid., 1/245.

74. Ibid., 1/166.

75. Ibid., 1/143 and comm.

76. Ibid., 1/140.

77. Ibid., 2/4-6.

78. Ibid., 2/1.

79. Pañcast., vol. 3, p. 2.

80. T.Ā., 1/145.

81. Ibid., 2/38.
82. Ibid., 2/9.
83. Ibid., 2/11.
84. Ibid., 2/14.
85. Ibid., 2/19.
86. Ibid., 2/28.
87. Ibid., 2/24-6.
88. *Anuttarāṣṭikā*, v. 1-3.
89. T.Ā., 1/242.
90. Ibid., 2/2.
91. See comm. to T.Ā., 2/2.
92. *Ratnamālā* quoted in M.M., p. 166.
93. T.Ā., 2/40.
94. T.Ā., comm. 2/2. The passage quoted here by Jayaratha is probably from the *Siddhayogeśvarīmata* which Abhinava tells us teaches the way of *Anupāya* called, in this passage, *Nirupāya.* Cf. T.Ā., comm. 2/40.
95. Sp.Saṃ., p. 25.
96. Ś.Dṛ., 7/5b-6; cf. ibid., 7/100b and T.Ā., 2/47.
97. We shall discuss this point more extensively in the companion volume of translations from the Spanda tradition.
98. Sp.Nir., pp. 25-6.
99. T.Ā., comm. 1/226: evaṃ ca nirvikalpātmā paraḥ prakāśa eva sarveṣām eṣām upāyaḥ.
100. T.Ā., 1/246-7.
101. Ibid., 1/212.
102. Sp.Kā., 36-7.
103. T.Ā., 3/108.
104. Sp.Pra., p. 84.
105. Sp.Kā., 22.
106. Ibid., 33-5 and Kallaṭa's *vṛtti.*
107. Ibid., 41. See also above p. 153.
108. P.T.V., p. 106.
109. M.V.V., 1/418.
110. Ī.P.v., comm. 1/5/11.
111. Sp.Pra., p. 46.
112. Ī.P., 3/1/3a.
113. Sp.Saṃ., p. 6.
114. T.Ā., 4/182b-3.
115. Ibid., 1/84b-6a.
116. Ibid., 1/87-8.
117. Pr.Hṛ., sū. 17.
118. M.V.V., 2/20b: jagadānandamayo 'sau sāmānyaspanda ityuktaḥ.
119. The concept of a 'super ego' (*ahaṃbhāva*) is unique to the Kashmiri Śaiva schools and those influenced by them. It has virtually no precedents, even in the *Śaivāgama.* The development of this important insight goes to the credit of the Pratyabhijñā theologians, particularly Utpaladeva and Abhinava-

gupta. It is therefore absent in the *Stanzas on Vibration* which predate them. We shall deal with this important point in the companion volume to this work.

120. Y.Hṛ., comm. 1/35.

121. T.Ā., 3/111.

122. Sv.T., I., p. 56: aśeṣaviśvasāmarasyavedanātmā.

123. K.K.V., v. 5.

124. T.Sā., pp. 14-5. The word *'pravekṣyati'* (here translated 'penetrates into') is presumably derived from the root *'viś'* in the sense of 'entering'. The third person singular should be *'praveśati'*.

125. T.Ā., 3/125; K.K.V., v. 7.

126. Ibid., 3/205b-8a.

127. Ibid., 3/283-5.

128. Sp.Kā., 51; Pr.Hṛ., sū. 20.

129. Commenting on Ś.Sū., 3/4, which belongs to the section of the *sūtras* that Kṣemarāja explains deals with the Individual Means, he says:

> [The Individual Means] is gross, it is therefore not included in the Doctrine of Vibration (*spandaśāstra*) which is concerned with explaining the Empowered Means. However, when dealing here [with any practice] that ultimately culminates in the Empowered and other Means we have corroborated [what we have said] with the *Stanzas on Vibration* and shall to a certain extent, continue to do so.
> Ś.Sū.vi., p. 38.

130. T.Ā., 1/202-4.

131. Ibid. 1/206.

132. Ibid. 1/217-8.

133. Sp.Kā., 46. The reader is referred to the introductory discussion at the beginning of this chapter.

134. M.V., 2/22.

135. Ī.P., 1/6/3-5; P.S., comm. v. 2; T.Ā., comm. 4/175; ibid., vol. 2, p. 199.

136. Sp.Pra., p. 105.

137. Ī.P.V.V., II, p. 15.

138. T.Ā., 10/200.

139. P.S., comm. v. 42.

140. T.Ā., 14/43.

141. T.Ā., 14/111b-3a; ibid., 5/2.

142. M.V.V., 1/988b-90; T.Ā., 10/201-3.

143. T.Sā., p. 23.

144. T.Ā., 5/5a.

145. T.Ā., 7/30b-2a.

146. Ī.P., 1/5/20.

147. Ī.P.V.V., I, p. 118.

148. Ibid., p. 246.

149. Y.Hṛ., p. 78.

150. T.Sā., pp. 22-3.

151. *Saṃvitprakāśa* quoted in M.M., p. 25.

152. T.Ā., 12/18b-21a. The context here is ritual. He who offers to the deity obnoxious substances or those normally considered improper must try to do so with his mind free of doubts and aversion.

153. T.Ā., 5/5.

154. Ibid., 15/269b-72.

155. Ibid., 4/2-5.

156. Ibid., 4/84.

157. Ibid., 4/203.

158. Ibid., 4/116b-7a.

159. Ibid., 4/120b-1a.

160. Ibid., 4/181b-2a.

161. Ibid., 4/194.

162. Ibid., 4/195-9.

163. Ibid., 4/200.

164. Ibid., 4/201-2.

165. Ibid., 4/205-9a.

166. M.V., 18/78-80 quoted in T.Ā., 4/218-20.

167. Ibid., 4/240-1a.

168. Ibid., 4/244.

169. Ibid., 4/243b-4a.

170. Ś.Dṛ., 3/68-70.

171. M.V.V., 1/1112.

172. T.Ā., 13/42.

173. P.S., p. 73.

174. Sp.Pra., p. 88.

175. T.Sā. quoted in P.S., comm. v. 33.

176. Ī.P., v. II, p. 129.

177. Sp.Pra., p. 88.

178. T.Ā., comm. 10/118.

179. Sp.Kā., 8.

180. Ibid., 3.

181. Ś.Sū.vi., p. 38: śāktopāyaprakāśātmani spandaśāstre. Kṣemarāja lays great stress on the importance of contemplation and mastery of the Wheel of Energies. As a result he affirms that Spanda practice belongs predominantly to the Empowered Means. The energies are aspects of the freedom of consciousness which Kṣemarāja identifies with the supreme goddess of the Krama school. Her Wheel is that of the twelve Kālīs who represent phases in the cognitive cycle (described above on p. 124). Abhinava gives pride of place to the contemplation of this Wheel in his treatment of the Empowered Means in the *Tantrāloka* (verses 4/122b-181a). Thus Kṣemarāja concludes his exposition of the Aphorism which declares that "when the Wheel of Energies is fused into one there follows universal destruction" (Ś.Sū., 1/6) by stating that this practice belongs to the Empowered Means and is also taught in the first and the last verses of the *Stanzas on Vibration* (Ś.Sū.vi., p. 10). Kṣemarāja maintains that because these verses refer to the Wheel of Energies the Doctrine of Vibration includes the esoteric teaching of the Krama school. Thus Kṣemarāja says that:

"In this way the venerable Vasugupta indicates how, through the introduction and conclusion [of the Stanzas, the Spanda teachings] embrace Krama doctrine (*mahārtha*), and so reveals that this [Spanda] doctrine (*śāstra*) is supreme amongst all secret Śaiva doctrine because it is the essence of [Krama]." (Sp.Nir., p. 74).

182. Sp.Kā., 21.
183. Ś.Sū., 9; Ś.Sū.vi., p. 11; see fn. 1 above.
184. Sp.Kā., 35.
185. Sp.Pra., p. 112.
186. Ī.P., 1/5/13-4.
187. Sp.Pra., pp. 120-1.
188. T.Ā., 11/66; Sp.Nir., p. 71.
189. Sp.Pra., p. 113.
190. Sp.Nir., p. 71.
191. T.Ā., 11/68b-9.
192. Ibid., 11/73-5.
193. Sv.T., comm. 11/199.
194. T.Ā., 3/198.
195. Ibid., 15/130b-1a.
196. See above p. 103.
197. The anonymous author of the Sanskrit notes on the Ś.Sū.vā. writes:

Inferior and superior knowledge correspond to the perception of division and the manifestation of unity, respectively. The power *mātṛkā* is the mother of the universe who sustains and presides over them both. [When giving rise to the] superior knowledge [of ultimate reality] she is the power called *Aghora* because she makes manifest both the inner reality [of undifferentiated consciousness] and the outer reality [of the All] as her own nature. Inferior [knowledge is the domain of the aspect of *mātṛkā*] called the power *Ghora* who directs the consciousness [of the fettered soul] out of itself when it fails to reflect upon the unity of reality and so obscures its Śiva-nature.
(Ibid., fn. 9 pp. 8-9).

198. Sp.Kā., 45.
199. Ibid., 47.
200. V.M., p. 3: pīṭhastu mātṛkā proktā.
201. Sv.T., I, p. 29. See also Jaideva Singh, *The Divine Creative Pulsation*, p. 158; also Sp.Nir., pp. 66-9 on Sp.Kā., 45.
202. P.T.V., p. 44.
203. Ś.Sū.vi., p. 8.
204. P.T.V., pp. 43-4.
205. T.Ā., 5/140-1.
206. T.Ā., II, p. 214: mananaṃ sarvavettṛtvaṃ trānaṃ saṃsāryanugrahaḥ.
207. M.M., p. 122.
208. M.M., v. 49.

209. Sp.Kā.vi., p. 82.
210. Ī.P.V.V., II, pp. 213-4.
211. M.M., p. 122.
212. T.Ā., II, p. 450.
213. "The functions of an externally directed Mantra are said to be its powers when it is introverted." T.Ā., II, p. 47.
214. Y.Hṛ., p. 180.
215. T.Ā., 7/3b-5a.
216. Ibid., IV, p. 2.
217. Ibid., 4/182b-3.
218. P.T.V., p. 4.
219. Sp.Nir., p. 66.
220. "O beloved, the Mantras whose seed phonemic powers (*bīja*) lie dormant will bear no fruit, while those mantras which are filled with consciousness are said to accomplish all things." K.Ā., 15/60.
221. *Śrīkaṇṭhīyasaṃhitā* quoted in Ś.Sū.vi., p. 24.
222. Sp.Kā.vi., p. 81.
223. *Śrītantrasadbhāva* quoted in Ś.Sū.vi., p. 23.
224. Pr.Hṛ., p. 93.
225. Sv.T., VI, p. 40.
226. Sp.Nir., p. 45.
227. Ibid.
228. Sp.Kā.vi., p. 80.
229. Ibid., pp. 83-4.
230. T.Ā., 11/86-9.
231. Ś.Sū.vā., fn. 1, pp. 29-30.
232. T.Ā., III, p. 1.
233. The *Stotrabhaṭṭāraka* quoted in M.M., p. 112.
234. T.Ā., 11/76.
235. Ibid., comm. 11/77.
236. Sp.Kā.vi., pp. 83-4.
237. Sp.Kā., 26-7.
238. Ś.Sū.vā., fn. 1, p. 30.
239. Sp.Kā.vi., pp. 83-4.
240. Ś.Sū.vi., p. 38.
241. We shall have occasion to discuss the relationship between the *Śivasūtra* and the *Spandakārikā* in our companion volume of *Translations.* Suffice it to say here that even though all commentators connect the two texts in various ways, their relationship is far from clear. Bhāskara thinks that the *Stanzas* are a part of a commentary on the *Aphorisms* (Ś.Sū.vā., p. 3). Bhagavatotpala consistently refers to the *Stanzas* as a synopsis (*saṃgrahagrantha*) by Kallaṭabhaṭṭa of the essential teachings of the *Aphorisms* (Sp.Pra., p. 83). Kṣemarāja similarly says in a number of places that the *Stanzas* convey the secrets of the *Aphorisms* (Sp.Nir., p. 2). At the same time, however, commentators think of the *Stanzas* as representing a 'separate system' (*svatantradarśana*) (Sp.Pra., p. 87) or what Rājānaka Rāma calls 'the philosophy of Spanda' (*Spandasiddhānta*) (Sp.Kā.vi.,

p. 12). Kṣemarāja, it seems, also implies this when he refers to the *Stanzas* as *'Spandaśāstra'* if we understand *'śāstra'* in its broadest sense to mean 'a school of thought' rather than just a 'book' (Ś.Sū.vi., p. 38; Sp.Nir., p. 1). It seems, therefore, that although the *Stanzas* and *Aphorisms* are closely related, the former marks the emergence of a distinct school, whereas the latter, although serving as the principle source of the *Stanzas*, does not belong to any particular school. This hypothesis is supported by the striking absence in the *Aphorisms* of a number of the fundamental terms and concepts in the *Stanzas*. A prime example is the term *Spanda* itself, and the teachings concerning the experience of *Spanda* in the first moment of perception when consciousness is in a state of propensity (*aunmukhya*) to manifestation (see above pp. 92-95).

242. Ś.Sū.vi., pp. 35-6.

243. Ś.Sū., 1/1: caitanyam ātmā.

244. Ibid., 3/1: cittam ātmā.

245. Sp.Kā., 49-50a.

246. T.Ā., comm. 13/188.

247. cittaṃ mantraḥ: 'the mind is Mantra' (Ś.Sū., 2/1). Bhāskara, commenting on this *Aphorism*, says: "One should know the mind itself to be Śiva, the subject free of all limitations, endowed with omniscience and every other divine attribute. Free of the differentiation (*kalanā*) of time and space, its inalienable quality is the experience of its own identity and so, as such, is said to be Mantra." Ś.Sū.vā., p. 30.

248. Ibid., p. 42.

249. Abhinava writes:

> This Supreme and authentic reality shines also in this, the unreal subject, immersed in the intellect, vital breath and the body because the vital breath and the rest are not independent of the Light which is pure consciousness alone (*cinmātra*).
> T.Ā., 5/7-8a.

250. Ibid., 1/164.

251. Ś.Sū.vi., pp. 38, 41.

252. Abhinava writes:

> [The state of] individualised consciousness (*aṇu*) coincides with the most fully evident manifestation of multiplicity (*bheda*). The Means proper to it is therefore called 'Individual'. It consists of representations and ascertainments of a discursive order [which culminate] ultimately in [a pure] undifferentiated awareness.
> T.Ā., 1/221.

253. Ś.Sū.vi., p. 8.

254. Ibid., p. 9.

255. Ibid., p. 22.

256. Ś.Sū., 1/20 and 3/5; 1/7 and 3/20.

257. Ś.Sū.vi., p. 40.

258. Ś.Sū., 2/2.

259. Ś.Sū.vi., p. 35.
260. Ibid., p. 24.
261. Ibid., p. 50.
262. Ibid., p. 12.

263. Śivopādhyāya, like Kṣemarāja, understands the liberated state as one of permanent contemplation (*nityasamādhi*). Those who achieve it are never again disturbed by the emergence of the ego (V.B., p. 64). Taking the *Vākyasudhā*, a lost work on Yoga, as his authority, Śivopādhyāya outlines the six types of contemplation (*samādhi*) which lead to it. Śivopādhyāya defines contemplation (*samādhi*) as 'the subtle state of the mind engendered by its undivided, non-dual nature' (ibid., p. 99). The first degree of contemplation is discursive (*savikalpa*) and associated with visible objectivity (*dṛṣyasampṛkta-samādhi*). It is developed by attending to the movement of the mind in moments of intense excitement or passion. As the *Vākyasudhā* says: "One should contemplate the mind as the witness of passion, etc., capable of being such because it has taken on their likeness." The second degree of contemplation is also discursive but associated this time with the Word (*śabda*) of consciousness. This state is "pure being, consciousness and bliss. Self-illuminating, free of duality and worldly ties it is pervaded by the Word 'I am'". The third degree of contemplation is free of thought-constructs. Unlike the previous level of contemplation, which can only be attained with much effort, this one dawns spontaneously when the other two have been achieved. Free of discursivity and objects of perception it is tranquil and steady like the flame of a lamp set in a windless place. The yogi who is absorbed in it relishes the aesthetic delight (*rasa*) of the glorious powers of his authentic nature. To these three levels correspond three others which are their fruits. Thus the first degree of contemplation frees the yogi from his attachment to name and form and so he participates in the transcendental freedom of his universal consciousness even while he views the world and acts in it. To the second degree of contemplation corresponds the uninterrupted reflection (*cintā*) of the undivided and unique aesthetic delight (*akhaṇḍaikarasa*) of being, consciousness and bliss. The next degree of contemplation develops when the mind resumes its original absolute (*brahman*) nature and savours the aesthetic delight which results from the cessation of thought-constructs. The highest level of contemplation is permanent and effortless. It consists of the direct vision (*sākṣātkāra*) of reality attained when the six degrees of contemplation have matured to perfection. Liberated from all identification with the body, the yogi realises his Supreme Identity (*paramātman*) and so passes freely from one form of contemplation to the other wherever the mind may happen to wander (V.B., pp. 100-1).

264. Ś.Sū., 2/10.
265. Ś.Sū.vi., p. 35.
266. Ibid., p. 46.
267. Jaideva Singh writes:

> Such a high state of realisation is not possible by Āṇavopāya. It is only possible by Śāktopāya. But Āṇavopāya is only a stepping stone

to Śāktopāya . It is not an end in itself. It has to end in Śāktopāya. (*The Yoga of Supreme Identity*, p. 150)

Kṣemarāja also says that "even the Individual Means culminates in the Empowered." Ś.Sū.vi., p. 41.

268. Y.Sū., 1/2.
269. T.Ā., 1/150-1 and comm.
270. Sv.T., 4/22 quoted also in N.T.U., I, p. 180.
271. T.Ā., I, p. 190.
272. Y.Sū., 2/30.
273. Ibid., 2/32.
274. Ibid., 2/46.
275. Ibid., 2/49.
276. Ibid., 2/54.
277. Ibid., 3/1.
278. Ibid., 3/2.
279. Ś.Sū.vi., p. 41. Kṣemarāja, like other Kashmiri Śaivites, knew Patañjali's system well. He was aware that it also distinguished between minor yogic attainments and the higher realisation which they obstruct. Thus he quotes the *Aphorisms of Yoga* as saying: "The obstacles which arise in the course of contemplation are the yogic attainments (*siddhi*) gained when one emerges from it." (Y.Sū., 3/37 quoted in Ś.Sū.vi., p. 28) He connects this with stanza 42 of the *Stanzas on Vibration* which says:

> Shortly after, from that [expansion of consciousness] arises the Point (*bindu*), from that Sound (*nāda*), from that Form (*rūpa*) and from that Taste (*rasa*) which disturb the embodied soul.

The Point, etc., represent visions of light, sound, form and taste, respectively.

280. N.T.U., I., p. 181.
281. N.T., 8/6-8a.
282. Ś.Sū.vi., p. 38.
283. Ś.Sū., 3/4.
284. V.B., v. 56.
285. T.Ā., 8/4.
286. Ibid., 8/7-8.
287. Ibid. 3/262-4; ibid. 3/286; M.V.V., 1/1091.
288. V.B., v. 52.
289. T.Ā., 8/20b-4a.
290. Ibid., 6/140b-2a.
291. Ś.Sū.vi., p. 39.
292. This account is based on N.T., 8/11-18 and Sv.T., 7/294-300, which are Kṣemarāja's sources. Although the N.T. gives the full complement of eight limbs, Kṣemarāja eliminates the first two, thus reducing the limbs to six. N.T., 8/10 defines the missing two as follows:

> The supreme and permanent form of restraint (*yama*) is said to be dispassion from profane existence (*saṃsāra*), while the [inherent]

eternal, discipline (*niyama*) is contemplation (*bhāvanā*) of the Supreme Principle.

293. T.Ā., 4/89-91.

294. Sv.T., 7/299b-300a quoted in Ś.Sū.vi., p. 39.

295. *Samādhi*, which literally means 'gathering together [of the faculties]', is here made to derive from the words *'samanā*, meaning equal', and *'dhī'*, meaning 'intellect' or 'awareness'.

296. T.Ā., 10/185; ibid., 10/309; M.V., 2/34b-5a.

297. M.M., p. 156.

298. Ś.Sū.vā., p. 11: svasvarūpaikaghanatāvimarśas turyabhūḥ smṛtā.

299. Sp.Nir., p. 13; P.S., p. 74-81.

300. T.Ā., 10/266.

301. Ibid., 10/271.

302. Ibid., 10/268-9.

303. Pr.Hṛ., pp. 46-7.

304. T.Ā., 10/273-4.

305. Ś.Sū.vi., p. 12.

306. Ibid., p. 53.

307. Sv.T., 7/250.

308. Ś.Sū.vi., pp. 41-2.

309. Abhinava writes:

> Beyond the subject stands the pure awareness (*pramā*) which, no longer detached, is intent on becoming full and perfect. That is said to be the Fourth State, considered to be penetration into the power [of consciousness] (śaktisamāveśa).
> T.Ā., 10/264b-5b.

310. Ś.Sū.vi., p. 52.

311. Ibid.

312. Ibid., p. 50.

313. V.B., v. 138.

314. Ś.Sū., 3/23; cf. ibid., 2/10.

315. Ś.Sū.vi., p. 51.

316. Kallaṭabhaṭṭa is frequently quoted as saying in one of his lost works "the vital breath is the first transformation of consciousness"—prāk saṃvit prāṇe pariṇatā.

317. Ś.Sū.vi., p. 53.

318. Ibid.

319. Ś.Sū., 3/34.

320. Ś.Sū.vi., p. 61.

321. V.B., v. 69-76 and comm.

322. See above p. 93.

323. Ś.Sū.vi., p. 64.

324. Ibid., pp. 64-5.

325. N.T., 8/8 quoted in Ś.Sū.vi., p. 66.

326. Ś.Sū., 3/42.
327. Ś.Sū.vi., p. 69.

BIBLIOGRAPHY

SANSKRIT TEXTS

Īśvarapratyabhijñākārikā by Utpaladeva. With own *vṛtti.* K.S.T.S., no. 34, 1921. Edited by M. S. Kaul.

———. with *Vimarśinī* by Abhinavagupta. vol. 1. K.S.T.S., no. 22, 1918. Edited by M. R. Śāstrī. Vol. 2. K.S.T.S. no. 33, 1921. Edited by M. S. Kaul.

———. English translation named *Pratyabhijñā Kārikā of Utpaladeva* by R. K. Kaw. Srinagar: Sharada Peetha Research Centre, 1975.

———. English translation of the *Vimarśinī* by K. C. Pandey. In *Bhāskarī* vol. 3. Sarasvati Bhavan Texts, no. 84, Benares, 1954.

———. *Vivṛtivimarśinī* by Abhinavagupta. (3 vols.) K.S.T.S., no.60, 1938; 62, 1941 and 66, 1943, respectively. All edited by M. S. Kaul.

Kāmakalāvilāsa by Puṇyānandanātha. With the commentary of Naṭanānadanātha. Translated with commentary by Sir John Woodroffe. Madras: Ganesh and Co., 1971.

Gurunāthaparāmarśa by Madhurāja. K.S.T.S., no. 85, 1960. Edited by P. N. Pushp.

Cittasantoṣatriṃśikā by Nāgārjuna (*Nāgabhaṭṭa*). Edited by R. K. Kaw. Srinagar: Sharada Peetha Series, 1962.

Cidgaganacandrikā. Edited by Swami Trivikrama Tirtha. Tantrik Texts 20. Calcutta: Āgamanusaṃdhāna Samiti, 1936.

———. with *Divyacakorikā.* In two parts with commentary by Karra Agnihotra Śāstrī. Letukuru, East Godavari District, 1943.

———. with *Kramaprakāśikā.* Commentary by Raghunātha Miśra. Sarasvatībhavanagranthamālā, no. 115. Benares, 1980.

Tantravaṭadhānikā by Abhinavagupta. K.S.T.S., no. 26, 1918. Edited by

M. S. Kaul.

Tantrasāra by Abhinavagupta K.S.T.S., no. 17, 1918. Edited by M. S. Kaul.

———. Italian translation entitled *L'Essenza dei Tantra* by R. Gnoli. Torino: Boringheri, 1960.

———. Translation into Hindi with commentary *Nīrakṣīraviveka* by Paramahaṃsa Miśra. Vol. 1. Benares: Śākti Prakāśana, 1985.

Tantrāloka by Abhinavagupta (12 vol.) with *viveka* by Jayaratha. Part 1 edited by M. R. Śāstrī; parts 2-12 edited by M. S. Kaul, K.S.T.S., no. 23, 1918; 28, 1921; 30, 1921; 36, 1922; 35, 1922; 29, 1921; 41, 1924; 47, 1926; 59, 1938; 52, 1933; 57, 1936; and 57, 1938.

———. Translation into Italian. Titled *La Luce delle Sacre Scritture* by R. Gnoli. Torino: Classici Utet, Boringheri 1972.

Nareśvaraparīkṣā of Sadyojyoti with commentary by Rāmakaṇṭha. K.S.T.S., no. 45, 1926. Edited by M. S. Kaul.

Netratantra with *uddyota* by Kṣemarāja. Vol. 1., K.S.T.S., no. XLVI, 1926; vol. 2, no. 61, 1939. Both edited by M. S. Kaul.

Pañcastavī Five hymns to the goddess, in three parts with Sanskrit commentary by Hara Bhaṭṭa Śāstrī. Part 1, K.S.T.S., no. 90, 1963; part 2, K.S.T.S., no. 92, 1962; part 3, K.S.T.S., 87, 1960. All edited by Dīnānātha Yakṣa.

Paramārcanatriṃśikā by Nāgārjuna (*Nāgabhaṭṭa*). Edited by R. K. Kaw. Srinagar: Sharada Peetha Series, 1962.

Paramārthacarcā by Abhinavagupta. K.S.T.S., no. 77. Edited by J. Zadoo. Srinagar, 1947.

Paramārthasāra by Abhinavagupta with *vivṛti* by Yogarāja. K.S.T.S., no. 7, 1916. Edited by J. C. Chatterjee.

———. English translation titled *The Paramārthasāra of Abhinavagupta* by L. D. Barnett. *Journal of the Royal Asiatic Society of Great Britain and Ireland.* London, 1910.

———. With annotated Hindi translation by Prabhā Devī. Kashmir: Īśvara Āśrama, 1977.

———. French translation titled *La Paramārthasāra* by L. Silburn. Paris: E. de Boccard, 1958.

Paramārthasāra by Bhagavadādiśeṣa with *vivaraṇa* by Rāghavānanda. Edited with Sanskrit notes by Sūrya Nārāyaṇa Śukla. Acyutagranthamālā, no. 9. Benares, 1932.

Parātriṃśikālaghuvṛtti by Abhinavagupta. K.S.T.S., no. 67, 1947. Edited by J. Zadoo.

———. Italian translation called *Il commento Breve alla Trentina della Suprema* by R. Gnoli. Torino: Boringheri, 1965.

———. A French translation by A. Padoux. Paris: E. de Boccard, 1965.

Parātriṃśikāvivaraṇa by Abhinavagupta. K.S.T.S., no. 18, 1918. Edited by M. S. Kaul.

———. Sanskrit text with Hindi translation and notes under the name *Śrīśrīparātriṃśikā* by Nīlakaṇṭha Guruṭū. Delhi: Motilal Banarsidass, 1985.

———. Italian translation titled *Il Commento di Abhinavagupta alla Parātriṃśikā* by R. Gnoli. Serie Orientale Roma 57, Rome, 1985.

Parātriśikāvivṛti by Lakṣmīrāma. K.S.T.S., No. 69, 1947. Edited by J. Zadoo.

Paryantapañcāśikā by Abhinavagupta. Edited with notes by V. Raghavan. Reprinted in *Abhinavagupta and His Works*. Varanasi: Chaukhambha Orientalia, 1981.

Pāśupatasūtram with *Pañcārthabhāṣya* by Kauṇḍinya. Translated with an introduction on the history of Śaivism in India by Haripada Chakraborti. Calcutta: Academic Publishers, 1970.

Pratyabhijñāhṛdaya by Kṣemarāja. English translation titled *The Secret of Recognition* with notes from Baer's German translation. Adyar: Adyar Library, 1938. References are from this edition.

———. Hindi translation with notes by Jaideva Singh. Delhi: Motilal Banarsidass, 1973.

———. English translation with notes by Jaideva Singh. Delhi: Motilal Banarsidass, 1963.

———. English translation and commentary named *The Secret of Self-Realization* by I. K. Taimni. Adyar, 1974.

Bodhapañcadaśikā by Abhinavagupta. K.S.T.S., no. 86, 1947. Edited by J. Zadoo.

Bhagavadgītā with *Sarvatobhadra* by Rāmakaṇṭha. K.S.T.S., no. 64, 1943. Edited by M. S. Kaul.

———. Edited by Śrīnivāsa Nārāyaṇa. Ānandāśrama Sanskrit Series no. 112. Poona, 1939.

———. Edited with English and Sanskrit introductions by T. R. Cintāmaṇi. Madras: University of Madras, 1941.

Bhagavadgītārthasaṃgraha by Abhinavagupta. Edited by Lakṣmaṇa Raina. Srinagar, 1933.

Bhāskarī. A commentary by Bhāskarakaṇṭha on the *Īśvarapratyabhijñāvimarśinī* by Abhinava. Edited by K. A. S. Iyer and K. C. Pandey. Three parts: parts 1 and 2, Sanskrit texts. Part 3, English translation of the *Vimarśinī* with *An Outline of the History of Śaiva Philosophy*. Sarasvatībhavana Texts no. 70, 1938; 83, 1950; and 84, 1954.

Bhāvopahāra by Cakrapāṇi with *vivaraṇa* by Rāmyadeva. K.S.T.S., no. 14, 1918. Edited by M. R. Śāstrī.

Mahānayaprakāśa. There are two widely differing texts published under this name. One is entirely in Sanskrit and appears in the Trivendrum Sanskrit Series, no. 130. Edited by K. Sāmbaśiva Śāstrī. Trivendrum, 1937. The other is also in verse, although not in Sanskrit, together with a Sanskrit commentary by Śitikaṇṭha. K.S.T.S., no. 21. Edited by M. R. Sāstrī, Srinagar, 1918.

Mahārthamañjarī and *Parimala* by Maheśvarānanda. K.S.T.S., no. 11, 1918. Edited by M. R. Śāstrī.

———. Edited by Gaṇapati Śāstrī. Trivendrum Sanskrit Series, no. 66, 1919.

———. Edited by Vrajavallabha Dvivedi. *Yogatantragranthamālā*, no. 5. Benares, 1972. This is the edition quoted in this book.

———. French translation with exposition titled *La Mahārthamanjarī de Maheśvarānanda* by L. Silburn. Paris: E. de Boccard, 1968.

Mātṛkācakraviveka by Svatantrānandanātha. With Sanskrit *bhāṣya* by Śivānanda and Hindi translation by Kṛṣṇānanda Budhauliyā. Datiya: Pītāmbara Saṃskṛit Pariṣad, 1977.

Mālinīvijayavārtikā by Abhinavagupta. K.S.T.S., no. 31. Edited by M. S. Kaul. Srinagar, 1921.

Mālinīvijayottaratantra. K.S.T.S., no. 37, 1922, Srinagar. Edited by M. S. Kaul.

Yoginīhṛdaya with commentaries *Dīpaka* by Amṛtānanda and *Setubandha* by Bhāskara Rāya. Sarasvatībhavanagranthamālā no. 7, 2d ed. Edited by G. Kaviraj. Benares, 1963.

Rājataraṅgiṇī by Kalhaṇa. In *A Chronicle of the Kings of Kaśmīr*. Translated, with introduction, commentary and appendices by M. A. Stein. 2 vols. Reprint. Delhi: Motilal Banarsidass, 1979.

Luptāgamasaṃgraha. Part 1 collected and edited by G. Kaviraja. Yogatantragranthamālā, no. 2. Benares, 1970. Part 2 collected by Vrajavallabha Dvivedi. Yogatantragranthamālā, no. 10. Benares, 1983.

Varivasyārahasya and its commentary *Prakāśa* by Bhāskararāya Makhin. Edited with English translation by S. Subrahmaṇya Śāstrī. Adyar Library Series no. 28. Adyar (4th ed.) 1976.

Vātulanāthasūtra with *vṛtti* by Anantaśaktipāda. K.S.T.S., no. 49, 1923. Edited with English translation by M. S. Kaul.

———. French translation called *Vātulanāthasūtra avec le Commentaire d' Anantaśaktipāda* by L. Silburn. Paris: E. de Boccard, 1959.

———. *Vāmakeśvaramata* with *vivaraṇa* by Jayaratha. K.S.T.S., no. 66, 1944. Edited by M. S. Kaul.

Vijñānabhairava with commentaries by Kṣemarāja (incomplete) and *Śivopādhyāya*. K.S.T.S., no. 8, 1918. Edited by M. R. Śāstrī.

———. With *Kaumudī* by *Ānandabhaṭṭa*. K.S.T.S., no. 9, 1918. Edited by M. R. Śāstrī.

———. French translation and exposition called *Le Vijñānabhairava* by L. Silburn. Paris: E. de Boccard, 1961.

———. English translation called *The Vijñānabhairava* by Jaideva Singh. Delhi: Motilal Banarsidass, 1979.

———. With subtitle *Samagra Bhāratīya Yogaśāstra* and two commentaries called *anvayārtha* and *rahasyārtha* in Sanskrit and Hindi respectively by Vrajavallabha Dvivedi. Delhi: Motilal Banarsidass, 1978.

———. *The Book of Secrets—Discourses on the Vijñāna Bhairava Tantra.* 5 vols. By Acharya Rajneesh. Edited by Ma Ananda Prem and Swami Ananda Teerth. Poona: Rajneesh Foundation, 1974.

Virūpākṣāpancāśikā with *vivṛti* by *Vidyācakravarti.* In *Tantrasaṃgraha,* vol. 1. Yogatantragranthamālā no. 3, pp. 1-22. Edited by G. Kaviraj.

Śāktavijñāna by Somānandanātha with *Parātriṃśikātātparyadīpikā.* K.S.T.S., no. 74, 1947. Edited by J. D. Zadoo.

Śivadṛṣṭi by Somānanda with *vṛtti* (incomplete) by Utpaladeva. K.S.T.S., 54, 1934. Edited by M. S. Kaul.

Śivasūtra with *Ṛjvārthabodha* by Pītāmbarapīṭhasthasvāmī. Datiyā, 1960.

———. Italian translation in *Testi dello Śivaismo* by R. Gnoli. Torino: Boringheri, 1962.

———. English translation and commentary under the title *The Ultimate Reality and Realization* by I. K. Taimni. Madras: Adyar, 1976.

Śivasūtravārtikā by Bhāskara. K.S.T.S., no. 4, 1916. Edited by J. C. Chatterjee.

Śivasūtravārtika by *Varadarāja.* K.S.T.S., no. 43, 1925. Edited with foreword by M. S. Kaul.

Śivasūtravimarśinī by Kṣemarāja. K.S.T.S., no. 1, 1911. Edited by J. C. Chatterjee.

———. Second edition with no title page. (This is the edition quoted in this book).

———. English translation by Shrinivas Iyengar. Trivandrum, 1912.

———. English translation named *Śiva Sūtras: The Yoga of Supreme Identity* by Jaideva Singh. Delhi: Motilal Banarsidass, 1979.

———. Italian translation named *Śivasūtra con il Commento di Kṣemarāja* by Raffaele Torella. Rome: Ubaldini Editore, 1979.

———. French translation and introduction named *Étude sur le Śaivisme du Cachemire, École Spanda, Śivasūtra et Vimarśinī de Kṣemarāja.* Paris: E. de Boccard, 1980.

Śivastotrāvalī by Utpaladeva. With commentary by Kṣemarāja. Edited with notes in Hindi by Swami Laksmanjoo. Benares: Chaukhamba, 1964.

———. *Śivastotrāvalī by Utpaladeva.* Sanskrit text with introduction, English translation and glossary by N. K. Kotru. Delhi: Motilal Banarsidass, 1985.

Sāṃkhyakārikā by Īśvarakṛṣṇa with *ṭippaṇī*, *Gaudapādabhāṣya* and Hindi translation by Ḍhuṇḍhirāja Śāstrī. Haridāsasaṃskṛtgranthamālā no. 120. Benares: Chowkhamba, 1953.

Sāṃbapañcāśikā edited with Hindi translation and notes by Swami Laksmanjoo. Srinagar, 1976. An edition with commentary by Kṣemarāja appears in the *Tantrasaṃgraha*, vol. 1. pp. 23-50. Edited by Gopinātha Kavirāja. Benares, 1970.

Siddhitrayī by Utpaladeva. This consists of three works: *Ajaḍapramātṛsiddhi*, *Īśvarasiddhi* and *Sambandhasiddi*. K.S.T.S., no. 34, 1921. Edited by M. S. Kaul.

Stavacintāmaṇi by Nārāyaṇabhaṭṭa with commentary by Kṣemarāja. K.S.T.S., no. 10, 1918. Edited by M. R. Sāstrī.

———. French translation called *La Bhakti: Le Stavacintāmaṇi* by L. Silburn. Paris: E. de Boccard, 1964.

Spandakārikā with *vṛtti* by Kallaṭabhaṭṭa. K.S.T.S., no. 5, 1916. Edited by J. C. Chatterjee.

———. Italian translation in *Testi dello Śivaismo* by R. Gnoli. Torino: Boringheri, 1962.

———. Hindi translation, introduction and notes by Nīlakaṇṭha Guruṭū. Delhi: Motilal Banarsidass, 1981.

———. Hindi translation by Pītāmbarapīṭhasvāmī. Datiyā, 1980. *Spandakārikāvivṛti* by Rājānaka Rāma. K.S.T.S., no. 6, 1916. Edited by J. C. Chatterjee.

Spandanirṇaya by Kṣemarāja. K.S.T.S., no. 43, 1925. Edited with English translation by M. S. Kaul.

———. English translation called *The Divine Creative Pulsation* by Jaideva Singh. Delhi: Motilal Banarsidass, 1980.

Spandapradīpikā by Bhagavatotpala. Published in the *Tantrasaṃgraha* vol. 1. Yogatantragranthamālā no. 3. pp. 83-128. Edited by G. Kaviraj. Benares, 1970. (This is the edition used in this book.)

———. Edited by Vāmana Śāstrī. Publishers not known. Islamapurkara, 1898.

Spandasaṃdoha by Kṣemarāja. K.S.T.S., no. 16, 1917. Edited by M. R. Śāstrī.

Svacchandabhairavatantra with *uddyota* by Kṣemarāja. 7 vols. K.S.T.S., 21, 1921; 38, 1923; 44, 1925; 48, 1927; 51, 1930; 53, 1933; 56, 1955. All edited by M. S. Kaul.

MANUSCRIPTS

Anuttaraparāpañcāśikā by Nāgānanda (alias Ādyānanda). Six MSs of this short work are in the Adyar Library, cat. no. 951-6. All are complete. Five are in Telugu script, one in Devanāgarī. Also commentary by Cidātmānanda called *Svarūpavimarśinī.* Two MSs cat. no. 957 and 958 (incomplete).

Īśvarapratyabhijñānvayadīpikā by Mahāmaheśvaranāthānanda. Government Oriental Library, Mysore, MS. no. B 167, 133 fol.

Cittānubodha by Rājānaka Bhāskara, Benaras Hindu University (B.H.U.), acc. no. C 784, s. no. 14/7598, 211 fol. Śāradā (complete).

Citspharasārādvayaprabandha by Sāhiṣkolānanda. B.H.U., cat. no. 14/7599, MS. no. C 3945, 10 fol. Śāradā (complete).

Jñānagarbhastotra by Nārāyaṇamuni. B.H.U., acc. no. B 900, s. no. 17/8528, 3 fol. Śāradā (complete).

Tantroccaya by Abhinavagupta. B.H.U., acc. no. C 1020, s. no. 14/7634, 14 fol. Śāradā (complete).

Niruttaravāda B.H.U., cat. no. 14/7674, MS. no. C-4720, 35 fol. Śāradā (complete).

Nirvāṇayogottara B.H.U., acc. no. C-4246, s. no. 14/7675 Śāradā, 8 fol. (complete).

Netroddyotavivaraṇa by Kalyāṇa Yarmā. B.H.U., acc. no. C-4394, s. no. 14/7679 Śāradā, 16 fol. (incomplete).

Prabodhapañcadaśā by Abhinavagupta(?) with comm. by Avadhūtamuni. Government Oriental Library, Madras. MS. no. D-15338, 13 fol. Devanāgarī (complete). Cat. no. 12303, MS. no. R-2701, 11 fol. Grantha, (complete).

Bahurūpagarbhastotra by Ānantaśaktipāda. 8 MSs in B.H.U. All in Śāradā; all complete except one. See, for example, acc. no. C-488, s. no. 17/8746, 9 fol. (complete with *ṭīkā*).

Bhedavilāsa B.H.U., cat. no. 14/7755 MS no. C-1533 114 fol. Devanāgarī (complete).

Madhyavikāsa, B.H.U., cat. no. 14/7759 MS. no. C-4393 98 fol. Śāradā (complete).

Mahādvayaśivavicāra Bhandarkar Oriental Institute, Poona MS no. 479 (1875-6), 2 fol. Śāradā (complete).

Ṣaṭtriṃśattattvadarpaṇa by Mañjunātha, Government Oriental Library, Madras, MS no. R-5042 (C), 11 fol. Devanāgarī, (complete).

Saṃvitprakāśa by Harṣadattasūnu, Bhandarkar Oriental Institute, Poona, MS no. 472 (1875-6) 2 fol. Devanāgarī (complete). B.H.U., acc. no. C-4003, s. no. 14/7893, 16 fol. Śāradā (up to 6th *prakaraṇa* only).

Siddhavīreśvarītantra (i.e., *Siddhayogeśvarīmata*). Asiatic Society of Bengal, Calcutta Cat. no. 5947, MS no. 3917 D, 2 fol. Bengali (incomplete).

Cat. no. 5948, MS no. 5465, 71 fol. Newārī (incomplete).

Siddhāntacandrikā by Vasugupta (?) Bhandarkar Oriental Institute, Poona, MS no. 501 (1875-6), 38 fol. Śāradā (complete).

Stavacintāmaṇi by Nārāyanabhaṭṭa with a commentary by *Rāma* (Rājānaka Rāma?). One MS in Baroda cat. no. S 54, MS no. 1821, 16 fol. Śāradā (incomplete).

Svarūpaprakāśikā by Nāgānanda with comm. by *Cidānanda* Government Oriental Library, Madras, cat. no. 24821, MS no. R-2159, 15 fol. Grantha (complete). Cat. no. 24822, MS no. R 3281, 31 fol. Telugu (complete). MS no. D 15328, 6 fol. Devanāgarī (complete).

Svātmopalabdhiśataka by Ācārya Millana. B.H.U., acc. no. C-4412, s. no. 14/7941, 28 fol. Śāradā (complete).

For notices of other unpublished Kashmiri Śaiva texts, see *Abhinavagupta and His Works* by Dr. V. Raghavan. Varanasi: Chaukhambha Orientalia, 1981. Chapter titled *The Works of Abhinavagupta*, pp. 17-32. Also *The Krama Tantricism of Kashmir* by N. Rastogi. Delhi: Motilal Banarsidass, 1979, pp. 225-7.

SECONDARY SOURCES—BOOKS

Beane, Wendell Charles. *Myth, Cult and Symbols in Śākta Hinduism: A Study of the Indian Mother Goddess.* Leiden: E. J. Brill, 1977.

Bhattacarya, K. C. *Studies in Philosophy.* 2 vols. Calcutta: Firma K. Mukhopadhyaya, 1959.

Cefalu, Richard F. *Shakti in Abhinavagupta's Concept of Moksha,* Ph.D. dissertation. New York: Fordham University, 1973.

Chatterjee, J. C. *Kashmir Shaivaism.* Research and Publications Department, Srinagar: 1st ed., 1914; 2d ed., 1962.

Dunuwila, Rohan A. *Saiva Siddhanta Theology: A Context for Hindu-Christian Dialogue.* Delhi: Motilal Banarsidass, 1985.

Dvivedi, Vrajavallabha. *Tantrayātrā—Essays on Tantra—Āgama Thoughts and Philosophy, Literature, Culture and Travel* (Sanskrit). Varanasi: Ratna Publications, 1982. *Āgama aur Tantraśāstra,* (Hindi). Delhi: Parimala Publications, 1984.

Francke, A. H. and Thomas, E. W. *The Chronicles of Ladhak and Minor Chronicles.* Antiquities of Indian Tibet, part 2. Asiatic Society of India, Calcutta New Imperial Series vol. 50 1926.

Gnoli, R. *The Aesthetic Experience According to Abhinavagupta.* Benares: Chowkhamba, 1968.

Haldar, Hiralal. *Realistic Idealism*. In *Contemporary Indian Philosophy*, edited by S. Radhakrishnan and J. H. Muirhead. 2d ed. London: George Allen and Unwin Ltd., 1952.

Kachra, Durgaprasad. *Utpala, the Mystic Saint of Kashmir*. Poona, 1945.

Kavirāja, Gopinātha. *Tāntrika Vānmaya Meṃ Śāktadṛṣṭi.* (Hindi) Patna: Bihāra Rāṣṭrabhāṣā Pariṣad, 1963.

———. *Bhāratīya Saṃskṛti aur Sādhanā* (Hindi, in two parts). Patna: Bihāra Rāṣṭrabhāsā Pariṣad, 1963, 1964.

Kaw, R. K. *The Doctrine of Recognition*. (Pratyabhijñā Philosophy). Hoshiarpur: Viśveśvarānanda Institute, 1967.

Jhā, Yaduvaṃśī. *Śaivamata*. (Hindi). Patna: Bihar Rāṣṭrabhāṣā Pariṣad, 1955.

Jung, C. G. *Psychology and Religion: West and East*. Vol. 11 of the *Collected Works*. London: Routledge and Kegan Paul, 1958.

Lorenzen, David N. *The Kāpālikas and the Kālāmukhas: Two Lost Śaiva Sects*. Berkeley: University of California Press, 1972.

Matus, Thomas. *The Christian Use of Yoga: A Theoretical Study Based on a Comparison of the Mystical Experience of Symeon the New Theologian and some Tantric Sources*. Ph.D. Dissertation. New York: Fordham University, 1977.

Michaël, Tara. *Corps Subtil et Corps Causal. Les Six Cakra et le Kuṇḍalinīyoga*. Paris: Courrier du Livre, 1979.

Murphy, Paul E. *Triadic Mysticism: The Mystical Theology of the Śaivism of Kashmir*. Delhi: Motilal Banarsidass, 1986.

Nadou, L. *Les Buddhistes Kaśmiriens au Moyen Âge*. Paris: Presses Universitaires de France, 1968.

Narasimhachary, D. M. *Contribution of Yāmuna to Viśiṣṭādvaita*. Madras: M. Rangacharya Memorial Trust, 1971.

O'Flaherty, Wendy Doniger. *Asceticism and Eroticism in the Mythology of Śiva*. Delhi: Oxford University Press, 1975.

Padoux, A. *Le Symbolisme de L'énergie de la Parole dans certains Textes Tantriques*. Paris: E. de Boccard, 1963.

Pandey, K. C. *Abhinavagupta: An Historical and Philosophical Study*. Benares: Chowkhamba, 2d ed., 1963.

———. *Indian Aesthetics*. Vol. 1 of *Comparative Aesthetics* 2 vols. Benares: Chowkhamba, 1950.

Pandit, B. N. *Kāsmīra-Saiva-Darsana*. (Hindi). Jammu, Shri Ranbir Kendriya Sanskrit Vidyapitha, 1973.

Pereira, José. *Hindu Theology: A Reader*. Doubleday Image Books, 1976. (pp. 381-8 contain a translation of Maheśvarānanda's *Mahārthamañjarī*)

Potter, Karl. *Presuppositions of India's Philosophies*. Reprint. Westport: Greenwood Press, 1976.

Raghavacharya, E. V. V. and Padhye, D. G. *Minor Works of Kṣemendra*. The Sanskrit Academy, Sanskrit Academy Series, no. 7. Hyderabad: Osmania University, 1961.

Raghavan, V. *Abhinavagupta and His Works*. Varanasi: Chaukhambha Orientalia, 1981.

Rastogi, Navjivan. *The Krama Tantricism of Kashmir*. Historical and General Sources, Vol 1. Delhi: Motilal Banarsidass, 1979.

Rolt, C. E. Translation of the *Divine Names* by Dionysius the Aeropagite. London, 1937.

Rudrappa, J. *Kashmir Śaivism*. Prasaranga, Mysore: University of Mysore, 1969.

Saksena, S. K. *The Nature of Consciousness in Hindu Philosophy*. Benares: Chowkhamba, 1969.

Schrader, F. Otto *Introduction to the Pāñcarātra and the Ahirbudhnya Saṃhitā*. Adyar Library Series, no. 5. Adyar (2d ed.) 1973.

Sharma, L. N. *Kashmir Śaivism*. Benares: Bhāratīya Vidyā Prakāśana, 1972.

Silburn, L. *Hymnes de Abhinavagupta*. Paris: E. de Boccard, 1970.

———. *Hymnes aux Kālī, La Roue des Énergies Divines*. Paris: E. de Boccard, 1975.

———. *La Kuṇḍalinī ou L'Énergie des Profondeurs*. Paris: Les Deux Oceans, 1983.

Temple, Richard Carnac, Sir. *The Word of Lalla the Prophetess*. Cambridge, England, 1924.

Tucci, G. *La Via dello Svat*. Bari, 1963.

Vail, M. *Heideggar and Ontological Difference*. Pennsylvania: Rider College, 1972.

ARTICLES

Alper, Harvey P. "Svabhāvam Avabhāsasya Vimarśam: 'Judgment' as a Transcendental Category in Utpaladeva's Śaiva Theology. The Evidence of the Pratyabhijñākārikāvṛtti." Unpublished.

———. "Śivā and the Ubiquity of Consciousness: The Spaciousness of an Artful Yogi." *Journal of Indian Philosophy* 1979 pp. 345-407.

———. "Understanding Mantras." Albany, N.Y.: SUNY Press. Forthcoming.

Basu, Arabinda. "The Religions". In *Kashmir Śaivism, The Cultural Heritage of India* 4 vols. Calcutta: The Ramakrishna Mission Institute of Culture, 1937-56. Vol. 4: pp. 79-97.

Bühler, George. "A Detailed Report of a Tour in Search of Sanskrit Manuscripts Made in Kashmir". *Journal of the Bombay Branch of the Royal Asiatic Society*, Extra number, 1877.

Chatterjee, J. C. "Śaivism of Kashmir". In *Sharada*, I, i: pp. 15-9. Delhi, 1952.

Gnoli, R. "The Śivadṛṣṭi of Somānanda". Canto I. Translation and notes in *East and West*, 8 (1957): pp. 16-22.

———. "Morte e Sopravivenza nello Śivaismo Kashmiro". *Ricerche e Studi Orientali*, (1957): pp. 101-2.

———. "Vāc. Il Secondo capitolo della Śivadṛṣṭi di Somānanda". *Ricerche e Studi Orientali*, (1959): pp. 55-75.

———. "Vāc. Passi scelti e tradotti del Parātriṃśikāvivaraṇa". Part 1. *Ricerche e Studi Orientali*, (1959): pp. 163-182; Part 2, *Ricerche e Studi Orientali*, (1965): pp. 215-45.

———. "Alcune techniche yoga nelle scuole Śaiva". *Ricerche e Studi Orientali*, (1956): pp. 279-90.

———. "Corrections and Emendations to the text of the Parātriṃśikāvivaraṇa". Miscellanea India: *East and West* (1959): pp. 192-212.

———. "Five Unpublished Stanzas by Abhinavagupta". *East and West*, New Series 9-3, 1958.

———. "Bhairavanukaraṇastotra by Kṣemarāja". *East and West*, New Series. 1958.

———. "Gli Āgama Scivaiti nell' India Settentrionale". *Indologica Taurinesia*, no. 1. Torino. (1973): pp. 61-69.

Kaul, B. N. "Shaivism in Kashmir" and "Tenets of Trika". *Research-Kashmir Trika Philosophy and Culture*, 1/1, 1959.

———. "Utpalacarya—The Mystic". *Kashmir Today*, (1960) and "The Doctrine of Self-Recognition". *Kashmir Today*, (1962): pp. 62-81.

Kaul, H. N. "Introduction to Trika Philosophy and Culture". *Kashmir Research Biannual*, I, i. Srinagar (1960): pp. i-iv.

Kaul, S. "Mahāmaheśvara Rājānaka Abhinavaguptācārya". *Kashmir Today*, 1961.

Kaw, R. K. "Finite Self in Pratyabhijñā System". *Indian Philosophy and Culture*, 1963, Institute of Oriental Philosophy, Vrindaban.

———. "Concept of Māyā in Kashmiri Śaivism". Ibid., 1968.

———. "Utpaladeva and his Philosophy". *Uttar Pradesh*, 1965.

———. "Nature of Mind in Pratyabhijñā". *Kashmir Research Biannual* 1, Srinagar, 1960.

Padoux, André. "Contributions à l'Étude du Mantraśāstra". EFEO 65. Paris, 1978.

———. "Contributions à l'Étude du Mantraśāstra II—Nyāsa". EFEO 67. Paris, 1980.

Sanderson, G. S. "Purity and Power Among the Brahmins of Kashmir". *The Category of the Person: Anthropological and Philosophical Perspectives*, Steven Lukes et al. Cambridge: Cambridge University Press. Forthcoming.

Torella, Raffaele. "Una Traduzione Francese Della Parātriṃśikālaghuvṛtti di Abhinavagupta". *Ricerche e Studi Orientali*, 54 (1980): pp. 171-200.

INDEX

A

A, first letter of *Ahaṃ*, 186-88
Ābhāsa, Pratyabhijñā conception of, 25. *See also* Appearance and Manifestation
Abhāva, 121. *See also* Non-being
Abhidharma, 1
Abhinavagupta, father of, 224; his life and works, 10-14; and Trika Śaivism
Abode, supreme, 159
Absolute, 34, 90, 113, 114, 127, 177, 193, 202, 257; as A, 186; bliss of, 116; concept of, 24, 38; cosmic play of, 188; experience of, 161; and finite, 24, 40; integral nature of, 38*ff.*; as Light and pulsation, 63-64; power of, 40-41; void of, 126; wheel of (*anuttaracakra*), 124, 125
Absorption, empowered (*śākta*), 201; introverted and extroverted, 157-58; mystical (*samāveśa*), three types of, 172. *See also* Contemplation
Action, 89, 91, 137; inner and outer forms of, 98, 152; relation to knowledge, 72, 80; limited, 137; limited power of, 150; organs of, 138; power of, 80, 90, 97-98, 108, 166, 173, 175, 176, 177, 181; power of, applied to yoga, 206; power of, as *bindu*, 186, 188; power of, contracted by thought-constructs, 190; temporal and eternal, 82-83; as *vimarśa*, 72, 113
Aesthetic experience, 148-50
Āgama, types of, 4-9, 232
Agency, 90, 98, 154, 164
Agent, 27, 98, 141
Aghora, 261. *See also* Benevolent powers
Agitation (*kṣobha*), stilling of, 201
Ahaṃ, 198; as Mantra, 202; symbolism and activity of, 185-88. *See also* 'I'-Consciousness; Ego; Egoity
Aiśvarya, 122. *See also* Sovereignty
All-Things (*sarvārtha*), 215
Alphabet, Sanskrit, 124
Āmardaka, 5, 18, 229
Ambā, 11
Anākhya. *See* Undefinable
Anāmakatantra, 12
Ānandabhairava, 145
Ānandabhairavī, 145
Ānandavardhana, 10
Ananta, 133, 211
Āṇavamala. *See* Impurity
Antaḥkaraṇa, 108
Antararthavāda, 46
Anupāya, 160, 173, 175-80, 206, 257; as fruit of *Kramamudrā*; two levels

C

D

J

K

L

Q

R

Sumati, 12, 13
Sun, 64, 125, 134, 144, 212
Superego, absent in original Spanda doctrine, 26-27; its origin in the Pratyabhijñā, 19
Supports, formation of (*sthāna-kalpanā*), 172
Supramental (*unmanā*), 215
Supreme, 173, 176
Svacchandabhairavatantra, 8, 14, 120, 121, 209
Svatantreśa, 133
Svātantrya. *See* Freedom
Svātmagraha. *See* Oneself, possession of
Svātmocchalattā. *See* Outpouring
Śvetāsvataropaniṣad, 26, 150
System, as specific term, 231-32

T

Tamas, 108, 133, 138
Tanmātra, 108
Tantra, 158, 171, 179
Tantras, 140, 142, 144, 145, 224, 226; their types, 4-9
Tantrāloka, 10, 11, 12, 14, 171, 172, 227
Tantraprakriyā, 13
Tantric lineages, 4
Tāratamya. *See* Hierarchy
Taste (*rasa*), 265
Tasting, (*āsvādana*), 147-48
Tattva. *See* Categories
Tattvayukti, 256
Tension, 93
Thon-mi Saṃbhota, 2
Thought-constructs, 126, 135, 136, 143, 159, 174, 208, 216, 217; affects not consciousness, 191-92; as binding and obscuring, 123, 165, 168, 185, 190, 191, 194; break up unity, 42, 69, 78; contemplation with and without, 264; like dreams, 163, 208, 254; generation of, 108, 119, 142, 153, 166, 182, 198; nature of, 192; purification, elimination and transcendence of, 142, 162, 173, 191, 192, 195, 203, 206; relation to speech, 185, 197
Tibet, 2
Time, 218; absent in consciousness, 81, 83, conquest of, 120; fire of, 143; generation of, 184; notion of, 82-83; power of, 93, 131
Totality, law of (*grāmadharma*), 184
Transcendence, 102, 113, 114, 120, 163, 209
Transformation (*parināma*), 88
Transmigration, 155, 156
Triad, 113
Trident (*triśūla*), 181
Trighaṇṭika, 15-16
Trika, 10, 11, 31, 171, 179; aims at realisation of absolute (*anuttara*), 257; categories of, 173; as independent school, 225, 226-27; goddesses of, 12, 15, 113; in Kashmir, 14-15; Kaula character of, 13, 16, 100; origins of, 12, 18; outside Kashmir, 17, 228; relation to Pratyabhijñā, 18, 229, 231
Trikamata, 228
Trikasāra, 12, 227
Tripiṭaka, 2
Triśirobhairavatantra, 14, 255
Truth, relative and absolute, 37-38
Tryambika, 18, 229
Tucci, 3
Tumburu, 6, 223
Turīya. *See* Fourth State
Turīyātīta. *See* Beyond the Fourth

U

Uḍḍiyāna, 3
Udyoga. *See* Exertion
Undefinable (*anākhya*), 124, 180
Unfolding (*unmeṣa*), 90; of becoming, 152; of cognition, 94-95, 96; of consciousness, 95